Art of
the Italian
Renaissance

André Chastel

Art of
the Italian
Renaissance

Translated by
Linda and Peter Murray

Arch Cape Press
New York

Frontispiece Andrea Mantegna. Camera degli Sposi, detail of the oculus. Before 1474. Fresco, Palazzo Ducale, Mantua. '...the remarkable works, worthy of admiration, which he painted earlier in our chapel and in the room in our palace...' (Decree of the Marquis Francesco, February 1492)

Jacket Art
front-Perugino. From *The Journey of Moses into Egypt.*
back-Piero della Francesca. *Baptism of Christ*

Translated from the French:

Chronique de la peinture italienne à la Renaissance 1280–1580

Copyright © 1983 Office du Livre SA Fribourg, Switzerland

English translation: Copyright © 1984 Linda and Peter Murray

This 1988 edition published by
Arch Cape Press, a division of dilithium Press, Ltd.
distributed by Crown Publishers, Inc.,
225 Park Avenue South, New York, New York 10003

Library of Congress Cataloging-in-Publication Data
Chastel, André, 1912-
    Art of the Italian Renaissance.

    Reprint. Originally published: A chronicle of
Italian Renaissance painting, translated from Chronique
de la peinture italienne à la Renaissance, 1280–1580.
    Bibliography: p.
    Includes index.
    1. Painting, Italian. 2. Painting, Renaissance—
Italy. I. Title.
ND615.C4313   1988   759.5   87-24176
ISBN 0-517-65686-8

Printed and bound in Hong Kong

h   g   f   e   d   c   b   a

Table of Contents

Introduction

Nothing is simpler than to write a history of Italian Renaissance painting. Everything is to hand: lists of works drawn up many years ago; major museum catalogues prepared with meticulous care; old and new guide-books of excellent quality; innumerable monographs (one might even complain of their endless proliferation); an inexhaustible fund of travellers' accounts, poetic commentaries, learned disquisitions... A kind of Aladdin's Cave of literature on art awaits the art lover, a treasure house which he can ransack at will, just as Stendhal did in his infelicitous *Histoire de la peinture en Italie* (1817) for which he ransacked the Abbé Lanzi's *Storia pittorica dell'Italia* (1789), which was itself compiled from earlier sources. The essential framework already exists, in that during the last two or three centuries scholars have established valid norms and criteria through their work in this one field. The universal prestige of Italian art, the abundance of works, the mass of documentation, attracted historians such as Burckhardt, art lovers such as Rumohr, and systematizers such as Taine. There is no need to expatiate on this: it is enough to record that *all* the useful ideas in the history of art have been formulated concerning Italian art.

But because of the rapidity with which scholarship was breaking new ground and becoming ever more specialized (the old classics by Crowe and Cavalcaselle established the groundwork for this over a century ago), the need arose for a simple account as a parallel development which would satisfy the demands of the non-specialist. What was needed was a sort of 'recitative' which would list the known names, the accepted dates, the most notable works, from Cimabue to the Carracci, in an arrangement as striking and evocative as possible. It is to supply this need that so many treatises, studies and books have been written. For some writers the aim was to define the *aura* of the works of art through the essence of the 'schools' of painting; into this category fall the famous, charming and misleading little treatises by Bernard Berenson. These seductive books endeavoured to depict (and to a certain extent were successful in so doing) the panorama of Italian painting from the single viewpoint of aesthetic sensibility, by using the language of a now rather old-fashioned psychology. For others it was important to establish the historical rhythm: to separate the 'primitive' Quattrocento from the 'classic' Cinquecento according to Wölfflin's ideas (1899), or to split the Cinquecento into two parts separated by 'Mannerism' according to the analysis of W. Friedländer (1925), etc.

As the literary accompaniment, or what may be called the poetic interpretation, became ever more dense, and as the literature of a more popular kind strove to cope with the demand, the gulf between the two types widened—between the so-called 'scientific' learning which grew ever more exact and detailed, and that of the more 'generalized' knowledge. An analogous evolution can be observed in the natural sciences; the ideas and aims of the amateur are no longer those of the researcher. There is a gulf between the two levels. Having worked in both fields, it seems to this writer interesting, not to bring together two systems which are mutually exclusive, but to clarify some of the preoccupations of the first by changing the tone of the second. This book proposes the experiment of opening up the laboratory so as to give the curious reader an idea of what is to be found inside.

If writing about Italian art is easy, this is because the Italians were the first moderns to consider that art deserved to be treated historically. In the mid-sixteenth century, when France, Germany, and Spain experienced an artistic activity as extraordinary as that in Rome or Venice, it never occurred to anyone to record the new developments, far less to include their creation in the chronicles of the time. The Italians assumed the task of teaching culture to the illiterate aristocracies and stolid bourgeoisies of the West; they found emulators, but they were somewhat surprised to find that even in educated circles the fundamental experiences offered by architecture and the representational arts were disregarded. For the Italians, things had always been ordered differently.

The first history of art was born, therefore, in Florence in 1550 with Vasari; it was partly the outcome of a massive retrieval of documents. From the thirteenth century onwards it was customary to establish proper contracts for important commissions. These documents were preserved in the archives of monasteries, confraternities and lawyers. During the period of the Grand Duchy, there was a methodical—and, for its date, early—amassing of these historical materials. A great deal of useful material was more or less accessible and had also been brought together: account-books, narratives and letters were all added to the archives. The art of the past was probably viewed with all sorts of prejudices, and no one hesitated to dismember or remove old altarpieces, as Vasari himself did when he restored churches in Florence and Arezzo. Yet there existed the elements for serious research—a sense of continuity, a popular interest, and a knowledgeable curiosity about 'Gothic' works of art as well as about less important or unusual artists. This tenderness of feeling and concern, which encouraged the growth of legends, has enveloped Italian art in an atmosphere of continuous interest and thought. There have been ups and downs; works have been neglected or sold off, but never systematically destroyed. During the French Revolution and in the nineteenth century, Italy became the happy hunting-ground for antiquaries and picture dealers on a scale which filled the museums of the world, but never ignorantly. The history of Italian art may be said to have advanced hand in hand with the art itself, and it was continuously perfected during its vicissitudes.

Italy has the privilege of conserving more works of art *in situ* than in museums. They exist in churches and houses according to a quite natural local distribution (once one allows for removals, re-sitings, etc.). In a particular place, the significance of the site is all-important, even though it destroys chronology, since in these buildings filled with works of art dates can well be approximative. They are of secondary importance; it is the continuity, the proliferation, the relationships created between objects by their very accumulation which really count. Whoever cannot appreciate this, will never be able to enjoy the singular atmosphere of Italy. A church like Santo Spirito in Florence, or the Minerva in Rome, or even the Sistine Chapel, offers works of very different periods; their arrangement is dictated by the site. But the moment comes when one needs to distinguish between the strata, and to identify, classify and arrange in a chronological order the works accumulated in this fascinating jumble from the past. This is when one turns to the vaunted documentation.

The primary function of documents was to establish legitimacy. They enabled confraternities, or founders of chapels, to establish their rights of possession, and through them allowed princes and collectors to display the origins of their decorations and the value of their objects. These private archives were later used only by historians to work out facts and dates. Vasari accumulated an enormous mass of precise information and he sometimes recorded his doubts and cited his references. He made many mistakes which the Sienese or the Venetians corrected. History is created by the continual, implacable, confrontation between documents and works. For instance, it was one day noticed that the contract for the so-called *Rucellai Madonna* was not signed by Cimabue, as Florentine

1 Interior of Santo Spirito, Florence (begun by Brunelleschi in 1444 and completed in 1487).
A church which presents a host of works of various dates.

tradition—including Vasari—asserted, but by the Sienese Duccio. Then critical opinion has to start afresh, and the old accounts have to be replaced by new ones.

Would it not be useful in a book which would still retain a 'general' character to go direct to the documents, present the actual deeds, indicate their origins, comment on their peculiarities, restate their arguments, and ask the obvious questions ? In short, to construct everything round those references which are found in the footnotes of serious books and which the other kind take on trust ? Removed from their learned cocoon, these documents by means of which various works are dated, distinguished and placed, would for once be the star turns of history, the focal points of discussion. Obviously, this would mean being involved in 'micro-historiography', but its interest would lie in drawing attention to the minor reasons for things at the expense of major causes such as the *genius loci*, the creative powers of a race, or the fortunate condition of a society. It would not be unsatisfactory if an awareness of the less important circumstances of artistic life threw some doubts on the validity of some of the convenient syntheses, even those which, for want of others are commonly used in any overall account because the very vocabulary—Renaissance, the cult of the Antique, the dawn of classicism—has implanted them in common processes of thought. The everyday preoccupations, some of which can be reconstructed round a famous work or a brilliant career, are of a quite different order. Consideration of the works and the artists as part of a great historical whole is so customary a process of thought that, as in ancient history or classical tragedy, the ordinary aspects of everyday life become incongruities. Small meannesses of ambition or private interest play second fiddle to the grand aspirations, so that the minor matters of the actual creation of a work never get a look in. For instance, Duccio's difficulties with the law (Ch. 1); Filippo Lippi's barefaced demands for rises in pay (Ch. 3); Perugino's blatant ambition (Ch. 6); these circumstances obtrude in the documents. The notarial deeds, the statements of witnesses, the letters all relate to small, clear-cut, often petty, problems which have nothing to do with critical dissertations. Contact with reality—with the trivial, the violence of feeling, the hesitancies, the constraints—makes for a realization that the normal method of approach is too much of a bird's-eye view. Instead of a more or less passing mention of Mantegna's *Triumph of Caesar*, which occupied the painter for ten years and was a matter for comment in the whole of cultured Italy, it is worth lingering over what is known about the progress of the work. It can then be isolated from the artist's biography and placed in its Mantuan context. The date and the place then work together so that one illumines the other.

Does insisting on this kind of viewpoint tend to demystify the 'greatness' and the 'miracles' which are the fabric of this history ? What is the point of knowing that Giotto's merit needed to be defended by the 'intellectuals' at the end of the Trecento (Ch. 2); that Piero della Francesca's contracts were no more honoured in their day than Perugino's (Chs. 4 and 6); that Mantegna, like Perugino, was very careful about money matters (Ch. 5); that Michelangelo was intolerant and crude (Ch. 7); that Venice saw a fight to the death between Pordenone and Titian (Ch. 8); that the Curia re-echoed for twenty years with vehement protests about Michelangelo's indecent nudities in the Sistine Chapel (Ch. 9) ? These facts are difficult to insert into an 'ordinary' history, but they throw into relief the problems of the day to day life of artists, their human nature, the importance attached to their work or simply to their behaviour, and the place which works of art occupied in everyday life and thought. It is possible to see some of the relationships from which the fabric of daily life was woven, and the sometimes terrible play of passions ceases to be a secondary affair. Often we are at the source of the legends. Raphael died suddenly on Good Friday, 1520 and his last work immediately became the supreme achievement of his art (Vasari); haled before the Inquisition, Veronese might have become the victim of Roman obscurantism (Ch. 10).

Such a 'direct' vision is possible only through confrontation with the original texts, which may indeed be hard work, though an indispensable task. The labours of earlier, and more recent, scholars have ensured that accurate versions of the sources exist, and it would

2   Attributed to Jacopo di Cione. *The Duke of Athens Driven out of Florence.* Mid-fourteenth century. Fresco. Palazzo Vecchio, Florence.
A fresco commemorating an important political event—the expulsion of the Duke of Athens in 1343 and the end of the aristocratic government. Art is used to give a lasting form to the event, with the model of the Palazzo Vecchio placed under divine protection.

3   Attributed to Jacopo Franchi. *The Feast of St. John.* Cassone. First half of the fifteenth century. Tempera. Museo Nazionale del Bargello, Florence.
A festival procession near the Baptistry, a religious and civic centre, with panels of decoration, emblems, and devotional images on the façades.

13

be churlish not to acknowledge gratefully the work of the archivists who have made these researches possible; what we have added is the translation. These Italian and Latin texts are often far from easy to interpret; the legal language is heavy, cumbrous and wearisome; the letters are often confused, and even great authors are capable of a verbiage which can be a challenge to clarity, but without clarity there would be little point in a translation. Every effort has been made to render this literature readable, it being understood that the original texts are always given in the relevant section.

Why bother to translate these contracts, which still have to be reduced to their essentials by cuts? Why not a resumé of their meaning in a few lines, as is so often done by writers who use them at first or second hand? Because these unyielding texts, laden with formulae, possess a picturesque quality which throws light on the mentality and social world of the time. For example: the confraternity commissioning a work from Duccio (Ch. 1), or the Florentine Signoria confronting Michelangelo and Leonardo (Ch. 7). Suddenly it is possible to see the place of these concerns in the life of a city or a capital like Siena (Ch. 1), Mantua (Ch. 5) or Perugia (Ch. 6). Above all, as in a political intrigue, the customary methods of proceeding which are designed to tie the artist to his commission are made plain. It is surprising to find that Piero did not keep to his undertakings, and that the great Florentine 'heroes' signed contracts, received substantial advances, began their work and then abandoned it. Are these cases exceptional? How were matters arranged in less important centres, or outside Tuscany? It is to questions such as these that an effort is here made to provide some kind of answer. As will be seen, the situation of the painter does not conform to the ready-made image which has so often been presented; nothing ever happens in a simple and foreseeable manner. Documentary analyses in many cases compel the art historian either to abandon commonly held opinions, or at least to modify them considerably. Yet it seems well worth while making an experiment which means asking 'How do we know what we know'?

Learned works so often give the impression that archival documentation is only useful in that it facilitates attributions and dating. It is usually from this standpoint that it is cited, and then only in summary form despite the fact that partial quotation can often cause many errors in the long run. But documents can play a larger role by restoring usages, modes of expression and conventions which were, after all, those of the world in which the craftsmen, great or small, lived. They give colour to the narrative, like a traditional costume.

These documents are linked directly to the juridical systems, to accounting methods, to the administrative and customary conduct of communal societies and merchant cities involved in establishing their ideology and their rules of conduct (Note). The early appearance of carefully drawn-up contracts replete with notarial formulae and technical repetitions which almost defy translation is in itself astonishing. All these precautions were taken by important men concerned with the management of public money or the funds of religious bodies, since artists already had the reputation of being unreliable and difficult to hold to their undertakings. Duccio, according to a mass of incontrovertible evidence, was particularly wayward about keeping to his contracts (Ch. 1). All through the Renaissance there were veritable battles round contracts made light-heartedly, or even cynically, and then treated cavalierly. The mid-Quattrocento provides any amount of instances of appeals and lawsuits which are very informative about the mentality of painters, and the risks entailed for commissioners, despite all the legal safeguards. In fact negotiations with notaries, like the arguments which followed, the acknowledgements of receipts for payments, etc., brought artists to the notice of administrators and, by degrees, to a wider public. The contracts help to explain the position occupied by artists in the social system; many names have survived because artistic activity was closely linked to the practices of a mercantile society.

In almost all the instances studied here, contracts and accounts are involved. They exist in quantity, but the way in which they are drawn up provides pitfalls for the historian. The

4 Bartolomeo Caporali. A Plague Banner. 1482. Tempera. S. Francesco, Montone.
Cities enclosed within their walls became privileged objects, offered humbly to the supernatural protecting powers.

5 Andrea Mantegna. *Triumph of Caesar: the Armour-bearers*. Detail. About 1490. Tempera on canvas. The Royal Collection, Hampton Court Palace.
A man carrying an antique trophy. The helmet and armour imaginatively restored owe their fantastic effect to art.

6 Sandro Botticelli. *Moses in Egypt*. Detail. 1482. Fresco. Sistine Chapel, Vatican.
A biblical water-carrier in an attentive and thoughtful pose, with a large gadrooned water-pot (modern), in contrast with Mantegna's virile style.

parties are generally defined in great detail, so far as the commissioner is concerned: the prior of a convent, for instance, or the representative of a congregation. Three important points are agreed upon: a programme, the time limit and the salary. Indications for the first point are usually deceptive; the description is almost always summary and conventional because a *disegno* existed—a small model annexed to the contract (very few of these survive)—or because the details still had to be discussed with a representative of a third party, whose role is often mentioned in the body of a contract. Even in the Quattrocento it often happened that the model was simply an earlier work which was to be replaced; this was the case, for instance, with the banner of the Annunciation ordered from Piero della Francesca.

The time limit allotted to the artist is always clearly stipulated, but this clause is the one most frequently broken. The unpunctuality of artists must have been so frequent and so well known that new contracts were commonly drawn up to reconsider the terms or redefine the delays, always in more imperative language. Such seems to have been the case for the Duccio *Maestà* (Ch. 1), for Piero's *Misericordia* altarpiece, and for the decoration of the Sistine Chapel (Ch. 4).

The payments are obviously the aspect which receives the most attention, but are easy to treat cursorily. No one will again make the mistake of a famous historian who, in commenting on the sum allocated to Botticelli *per suo pennello*, assumed that this ready-made formula was a homage to the painter's talent. In effect, besides the sum due to an artist there was usually a credit assigned for materials, which might be very expensive, if ultramarine and gold were involved. These costly materials were always mentioned during the Quattrocento, until the time when more modern painters campaigned to reduce their use, since they were regarded as unworthy of a great artist (Ch. 4). What is very striking, however, is the unevenness of the fees proposed and the diversity in the manner of payment. In the case of Duccio's *Maestà* (Ch. 1) it is obvious that things were so arranged as to constrain the painter; he was to be paid sixteen Sienese soldi for every day that he worked. Filippo Lippi received forty florins for the Barbadori Altarpiece (Ch. 3) but asked for more money in begging letters to Piero de' Medici.

Fame brought better prices. Mantegna had agreed to 150 ducats for a large picture for the Cornaro family, but was then dissatisfied (Ch. 5). Important mural paintings involved more expense: Perugino first asked 300 ducats to work in the Sala Grande of the Doges' Palace in Venice, but then asked for 600, which was refused (Ch. 6). The big stars received very large sums.

One of the problems is to work out a scale of equivalents. Allowing a large margin for approximation, and taking into account the slow devaluation of money, one can equate the Venetian ducat with the Florentine gold florin. The hire of a house and a workshop for an artist cost between seven to ten florins a year; a house could be bought for between 100 and 300 florins. The basic minimum for living was reckoned at fourteen florins a year (or three soldi a day) according to the Florentine *catasto* or tax schedules. The average salary for a scribe or secretary was six florins a month (one lira a day). This enables one to agree with Ugo Procacci that, in contradiction to the pessimistic tax declarations, the average condition of artisans was good, and for many painters was excellent.

In the usual extensive conspectus everything seems as if prearranged, and the artists appear one after the other as if in a procession. 'Micro-history', which resists these conventional forms, tends to isolate contradictory views. Instead, therefore, of a continuous narrative, the reader will find a series of separate episodes; ten short stories rather than a novel.

Why episodes rather than a continuous narrative? This arrangement soon appeared as an inevitable result of the initial choice. Continuous narrative ceases to be possible the moment documents are inserted into it, and the works are discussed solely from the standpoint of the light that the documents throw upon them. To see how history is made, and how problems arise and answers to them are found in the context of a great painting or a remarkable episode, seen from the standpoint of the relevant documents, requires a leisurely approach which concentrates attention on a small number of facts and names.

It was also necessary for the episodes to be chosen so as to offer a range of scenarios capable of suggesting the sequence of generations, and also certain constant themes. The advantage of this method is that it seizes upon certain recurring situations, analogous reactions and permanent preoccupations. The discontinuity of the episodes may be compensated for by the recurrence of the same themes and the same reactions. This helps towards an understanding of the question why the history of Italian art forms an entity, in which the important events and the sequence of famous personalities stand out in distinct and characteristic relief. Knowledge of the period cannot lose anything by this piecemeal presentation.

Two guidelines are proposed. Firstly, 'art in the street', or, if preferred, in front of the public. The first example deals deliberately with the phenomenon of altarpieces carried in procession in Siena at the turn of the thirteenth century (Ch. 1); it was repeated in 1494 in Mantua with the *Madonna of Victory* (Ch. 5); and again in 1504 when Michelangelo's *David* was carted across Florence (Ch. 7). These spectacular manifestations not only form part of civic life; they define it and express it. The authorities took particular care that the transportation of a masterpiece should be a festivity for the whole community, like the processions on the feast of the city's patron saint, St. John the Baptist. They hoped—and knew—that they would derive a great deal of prestige from this. What could be more natural than that those in power—a city council, a prince, the Church—should also participate in artistic activity? Paul Veyne has established very clearly in *Le Pain et le Cirque* the position in Rome and the world of Antiquity: the Mediterranean has not changed all that much. It is not purely fortuitous that the model of Antiquity is constantly recalled by princes and nobles from the fourteenth century onwards. There is even a case where a magnate and an artist shared for ten years or so in the reconstitution of the striking cycle of a Roman Triumph (Ch. 5).

From the moment when expenditure for a cultural purpose was justified by the idea of obligatory magnificence, artists took care to encourage—even to flatter—those in power who felt it their duty to commission new and original works. It is in this reciprocal movement that the great expansion which is loosely called the Renaissance was achieved. A society creates for itself both a spectacle and a mirror—though not without protests, it must be admitted. There could well be an inverted history, negative and critical, but that is none of the business of this book. One aspect of it can be seen in the 'scandal' of the *Last Judgement*, the importance of which it is difficult to exaggerate (Ch. 9). It was a case of defining clearly what could be tolerated in a church. Art enjoyed a kind of autonomy of action; it is possible to show elsewhere how, from the thirteenth century onwards, the right, if not to iconographical invention, at least to original composition, was sometimes claimed—when necessary—by innovative masters and their workshops. To this end a slogan taken from Horace was used: *pictoribus ac poetis... quidlibet audendi potestas*—a formula which was invoked spontaneously by Veronese in his reply to the Inquisitor.

The notion of 'competition' between artists, workshops, religious houses, cities, princes and prelates—that is, among practically all the bodies interested in artistic activity— has not been brought out as much as it should have been. In the modern world this phenomenon is familiar; it is not only commercial concerns that keep a close eye on one another. The initiative of a successful exhibition in one country stimulates a similar one in a neighbouring country. Cities behave in the same way. Nothing is better publicized than the sometimes violent disagreements between artists which are treated as eminently newsworthy: Ingres and Delacroix during the last century; Matisse and Picasso in this (after a brief moment when the rivalry seemed to be rather between Derain and Picasso).

Things were no different during the Renaissance. All that is necessary is to allow for a less extensive commercial organization, a more complex social structure, and a smaller

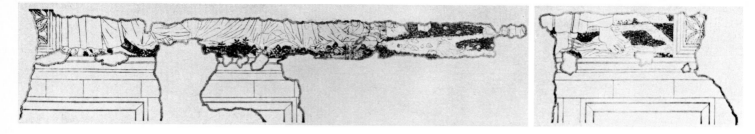

7 Domenico Veneziano. Frescoes in Sant' Egidio, Florence. 1439. Drawing of some part of the fragments.
Test borings have revealed vestiges of the work which has been lost since the seventeenth century: feet on a tiled floor are sufficient to establish the rigorous perspective system of the whole.

volume of trade. Once this has been realized, it is fascinating to observe similar phenomena, with the antagonisms displayed as strongly and as fiercely. Each episode will bring out one of the facets of this emotional dynamism which Italy has always displayed. One success stimulates another (Ch. 1); an aspiring painter intrigues to thrust himself on two of his colleagues (Ch. 3); an astute impresario contrives through a carefully organized publicity campaign (Ch. 6) to obtain a series of commissions which he then cannot properly undertake. The appearance after 1500 of important, dominating figures multiplies the opportunities for conflicts, often embittered by personal hatreds (Ch. 7), the strife of partisans, or by the ambition to achieve exclusive predominance (Ch. 8). The aim here is to provide, by means of striking examples chosen among the most famous names, convincing information about this aspect of artistic life in Italy. Nowhere else, it seems, did deliberate competition reach such proportions. In his Life of the painter Francia, which represented in his eyes a model of a well-conducted career, Vasari has a typical phrase: '...his reputation as an excellent master spread and cities competed (*facevano... a gara*) to acquire his works.' At first it might be thought that this was simply a matter of increasing the speed of production, but in fact the result was also a more exacting attitude and therefore a higher quality. The example of Siena is revealing (Ch. 1), as is also that of Florence in 1500. The boring stereotypes which can stem from multiple repetitions (Ch. 6) are countered by a concern for the work as a whole, for the complete synthesis and, briefly, by a more successful result which has nothing to do with a master-work in the craft sense of the word.

This dramatized presentation has the advantage of reminding one that artists during the Quattrocento and Cinquecento were caught up in the often turbulent life of the times. They did not live in a world apart, without risks and problems. There has been too strong a tendency to dismiss the strains, and it is clearly inadequate to say merely that the workshops suffered the consequences of these; the political, religious and social upheavals of the age were by no means trivial. Foreign wars and dynastic intrigues broke out everywhere; hostility towards Rome increased as the Papacy became more dominant, spiritually and politically. The great artistic enterprises, and even less important ones, became the field for battles over prestige. For artists the important event of the day was whatever enabled them to become known (Ch. 3) and to obtain substantial commissions (Ch. 7). But in the realm of spectacular works, reflecting the concern of a whole city (Ch. 1) or a dynasty in the process of establishing its cultural authority (Ch. 5), the new work of art became a real event, written about, visited, and, if it were a new creation in the papal city, it immediately acquired decisive importance (Ch. 4), its production followed and appraised stage by stage. It could even become, as happened in one admittedly exceptional case, an event in the history of the Church itself, a scandal for some and an object of admiration for others (Ch. 9). Works of art were real news in Italy, as nowhere else. Proof of this will follow.

8 Michelangelo. *The Last Judgement.* Detail: *St. Catherine.* 1534–41. Fresco. Sistine Chapel, Vatican.
Draperies added by Daniele da Volterra —a particularly indicted example of the alterations intended to do away with the nudity thought to be provocative.

Except in the case of one of the episodes (Ch. 5), the subjects treated here are all religious works. It is generally believed—since the works of Emile Mâle are usually accorded an absolute authority (which they cannot have)—that works of art destined for churches were under the strict control of the Church, and followed implicitly an iconographic canon laid down by theologians. These two propositions are the origin of a

9 Neri di Bicci. *Annunciation*. About 1460. Tempera on panel. Galeria dell' Academia, Florence.

A work *all'antica*, '... with an Annunciation... of the same treatment and decoration as the *pala* di San Remigio'. (Neri di Bicci, *Ricordanze*, 237.)

whole family of false problems which have to be rooted out. After the bitter conflict of iconoclasm, Greek Christianity elaborated a comprehensive doctrine concerning images which was never developed in Latin Christianity. The doctrine of the Eastern Church was based on an order, a hierarchy, a catalogue, and a definition for all sacred representations for which there was no parallel in the West. What counted in Italy—as elsewhere for that matter—were local customs, the initiatives of bishops, rivalry between religious orders, and the individual concerns of confraternities or, of course, the 'cultural' politics of civic authorities.

The fashion for large altarpieces (*pale*) of the Madonna (Ch. 1) before 1300 is a good example of regional developments. From 1400 onwards the artistic model—that is, the Giottesque style—was followed without any attention being paid to the devotional model (Ch. 2). Of course, a major religious event might well be echoed—if only temporarily—in the formulae for religious painting (Ch. 3). The programmes of larger works—polyptychs or fresco cycles—were carefully worked out; a case in point is the recent sensational demonstration with regard to the cycle in the Sistine Chapel, the true theme of which no one had previously been able to elucidate or reconstruct (Ch. 4). Historians who believed that this aspect of their research could be brushed aside were neglecting one of the major constituents of art. Yet there is no question of an immutable iconographic system established by higher authority, but of representations required by religious orders or confraternities, or by a pontiff anxious to reaffirm his authority. The evolution of iconography is sufficient in itself to indicate that *there is no fixed system* in Christian art. After 1520 the crisis in the Church—of which the overriding aspect was the violent disputations with the Reformers—led prelates and theologians to discover with astonishment the variety of customs and the absence of an official doctrine. The affair of the *Last Judgement* corresponds to a dramatic realization of the conflict that was possible between the artistic order and the sacred one (Ch. 9). Hence its importance. The interrogation of Veronese by the Inquisition is a consequence of this at a time when, even in Venice, the question was being asked what should be done to control the one and strengthen the other (Ch. 10). Above all, it is the circumstances surrounding the creation of works of art, their elaboration and the material vicissitudes which they underwent, that an endeavour has here been made to provide useful information, seen in a totally different light. A great painting (Ch. 1) or sculpture (Ch. 7) presupposes a workshop in the city, transportation through the streets attracting the public, and an unveiling which excites considerable interest. Certain works have been confused with others (Ch. 1), whitewashed over (Ch. 3), or destroyed (Ch. 8); some important but now vanished works have also been included to serve as reminders of the gaps in our knowledge, and to insist that history should never skate over them too quickly.

A decisive piece of information sometimes hangs by a single thread lost in a jumble of documents; only patient sifting and extreme vigilance brings it to light almost by a miracle. The best account possible has been compiled for Duccio (Ch. 1), and also for Piero della Francesca (Ch. 3). Nothing is known about Piero's early years, but a receipt for a payment buried in the accounts of the Hospital of Sta. Maria Nuova (formerly Sant'Egidio) brought his name to light as an assistant to Domenico Veneziano, who was responsible for the decoration. The work itself had vanished by the seventeenth century, and no one knows what the young Piero was working on; nevertheless, there are works which can be associated stylistically with the lost work (its history is complicated, for at least three painters and their assistants were engaged on it). Recently technical investigations have revealed a fragment of it: some feet on a tiled floor. This allows an opportunity to consider the art of Domenico Veneziano and the beginnings of that of Piero. In this way knowledge is increased by tiny steps, forwards and backwards, either in the presence of works or in their absence.

None of the documentary compilations here can—or even pretends to—be complete. But at the heart of each one of them is a small problem which has directed the collection

of the documents and the selection of its principal elements. Frequently more or less new questions are asked: How did Giotto's fame evolve (Ch. 2)? How did Perugino gain such an immense reputation (Ch. 6)? Was a summons to appear before the Inquisition a piece of petty persecution (Ch. 10)? Each chosen episode is underpinned by an exercise in research. It was less important to find an answer than to show, by bringing together the documents, how concurrent historical events provide the best answer. It is only necessary to look at the sequence of historical events: the return to Giotto and the new 'cultural' conscience of the Florentines (Ch. 2); the presence of Eugenius IV in Florence and the city's prestige and power of attraction (Ch. 3); the Gonzagas begrudging nothing for the glory of Mantegna, the acknowledged master of the Antique (Ch. 5), nor was it purely by accident that Michelangelo and Leonardo came face to face three or four times (Ch. 7); after Lepanto (1571) the triumphalism of Venice found its most accomplished interpreter in Veronese (Ch. 10).

The works around which each dossier has been accumulated are all famous ones. There may, therefore, be, an impression of staleness, of *déjà vu*. However, the gain from the analysis of the texts will be even greater as a result. The sources will serve to stimulate historical imagination by a kind of physical contact with the very bedrock of research.

To put it briefly, the 'micrographic' vision, by its close adherence to the document, brings to light the unexpected, the accidental, the play of passions, the interweaving of personal interest and pride, the intrigues, the bouts of impatience, the delays, so that each episode can then, so to speak, be gauged at its true temperature. But at the same time the part played by pure accident, in the sense of the multiplicity of causes and the unforeseeable aspects of the results, becomes much more evident. The picture thus presented may well be more truthful than that painted by a continuous narrative. The historical situation, loaded as it may be by customs, rules or conflicting impulses, is always new; by perceiving its actual workings it is possible to grasp the contingent nature of initiatives and achievements. This form of enquiry is more satisfying, through its adherence to what really happened, and conforms more closely with modern epistemological practice, characterized as it is by a tactical withdrawal to more limited fields of research, by the observation of localized phenomena, and by the analysis of individual incidents at the expense of a generalized conspectus. All general views, dependent on successive occurrences treated as a concatenation of events, rationalize evolution, which then becomes subject to the necessity of historical logic.

Need one add that this book is not a learned work? Its special quality is to give an idea of the detours, the hazards and the perplexities of historical research; it opens a window on the processes of erudition. But, in the choice of episodes, a deliberate selection has been made of the great names and the great events. In writing this book the author has avoided developing critical analyses in their minutiae and their accumulation of detail. It is hoped that the limited apparatus will still be sufficient to engage the interest of readers in these processes, without this simplification appearing unworthy to colleagues and to experts.

Note

There is a good example of this in the entries in the famous *Libro delle Ricordanze* of the Florentine Neri di Bicci. Known to historians from the eighteenth century onwards, Book D, which runs from 1453 to 1475, contains the money accounts for commissions and deliveries by the workshop.

13 December 1458: Record of the commission for the altarpiece for Mosciano: Doc. 1

Wednesday, 13 December 1458: Accepted: the altarpiece for Mosciano to be constructed and painted.

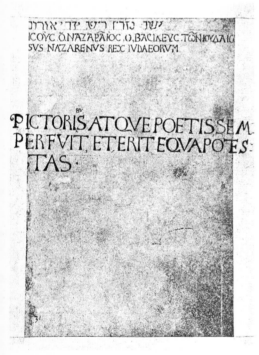

10   Benozzo Gozzoli. Sketchbook, fo. 31. About 1460. Pen on paper. Museum Boymans-van Beuningen, Rotterdam. Cover of a sketchbook containing studio drawings, with the trilingual *titulus* of the Cross and the *dictum Horatii*: 'Painters and poets have always had and will always have the same right (to invention).'

Note. The said day, I agreed to have made in wood and painting for Giano di Simone da Mosciano, Chamberlain of the company of Sta. Maria at Sant' Andrea of Mosciano and Checho d'Antonio, master mason, and Orlandino di Leonardo, all of Mosciano. This altarpiece, I have to create it at my own cost in wood, with gold, blue, and every other colour or substance necessary for the said retable. [It will] be made and composed exactly on the model of the retable made for Bernardo Gherardi and Ormanozo Detti at S. Romeo of Florence, with an Annunciation as in that one, the same workmanship and decoration as that, and of about the same size and dimensions, except that the afore-mentioned persons wish it to be a little smaller. The afore-mentioned Giano, Antonio and Orlandino have to give me for the wood, the gold, the colours and the execution of this retable twenty-eight florins, divided by contract as follows: for December five fl., January nine fl., in all fl. fourteen, the half of the twenty-eight fl. The rest has to be paid me in October 1459. Thus runs the contract with the afore-mentioned Giuliano, Francesco and Orlandino on the afore-mentioned date...

11 Piero della Francesca. *Polyptych of the Misericordia.* 1460. Tempera on panel. Palazzo Comunale, Sansepolcro.
'The said Piero has promised to paint and ornament the said panel and to adapt it in width, height, and type to the already existing work in wood.' (Contract of 11 June, 1445.)

The clients are identified, the model specified exactly, the financial considerations are perfectly clear... In an artisan world the rules of production take precedence of artistic preoccupations. As is now well established, the carpentry work—the planing and assembly of the planks of wood—was usually done in the *bottega* as part of the responsibility of the head of the enterprise, and it was by no means the least important part of the job; far from it. But the frame was often sub-contracted. This was the case, as is indicated by entry No. 237 of the *Ricordanze*, where is recorded the order to Giuliano da Maiano for the work *al'antica* on the exact model of the earlier *pala* for S. Remiglio. Other important points to be settled concerned the colours, which were expensive, and even very expensive: ultramarine blue *(azuro)* and gold. They are always the object of precise stipulations.

However, no indication is given of the iconographic programme, other than the generic formula: 'with an Annunciation...' and for the subject, 'of the same manufacture and decoration' as the *pala* for S. Remigio. The entry for 1 September 1455 concerning this *pala* is itself laconic on all these points: however, it mentions that the retable shall be

12   Piero della Francesca. *Polyptych of the Misericordia.* Detail: *St. Sebastian* and *St. John Baptist.* About 1460. Tempera on panel. Palazzo Comunale, Sansepolcro.
'The images, figures and ornaments will be determined by those responsible.' (Contract of 11 June, 1445.)

al'antica—that is with columns, architrave and cornice, and shall contain three 'histories' in the predella, with the coat of arms of the commissioner, Ormanozo Dati. Since both these altarpieces have been identified, one (that of 1455) in Sta. Maria Novella, the other (that of 1458) in the gallery of the Accademia, they offer an excellent opportunity to compare two works of current production, or rather the stereotyped, average productions of a well organized *bottega*.

The contract concerning the first commission known to have been given to Piero della Francesca, dated 11 June 1445, includes conditions of the same kind; this is for the polyptych of the *Misericordia*. The 'images, figures and ornaments' will be decided by the officials of the Confraternity, and the contract does not define them further. But it is exactly laid down that 'the said Piero has promised to make, paint and ornament the said panel and to adapt it in width, height and type to the pre-existing work in wood', within three years. This *pala* was therefore destined to occupy an already existing frame, doubtless as a replacement for an earlier work.

Despite all the precautions taken by the members of the Confraternity, Piero never observed the time limit. A new contract signed in January 1454 included precise threats of a financial character:

Doc. 2   14 January 1454: New contract for the polyptych of the Misericordia:

> The 14 January in the pharmacy of the abbey where was [Ser] Mary notary in the presence of Cristoforo da Viterbo and Antonio and Angelo Franceschi, summoned to serve as witnesses.
>
> It being given that Pietro di Benedetto di Borgo has received a certain sum to make the panel of the confraternity of Sta. Maria della Misericordia, according as appears to the hands of Ser Mary, written and signed from the hands of the said Pietro di Benedetto [...] if the said Pietro does not return during the coming Lent, the said Benedetto will be held to return the said sum as foreseen in the said deed.

This document is important, if it in fact concerns this particular retable. The repayment of the fifty florins given as an advance is imperatively demanded. A strict time limit is given to the painter, and impatience is noticeable after a nine years' wait. The allusion to a private contract made in the meantime does not permit an exact understanding of the position. Was the work completed in 1455? This has been supposed, but a docket for payment of fifteen lire in 1462, almost certainly for the cost of varnishing, suggests that seven more years passed before everything was complete. In any case, it is clear that new contracts could always intervene to interpret—or annul—the clauses of a strict contract. The juridical framework for contracts was perhaps not so strictly operational as one might suppose.

Perhaps an intervening contract (1451), now lost, may have authorized recourse to an assistant, in order to expedite matters. According to C. GILBERT, *Change in Piero della Francesca*, New York, 1968, this may deal with another *pala* than that of the 1445 contract. There is, in fact, a difficulty about the *St. Bernardino* represented in the final version of the polyptych: he was not canonized until 1450 and he must have been added to the programme in a symmetrical position to the *St. Matthew*, who corresponds to the name of the Prior, as has been observed by E. Battisti.

Chronological Table 1230–1400

x	*C.* 1230	Siena	*Pala* (altarpiece), so-called *Madonna degli Occhi Grossi* (Madonna with the Large Eyes), for the Cathedral (now Museo dell'Opera, Siena)
	1260	Pisa	Nicola Pisano, completion of the Baptistery Pulpit
	1284–1299	Siena	Giovanni Pisano, Cathedral façade
x	1285–1290	Siena	Duccio, *Madonna of the Badia a Isola* (SS. Salvatore e Cirino); *Rucellai Madonna* (Uffizi, Florence); *Madonna of the Franciscans* (Pinacoteca, Siena)
	C. 1290–1295	Assisi	St. Francis Cycle, Upper Church
	1290 et seq	Rome	Pietro Cavallini, mosaics in Sta. Maria in Trastevere
	1291–1295	Rome	Jacopo Torriti, mosaics in Sta. Maria Maggiore
	1296	Florence	Building of the Cathedral begun under Arnolfo
	1298–1301	Pistoia	Giovanni Pisano, pulpit in S. Andrea
	1300	Rome	Giotto, fresco of Boniface VIII, S. Giovanni Laterano
	C. 1305	Padua	Giotto, frescoes in the Scrovegni Chapel in the Arena
x	1302	Siena	Duccio, *Maestà* (lost) for the chapel of the Nine in the Palazzo Pubblico
x	*C.* 1310	Florence	Giotto, *Ognissanti Madonna* (Uffizi, Florence)
x	*C.* 1310	Rome	Giotto, *Navicella*, St. Peter's
	1311	Pisa	Giovanni Pisano, completion of the Cathedral pulpit
x	1311	Siena	Duccio, completion of the *Maestà* for the Cathedral (now Museo dell'Opera)
x	1315	Siena	Simone Martini, *Maestà* in the Palazzo Pubblico
	1317	Naples	Simone Martini, *St. Louis of Toulouse Crowning Robert of Anjou* (Museo di Capodimonte, Naples)
x	*C.* 1318	Florence	Giotto, fresco cycle of the *Life of St. Francis*, Bardi Chapel, Sta. Croce
x	1320	Florence	Giotto, *Peruzzi Chapel*, Sta. Croce
	1324	Venice	Paolo Veneziano, *Coronation of the Virgin* (National Gallery, Washington)
	1325–1338	Naples	Tino da Camaino, Angevin tombs in Sta. Chiara
	1326	Assisi	Simone Martini, frescoes in the Lower Church
x	1330–1333	Naples	Giotto, gallery of 'Illustrious Men' in the Castel dell'Uovo (lost)
	1330–1336	Florence	Andrea Pisano, First Baptistery Door

x works mentioned in the text

	1333	Venice	Paolo Veneziano, *Death of the Virgin* (Museo Civico, Vicenza)
	1333	Siena	Simone Martini, *Annunciation* (Uffizi, Florence)
x	1334	Florence	Giotto directs building work at the Cathedral
	1335	Pisa	Orcagna, *Last Judgement* in the Campo Santo
x	1336–1338	Florence	Presumed portrait of Giotto in the Chapel of the Bargello
x	1337–1339	Siena	Ambrogio Lorenzetti, political allegories in the Palazzo Pubblico
	1339–1348	Florence	Andrea Pisano, bas-reliefs on the Campanile
	1339–1344	Avignon	Simone Martini, works in Notre-Dame-des-Doms
	1340–1345	Venice	Paolo Veneziano, polyptych of the *Coronation of the Virgin* (Accademia, Venice)
	1342	Siena	Ambrogio Lorenzetti, *Presentation in the Temple* (Accademia, Florence)
	1343–1345	Naples	Tomb of Robert of Anjou in Sta. Chiara, by a Florentine workshop
	1345	Venice	Paolo Veneziano, painted cover for the *Pala d'Oro* of S. Marco
	1346–1365	Venice	Earliest sculpture for the façade and the capitals of the Doges' Palace
	C. 1350	Assisi	Pietro Lorenzetti, frescoes in the Lower Church
	1352	Treviso	Tommaso da Modena, *Dominican Saints* in the Chapter House, S. Niccolò
	1353	Bologna	Vitale da Bologna, polyptych of S. Salvatore
x	1354–1357	Florence	Orcagna, polyptych of the Strozzi Chapel, in Sta. Maria Novella
	C. 1357	Florence	Nardo di Cione (*St. Thomas Aquinas and the Virtues*) and Orcagna (*Last Judgement, Paradise, Hell*), frescoes in the Strozzi Chapel in Sta. Maria Novella
x	1359	Florence	Orcagna, *Death of the Virgin*, tabernacle in Orsanmichele
x	1360	Florence	Taddeo Gaddi, frescoes in the crypt of S. Miniato
	1365	Venice	Guariento, fresco of *Paradise* in the Doges' Palace
x C.	1365	Florence	Andrea da Firenze, Dominican frescoes in the Spanish Chapel, Sta. Maria Novella
	C. 1368	San Gimignano	Barna, frescoes in the Collegiata
	1375	Pisa	*Triumph of Death* in the Campo Santo
	1376–1381	Florence	Loggia in the Piazza della Signoria
	1377–1384	Padua	Altichiero, frescoes in the Oratory of St. George in S. Antonio (the Santo)
x	1385–1390	Florence	Agnolo Gaddi, fresco cycle of *The True Cross* in Sta. Croce
	1386	Milan	Work begun on the Cathedral
x	1387	Florence	Spinello Aretino, fresco cycle of the *Life of St. Benedict* in S. Miniato
x	Late 14th century	Florence	Cennino Cennini, *Libro dell'Arte*
	C. 1400	Milan	Debate between Lombard, French and German technicians about the Cathedral

Chapter 1
The Altarpiece in the Street (1285–1315)

The history of Italian painting begins with public celebrations, which have never been forgotten. In the last quarter of the thirteenth century works destined for major churches were sometimes carried across the city in triumphal processions. It is not difficult to see in this a revealing indication of a new political and social context, as much as a form of ardent devotion to the Madonna; the splendour of the pictures was indispensable to the double celebration of the city and its heavenly protectress. Ghibelline feudal domination had receded with the collapse of the Hohenstaufen Empire in 1268. 'Popular Guelphism', linked with the Church, encouraged a new activity with the autonomy of cities, though not without the fits and starts and the revolts with which the chronicles are filled. There was a new and precise realization of civic consciousness, and it is no accident that cities packed closely within their walls are often represented in religious pictures, as Duccio was to do in one of the panels of the *Maestà;* likewise Siena, in Ambrogio Lorenzetti's huge fresco of *Good Government* (1337–9), became the image of the happy city.

The centres of power and of the Church began to be embellished and renewed. The art which glorified them and organized them formed part of the essential needs of a burgeoning society. The production and display of remarkable works, admired by all, are indispensable to a collective affirmation and to civic pride. Here is one of the most famous examples:

1285: The *Rucellai Madonna* enters Sta. Maria Novella (from Vasari, 1568):   Doc. 1

> He then made for the church of Sta. Maria Novella the picture of Our Lady, which is placed high up between the chapel of the Rucellai and that of the Bardi da Vernio; which work was of great size and larger than any done up to that time; and some angels which surround her show that, although he still used the Greek manner, he was approaching the lineaments and style of the modern manner; for this reason this work was such a marvel to the people of the time, because nothing finer had been seen up to then, that from Cimabue's house with great festivity and with trumpets it was carried to the church in solemn procession, and he was greatly rewarded and honoured for it.

The story is a classic one. Four and a half metres high by 2.9 m. wide, the *Maestà*, which had been commissioned by a confraternity of the Madonna for its chapel in Sta. Maria Novella, was certainly the largest altarpiece that had ever been seen; a wall raised at the back of the chapel. The seated Virgin, surrounded by three angels on either side of her throne, presented for the first time in a gigantic panel the equivalent of the large figures in the apses of churches. The crowd reacted enthusiastically; the installation of the picture became the occasion for a civic and religious festivity. A new image of the Madonna, protectress of the city, assuming this extraordinary, monumental, modern aspect, seemed

13   Duccio. *Christ Tempted on the Mountain*, panel from the *Maestà*. Detail. 1311. Tempera on panel. Frick Collection, New York.
A view of a fortified town.

to promise even more firmly the favour of the Virgin, and to unite her more closely with the citizens. This is the meaning of the popular joy and demonstrations.

This archetypal anecdote appeared in the Life of Cimabue more than two and a half centuries later. Vasari obviously did not invent it, and everyone was willing to believe it. But by ill luck, during the last century, a contract for this *Madonna* was found in the archives of Florence, and the painter mentioned is not Cimabue, but the Sienese Duccio.

> 15 April 1285: Commission for a large panel for the Confraternity of Sta. Maria,   Doc. 2
> patron of the chapel in Sta. Maria Novella, to Duccio di Boninsegna, painter of
> Siena:
>
> [Lupo Ugolini, Master Guido, Master Corsi, Dino Benivieni], acting in the name of
> the said Confraternity for the work which is hereafter destined to it, commissioned
> the creation in fine painting of a large picture especially for the said Confraternity,
> in honour of the Blessed and Glorious Virgin Mary, from Duccio di Boninsegna,
> painter of Siena, engaging themselves to remit to him, or to his heirs, or to anyone
> to whom he shall have given title, as the named price of the painted picture and
> realized by the undersigned, when it shall have been completely painted, 150 lire of
> common florins [....]
>
>   In return, the said Duccio, invited to create a painted picture for the afore-mention-
> ed who are responsible for the commission, has promised and agreed to paint
> and ornament the said picture for the commissioners themselves and for their
> Confraternity, with the figure of the Blessed Virgin Mary and her omnipotent Son,
> and other personages, according to the desire and pleasure of the said
> commissioners, and to gild it and make all the details necessary for the beauty of the
> picture, all at his own cost and expense. With this clause and condition, that if the
> said picture be not painted and elaborated according to the desire and pleasure of the
> commissioners, they will not be held to this payment and to the reimbursement of
> any expense incurred by him, and the picture will remain Duccio's [...]

Contracts in due form for works of art appeared from the thirteenth century onwards in central Italy. They may be considered as the distant forerunner of the festivities of inauguration. The stipulations make it clear that it is a serious operation, destined to cause much comment, and thus to be conducted with care. The texts always mention the pious and honourable purpose and, in consequence, the public and collective character of the affair. The financial clauses are designed to bind the painter definitely to a work which was a long-term undertaking.

The altarpiece, which would later be called a retable, is termed a *tavola*, that is a panel or board, even if it is to consist of an assemblage of planks. In the chronicles one finds the terms *Maestà*, Virgin of majesty, Virgin enthroned, since it almost always consisted of representations of the Virgin, whose cult during the thirteenth century came to occupy a very important place on altars.

Duccio therefore received 150 lire to paint the *pala* of the Confraternità dei Laudesi at Sta. Maria Novella. This was founded in 1243 and met in a chapel in the left transept (which it abandoned in 1335 for a foundation of the Rucellai family). But why choose a Sienese ? This raises the question of the situation of painting in Tuscany around 1280, which has not yet been entirely clarified. A lively interest in a new *maniera* was appearing everywhere, but particularly in Florence. Cimabue, who also worked in Siena, was considered to be the leader of a school. It is generally agreed that Duccio, who was born about 1260, paid great attention to these examples of a carefully constructed, virile, strongly modelled art, either because he had been a member of Cimabue's team in Assisi, as Roberto Longhi has proposed, or because he had studied it for himself.

The so-called *Rucellai Madonna* must therefore be considered as a variant, an original interpretation of the creations in the new style. It has not been difficult to identify the Sienese characteristics: the type of the angels, the arcading and the delicate woodwork of the throne, the tenderness of the Madonna, the capricious fluttering of the gilded hem of her mantle, compared with the Florentine characteristics: the obliquity of the throne, the strict symmetry of the acolyte angels, the powerful composition of the *Maestà*, and also, probably, the rhythmical alternation of the medallions in the frame with busts of saints and prophets.

The name of Duccio was quickly forgotten in Florence: from 1312 the *pala* is cited without any mention of the author's name. The success of Giotto and his school helped in

14 Duccio. *Christ Tempted on the Mountain*, panel from the *Maestà*. 1311. Tempera on panel. Frick Collection, New York. The 'synthetic' towns symbolize the goods of this world, which Satan thought to have at his disposal, as well as civic power.

33

this, in that all initiative must have been Florentine and the name of a Sienese was even less likely to survive for long, in that the Sienese School, now very distinctive, considered Duccio to be its founder. But for the Florentines the only predecessor of Giotto worthy of notice had to be Cimabue. Since the great *pala* of 1285 was manifestly halfway between the *maniera greca* and Giotto's powerful style, which was affirmed with the Ognissanti *pala*, its author, if it were absolutely essential to name one, could only be the master of Giotto: Cimabue. This is the version which Vasari took over; it became Holy Writ.

But in the case of the *Rucellai Madonna* everything is apocryphal. In fact the historian continues:

Doc. 3   *C.* 1285: Visit of Charles of Anjou to Cimabue (from Vasari, 1568):

> It is said, and in certain memoirs of old painters it is written, that when Cimabue was painting this picture in some gardens near the Porta San Piero, King Charles the Elder of Anjou passed through Florence, and among the many receptions given him by the men of this city, he was taken to see the picture by Cimabue; and because it had not yet been seen by anyone, when it was shown to the king all the men and women of Florence gathered there, with much festivity, and with the greatest crowd in the world. Because of the rejoicing of the neighbours, this place was called Borgo Allegri, and, when it was enclosed within the city walls, it always kept this name.

The anecdote is every bit as revealing as the preceding one; it now consists of a consecration of the artist by the attention paid to him by a great foreign lord. It was not enough that his fellow-citizens honoured him by accompanying his work in a procession;

15 Duccio. *Madonna and Child with Angels.* Before 1285. Tempera on panel. SS. Salvatore e Cirino, Badia a Isola (Abbadia Isola, Monteriggioni).
Duccio's manner at the beginning of his career: the folds are typically Byzantine.

16 Giotto. *Pala d'Ognissanti.* About 1310. Tempera on panel. Galleria degli Uffizi, Florence.
Giotto's strong style is affirmed here as a profession of order and measure. The angel acolytes stand out like statues.

17 Duccio. *The Rucellai Madonna.* 1285. Tempera on panel. Galleria degli Uffizi, Florence.
The largest picture painted on panel up to that date. There are four different systems of drapery folds—the cloth of honour, the angels' robes, the Madonna's dress and the Child's tunic.

18 Duccio. *The Rucellai Madonna.* Detail: *An Angel.* 1285. Tempera on panel. Galleria degli Uffizi, Florence.

19 Giotto. *Pala d'Ognissanti.* Detail: *An Angel.* About 1310. Tempera on panel. Galleria degli Uffizi, Florence.
Duccio preferred to retain the three-quarters view of the head, used by the Byzantine artists, with a sideways glance. Giotto adopted the clearly-defined profile and direct glance, at the same time giving the angel a much more sober robe.

20 Duccio. *Maestà*. 1311. Tempera on panel. Museo dell'Opera Metropolitana, Siena.

The *Maestà* consists of a Madonna enthroned in glory, surrounded by an immense group of the saints venerated in Siena, and, on the back, a striking assembly of biblical images.

21 Duccio. *Maestà*. Detail. 1311. Tempera on panel. Museo dell'Opera Metropolitana, Siena.

'The said Duccio has promised to paint the said retable to the best of his ability and knowledge and as the Lord shall inspire him.' (Contract of 1308.)

it now excited the curiosity of important visitors, and the crowd of the well-born rushed to see it in their turn. One is here in the presence of a sterling scenario, one willingly repeated by popular enthusiasm and recorded by chroniclers: the king who renders homage to talent. It is enough to imagine the scene—as Vasari evokes it—several years before 1300, in order to grasp what it meant to the prestige of the artist and of painting in general. A natural enough occurrence in the southern world, such a manifestation is inconceivable in the Gothic world. It is, in fact, a well-known commonplace of Italian historiography, which never missed a chance to exalt cultural glories. But here we even have an extra legend: the suburb of the Allegri, if one traces it back, owes nothing to the joy of the crowd and is to be explained by the memory of former proprietors. The story does not hold together; Charles of Anjou, the brother of St. Louis, did pass through Florence, but in 1267. If he were to have visited an artist in his studio, there is no question of his having been to see the *Maestà* (by Duccio), and it is not even probable that his visit was to Cimabue either (he was born about 1250, and was therefore a youth). So the history of Italian painting begins with an account which resolves itself into a symbolic arrangement, as misleading as it is suggestive, and because of this doubly revealing.

Incidentally, it is not absolutely certain that the *Madonna* placed in the Rucellai Chapel is in fact the *pala* which is the subject of the 1285 contract. The arguments over attribution, even in cases as favourable as this, almost always bring about counter-propositions, over which one should not linger too long, but which cannot always be ignored. Some historians, struck by the style of the work, which is at the same time both robust and delicate, have suggested that the Rucellai *pala* might rather be by a Florentine working about 1300 and with a knowledge of Duccio (P. Toesca, 1951). What is needed is to compile a classified index of the large number of similar yet distinct *Madonnas*. Their chronology is very tight, and the balance can be shattered by making them originate from a Sienese or a Florentine workshop. In order better to grasp Duccio's manner at the beginning of his career, the *Badia a Isola Madonna* has been placed just before 1285, since it presents, together with a generally analogous structure, a very different treatment of the mantle woven with gold flecks, and, being much smaller, has only two angels (E. Carli, 1952). The tiny little panel of the *Madonna of the Franciscans* (Pinacoteca, Siena) would be an

22 Duccio. *Maestà*. Detail of the reverse: *The Crucifixion*. 1311. Tempera on panel. Museo dell'Opera Metropolitana, Siena. The group of female saints to the right of Christ and the Jews reproved at His left are based on Byzantine models. The figures, charged with expressive intensity, are diversified among themselves.

23 Duccio's Workshop. *Maestà*. Detail of the reverse: *The Capture of Christ in the Garden*. 1311. Tempera on panel. Museo dell'Opera Metropolitana, Siena. A striking rhythmical effect of movement accompanied by the verticals of the lances and tree-trunks.

example of Duccio's refinement and the preciosity of his art, just after his experience of working monumentally in 1285. But it still remains to be explained why a Sienese should have been chosen in a city as jealous and proud as Florence for a commission of such importance. Only one hypothesis is plausible: Duccio must have been either a pupil or a collaborator of Cimabue. The hypothesis has been boldly formulated, and this could not be otherwise: Duccio must have been a disciple of Cimabue even before the arrival of Giotto, and it must be possible to discover his traces at Assisi, where he could logically have worked alongside his master (R. Longhi, 1948). Thus everything can be explained, in assigning to the same innovating teaching—Cimabue's—the two great forces which were to diverge after 1300: Giotto's, more classical and sculptural, which became the Florentine style, and Duccio's, open to neo-Byzantine colour and Gothic elegance, which went on to make Siena a sort of citadel of 'precious' taste and tender painting. But is it necessary to stress that no document, no reference to a role or any note of payment, exists to back up this reconstruction of events between 1280 and 1290?

24 Duccio's Workshop. *Maestà*. Detail of the upper part: *Christ Appearing to the Apostles*. 1311. Tempera on panel. Museo dell'Opera Metropolitana, Siena.
The drapery folds hatched in a conventional Byzantine manner indicate the supernatural nature of the figure of Christ.

25 Duccio. *Maestà*. Detail of the reverse: *Agony in the Garden*. 1311. Tempera on panel. Museo dell'Opera Metropolitana, Siena.

Art historians work in the gaps left by the silence of archives, in the midst of the evidence, often contradictory, supplied by the works whose fascination does not permit them to remain silent.

5 June 1294: Duccio condemned to pay a fine: Doc. 4

Item XIII soldi IV denari on the same day for the painter Duccio for a fine of X soldi increased by one-third for not having sworn the oath to the Captain of the People during the time of the government of the Lord Baron (repeated from fo. 51)

Duccio figures particularly in the archives by the astonishing number of his fines and condemnations. They run from 1280 onwards and continue throughout his life, which suggests a character defiant of civic regulations, given to absenteeism, disturbing traffic, not paying either debts or taxes, and becoming the bane of municipal functionaries, who never ceased to denounce him. In 1289 the Podestà for the second semester was a Baron Mangiadori di San Miniato. Duccio was absent from a meeting of the Consiglio and, not having an excuse, was fined 5 soldi, with a supplement of 10 soldi for not having sworn the usual oath. The fine was reimposed in 1294 for the same negligence (the text cited is copied from the official Register of Condemnations). The most curious point is that these fines alternate in the books of the *Biccherna* with payments made to Duccio for the painted decoration of the collections of official papers. This suggests at least that the condemnations were not considered as serious or dishonourable. He seems also to have travelled considerably, in particular during the period from 1295 to 1302, when he may perhaps have gone to Paris. In 1296 and 1297 there appears in the register of taxes for the parish of Saint-Eustache a 'Duch de Siene' who pays—regularly, this time—70 sous in taxes. If this in fact refers to Duccio di Buoninsegna the link with Parisian illumination is established, and above all the knowledge which the artist had of the new masterpieces of Gothic stained glass, in particular Chartres: the 'Belle Verrière' might even be one of the sources of the *Rucellai Madonna* if Duccio had already been in France about 1280.

In 1302 Duccio painted for the chapel of the Nine in the Palazzo Pubblico a *Maestà*, now lost; it has been considered less as an intermediary between the Rucellai *pala* and the *Maestà* of 1311 than as evidence of a move closer to the lively Gothic style, judging by the echoes apparently made by the seven scenes from the predella showing incidents from the Passion.

Duccio had more luck with the *Maestà* for Siena Cathedral, about twenty years later than the *Rucellai Madonna*. The work has always been considered as his masterpiece and the document for the commission exists:

9 October 1308: Jacomo de Gilberto Mariscotti commissions from Duccio di   Doc. 5
Buoninsegna the retable for the high altar:

In the year of Our Lord 1308, on 9 October, let it be known to all that Jacomo de Gilberto Mariscotti, member of the Opera of Sta. Maria of Siena, acting in the name and place of the said *fabrica* on the one hand, and of the painter Duccio di Buoninsegna, citizen of Siena on the other hand, the said Duccio having received from the said member of the Opera the commission for a retable destined for the main altar of the cathedral of Our Lady of Siena, they have agreed between them the clauses hereafter mentioned and have made reciprocal engagements for the execution and finishing of this retable, according to what is later laid down. Firstly, the said Duccio has promised and agreed with Master Jacoppo [*sic*] of the Opera, acting in the name of the Opera of Sta. Maria, to create in painting the said retable to the best of his powers and knowledge and as Our Lord has enabled him; to work

26 Duccio. *Maestà*. Detail of Plate 25.

27 Unknown. *Christ Tempted on the Mountain*. About 1300. Mosaic. Kahriye Camii, Istanbul.
One must suppose that there was a common Byzantine model for the mosaic in Constantinople and Duccio's composition, where the same biblical episodes are treated identically.

continuously on this retable in all the periods when he is able to work; not to accept and produce any other work, for as long as this retable shall not be completely finished. The said Master Jacoppo, member of the Opera, in the name of the said Opera, has promised to give in payment to the said Duccio as salary for this work, sixteen soldi denari Sienese for each day on which the said Duccio works with his hands on the said retable. In default of which, should he lose some part of a day, there shall be deducted from the said salary *pro rata* to the time lost. This salary the member of the Opera above-named is held to pay and engages himself towards the said Duccio as follows: each month when the said Duccio shall have worked on the said retable, to give to the said Duccio ten pounds denari in ready money, and the shortfall of the said salary counted in denari the said Duccio is bound to restore to the above-mentioned Opera of Our Lady. *Item*, the said member of the Opera has contracted to furnish and procure all that shall be necessary for the work on the said retable; *item*, the said Duccio is held not to cause to intervene anyone but his own person and his work…

[Penalties for the non-accomplishment of these engagements are provided for. Duccio swore an oath on the Gospels. The notary registered the agreement before witnesses.]

The text of this contract presents several curious details. The programme of the work is not mentioned, which suggests that other legal documents have disappeared. The master contracts to paint the whole work on his own, which suggests that he had a workshop with assistants, but the commissioners were anxious to have an 'autograph' work. Finally, the restrictive clauses about payment are recorded with extreme precision, if not with lack of confidence, which can only be explained by the fact that Duccio, in the course of the last ten years had incurred innumerable fines for divers reasons; perhaps the authorities mistrusted him.

There were in fact several complementary agreements, which stipulated the disposition of the panels on the reverse, set out in a document of 1309 or 1310, of which the original has disappeared, but which is known from a copy: 'there will be thirty-four principal scenes and the little angels at the top, and perhaps some other paintings, so that there will be thirty-eight pictures… Duccio will receive 2½ gold florins for each scene, but will furnish all that is necessary for the painting.' Conditions had therefore evolved during the course of three years' work.

A chronicler, Tora del Grasso, has affirmed that 'this retable, the most beautiful that has ever been seen or made, cost more than 3,000 gold florins, it is the work of the painter Duccio'. This time, everything seems to hold together; and it is known, too, that the reception of the work was unforgettable:

8 June 1311: The *Maestà* of Siena enters the cathedral (from an anonymous Sienese chronicle):   Doc. 6

At this time the Signoria decided to change the panel over the high altar and they removed the one which is now placed on the altar of St. Boniface: the 'Madonna with the Large Eyes', or 'Madonna of Grace'. It was the Madonna who heard the prayers of the people of Siena in the defeat of the Florentines at Montaperti. This panel was therefore changed by commissioning a new one far more beautiful, larger, and full of devotion, with scenes of the Old and New Testaments on the back. On the day of its transfer to the cathedral all the shops were shut; the bishop asked for a large and pious escort of clergy, priests and monks, with a solemn procession led by the Nine, all the magistrates of the city, and all the population; one after another, all the notables were close to the panel, lighted torch in hand; behind them were women and children, all in the greatest devotion. They accompanied the picture as

28 Simone Martini. *Maestà*. 1315. Fresco. Museo Civico, Palazzo Pubblico, Siena. The inscription makes the Madonna speak as protectress of the poor and the weak and guarantor of the weal of the district.

29 Simone Martini. *Maestà*. Detail: *A Saint*. 1315. Fresco. Museo Civico, Palazzo Pubblico, Siena.

far as the cathedral, going round the piazza as was the usage; all the bells rang out to celebrate piously so noble a work. The panel was the work of the painter Duccio di Nicolò, who created it in the house of the Mocatti, outside the Porta Stalloreggi. All day long there were prayers and many alms given to the poor, asking God and His Mother, our Patroness, to protect us in His infinite mercy against all adversity and evil, saving us from traitors and enemies of Siena.

The details given by the author of the municipal chronicle about the 'civil and religious festivity' of the *Maestà* are valuable, in particular the order of the procession. There is no doubt that the authorities paid for most of it. The invoices exist for reimbursement of expenses for the drums and trumpets of the Signoria, and also for the town-criers, whose duty it was to announce and accompany the procession. This striking recital has been mentioned by all writers on the subject, many of whom added commentaries. For example, in the Sienese chronicle of Sigismondo Tizio the following appears:

Doc. 7   The *Maestà* of Siena in the cathedral (from Sigismondo Tizio):

On Wednesday the 9th June [1311], the panel of the Madonna was transported from the Laterini quarter, where it was painted, to the high altar of the church, with a grand accompaniment of honour and piety. This retable was painted by Duccio of Siena, who was then the first among all the painters; and from his workshop there came, as from the Trojan Horse, the finest artists.

The final invocation of the anonymous chronicler stresses the political aspect of the inauguration of the *Maestà*, the Madonna being in some way the 'poliad' divinity of Siena. No better way existed of honouring the Virgin than to consecrate a new work to her, in the place of honour, the high altar of the cathedral, once the old altarpiece appeared antiquated and outworn. The *Maestà* took the place of the *Madonna with the Large Eyes*, associated by the people with the victory over the Florentines in 1261, which assured three centuries of independence to the city. The new *Maestà* inherited in some way the virtues of the preceding one. But, even more than in Florence, it is the surge of devotion, the participation of the civic and religious authorities, the general fervour of the city, where all activity was suspended in honour of the new picture, that is emphasized here. Duccio's *Maestà* appeared as the final metamorphosis of the Heavenly Patroness.

The structure of the work in multiple elements required a large frame, constructed like a Gothic façade with its various crowning features, in a rectangle nearly 4 metres high by nearly 5 metres wide. On the front the Madonna, surrounded by saints—with the four protectors of Siena in the foreground—occupies a surface of 2.14 by 4.12 metres achieved by joining eleven planks of poplar wood 7 centimetres thick. The twelve pictures in the lower part, separated by standing figures of prophets, forming a predella, illustrate scenes of the infancy of Christ, among which is a tender and famous *Nativity*, very Byzantine in structure. The back of the altarpiece comprises in the central part twenty-six scenes from the Passion, between incidents from the public life of Christ in the predella, and episodes from His appearances after the Resurrection. The removal of the altarpiece in 1506, followed by its dismemberment in the eighteenth century, led to the disappearance of the frame and seriously damaged the work, some parts of which were dispersed and several portions lost. But the *Maestà* remains, especially since the restoration done in Rome in 1953–8, the most striking repertory of scenes from the Gospels ever assembled on an altar round a Madonna enthroned in glory.

The most recent research has established the chronology of this unusual work which transposes the diversity and size of a monumental cycle within the dimensions of a *pala*, admittedly an exceptional one. The difficulty consists in the very precision of the dates: between the contract of October 1308 and the public ceremony of June 1311 there were

30 Duccio. *Maestà*. Detail: *St. Catherine of Siena*. 1311. Tempera on panel. Museo dell'Opera Metropolitana, Siena.
Variations on the theme of the female saint, complete with accessories such as the nimbus, veil, ornaments and pose.

only two years and eight months. This is a very short time indeed for such a creation, and it has led to the claim that the Sienese could work with great speed (J. White, 1979) or to the hypothesis that Duccio used a number of collaborators (J. Stubblebine, 1980), one explanation not necessarily excluding the other. In effect there remains the possibility that the contract of 8 October, very strict in its financial clauses but very vague in setting out the programme, is the expression of a second agreement, made two or three years after the usual contract which defined the work in detail (J. Pope-Hennessy, 1980). It must be presumed lost or, more simply, replaced by the document known to us. This attractive explanation would also accord well with the known turbulent character and 'irregular' business methods of the painter; other cases exist—later ones it is true (Ghiberti, Piero della Francesca)—where a new contract replaced a first agreement.

All the phrases used by chroniclers describe the work as the largest, the most beautiful, the most devotional. Comparison with the *Madonna with the Large Eyes*, a rather rustic and unambitious icon (*c.* 1250), proved to everyone that Siena had been able to react to the immense changes in artistic culture achieved in Rome, Florence and Assisi over the last thirty years, by responding in an original way to the general movement without aligning itself with any of the important rival centres. Whatever may have been Duccio's obviously complex training, something more was expected of him than a local version of the monumental style developed in the great basilicas of Trastevere and in the Franciscan capital around 1300. In contrast to the apsidal mosaics and fresco cycles, the structure of the *Maestà* evoked an iconostasis. A similar screen of images closing the choir of the sanctuary with thirty or forty juxtaposed scenes existed only in the Byzantine world. Yet Duccio's manner is a decidedly narrative one; he does not present hieratic figures, but the agents of Salvation and true-life episodes; in this he conforms to the now established 'Latin' evolution. But—leaving aside the Madonna surrounded by saints—the format and the poetry even of these panels recall icons, and it has not been too difficult to find in the manuscripts of Mount Athos and in precedents close to Byzantium, if not the models which he used, at least their equivalent. Like the *Nativity* on the front, dominated by the red bed of the Virgin, the *Raising of Lazarus* on the back is a purely Greek formula. Other details from the *Washing of the Feet*, or from the *Agony in the Garden* for instance, have prototypes in recent Byzantine iconography.

Sienese originality lay in turning to innovators who had nothing in common with Torriti or Giotto, not merely in the articulation of scenes but in their disposition, their harmonization and their range of colours. One detail shows Duccio's ingenuity: in all the scenes in which the Resurrected Christ appears, now 'the glorified body', the painter has shown Him as in the scenes of the Passion, with a black mantle and a red toga, but he has covered them with gold hatchings, following the typical Byzantine practice, destined to remain a permanent feature of icons. Everywhere else Duccio had avoided it, at least after the youthful work of the *Crevole Madonna*. The old technique is revived exclusively to symbolize the supernatural condition, by an intelligent reinterpretation of traditions. The work remained unique; there is no other retable of the same type. It gave to the Sienese community the consciousness of its own originality, as was shown in the festivity of 1311. The work did not leave its place on the high altar until the sixteenth century, in 1506, as Vasari correctly records.

Nevertheless, even before Duccio's death, which took place in 1319 or 1320, a new version of the *Maestà* had been created by Simone Martini in the Palazzo Communale. This time it was a fresco, dated June 1315 by an inscription; its composition is more open, the handling larger, less precious. The idea of a dais forming a baldaquin is a new device which transforms the whole scene by deepening and unifying the pictorial space. Before the blue background was obscured, the articulation of the forms must have been striking. A huge painted frame enclosing large medallions surrounds the whole, according to Tuscan fashion. The throne is treated positively as a piece of Gothic furniture, which denotes quite clearly Simone's orientation.

Doc. 8   1315: Inscriptions on Simone's *Maestà*:

The flowers of the angels, roses and lilies,
With which the celestial meadow is decorated,
Do not please me more than good counsels.
I see people who for their own ends
condemn me and betray my land.
The more one vilifies, the more one is praised.
Let them beware, those who read and condemn my words.

[The Madonna's answer to the saints]
My dearly loved, remember
That I will grant according to your wishes,
Your devout and honest prayers.
But if the strong torment the weak
Your prayers are not for them
Nor for any who do harm to my land.

This inscription makes the Madonna speak as the protectress of the poor and the weak as much as a guardian of the country.

Being situated in the Sala del Mappamondo of the Palazzo Pubblico, and since it was also part of the wall, the work could not give rise to a procession, which would have repeated, four years later, the one which honoured Duccio. But a municipal festivity can be imagined—a public manifestation. This was even more probable since the Sienese, having borne the Madonna to the cathedral, must have been happy to honour her presence also in the palace of the Signoria. A kind of equilibrium is thus established, the two powers, religious and civil, each having received its titular image.

The names of the artists have been carefully transmitted, a remarkable fact in itself. From the thirteenth century onwards, by comparison with the customs of other countries, the mass of artists identified and recorded by tradition, by chronicles or by narrators far surpasses the anonymous ones whose names have not been recorded. In Tuscany the works have authors. The practice of making contracts with artists—the importance of which has just been shown—coincides with their mention in the chronicles.

One last point should be noted. The two legal documents presented here contain two similar formulas: *et omnia et singula facere que ad pulcritudinem dicte tabule spectabunt* (1285)—'execute in general and in detail all things necessary for the beauty of the said *pala*'; '*pingere et facere dictam tabulam quam melius poterit*' (1308); 'paint and create the said *pala* as finely as possible'. The stress is on the quality of the work. But one should not rush to see in this a precise aesthetic requirement, which would reveal a precocious respect for the artist. The formula bears the character of a rule for artisans, and nothing more. It is to be found in innumerable agreements until the sixteenth century and even beyond it. The author remains an *artifex*. As such he may have more or less prestige; the enthusiasm evoked by a work mixes political, social, religious and artistic considerations indiscriminately. Italy is like that.

Chapter 2
Giotto and his Legend (1360–1400)

Florentine poets and writers paid a certain amount of attention to artistic activity from the end of the thirteenth century onwards. Nevertheless, it would be a mistake to imagine a unanimous world, as if a general accord reigned over the modalities of the new art. The texts have often been falsified and badly interpreted by historians enamoured of a simplistic image of the Renaissance. Reading them in the context of the culture itself indicates something quite different: a long polemic about Giotto, whose reputation was not really established until the end of the Trecento. This glorification is associated with the claims on behalf of the *maniera latina*, the existence of which is now clear, but whose definition is far from being evident. The precise data of the vicissitudes between the years 1380 and 1420 reveal that the 'neo-Giottesque' trends of painting needed support and the publicity provided by the intellectuals.

> *C.* 1312: Dante, *Purgatorio*, XI, 94–6:   Doc. 1
>
> Cimabue thought that in painting he led the field,
> But now the cry is for Giotto, so that his fame is obscured.

31 Andrea da Firenze. *Via Veritatis.* 1365. Fresco. The Spanish Chapel in Sta. Maria Novella, Florence.

On the ledge of Purgatory, where he advanced with slow steps, Dante looked at the proud bent under huge stones, which forced their heads down. He interrogated one of them, Oderisi, whose fame had been surpassed by that of a rival, Franco; in the same way, that of Cimabue had ceded its glory to Giotto, as in poetry Cavalcanti moved ahead of Guinicelli, expecting that another would surpass them both (which has always been understood as an allusion to Dante himself). The moral is pronounced by Oderisi:

O vana gloria de l'umane posse !
'Oh, vain glory of human power.'

In the general economy of the *Commedia*, each region of the hereafter has its privileged inhabitants; in the rocky escarpment of Purgatory cultural allusions abound, writers and artists being without doubt predisposed to sin through pride. From this came a kind of promotion of painters and miniaturists against which, as will be seen, commentators protested, surprised to see artisans from a lower class mixed up with intellectuals. On the other hand, since explanations were necessary, some information about these persons had to be supplied, and the name of Giotto was regularly cited by the commentators, who then were obliged to say something about the subject. The simplest thing was to write, as did the author of the *Ottimo commento* (*c.* 1333): 'Giotto is the most eminent among known painters.' Dante never said anything of the sort, but the commentators saw no other explanation possible, all the more so since the writing of *Purgatorio*, about 1312, time had elapsed without damaging—to the contrary—the reputation of the artist. It was as if, to give the lie to Dante and his moral lesson, no one had yet surpassed Giotto.

32 Andrea da Firenze. *Via Veritatis*. Detail: *Triumph of the Dominican Order*. 1365. Fresco. The Spanish Chapel in Sta. Maria Novella, Florence.
In the Spanish Chapel, adjoining the church of the Dominicans, the cathedral is taken as a spatial symbol of the Christian city, in front of which contemporaries are represented, along with the clerics who care for their salvation.

1334: The City Council nominate Giotto as architect in chief of the cathedral and the city:

Doc. 2

The Priors of the Guilds and the Gonfalionier, with the Committee of the Twelve, desirous for the honourable and suitable development of the works in progress or still to be done in the city of Florence, which cannot be perfectly realized without an expert and a celebrated man at the head of these services, since it is not possible to find in all the world a person more able in this and other things than the painter Master Giotto di Bondone, he must be treated as a great master in his country and held in great affection...

Giotto had at that moment returned from Naples, where he had been in the service of King Robert. For the Signoria of Florence, it was a question of retaining the great man in his city, by confiding to him a sort of artistic superintendence. The fulsome terms of the appointment are to be explained by this political background. But the artist immediately achieves an even greater degree of celebrity; he would thereafter be closely associated with Tuscan history. The Campanile appeared as a symbol of Florentine power and, with its decoration, of the cultural abilities which the city claimed:

C. 1335: from Ghiberti's *Commentarii, c.* 1450:

Doc. 3

[Giotto] was very worthy in all kinds of art, including sculpture. The first histories on the edifice which he built, the campanile of Sta. Reparata, were drawn and carved by him. I have seen preparatory studies from his hand for these histories, very remarkably drawn.

33 Unknown Italian artist. Illustration to Dante. Third quarter of the fourteenth century. Miniature in MS. Holkham misc. 48, p. 78. Bodleian Library, Oxford.
On the Circle of Purgatory, where Dante walked with slow steps, he looks on the proud, bowed beneath huge stones.

This piece of information is sufficiently clear to make Giotto be seen, if not as the architect

34 Andrea Pisano. *The Sculptor*. 1337–45. Sculpture in relief. Campanile, Florence.

35 Andrea Pisano. *The Painter*. 1337–45. Sculpture in relief. Campanile, Florence. Among the symbols of the mechanical arts those of painting and sculpture are introduced and commended.

36 Attributed to Giotto. *The Ploughman*. 1337–45. Sculpture in relief. Campanile, Florence.
'[Giotto] was most remarkable in all forms of art, including sculpture... I have seen sketches by his hand for these medallions, very remarkably drawn.' (Ghiberti, *Commentarii*, about 1450–5.)

and decorator of the campanile, at least as the author of the design of this unusual building and its equally original sculptural programme, both of which were realized in their essentials by Andrea Pisano after the master's death. The proof of Giotto's intervention is in the existence of the *provvedimenti* indicated by Ghiberti: drawings, models and measurements. Moreover, a near-contemporary noted:

Mid–14th century: Antonio Pucci, *Centiloquio*, LXXIX.vv. 84–6:   Doc. 4

For Master Giotto, subtle painter,
Who so well directed the work
That he made the first reliefs in his beautiful style...

37 Mosaic (restored in the seventeenth century) of the *Navicella*. St. Peter's, Rome. The masterpiece by Giotto was radically reworked, but was preserved in the new St. Peter's.

The first reliefs? By this must be meant the lower range of medallions, with motifs of the Arts and Techniques, carved with grace and a fine formal economy in the hexagons above the series of the Planets, Virtues and Sacraments. The probable work of Giotto has

38 Parri Spinelli. *The Navicella*. Copy after Giotto's mosaic in St. Peter's. First half of the fifteenth century. Pen and bistre. Metropolitan Museum, New York. 'Giotto, apart from painting, was a man of great ingenuity and capable of many things... In Rome, in the atrium of St. Peter's, for example, where he represented in mosaic with great skill the ship of the Apostles in peril...' (Villani, *De origine civitatis Florentiae*, about 1380).

39 Unknown artist, after Giotto. *The Navicella*. Fourteenth century. Drawing. Pinacoteca Ambrosiana, Milan.

been plausibly identified with the scene of the smith Tubal-cain, the labourer, rather than with the scene of the sculptor, which is closer to the style of Andrea.

In the middle of the fourteenth century, in Florence, reference was always made to Giotto either to approve or to criticize modern style. Boccaccio himself echoes this in the passage:

C. 1350: Boccaccio, *Decameron*, VI, 5: Doc. 5

And he [Giotto] having by these means restored that art to the light, which for many centuries had been buried under the errors of those who preferred to satisfy the eyes of the ignorant rather than to please the intellect of the wise, may justly be called one of the luminaries of Florentine glory; and the more so, when with the greatest humility, he acquired even more [glory] by always refusing to be called master; which title though refused by him was the more striking in that it was so sought after by those who knew less than him, or by his disciples was enviously usurped.

Boccaccio praises the intelligence, the intellectual largeness of mind, and the 'naturalistic' power of Giotto, but underlines his modesty; he gave, in fact, so little occasion to the suspicion of *superbia* that he allowed lesser artists to thrust themselves forward beside him. Boccaccio, while recording the painter's renown, seems to be trying to redress the historical perspective. And here a new step is taken. For the first time Giotto appears as the instigator of the modern revolution which had revived great art: a painter with a formidable historic importance. In the middle of the fourteenth century a master writer, who appeared to express fully the opinion of cultivated people, considered the style introduced by Giotto as the beginning of a new era. The reasons for this are still somewhat unclear.

Petrarch, like Boccaccio, placed Giotto very high (even if he did prefer the Sienese Simone Martini). As early as 1358 he urged a friend of his not to miss going to see the frescoes of 'the prince of painters' in Naples. But above all he explained in the evening of his days that the painter had always had his detractors:

1361: Petrach's Will: Doc. 6

I bequeath my picture or icon of the Virgin Mary, work of the eminent painter Giotto, which was sent to me from Florence by my friend Michele Vanni; its beauty is not understood by the ignorant, but astonishes the masters of art. I bequeath this icon to my Lord [Francesco di Carrara] so that the Blessed Virgin will intercede for him to her son Jesus Christ.

The poet appears to believe that the beauty of the image of the Virgin gives it greater power for piety; a very Italian trait. But above all he protests against the criticisms of the ignorant, and it has been necessary to try to fin out which circles had opposed the modern style. The hostility of religious groups comes readily to mind, in particular those Franciscans who disapproved of the 'luxury' of Assisi and the churches of the Order. But it must be remembered that the years 1340–50 saw changes in taste, with a turning towards a more austere, archaizing and dogmatic art. Giotto's glory was an established fact, but the clergy, the commentators, still questioned each other about him:

C. 1376: Benvenuto da Imola, Commentary on the *Divina Commedia*: Doc. 7

Observe this: certain people in their ignorance are astonished and ask why Dante had mentioned men with unknown names, working in inferior occupations, when he might have evoked those of superior men, desirous of glory and authors of fine

40, 41 Andrea da Firenze. Vault of the Spanish Chapel. 1365. Fresco. Sta. Maria Novella, Florence.
One of the four sections of the vault is dedicated to the *Navicella* in St. Peter's, showing the saving of St. Peter on the right and the angler, emblem of idle amusement, on the left.

42 Giotto. *The Last Judgement*. Detail. 1303–5. Fresco. Cappella degli Scrovegni, Padua.
According to one suggestion—not really very likely—this group contains the portraits of Giotto, Dante and Giovanni Pisano.

43 Pseudo-Giotto. *The Last Judgement*. Detail: *Portrait of Dante*. Fourteenth century. Fresco. Cappella del Podestà, Museo Nazionale del Bargello, Florence.
'He also painted his own portrait, using a mirror, and that of his contemporary Dante Alighieri on a wall of the chapel in the Palazzo del Podestà.' (Villani, *De origine civitatis Florentiae*, about 1380.)

actions worthy of fame. In effect, the poet has here shown himself clever and judicious, for he has thus allowed it to be understood implicitly that the appetite for glory is found equally among all men, so that even minor artisans aspire to it with ardour, and we thus see painters putting their signatures at the bottom of their works... Our poet is right to praise Giotto because of his city, his talent, their friendship... Giotto is always the first, even though there were sometimes serious mistakes in his pictures, as I have heard said by very clever men.

Giotto's legend has here taken another turn. First, there is a justification for the mention of artisans of an inferior class in the poem. The commentary completes the reference to renown by the mention of a friendship between the painter and Dante, which had never been mentioned before. A certain number of anecdotes were current, such as the famous reply by Giotto about his children, who were considered to be so ugly in comparison to the beautiful figures he created: 'I paint during the day; I make them at night.' Soon, a figure by Giotto in the Bargello would be pointed out as a portrait of Dante. His work would be copied during the rest of the century.

It was during the last years of the Trecento that, generally, there would be a 'return to Giotto', in which it is possible to see a basic cycle of Florentine cultural history.

C. 1380: Filippo Villani: *De origine civitatis Florentiae*: Doc. 8

The Ancients, authors of remarkable chronicles, have included in their works the best painters and sculptors among the notables... So may I be permitted, with all deference to the mockers, to give space to the great Florentine painters who have restored life to an art exhausted and nearly dead.

First among them Giovanni, called Cimabue, has by his talent recovered the decadent painting which strayed strangely far from the imitation of nature; before him, during long centuries, in the Greek and Latin world, this art was the prey of mediocre artisans, as is shown by the figures and images which decorated the panels and walls of churches.

After him the road to innovation was open. Giotto, who is to be compared to the Ancients, not only for the brilliance of his fame, but is to be placed above them by his talent, restored painting to its erstwhile dignity and prestige. The figures born of his brush agree so well with the lineaments of nature that they appear to the spectator as alive and breathing, adapting their gestures and movements so exactly that they can be seen speaking, crying, laughing, and acting to the satisfaction of the spectator filled with enthusiasm by the genius of the artist. Many considered, and not without reason, that painters are not intellectually inferior to those whom the liberal arts have enabled to become masters; these have acquired by study and instruction the rules of their profession through books, but the others have had to learn the rules which they know of their art solely by the force of their talent and the tenacity of their memory.

Giotto, apart from his painting, was a man of great wisdom and capable of many things. Thanks to a faultless knowledge of history he rivalled the poets so well that perceptive critics esteemed that he represented what they recounted. He was, moreover, as befitted a man of great sense, more attracted by glory than gain. Careful to make his name known, he painted a work in a noticeable place in all the most important cities of Italy. In Rome, in the atrium of St. Peter's, for example, he represented with great art in a mosaic the ship of the Apostles in peril, to show the power of his art before the eyes of the crowds that flock to the city from all over the world. He also painted his own portrait, using a mirror, and that of his contemporary Dante Alighieri on a wall of the chapel of the Palazzo del Podestà. [Later there is mention of the rivers issuing from this 'pure and abundant spring': Maso, Stefano, Taddeo.]

It is important to know this text because, twenty or thirty years before what is now agreed to be the beginning of the Renaissance, it clearly establishes a new type of relationship between art and culture, without which the Renaissance could not have flourished. First, a place is made for artists among the great men of the city; this is an extraordinary innovation. Villani, son and nephew of historians and chroniclers, is very conscious of his audacity; he explains his action, and his justifications constitute a remarkable plea on behalf of the intellectual dignity of painting. If one thinks of the gifts which it presupposes, the masters of painting may reasonably be compared with the professionals in the liberal arts. Not everyone agrees with this—Villani stresses the point—and here in effect is the opening move in a polemic which will echo all through the Renaissance. If it appears with such clarity about 1380, this is largely due to the comments which continued to be made on the case of Giotto, who is spoken of more and more, at a time which sees the initiation and the development around 1390 of a veritable 'return to Giotto', which will be discussed later.

With the firm and well-written exposition by Villani, the historical dignity of Giotto and the primacy of Florence in painting were definitely associated and no one will again

44 Orcagna. *The Last Judgement*. Detail. Fourteenth century. Fresco. Strozzi Chapel, Sta. Maria Novella, Florence. The Resurrection, with Dante praying in profile, and the painter at the right.

45   Jacopo del Casentino. *Dormition of the Virgin. C.* 1320. Tempera on panel. Loeser Collection, Florence.

46   Giotto. *Dormition of the Virgin.* Detail. *C.* 1315. Tempera on panel. Gemälde-galerie, Staatliche Museen Preussischer Kulturbesitz, Berlin.

47   Agnolo Gaddi. *The Legend of the True Cross.* 1390. Fresco. Sta. Croce, Florence. Agnolo Gaddi's pictures of the cycle of the Cross show a taste for narrative and an aptitude for managing large scenes, gov-erned by the memory of Giotto, in spite (according to Vasari) of a certain weak-ness in draughtsmanship, compensated for by a good colour sense.

contest them. In this sketch of the history of art Filippo achieved an unpretentious work, which turns this mediocre Latinist into an adept of would-be antique humanism. He places his panorama under the patronage of an antique model, that is, Pliny, whose Book XXXV on artists supplied the scheme which permitted—as Baxandall has shown—the organization of the narrative: the precursor, the advent, the disciples. Giotto's name occurs as a reminder of a strong style to be recovered. Villani in effect is a pessimistic chronicler; like so many clerics and poets of the second half of the fourteenth century in the West, he takes a gloomy view of the world and his own times. He writes: 'we have arrived at such a point of villany and inertia that it is indispensable to remember, as a counter to the present degradation, the memory of the virtues of bygone days.'

The mention of a portrait of Dante by Giotto in the Bargello appears for the first time in Villani. It was taken up again by Ghiberti some fifty years later, and became the occasion for an imposing development by Vasari about a century after that. The chapel of the Bargello, where it was thought possible to rediscover, in the last century, the image of Dante, was built and decorated between 1336 and 1338. It is not impossible that, before his death, Giotto was involved in the work, but improbable that an exile, whose condemnation had not yet been abrogated, should have been represented in a place of honour. Moreover, the friendship between Dante and Giotto is a pious legend elaborated during the century, as a result of the haunting verse in *Purgatorio.* In any case, the interesting fact is this insistence on Giotto's gifts as a portraitist; the great merit of his art

48   Agnolo Gaddi. *The Legend of the True Cross: Entry of Heraclius into Jerusalem.* 1390. Fresco. Sta. Croce, Florence.
The composition gathers two episodes into a single fresco, articulated by the architecture: there are two self-portraits, at the sides (cf. Pls. 53, 54).

is to produce the appearance of life, and to give, in this way, a sort of survival to the illustrious dead by the striking presentation of their features. This is held to be the fundamental aim of art; the Italians will never give this up.

The people were emerging from a period dominated by the Black Death, when painting had been led back to a hieratic style, to austere formulae, to more dogmatic devotional themes, of which the great altarpiece by Orcagna in Sta. Maria Novella (1354–7) could be considered typical. This severe art contained an implicit criticism of Giotto's ample and vivacious manner. Conversely, it was a denunciation of the feebleness of the art of the day to appeal from it to the master of the Bardi Chapel and the *Navicella.* This evocation of *Peter's Barque* was a reminder of St. Peter's in Rome and of papal authority. It reappears in one of the smaller vaults of the Spanish Chapel (*c.* 1366–8) where Andrea da Firenze had illustrated Dominican orthodoxy in a celebrated work.

C. 1390: F. Sacchetti, *Novella 136:*   Doc. 9

In the city of Florence, ever rich in men of original talent, there were painters and other masters in a place called S. Miniato al Monte to work on paintings and other requirements for this church. After having dined with the Abbot, eaten well and drunk deeply, they started to talk. Among other questions, one of them, named

Orcagna, head of the workshop of Nostra Donna d'Orto S. Michele, asked: 'Who was the greatest master of painting, who else has there been since Giotto?.' Some said that it was Cimabue, some Stefano, some Bernardo and some Buffalmacco; some said this one and some another. Taddeo Gaddi, who was of the company, said: 'Certainly there have been many able painters, who have painted in a manner which it is impossible for human beings to equal; but this art has now begun to decline and continues to do so day by day.'

One named Master Alberto, who was a great master of marble sculpture, said: 'I think that you are very wrong, and I will show you that never was Nature so delicately rendered as nowadays, especially in painting and in the making of sculptures.' Hearing him all the masters laughed, as if he had taken leave of his senses...

[Alberto then explained that, if God is an unsurpassed painter, Florentine women are even better, since they know how—thanks to paint and the processes of their toilet—to improve on Nature better than any painter or sculptor. And the whole company, convinced, under Alberto's rule began to drink.]

49 Orcagna. *Death of the Virgin.* Detail: *Self-portrait.* 1352–9. Sculpture. Tabernacle, Orsanmichele, Florence.
In the great central composition in marble, the self-portrait is slipped in among the group of the Apostles: 'a hood round his head, a short beard, the face round and flat...' (Vasari).

Sacchetti is one of the best collectors of anecdotes about Florentine life. He wrote towards the end of the fourteenth century. Skilfully he brings on the scene celebrities and ordinary people concerned with current problems and familiar events. It is even more interesting that several times he concerns himself with Giotto, who obviously frequently entered into the stories and the conversation of Tuscans. But at first sight the 'pessimist' declaration by Taddeo Gaddi surprises one and requires explanation.

Orcagna had died in 1366; *capomaestro* at Orsanmichele from 1355 to 1359, he had carved the altar of the Madonna, after having completed the retable in the Strozzi Chapel in Sta. Maria Novella. The conversation took place about 1360, a date confirmed by the works at S. Miniato, in particular the crypt which Taddeo Gaddi executed. The jovial Master Alberto, who interprets in his own way the vitality of painting, seems to have been the Lombard Arnoldi, who also died about 1360. The reunion at S. Miniato has nothing unreasonable about it. It serves as a serious starting-point for a rather cynical evocation of the coquetry of Florentine women. The opinion of Taddeo Gaddi is not cited as an historical fact, but as a judgement of the moment, which the *novellista* was quite willing to take over, since he shared the pessimistic attitude of the Trecento. If he writes entertaining stories, sometimes rather free ones, it is to amuse, 'thanks to which in the mass of woes there is a little laughter' (Prologue to the *Trecento Novelle*).

But in reality a desire to restore style by a return to Giotto was now appearing, and historians have now well charted its course. A painter like Spinello Aretino painted in 1387 a cycle of the Life of St. Benedict at San Miniato, which can only be properly understood by comparing the types, the draperies and the management of the forms with those in the Peruzzi Chapel in Sta. Croce (*c.* 1320), for example. The works by Agnolo Gaddi on the cycle of the history of the True Cross (1390) display a taste for narrative and a skill in articulating large scenes which certainly lack amplitude, but betray the same model. Around these dates the references to Giotto multiply. The legend of the great Florentine is filled out in several ways. First, from the standpoint of the humanists:

Doc. 10   *C.* 1397: Cino Rinuccini, *Responsiva alla Invettiva di Messer Antonio Lusco:*

[Giotto] represents human figures in such a way that he continually incites us to virtue; he surpasses not only Cimabue, but also the Ancients, Scopas, Polyclites and Praxiteles.

This comparison with antique sculptors seems odd; but they belong to the traditional types of artists who are mentioned with confidence in order to exalt Cimabue's successor.

50 Giotto. *The Visitation*. About 1300.
Fresco. Basilica di S. Francesco, Assisi.

51 Unknown artist, after Giotto. *The Visitation*. Second quarter of the four-teenth century. Drawing. Gabinetto dei Disegni, Galleria degli Uffizi, Florence.
A studio version or a copy after an original by Giotto, which recalls the principle of a frieze-like composition in the simplification of the building and land-scape.

Even more curious is the care taken to underline his modernity by the stimulating effect which the seriousness and moral dignity of his types convey. This is probably an answer to the criticisms of the sanctimonious, who failed to find enough pious concentration in the works of the master, and in particular in those of his first disciples.

Paduan circles did not hang back; a northern humanist makes this clear in a digression in a letter:

Doc. 11   1404: Letter from P. P. Vergerio:

One must do as the painters of today, who, while looking with care at the celebrated works of other artists, nevertheless hold only to the models of Giotto.

The importance of the frescoes in the Arena Chapel for Paduan workshops is obvious, if one considers the activity of Altichiero, with whom is achieved—as with Spinello Aretino in Florence—a return to the ample style of Giotto; as in the *Beheading of St. George* (1377) in the oratory grafted on to the side of the Basilica of Sant'Antonio. This is also probably the moment when people began to examine frescoes in order to identify the personages

52   Spinello Aretino *Miracle of St. Benedict.* 1387. Fresco. S. Miniato al Monte, Florence.
A return to the broad distribution of figures and Giottesque types, praised by Vasari as 'great knowledge and capacity to give force to his colours, which came from long practice'.

represented. As in Sta. Maria Novella, there were efforts to find Dante in the *Last Judgement*. Recently a suggestion has been put forward which, in the spirit of the tradition, would discover among the Elect a group containing Dante, Giotto and perhaps Giovanni Pisano.

The artists of the new generation had found their hero. This movement of return towards the art of the beginning of the fourteenth century found its classic formulation with Cennino Cennini:

C. 1400: Cennino Cennini, *Il Libro dell' Arte:* Doc. 12

As a minor member exercising the art of painting I, Cennino, born of Andrea Cennini da Colle di Valdelsa, was taught the said art for twelve years by Agnolo di Taddeo da Firenze my master, who learned the said art from Taddeo his father, who was held at the baptismal font by Giotto and was his disciple for twenty-four years. This Giotto changed the art of painting from Greek to Latin and made it modern; and his art was the most perfect that anyone had ever practised.

This declaration is placed at the beginning of his book, a collection of recipes, which is important for the correct technical analysis it permits. It is very remarkable that its author traced a kind of genealogy which guaranteed an incontestable title of nobility to his work and his craft. Everything is said with simplicity, in recalling that Giotto is the one who brought back painting from 'the Greek to the Latin'. Thereafter the formula never changed.

Cennino's own manner is not well enough known for him to be included among the initiators of the return to Giotto, other than morally. But there is certainly a fresh start. By appealing to Giotto, the painters of the younger generation were leaning on the authority of a grand style, well articulated in a strictly defined space, in order to organize their large narrative scenes.

Giotto was particularly useful as a justification of the new practice of including portraits within compositions. The renown of the 'restorer' of painting gave legitimacy to the contemporary effigies which he liberally included in his frescoes. The most famous of these was the double portrait in the Bargello. Giotto's renown was thus a double benefit for painters, in promising them an intellectual status less humble than that of mere artisans, and by authorizing them, on his example, to introduce, with the portraits of their contemporaries, their own portraits, in carefully thought-out places in large compositions. The habit of indicating them in frescoes seems to be justified in this way. Later chroniclers recorded this practice quite happily:

C. 1385: Self-portrait of Agnolo Gaddi (from Vasari, 1568): Doc. 13

His self-portrait can be seen in the Alberti Chapel in Sta. Croce in the scene of the Emperor Heraclius carrying the Cross; he is near a door, in profile, with a little beard, wearing the pink hood that was then fashionable.

53, 54   Agnolo Gaddi. *The Legend of the True Cross: Entry of Heraclius into Jerusalem.* Details. 1390. Fresco. Sta. Croce, Florence. Details from Plate 48, showing the two self-portraits: '...in profile, with a small beard and a rose-coloured hood as was then the fashion'. (Vasari, *Life of Agnolo Gaddi.*)

The group is famous. The two profile portraits of the painter in his pink hood and his neighbour, who wears a felt hat, are of a remarkable vivacity. They are placed at the side of the scene, as casual onlookers. This is where, for more than a century, painters were accustomed to place themselves, without any manual, treatise or official document inviting them to do so. Thus the self-portrait *in assistenza* was born in the heart of the Florentine artistic community, thanks to the authority firmly established by Giotto, the 'master of masters'.

Chronological Table 1400–1500

	1403–1424	Florence	Ghiberti, north door of the Baptistery
	C. 1406	Lucca	Jacopo della Quercia, tomb of Ilaria del Carretto in S. Martino
	1409	Florence	Donatello, marble *David* for the Cathedral
	1416–1425	Florence	Donatello, *Prophets* on the Campanile (now Museo dell'Opera)
	1417–1446	Florence	Brunelleschi, dome of the Cathedral
	1420	Rome	Masolino, fresco cycle of *St. Catherine of Alexandria* in S. Clemente
	1423	Florence	Gentile da Fabriano, *Adoration of the Magi* for Sta. Trinità (Uffizi, Florence)
	1423–1428	Florence	Masolino and Masaccio, frescoes in the Brancacci Chapel in the Carmine
	C. 1425	Rome	Masolino and Masaccio, polyptych for Sta. Maria Maggiore
	1425–1452	Florence	Ghiberti, *Gates of Paradise* for the Baptistery
	1428	Florence	Masaccio, *Trinity* in Sta. Maria Novella
	1428–1435	Castiglione d'Olona	Masolino, frescoes in the Baptistery
	1429–1430	Verona	Pisanello, *St. George and the Princess* in Sant'Anastasia
x	*C.* 1430–1435	Florence	Domenico Veneziano, *Adoration of the Magi* (Berlin)
	C. 1430–1437	Bologna	Jacopo della Quercia, portal of S. Petronio
	1431–1435	Florence	Luca della Robbia, reliefs for the *Cantoria* of the Cathedral (Museo dell'Opera)
	1433–1439	Florence	Donatello, reliefs for the *Cantoria* of the Cathedral (Museo dell'Opera)
	C. 1435	Fiesole	Fra Angelico, *Coronation of the Virgin* for S. Domenico (Louvre, Paris)
	C. 1435	Florence	Donatello, bronze *David* (Bargello)
x	1435–1436	Florence	Alberti, *Trattato della Pittura* (Treatise on Painting)
	C. 1435–1444	Florence	Paolo Uccello, frescoes in the Chiostro Verde in Sta. Maria Novella
x	*C.* 1436	Prato	Fresco cycle of the *Life of the Virgin* in the Cathedral
	1436	Florence	Paolo Uccello, fresco of *Sir John Hawkwood* in the Cathedral
x	1437	Perugia	Fra Angelico, triptych for S. Domenico (Galleria Nazionale dell'Umbria, Perugia)
x	1437 et seq.	Florence	Filippo Lippi, *Barbadori Altarpiece* for Santo Spirito (Louvre, Paris)

	1437–1444	Siena	Sassetta, polyptych of S. Francis (various museums)
	C. 1437–1445	Florence	Fra Angelico, frescoes in the convent of S. Marco
x	1438–1445	Florence	Domenico Veneziano and Piero della Francesca at Sant' Egidio
x	1439–1440	Florence	Fra Angelico, altarpiece for S. Marco
	1439–1445	Rome	Filarete, bronze doors for St. Peter's
	C. 1440 (?)	Mantua	Pisanello, Arthurian fresco cycle in the Ducal Palace
	1440–1443	Florence	Donatello, bronze *Judith* (Piazza della Signoria)
	1443–1450	Padua	Donatello, statues and panels for the high altar of the Santo
x	before 1445	Sansepolcro	Piero della Francesca, *Baptism of Christ* for the Priory of S. Giovanni Battista (National Gallery, London)
x	1445–1462 (?)	Sansepolcro	Piero della Francesca, polyptych of the *Madonna della Misericordia* (Museo Civico)
	1447	Orvieto	Fra Angelico, *Last Judgement* and *Prophets* in the vault of the Chapel of S. Brizio in the Cathedral
	1447–1453	Padua	Donatello, equestrian statue of Gattamelata
x	1449–1450	Padua	Mantegna, frescoes in the Eremitani
	1449–1455	Rome	Fra Angelico, fresco cycles of *SS. Lawrence and Stephen* in the Chapel of Nicolas V (Vatican)
	before 1450	Urbino	Piero della Francesca, *Flagellation of Christ* (Galleria Nazionale delle Marche, Urbino)
	C. 1450	Florence	Andrea del Castagno, *Last Supper* in the refectory of Sta. Apollonia
	1451	Rimini	Piero della Francesca, *St. Sigismond and Malatesta*, in the 'Tempio Malatestiano'
x	1451–1453	Florence	Andrea del Castagno, frescoes in Sant' Egidio (lost)
	1452–1458	Arezzo	Piero della Francesca, *Legend of the True Cross*, S. Francesco
	1452–1458	Naples	Francesco Laurana, etc., Triumphal Arch of Alfonso of Aragon at the Castelnuovo
	1454–1464	Sansepolcro	Piero della Francesca, polyptych of S. Agostino (now in various places)
x	1455	Florence	Neri di Bicci, *S. Remigio Altarpiece*
	C. 1456–1470	Florence	Paolo Uccello, *Battle Scenes* for the Medici Palace (now Uffizi, Florence; Louvre, Paris; National Gallery, London)
	after 1456	Florence	Donatello, *St. Mary Magdalen*, Baptistery
	C. 1457–1459	Verona	Mantegna, *S. Zeno Altarpiece*, S. Zeno
x	1458	Mosciano	Neri di Bicci, altarpiece for S. Andrea (commission date)
x C.	1459–1463	Florence	Benozzo Gozzoli, decoration of the chapel of the Medici Palace
	1460	Florence	Alesso Baldovinetti, *Nativity* in SS. Annunziata
x	1461–1474	Mantua	Mantegna, *Camera degli Sposi*, Ducal Palace
	1463	Bologna	Niccolo dell'Arca, *Pietà* in Sta. Maria della Vita

	1466–1468	Arezzo	Piero della Francesca, gonfalone (banner) of the Nunziata (lost)
	C. 1467	Milan	Vincenzo Foppa, decoration of the Portinari Chapel in Sant' Eustorgio
	1467–1484	Pisa	Benozzo Gozzoli, frescoes in the Campo Santo
	1468 et seq.	Ferrara	Ercole de' Roberti and Francesco del Cossa, *Sala dei Mesi*, Palazzo Schifanoia
	C. 1470 (?)	Venice	Giovanni Bellini, *Pietà* (Brera, Milan)
	1472–1474	Urbino	Piero della Francesca, the *Brera Altarpiece (Madonna di Federico Montefeltro)* (Brera, Milan)
	1473	Pavia	Work on the façade of the Certosa
	1473	Ascoli Piceno	Crivelli, Cathedral polyptych
	C. 1474	Naples	Antonello da Messina, *St. Jerome* (National Gallery, London)
	1474–1477	Urbino	Justus of Ghent and Pedro Berruguete, decoration of the *studiolo*, Ducal Palace
	before 1475	Florence	Verrocchio and Leonardo, *Baptism of Christ* (Uffizi, Florence)
	before 1475	Ferrara	Cosmè Tura, *Roverella polyptych* (various museums)
	C. 1475	Florence	Botticelli, *Adoration of the Magi* for the Medici (Uffizi, Florence)
x	1477	Rome	Melozzo da Forlì, decoration of the Vatican Library
	1477–1478	Florence	Botticelli, *Primavera* for the Villa Castello (Uffizi, Florence)
	C. 1478	Florence	Arrival of the *Portinari Altarpiece* by Hugo van der Goes
	C. 1478	Venice	Antonello da Messina, *S. Cassiano Altarpiece* (Vienna)
x	1479	Rome	Perugino, apse frescoes in the choir of Old St. Peter's
	1480	Florence	Ghirlandaio and Botticelli, frescoes in Ognissanti
	C. 1480	Mantua	Mantegna, *St. Sebastian* (Louvre, Paris)
	1481–1483	Florence	Leonardo, *Adoration of the Kings*, unfinished (Uffizi, Florence)
x	1481–1483	Rome	Perugino, Botticelli, Domenico Ghirlandaio, Cosimo Rosselli, Signorelli, etc. execute the fresco cycles in the Sistine Chapel
x	1482	Florence	Commissions to Domenico Ghirlandaio, Botticelli, Perugino, Piero Pollaiuolo for decorations in the Palazzo della Signoria
	1482–1486	Milan	Bramante, Sta. Maria presso S. Satiro
x	1483	Volterra	Botticelli, Perugino, decoration of the Villa Medici at Spedaletto
	1483–1486	Florence	Ghirlandaio, Sassetti Chapel in Sta. Trinità
	1483–1488	Florence	Filippino Lippi, *The Virgin Appearing to St. Bernard*, Badia
x	1484–1495	Mantua	Mantegna, *The Triumphs of Caesar* (The Royal Collection, Hampton Court Palace)
	C. 1485	Florence	Filippino Lippi, frescoes in the Brancacci Chapel in the Carmine
x	C. 1485	Mantua	Mantegna, *Madonna and Angels* (Brera, Milan)

x	1485–1490	Florence	Ghirlandaio, choir frescoes, Sta. Maria Novella
	1485–1500	Treviglio	Butinone and Zenale, *S. Martino Polyptych*
	C. 1486	Florence	Botticelli, frescoes in the Villa Lemmi (Louvre, Paris)
	1486–1487	Venice	Giovanni Bellini, *S. Giobbe Altarpiece* (Accademia, Venice)
	1488	Venice	Verrocchio, equestrian statue of Colleone, finished by Leopardi
	1488–1489	Rome	Filippino Lippi, frescoes in the Carafa Chapel in Sta. Maria sopra Minerva
x	1488–1497	Fano	Perugino, altarpiece for Sta. Maria Nuova
	C. 1490	Siena	Francesco di Giorgio, *Nativity*, S. Domenico
	1490 et seq.	Venice	Carpaccio, cycle in the Scuola di Sta. Orsola
x *C.*	1490–1498	Milan	Leonardo, projects for the equestrian statue of Francesco Sforza
x	1492 et seq.	Rome	Pollaiuolo brothers, *Tomb of Innocent VIII*, St. Peter's
x	1493–1494	Rome	Pinturicchio, decoration of the Appartamento Borgia in the Vatican
	before 1494	Florence	Michelangelo, reliefs of the *Madonna of the Stairs*, and the *Battle of the Centaurs* (Casa Buonarroti, Florence)
x	1494		Dürer, copies after prints by Mantegna
x	1494–1495	Perugia	Perugino, *Polyptych for S. Pietro*; altarpiece for the chapel of the Priors
	1495	Bologna	Michelangelo, figures for the Shrine of S. Domenico
x	1495–1497	Milan	Leonardo, *Last Supper* in Sta. Maria delle Grazie
x	1496	Mantua	Mantegna, *Madonna of Victory* (Louvre, Paris)
x	1496–1500	Perugia	Perugino, fresco cycle in the Cambio
	1497–1501	Monte Oliveto Maggiore	Signorelli, *Life of St. Benedict*
	1499–1502	Orvieto	Signorelli, frescoes in the Chapel of S. Brizio in the Cathedral
	1498	Rome	Michelangelo, *Pietà* in St. Peter's
x	1500	Vallombrosa	Perugino, *Assumption* (Uffizi, Florence)

Chapter 3

The Events of the Years 1438-1440 in Florence: Domenico Veneziano and Piero della Francesca

After a short exile in Venice, Cosimo de' Medici, recalled by the Signoria, returned to Florence in October 1434. His recovery of political power was followed or, more exactly, marked by many initiatives of a cultural nature. They comprised public buildings and above all a convent—that of the Dominicans of S. Marco, to whom Cosimo always remained particularly attached. The convent was a branch of the reformed Order, known as the Observance; one of the priors was Giovanni da Fiesole—Fra Angelico.

Cosimo followed in this the directives of Pope Eugenius IV, who was a client of the Medici bank, and for whom Florence was his most solid support. The pontificate came during a period of many difficulties which led Eugenius IV to leave Rome and to avoid the Council of Basle. He was counting on a positive renewal of authority through the reunion of the Greek and Latin churches, in which cause he was very active. Everyone was asking where and when the historic Council would take place. Eventually Ferrara was chosen, where the Este made spectacular plans for the reception of the Orthodox clergy and the Byzantine court, whose great style and luxurious pomp astonished and even rather intimidated Latin princes and dignitaries. Florence, where the Pope was living, was waiting to see what would happen. In the pontiff's suite there was a young secretary, educated in the north Italian universities; his family, long banished from Florence, had been able to return after 1428. He was called Leon Battista Alberti and he was born in 1404. He believed that this was the moment to announce the arrival of a new era in painting, more intellectually satisfying, more complete and much stronger. In 1435 he therefore published a little *Treatise on Painting*, with a dedication to Gianfrancesco Gonzaga for the Latin version, and in 1436 an Italian version dedicated to Brunelleschi.

1436: Dedication of Alberti's treatise: Doc. 1

> On returning from the long exile in which we Alberti have grown old, here in this city above all others distinguished, I perceived in many, but first in you Filippo, and in our close friend Donato the sculptor, and in those others, Nencio and Luca and Masaccio, that they are in every praiseworthy thing of a talent not to be placed behind anything which is antique and famous in these arts.

55 Jacopo del Sellaio. *St. John the Baptist.* Detail. About 1460. Tempera on panel. Samuel H. Kress Collection, National Gallery of Art, Washington D.C.
S. Giovannino, protector of Florence, indicates the city, seen on the other side of the Arno, with the dome of the cathedral, the campanile and the tower of the Palazzo della Signoria.

Gloom was no longer fashionable. Outside Florence it might be believed that the arts were inexorably in decadence, but on his return to his homeland Leon Battista saw, thanks to his friends, another future and hastened to explain the formula for the renewal of painting. Masaccio had died in Rome in 1428. It has occasioned some surprise that Alberti did not think fit to mention the two most notable figures of the day: the Dominican Fra Angelico and the younger Carmelite, Fra Filippo Lippi. If he felt that he had the right to mention his architect and sculptor friends while discussing painting, yet he mentioned only one dead painter—Masaccio—in his dedication; and in the text itself one great man from the

56 The Adimari Master. *A Florentine Wedding Procession.* Mid-fifteenth century. Tempera on panel. Galleria dell'Accademia, Florence.
A procession on a raised platform, covered with an awning, outside the Baptistery, on the occasion of a secular celebration.

past—Giotto, author of the *Navicella*—in the midst of references to painters of Antiquity. Alberti's short treatise indicates, however, that it was felt that important things were about to happen.

First came the building of the dome of Florence cathedral, the crowning glory of Brunelleschi's achievement, which was consecrated the following spring.

25 March 1437: Consecration of Sta. Maria del Fiore (from Leonardo Bruni):   Doc. 2

At this time the basilica of Florence was solemnly consecrated by Pope Eugenius [IV]. A wooden bridge was built, with unbelievable speed and marvellous workmanship, from the church of the Friars Preachers [Sta. Maria Novella] where the Pope was living, as far as the basilica to be consecrated. This bridge was not only for magnificence, but also for utility. The day of the dedication, there were such crowds from the countryside, from neighbouring towns, from the mass of the city, that all access, all the roads were filled; this enormous crowd would never have permitted the Pontiff or his cardinals and his prelates to pass without the suspended passage which this bridge gave them [...]

Unfortunately, there are no more precise documents on the arrangement of this 'aerial bridge' between Sta. Maria Novella and the cathedral. The ceremonies depicted on some of the *cassoni* of the period give an idea of the arrangement of the awnings and the platform erected in front of the Baptistery. In view of the value which the Florentines attached to their cathedral—still unfinished—this pontifical consecration was of great significance. The wooden bridge was a technical discovery along the same lines as Brunelleschi's dome. The ceremony strongly consolidated the power of Cosimo de' Medici, who was linked to Pope Eugenius by all sorts of ties—religious, political and financial. Florence would become a sort of provisional capital of Christendom if the Council could be induced to come to the city. In any case it had now become as Alberti had foreseen, a focus of attraction for all serious artists. The proof is found in a rather unexpected document dating from the following spring.

1 April 1438: Letter from Domenico Veneziano to Piero de' Medici: Doc. 3

Most honoured and noble lord,
   Thanks be to God, I am well and hope that my letter finds you in good health and happy. Many, many times I have asked for news of you and have not had any, except by Manno Donati who told me that you were in Ferrara and that you were well. I

was comforted by this and, knowing where you are, I write to you for my comfort and duty. God knows that my humble position does not justify my writing to your lordship, but my affection for you and for all your family emboldens me to do so as liege and duty-bound.

I have now heard that Cosimo has decided to have a retable made, which he wishes shall be magnificent. I am very pleased about this and I would be even more so, if it were I who could paint it, thanks to your intervention. If that came about, I could—with the help of the Lord—produce something magnificent comparable to

57 Domenico Veneziano. *Adoration of the Magi.* About 1440. Tempera on a circular panel. Gemäldegalerie, Staatliche Museen Preussischer Kulturbesitz, Berlin.
This picture was probably offered to the Medici, since Cosimo was a protector of the Confraternity of the Magii (see Pl. 58). A fresco of the same subject adorned the wall of the cell which was kept for him in the Convent of S. Marco.

the work of good masters like Fra Filippo and Fra Giovanni, who have a lot of work. Above all, Fra Filippo, with the picture for Santo Spirito on which he works day and night, but which he will not finish in under five years; it is a very large work. Even if the wish to serve you makes me presumptuous in offering my services, and in risking doing less well than the others, I want to seize every occasion to gain merit and act gloriously.

If the work is so large that Cosimo decides to give it to several masters, I beg you, in the measure in which a servitor can beg his master, to be willing to incline your noble spirit to help me to obtain this favour and to take part in the work. If you knew my desire to create a masterpiece, in particular for you, you would help me here and, I am sure, without having to regret it. I pray you to do everything possible; my work, I promise it, will do you honour...

Domenico Veneziano, whose name indicates his origin, was not far off thirty. It would be interesting to know what his training had been, his early work, and the spirit of his art. If he addressed himself with some assurance to Piero, it must be because he had known him during the Medicis' stay in the Veneto; he must also have already proved himself and could no longer be considered as a beginner. His letter was written from Perugia; this suggests that Domenico had useful contacts in Umbria. But why write to Piero, if it were for a request to Cosimo?

Perhaps the statesman himself was not very approachable. Cosimo, on whom all depended, concerned himself, it appears, with matters of architecture and town planning. Historians have gained the impression that he left the care of the rest to his sons Piero and Giovanni. This is rendered more likely by the fact that around 1440 several painters solicited the intervention of Piero. If they acted thus it can only be because they had already had dealings with him and found him more accessible than the master of Florentine politics. In 1438 Piero was twenty-two; perhaps he was already becoming a collector, as he did later when illness immobilized him and he became for the people 'Piero il Gottoso'—the Gouty. At the death of Cosimo in 1464 he was already almost an invalid and he died in 1469. But thirty years earlier he appears to have played an interesting role, at a moment when Florence was becoming for a time the centre of ecclesiastical affairs.

Did Domenico propose himself as a candidate because he painted like Angelico and Lippi, or because he could introduce a style which was more seductive and new for Florence? The matter is not without importance. One of the most admired painters in the north, in Venice and in Ferrara, was Pisanello, whose lively and charming art was fashionable. On the other hand, Domenico was well aware of the brilliant and 'precious' works of Gentile da Fabriano, which were not without connections with Pisanello, and he may have felt that a style at once narrative and graceful stood a chance in Florence. This would have been proved by the *tondo* of the *Adoration of the Magi* (Berlin), now attributed to Domenico, and may well have been a kind of demonstration-picture offered to the Medici. In it may be seen the ornamental motif of the seven balls (*palle*) which are to be found twenty years later on the caparison of the young Lorenzo in the cavalcade by Gozzoli in the Medici Palace.

Unfortunately, it is not known to what important *pala*, desired by Cosimo, Domenico was referring. It looks as if he believed that there was a kind of void in Florence. He mentions only two colleagues, whom he confidently declares to be too busy. As regards Angelico, it is true that there is no lack of works; he was in Perugia in 1437 to do an altarpiece for the high altar and a *pala* of St. Nicholas in a chapel. The allusion by Domenico confirms that he occupied a place of importance and was appreciated for the 'modern' quality of his art. Their contacts in 1438 therefore bear looking into. As to Fra Filippo, he had indeed been busy since 1437 on the *Barbadori Altarpiece* (Louvre), where his manner is rather lacking in flexibility, though not in delicacy, with a curious dreamy

58   Domenico Veneziano. *Adoration of the Magi*. Detail. About 1440. Tempera on panel. Gemäldegalerie, Staatliche Museen Preussischer Kulturbesitz, Berlin.
This detail from Plate 57 allows one to see the ornamental motif of the seven *palle* (balls, the Medici arms) on the belt of the man at the right.

59 Filippo Lippi. *The Barbadori Altarpiece.* Detail: *Self-portrait.* 1437. Tempera on panel. Musée du Louvre, Paris.
Filippo Lippi, working on the Barbadori Altar from 1437, painted his own portrait in the monk at the left, seen in three-quarter view looking at the spectator.

self-portrait in the monk on the left. But what were Domenico's advances going to lead to, since he did not hesitate to substitute himself for the two painters?

Events were moving fast: the solemn opening of the Council at Ferrara on 8 January 1438; departure from Ferrara to Florence, January/February 1439; first session in Florence, 2 March 1439; solemn session of union, 6 July 1439.

1438–9: Council of Florence (from Vespasiano da Bisticci, *c.* 1480–90):   Doc. 4

Pope Eugenius had the idea of bringing to Italy at his own expense the members of the Greek Church so that they should unite themselves to the Roman one. The Emperor of Constantinople and the Patriarch made the journey with all the worthy prelates of that nation. They came to Ferrara in great numbers at the Pope's expense. But plague having broken out in Ferrara, the Pope came to Florence and there had made ready lodgings for the Greeks and settled their bills month by month [...]

A very fine installation of benches and seats was made at Sta. Maria Novella; it was called the Council of the Greeks [...]

Then arrived some Jacobites and some Ethiopians sent by Prester John; they came to the Pope who invited them at his expense. All the learned men of Italy and from abroad were invited [...]

Finally, one day, the Pontiff came solemnly with all the Roman Curia and the Emperor of the Greeks, as well as the Latin prelates, to Sta. Maria del Fiore, where there was an installation which allowed the prelates of both churches to have their seats [...]

The Pope was wearing pontificals, all the cardinals wore copes, the cardinal bishops white damask mitres, and all the bishops both Greek and Latin mitres of embroidered white lawn, Latin bishops copes and the Greeks robes of very rich silk in the Greek fashion, and the style of the Greek robes appeared far more dignified and solemn than those of the Latin prelates [...] The place of the Emperor was, for this solemnity, on the Epistle side of the High Altar and on the same side were the Greek prelates. A great crowd had come to Florence to see so remarkable an event. In an armchair placed in front of the Pope's, draped with silk, was the Emperor in a very rich vestment of damasked brocade and with a Greek style of hat with a very beautiful jewel at the top. He was very fine, with a Byzantine type of beard...
[There then follows an account of the ceremony of union and the nomination of new cardinals.]

The account given by the old Florentine bookseller, a great supplier to pontiffs and princes, is confirmed by contemporary documents, in particular by the memoirs of Bruni. Vespasiano has naturally noted the huge costs incurred by the Pope, who could not have been able to manage without the help of the Medici bank. But these memoirs also serve to illustrate the spectacular character of the Council and its ostentatious displays for the Florentine crowd, among whom was Domenico Veneziano, accompanied—as is now known—by the young Piero della Francesca. The elaborate dress of the Greeks and the vestments of the foreign visitors were quite properly the object of precise drawings made by another notable spectator, Pisanello, who, first in Ferrara and then in Florence, recorded the event in a series of detailed drawings. At the same time he produced medals destined for the participants in the meeting, thus confirming his eminent position in Italian art. Is it surprising that other painters did not also participate? Perhaps it is merely that their records have not survived. Even before the Council ended on the spectacular day of 15 August, important works had been started in the chapel of the Hospital of Sta. Maria Nuova, also called, because of an earlier church on the site, Sant'Egidio. Documents of payments have established that the decoration of the choir had been begun as early as May 1439 with Domenico Veneziano.

Doc. 5   1439–40: Frescoes in the Chiesa Nuova, Sant'Egidio (from Vasari, 1568):

Domenico painted in oil Joachim visiting his wife St. Anne; beneath it was the birth of Our Lady, represented in a very ornate room, and a little boy who knocks on the door with a door-knocker, with great charm. Lower down still he painted the Marriage of the Virgin, with a large number of portraits painted from life; among them was Messer Bernardetto de' Medici, Constable of Florence, in a red hat; Bernardo Guadagni, who was the Gonfalonier; Folco Portinari and others from that family. He also placed there a dwarf who breaks a little rod, in a very lively fashion; and some women wearing graceful dresses of an unfashionable design, such as were worn at that time. But this work remained unfinished... [The rest of the description is about the *Death of the Virgin*, painted later by Andrea del Castagno with a striking perspective of the bier and also an array of portraits.]

The attention given by Vasari to this work is somewhat spoilt by the tale of the dramatic rivalry between Domenico and Andrea del Castagno; if Vasari were to be believed, Castagno ended by murdering his colleague, something that agrees neither with the dates nor with any known facts. To judge from the accounts, the work in Sant'Egidio, begun in all probability during the winter of 1438–9, seems to have been continued actively from May to September 1439, and then to have been interrupted until June 1441, when it was resumed for a year. In June 1445 there is mention of another fresco, the *Marriage of the Virgin*, which was never finished since Domenico, for unknown reasons, abandoned the enterprise. The tale of Andrea's crime can be fairly easily explained. Domenico never finished his work at Sant'Egidio; in 1445 he was a debtor for ten florins, and does not again appear in the accounts up to his death in 1461. Meanwhile, Castagno who was working on the opposite wall in 1451–3, completed his programme: the *Annunciation* and the *Presentation in the Temple*. Finally, in 1461 Baldovinetti finished the work which Domenico had begun.

Thanks to the historians it is possible to get a good enough idea of the general air of the compositions to divine their interest: buildings in perspective, effects of shadow, care

60   Pisanello. Medal of John VIII Palaeologus. 1438. Museo Nazionale del Bargello, Florence.
'...and there was the Emperor, in a brocaded damask robe of the greatest luxury and a Greek hat with a very fine jewel on top. He was very handsome, with his beard in the Byzantine manner...' (Vespasiano da Bisticci, *Life of Eugenius IV.*)

61   Pisanello. *The Patriarchs of Constantinople*. 1438–9. Pen drawing. Art Institute, Chicago.
'The Greeks wore sumptuous silk vestments in the Byzantine manner, and the style of their vestments seemed to have more gravity and dignity than that of the Latins...' (Vespasiano da Bisticci, *Life of Eugenius IV.*)

taken with the daylight suitable for a light coloured picture; also the odd anecdotic figures placed in each scene, and the individualized faces representing the friends of the Medici. From the winter of 1438–9, therefore, the decoration of the choir of Sant'Egidio was allotted to Domenico, and his entry into Florence under Piero's patronage had thus succeeded. But it has been asked how it was possible to give such an important commission to a non-Florentine. The descendants of the Portinari family having transferred their right of patronage from the nearby hospital to the *cappella maggiore* of Sant'Egidio, there is the possibility that they were then able to act in a way that escaped the control of the guilds. In this case it is possible that the decision emanated from the Medici—and hence from Piero—acting in the name of the heirs of Folco Portinari (*d.* 1431) who were still minors. The accounts of the hospital were well kept, and historians who have gone through them carefully have found an interesting remark in them.

September 1439: Cash docket for Sant'Egidio: Doc. 6

Master Domenico di Bartolomeo da Venezia who is painting the choir of Sant'Egidio, is debited on the 12 September 44 florins, credited in the receipts in the ledger marked DDC.185 [...] He is debited on the 12 September 2 florins 15 soldi *a oro* taken by Pietro di Benedetto da Borgo San Sepolcro who is with him. That is 2 florins 3 livres 3 soldi.

This is one of the seven or eight dockets for payments which concern either the salary of the head of the team or reimbursements for expenses. The young Piero di Borgo may have been given the job of preparing certain colours. This poor little indication covers one of the remarkable points in the history of painting in central Italy, but also, in the absence of works, one of the most difficult to unravel. It is by no means absurd to compare the void caused for the middle of the Quattrocento by the disappearance of this cycle in Sant'Egidio to the confusion which would be created by the absence of the Brancacci Chapel in the Carmine for the immediately preceding generation. In 1439 there appeared suddenly in Florence this assistant to Domenico, whose activity and movements in the preceding years are unknown. The self-confidence of Domenico, the chief exponent of painting in a high key and also of new techniques, cannot but have impressed the young artist Piero della Francesca—but where is the echo of this to be found?

The ensemble described by Vasari, which was seriously damaged during the seventeenth century, disappeared for good during the eighteenth. The few traces of the lowest range, found just before 1955, do not allow for more than very limited hypotheses. Only old copies, or works which can at least be seriously considered as having derived from the cycle, would shed any light on the problem. It has been suggested that the perspectives, the articulation of architectural forms, and details of the costumes, have been reflected in the work of some of the *cassoni* painters. The work of the anonymous painter known as the Pratovecchio Master has also been considered (R. Longhi), which would be extremely important for the formation of the painter—also anonymous—of the Barberini Panels (F. Zeri); this is not an unacceptable idea. But the most likely link is to be found rather in the celebrated cycle of the *Life of the Virgin* at Prato.

For some this group—or more precisely the frescoes of the *Birth of the Virgin* and the *Presentation in the Temple*, which are somewhat distinct from the others—cannot be explained without Domenico. For others, on the contrary, the Prato cycle, earlier than the works at Sant'Egidio and the arrival of Domenico, are the work of Uccello, helped perhaps by the young Piero; but is it reasonable to transfer to another work and another workshop leader the elliptical reference of 1439 concerning Piero's presence? It would appear more correct to discern in the easy compositions the blond colour and the kind of joyousness and playfulness so appreciable at Prato, a precocious echo of the lost work at Sant'Egidio, which the ambitious Domenico abandoned in 1442 or 1443.

62 Piero della Francesca. *Baptism of Christ*. Detail. About 1450. Tempera on panel. National Gallery, London.
In the group of Orientals reflected in the calm loop of the river Jordan, beyond the catechumen, we can recognize the silhouettes of Byzantine prelates.

During this same extraordinarily active summer of 1439 Piero de' Medici continued to be besieged by painters:

13 August 1439: Letter from Filippo Lippi to Piero di Cosimo, at Trebbio, in the Mugello:　　　Doc. 7

The answer to a letter which I sent you, I only had it after thirteen days, which has occasioned me much harm. You tell me in conclusion that you can agree to no other price for the picture and that I should keep it for you [...] This has pained me for more than one reason; and this is one of them, since it is certain that one of the poorest friars in Florence is myself, for God has left me six nieces to marry, all ill and useless, and that small sum means much to me, seeing what I am. If you could give me at your house a little wheat and wine, which you can sell me, it would be a great joy to me, putting it to my account. I have tears in my eyes that if I died I would leave these poor girls [...] I beg you to take the trouble to write two lines to him, to Ser Antonio, that you have recommended me. And may your reply be quick; for it is clear that eight days from now I shall be dead; I am very afraid. For God's sake reply to the house, where I am writing to you, so that I receive it, so that what happened to my last letter shall not happen again.

However in 1437, the contracts concerning the Barbadori Altarpiece for a chapel in Santo Spirito foreshadowed substantial fees:

8 March 1437: Sum allocated to Fra Filippo by the Company of Or San Michele:　　　Doc. 8

The 8 March 1436 [Old Style 1436 = New Style 1437], Jacopo Filippi, goldsmith, of the parish of S. Nicolas, of Florence, promises that Fra Filippo di Tomaso, of the Carmelite Order, will receive an advance of 40 florins in good money which he is due from the said society [of Or San Michele] for the painting of the altarpiece in the chapel of Gherardo Barbadori. Otherwise he [Jacopo Filippi] will make good the sum from his own pocket. Promise, obligation, made in the presence of the said Fra Filippo with confirmation of his promise, Maso Pieri and Marcho being witnesses.

The emotional and whining letter of August 1439 has never been taken very seriously by historians, and the protectors of the friar themselves do not seem to have been very moved by his jeremiads— any more than by his escapades. This 'poor monk' had just received 40 gold florins. It was something of a mania of his to cry misery so as to attract attention, but the tone which he uses presupposes a certain confidence in the patience of his correspondent and a rather interesting familiarity.

Cosimo had occasion to show a great deal of indulgence towards Fra Filippo, but the painter he preferred was the Dominican from Fiesole, who was then decorating the restored convent of S. Marco.

1439–40: Altarpiece in S. Marco painted by Fra Angelico (from Vasari, 1568):　　　Doc. 9

The altarpiece of the high altar of this church in particular is of marvellous beauty; the pure simplicity of the Madonna inspires the spectator with piety, and the saints who surround her are like her; the predella, with scenes of the martyrdoms of SS. Cosmas and Damian and the others, is so well done that one could not imagine it possible to see anything better finished or more delicate or better understood than these little figures.

63　The Prato Master. *Presentation of the Virgin in the Temple*. Fifteenth century. Fresco. Chapel of the Assumption, Prato Cathedral.
A composition strongly articulated by the architectural elements.

The altarpiece which was to excite so much enthusiasm was in some measure the crowning achievement of Medici patronage. In 1436 Eugenius IV had decided on the installation of the Dominicans of the Observance in the convent of S. Marco, and Cosimo de' Medici entrusted Michelozzo with the reconstruction of the church and the convent. Fra Angelico was responsible for the painted decoration and in particular for the retable of the high altar of the new church. Because of this concern for unity and 'modernity', Lorenzo di Niccolò's picture of the *Coronation of the Virgin*, even though it was not very old (1402), was removed and its dispatch to Cortona was decided upon in 1438. The large work which replaced it was an early example of a *pala* with a central aedicule and with symmetrical groups on either side arranged according to a rising perspective. This was of great importance for later altarpieces: the Barbadori Altarpiece, for example, was rather differently arranged. The present poor condition of the S. Marco Altarpiece only allows guesses at the harmonious charm of this celestial enclosure, where the Oriental carpet, the garlands and the little wall define the space around the Madonna. The movement of the two doctor saints (Cosmas and Damian, 'Medici' in Italian), ready-made patrons of the dominant family, draw the spectator towards the centre of the scene; a tone of gentle devotion, linked to a simple arrangement in conformity with the 'modern' perspective, has

64 Fra Angelico. *The S. Marco Altarpiece.* Detail of the predella: *Life of SS. Cosmas and Damian.* 1439–40. Tempera on panel. Alte Pinakothek, Bayerische Staatsgemälde-sammlungen, Munich.
'The predella, with scenes of the martyr-dom of SS. Cosmas and Damian, is so well executed that one cannot imagine any-thing more careful, more delicate, or better understood, in small-scale figures.' (Vasari, *Life of Fra Angelico.*)

65   Fra Angelico. *The S. Marco Altarpiece.* 1439–40. Tempera on panel. Museo di San Marco, Florence.
'The altarpiece on the High Altar, in particular, is of marvellous beauty; the pure simplicity of the Madonna inspires piety in the spectator...' (Vasari, *Life of Fra Angelico.*)

assured that this work should enjoy over the generations a prestige which already in Vasari's time made it an unforgettable masterpiece of the Florentine Quattrocento.

Piero de' Medici continued to protect his painter friends; his correspondence with some of them is interesting because it is concerned with technique.

1441: Letter from Matteo de' Pasti to Piero de' Medici: Doc. 1●

Magnificent and honoured lord,

By this letter I wish to tell you how I have learned since I have been in Venice something which cannot be bettered for your work, as you will see; and this is powdered gold, which I paint with as with any other colour, and I have begun to ornament these [i.e. the *Triumphs*] which are made so that no one has ever seen such a thing. The plants are all touched with powdered gold and I have made a thousand embroideries on the damsels. So I beg you urgently to send me instructions for the other fantasies, so that I may finish them; and if you wish me to send you these, I will send them, if you command; whatever is your pleasure that I do, I am ready to obey you in anything that pleases you [...]

If it please you, tell me to do likewise with the *Fame*, because I have the design for it, except that I do not know if you wish the seated lady to be in a dress or in a mantle, as I would prefer; for the rest, I know what to do, that is the chariot drawn by four elephants: and I do not know if you want esquires and damsels behind, or perhaps famous old men; so advise me of everything so that I may do something

A poi che morte tri
umpho nel uolto.
Che di me stesso trium
phar solea.

66 Unknown Florentine Artist. *The Triumph of Fame.* Mid-fifteenth century. Miniature. MS. Pal. 192 c., 34r. Biblioteca Nazionale Centrale, Florence.
'Give me an indication... how to continue the Triumph of Fame...' (Letter from Matteo de' Pasti, 1441.) An example of this allegory with a naïve but striking effect of perspective.

beautiful with which you will be pleased. And you will forgive me all this, and one that I do now will be worth more than all those that have already been done...

This letter will suffice to end the episode studied here; it shows a young artist working for Piero submitting to him both questions of style and problems of composition. The interest of Cosimo's son in painting can no longer be doubted; in fact, he follows the course of works closely, and if Matteo rather overdoes the conventional courtesies, he must have known that he had to work in close agreement with Piero. Greater importance should, therefore, be attached to these successive letters than has been the case up to now; they are the vestiges of an active correspondence which establishes the role of Piero de' Medici in the period which coincides with the Council of Florence. The 'cultural' role of Medici power, which the reign of Lorenzo would completely illustrate twenty years later, had been already inaugurated about 1440 by his father.

Moreover, the letter deals with processes which permit the distribution of gold powder on a composition, a technique which Matteo had learned in Venice. Exchanges with the

67 Piero della Francesca. *Baptism of Christ*. Detail. About 1450. Tempera on panel. National Gallery, London.
A view of Borgo San Sepolcro, a privileged *borgo* set on the banks of the Jordan.

north continued, therefore, and with preoccupations—such as the use of gold—which have nothing to do with the purely intellectual reform of painting advocated a few years earlier by Alberti. The work for which Matteo consults Piero on its method and design was almost certainly a miniature, where precious effects are proper. Finally, the arrival of Domenico must be considered as an encouragement given not only to the rising vogue for pale colour, either in Lippi or Angelico, but also for picturesque costumes, variety in the details, and brilliance in the painting. It may even be that Pisanello—who was certainly present in Ferrara—accompanied the Council to Florence and ensured its 'reporting'. This is not improbable. But 1439 was in Florence the occasion of an important experience for artists. The work of the young Benozzo di Lese, called Gozzoli (*b.* 1420), was to demonstrate this, as did probably that of his contemporary, Piero della Francesca. According to Vasari, Piero followed Domenico Veneziano in the Marches, to Spoleto, Ancona and Loreto. Before he reappeared in 1445 in Borgo San Sepolcro, to paint a polyptych for which his compatriots defined the conditions with great precision, he had painted the panel of the *Baptism of Christ* which was found in the Priorato of S. Giovanni Battista in San Sepolcro.

One of the many problems debated in the Council of Florence concerned—disastrously—the Three Persons of the Trinity. The doctrinal point which earlier had provoked the Byzantine schism was explicitly recalled.

6 July 1439: The decree *Laetentur caeli*: Doc. 1

...We declare moreover that the explicit terms: *filioque*, in view of the truth and according to the necessity which compelled it, has been legitimately and reasonably added to the Creed [of the Apostles]...

The episode of the Baptism in the Jordan is, in the Gospels, one of the rare divine manifestations of all three Persons. Hence the interest of the representation of this subject during the crucial phase of the debate. Piero's work, full of pictorial and iconographic novelties and of a marvellously poetic quality, can appear doubly as the conclusion of his Florentine episode, where he was in close contact with Domenico and where he was present at the conclusion of the Council. The view of San Sepolcro is in the centre, at the same level as the side of Christ. The pure light, the rosy and blond colour, the freshness and clarity indicate the recent memory of Domenico; the geometric structure tenderly interpreted by the repeats, the counterpoint, and the formal sequences of movement, express the contact with the powerful Tuscanism of Masaccio, suggested by the figure of Christ. But too many subtle notes have been observed for there not to be also a recognizable reference to motifs set in train by the meeting of the Council: the 'trinity' of angels in which there can be seen three different hair styles, three colours, three different poses, forming, so to speak, a unity in three-time, has to have an emblematic value since these heavenly servitors do not act here, as they usually do, as the bearers of Christ's garments. Beyond the catechumens—derived from, or rather lifted from, Masaccio—a group of Orientals is reflected in the calm loop of the Jordan; in them can easily be recognized the figures of the Byzantine prelates. Their picturesqueness was even less likely to escape Piero's attention in that they supplied the means of associating them explicitly with the scene of the Baptism, recognized by the Council as valid equally according to the Greek or the Latin rite.

68 Piero della Francesca. *Baptism of Christ*. About 1450. Tempera on panel. National Gallery, London.
One of the rare mentions in the Bible of all three Persons of the Holy Trinity is in the account of the Baptism of Christ in the river Jordan.

Chapter 4
Tuscans and Umbrians in the Service of Sixtus IV (1480-2)

69 Melozzo da Forlì. *Sixtus IV Inaugurating the Vatican Library.* Detail. 1474. Fresco. Pinacoteca, Vatican.
A portrait of the founder of the great library, decorated with frescoes by Melozzo da Forlì, assisted, no doubt, by Antoniazzo Romano.

Francesco della Rovere, who in 1471 became Pope with the title of Sixtus IV, had very high ambitions for the city of Rome; the bull *Etsi universis*, announcing the Jubilee of 1475, bears witness to this. In thirteen years he achieved a great deal. His was a strong government, in the temporal more perhaps than in the spiritual sense; a detailed 'budget' exists for the year 1480–1, which gives an idea of the complex way in which papal finances worked. The Camerlengo was a Norman cardinal, Guillaume d'Estouteville; he had the advantage of himself being very wealthy, and he became in 1480 a kind of town-planner in chief, using a high hand with the *magistri aedificiorum et stratorum Urbis*. The Ponte Sisto was ready in time for the Jubilee; the Hospital of Santo Spirito, at the entrance to the Borgo, was given new buildings in 1477. The Pope ordered a spectacular translation of what can best be described as the 'pagan relics' of Rome; they were gathered together and exhibited at the Capitol, in one of the most significant acts of the 'imperial' exaltation of the Roman See. No less remarkable were the transformations in the Vatican, with the great library decorated with frescoes by Melozzo da Forlì, assisted no doubt by Antoniazzo Romano (the commemorative panel dates from 1477), and the creation of the palace chapel. The construction of the chapel must have been finished by the end of 1480 or the beginning of 1481, and it was then necessary to give thought to the grand decoration foreseen for the exceptional arrangement of the unified space of this large chapel. The consolidation of the papal finances allowed rapid progress to be made.

Two other facts have to be taken into account to complete this summary of the 'Sistine' renewal of Rome. In 1478 there occurred the horrible affair of the Pazzi conspiracy, instigated by Sixtus so as to strike at the Medici and block Florentine expansion. It failed; a general crisis followed in 1479. To everyone's relief, Florentine political wisdom averted a conflict, and the octagon of Sta. Maria della Pace in Rome was begun, possibly soon after 1480, as a thanksgiving. Under these conditions the dispatch to Rome in 1481 of a strong team of painters must be considered as a political gesture of a kind that was common with Lorenzo de' Medici. During these same difficult years a sort of panic spread through Italy and the Vatican itself, because of the Ottoman descent on the south of the peninsula and the massacres of Otranto. Emotion—and fear—were running high in Italy, particularly in the Vatican. The menace of Islamic expansion made even more essential the affirmation of the divine foundation—and hence protection—of the Roman church and its monarchy. The programme of decoration of the new chapel had to contain allusions to these preoccupations.

The workshop master most sought after and most docile, particularly if he were paid a large salary, was already Pietro Vannucci, called Perugino. Vasari, who detested him had to record the fact, placing the moment of his greatest glory around 1480.

1481: Perugino in the Sistine Chapel (from Vasari, 1568): Doc. 1

The fame of Pietro spread across Italy and outside it, so much so that Pope Sixtus

IV invited him with great honour to Rome to work in his chapel in company with other excellent artists. He executed, with the help of Don Bartolommeo della Gatta, abbot of S. Clemente at Arezzo, the scene of the *Giving of the Keys to St. Peter*, as well as the *Nativity*, the *Baptism of Christ*, and *Moses Saved from the Waters* by Pharaoh's daughter. For the wall behind the altar he made an altarpiece in fresco of the *Assumption of the Virgin*, in which he represented Pope Sixtus on his knees.

The importance attached after 1480 to the 'modern manner' of Perugino cannot be doubted. The insipidity of his later compositions has prejudiced a proper view of his art. It is enough to look at the *Giving of the Keys* to understand the general admiration: an amplitude in the forms, a space airy and taut at the same time, in which the figures glide like living ornaments to accentuate by their elegance the impact of the paving and the architecture.

The invitation to Perugino is confirmed by another piece of information: in 1479 the painter decorated the apse of the choir chapel of Old St. Peter's, where he had already

70 Hartmann Schedel. *Liber Chronicorum*, pp. LVII-LVIII. *View of Rome*. Detail: *The Borgo*. 1492. Woodcut.
The Hospital of Santo Spirito at the entry to the Borgo, at the left, was endowed with new buildings, begun in 1477. To the right of St. Peter's are the buildings of the Pontifical palace.

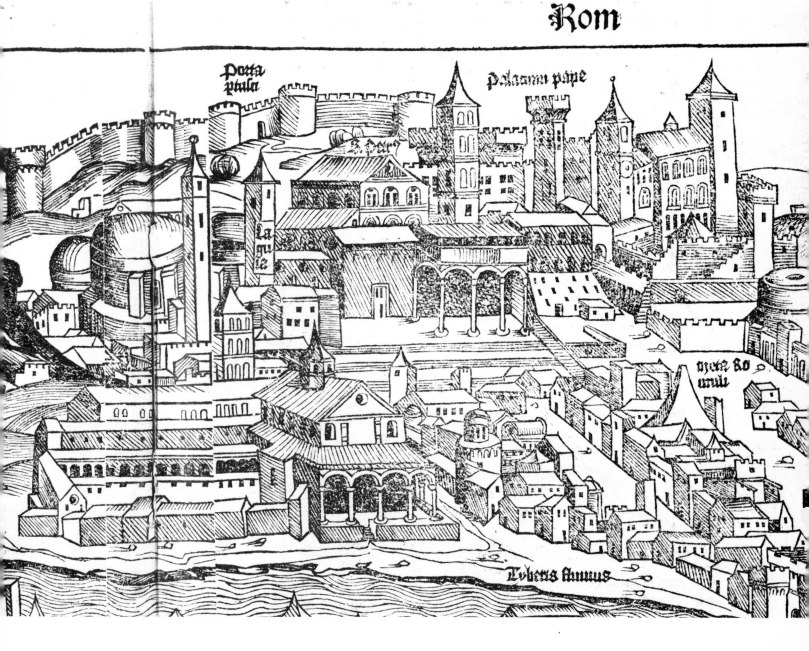

represented the Madonna with the kneeling Pope. This he repeated in the Sistine Chapel, but with a large composition of the *Assumption* (a frescoed altarpiece painted on the wall, and not an independent wooden panel). On this same wall, on the right was the *Nativity*, and on the left *Moses Saved from the Waters*, that is the two starting-points of the two parallel series which were to confront each other on the long side walls of the chapel and on the end wall: the 'Life of Moses' on the left and the 'Life of Christ' on the right. The contract concerning the pictures in the Sistine Chapel is in the Vatican archives:

71 Reconstruction (after E. Steinmann) of the Sistine Chapel in 1483.
'...the Pope has... agreed and contracted... with suitable people: the Florentines... to paint in the principal chapel of the said palazzo apostolico, starting from the altar, that is to say, ten scenes from the Old and New Testaments, with curtains below them...' (Contract for the painting of the Sistine Chapel, October 1481.)

72 Unknown Italian Artist. *Pope Sixtus IV in the Sistine Chapel.* About 1490. Tempera on panel. Musée Condé, Chantilly.
A conventional representation, showing the altar, the altarpiece of the *Assumption*, and the papal *baldacchino*, but not the fresco cycle.

73 Perugino. *Assumption*, a sketch for an altarpiece. 1481. Drawing in metal-point, pen and wash, heightened with white. Graphische Sammlung Albertina, Vienna. 'For the wall behind the altar he made an altarpiece of the Assumption of the Virgin, in which he represented the kneeling figure of Pope Sixtus IV.' (Vasari, *Life of Perugino*.)

Doc. 2   27 October 1481: Contract for the paintings in the Sistine Chapel:

[Commission for painting in the principal chapel of the new Apostolic palace.]
27 October 1481. Given at Rome in the Apostolic Chamber, in the eleventh year of the pontificate of the most Holy Father in Christ and Lord Pope Sixtus IV. In Rome in the Apostolic Palace, Master Giovanni di Pietro dei Dolci, a Florentine, acting in Rome as the superintendent or commissioner of works in the Apostolic Palace, according to his mandate and commission from our Holy Lord the Pope, in the presence of myself as notary public and of the undersigned witnesses [...] has made an agreement and contract and agrees and contracts to competent persons: the Florentines Cosimo di Lorenzo [Rosselli], Filippo Rosselli, Sandro Mariani [Botticelli], Domenico di Tommaso di Corrado [Ghirlandaio] and the Perugian Pietro di Cristofano of Castel della Pieve, painters living in Rome, to paint in the

74 Perugino. *The Giving of the Keys*. 1481. Fresco. Sistine Chapel, Vatican.
'The fame of Pietro [Perugino] spread throughout Italy and abroad, so that Pope Sixtus IV invited him most honourably to Rome to work in his chapel... there he made... the scene of the Giving of the Keys to St. Peter...' (Vasari, *Life of Perugino*.)

75 Perugino. *The Giving of the Keys*. Detail. Fresco. 1481. Sistine Chapel, Vatican.
The figures glide like living ornaments to set off the pattern of the pavement and the buildings.

76 *Electio Papae Leonis Decimi*, frontispiece. 1513. Biblioteca Apostolica, Vatican.
Pamphlet on the Conclave of 1513, with the arms of Leo X (Giovanni de' Medici).

77 *Electio Papae Leonis Decimi*, fo. 1ᵛ. 1513. Biblioteca Apostolica, Vatican.
The lists of the *tituli* corresponding to the frescoes in the Sistine Chapel, with the names of the prelates whose thrones were placed below each of them for the Conclave of 1513.

principal chapel of the said Apostolic Palace, starting at the altar, to wit: ten histories from the Old and New Testaments with the curtains underneath, to paint with diligence and conscience to the best of their ability, themselves, each with his assistants, according to what has already been begun.

The said painters agree and promise to the same Master Giovanni di Pietro, responsible for the contract in the name of the said most Holy Father our Lord, to paint and finish the said ten scenes with their curtains as previously mentioned, by the 15 March of next year, with payment according to the valuation of the scenes already realized in the said chapel by these same painters, under pain of a fine of fifty gold ducats, fifty *ducati di camera*, for any contravener, a fine which they have willingly agreed shall be imposed and do agree in the case of non-execution, by the *fabrica* of the said chapel, etc.

For each and every one of the above clauses, each of the painters has engaged his person with all the goods present and future which are proper to him; and each one among them is bound for the non-execution of any one among them, in non-conformity with the clauses above mentioned, or conforming [...] according to the best or strictest form of the Chamber, etc. They have agreed, made public, constituted an accounting agent, and have sworn an oath. Fuller formulation has to be made.

By the same contract they are agreed that the obligations made by the said painters with the said Giovanni di Pietro, superintendent of the sums received or to be received by them for the said painting, remains valid and in force.

Being present the Venerable Masters Marino de Monte Alto and Battista di Spello, notaries of the Apostolic Chamber, and witnesses and myself, Giovanni di Girone, Delegate Notary of the said Chamber.

This certainly refers to the double cycle of the Histories from the Old and New Testaments on the walls of the chapel, but it is very difficult to explain the number of ten scenes. The complex involved two sets of six on the long sides, and two sets of two, plus

the *Assumption* on the short sides: that is, sixteen histories in all. Even if one takes into account only the compositions on the side walls, the sum is only a part. This would not be the first time that a *lapsus* has slipped into a contract. But it must be supposed rather that the agreement only concerned a portion of the work, which had to be completed by other agreements; or else, more probably, six of the sixteen scenes provided for had already been painted. The text, distinctly urgent, provided for an important forfeit as well as a kind of collective responsibility. The constraints must have worked, since a deed for payment from January 1482 provided, after inspection, for a settlement of the fees foreseen for four of the ten frescoes. It is also known that the Pope was becoming impatient.

End of 1481: Chronicle of Jacopo da Volterra: Doc. 3

The big chapel is not yet finished; the continuous decoration of emblems and pictures continues.

According to the contract of 27 October 1481 the work was to have been finished by March in the following year, which would have been a record, unless the number of painters had been increased, because each of the frescoes required at least four months' work. From this it has been concluded that the works were already far advanced by the autumn of 1481; to judge by what had already been begun, the contract comes in the midst of the campaign in order to establish new terms. It was probably not the last contract, since it does not mention Signorelli, who was to paint two frescoes a little later.

The list of the four painters cited in the contract presents no problem; the panels in the manner of Cosimo Rosselli and his brother Filippo, Botticelli, Ghirlandaio and Perugino can be recognized without difficulty. But there is still a small problem, stemming from the fact that Vasari, paying no attention to what has been said of Perugino, cites Botticelli as the head of the enterprise:

Botticelli in the Sistine Chapel (from Vasari, 1568):   Doc. 4

Pope Sixtus IV, having built the chapel which he had in his palace in Rome and

78   Sandro Botticelli. *The Life of Moses in Egypt.* 1482. Fresco. Sistine Chapel, Vatican.
A rustic setting for the scene of Moses at the well with the daughters of Jethro, and other scenes in the background.

wishing to have it decorated, ordered that Botticelli should direct the works. He therefore painted the following scenes: that is, the *Temptation of Christ, Moses Killing the Egyptian and Receiving Water from the Daughters of Jethro the Midianite*, and similarly in the scene of the *Sons of Aaron Sacrificing* there came fire from Heaven, as well as some holy Popes in the niches over the frescoes. Having become famous and having made a name with his Florentine assistants, he received from the Pope a large sum of money which he quickly dissipated in Rome, because he was in the habit of living from day to day. Once the part which was done by him was finished and unveiled, he immediately returned to Florence.

79 Perugino. *The Journey of Moses into Egypt*. Detail. 1481–2. Fresco, Sistine Chapel, Vatican.
The crowd of the Jews on their journey is symbolized by additional figures, a family and a woman carrying a vase.

A very odd and bohemian workshop leader! Was his precipitous return due to some vexation, or even to a conflict with his colleagues? It is very unlikely that Perugino, who had the place of honour on the altar wall, would have agreed easily that the direction of the work should go to another. The account does not hold water. But it is a pity that the historian made no comment on Botticelli's manner; his adaptation . to Roman surroundings is marked by the introduction of remarkable architecture, powerfully symbolic: the Arch of Constantine, the Portico of Santo Spirito. The emblematic value of the compositions is thus affirmed with an authority which shows the capacity of the painter to grasp this aspect of things. But it is very remarkable that his frescoes—and Signorelli's too, incidentally—are ostensibly treated as an assembly of multiple scenes set in a landscape, a setting amenable to narratives in friezes. This form has, not without reason, been compared to the practice of *cassoni* painters, who never saw the need for any unity of place in their panels.

Perugino was therefore the head of the enterprise and Botticelli one of the narrators, though the most independent in tone and in life. If the accounts are accurate, something even more curious happened: a kind of 'prize' was announced by the Pope. It was not won by the one who was believed to be the winner, but the intrigue set up by the colleagues of Cosimo Rosselli turned to his advantage, by demonstrating incidentally the mediocre artistic taste of Sixtus IV. This strange vicissitude was also known to the tireless Vasari:

1481–2: Cosimo Rosselli carries off the prize for the Sistine Chapel (from Vasari, Doc. 5
1568):

Summoned with the other painters to the work which Pope Sixtus IV had made in the chapel of the palace, he painted in company with Sandro Botticelli, Domenico Ghirlandaio, the abbot of S. Clemente [Bartolommeo della Gatta], Luca da Cortona [Signorelli] and Pietro Perugino, three scenes: the *Crossing of the Red Sea*, with the destruction of Pharoah's host, *Christ Preaching to the Crowd on the Banks of the Sea of Tiberias*, and the *Last Supper* with the Apostles and the Saviour. In this last he drew in perspective a table in eight sections and above it a ceiling, also in eight sections forming an octagon, and he managed the foreshortenings as well as any other painter.

80 Sandro Botticelli. *The Punishment of Corah*. 1482. Fresco. Sistine Chapel, Vatican.
The most violent scene in the cycle: in front of the Arch of Constantine, the symbol of Antiquity and of Rome, the rebellious Levites are punished by fire from Heaven on the appeal of Moses.

▷

81 Sandro Botticelli. *The Punishment of Corah*. Detail. 1482. Fresco. Sistine Chapel, Vatican.
The Arch of Constantine, backdrop for the tragic biblical event, stands on the seashore.

82 Perugino. *Baptism of Christ*. Detail.
1481. Fresco. Sistine Chapel, Vatican.
Signed in Roman lettering: OPUS PETRI
PERUSINI CASTRO PLEBIS.

The Pope had decided, it is said, to give a prize to the painting which he judged to be the best. The painting of the scenes finished, His Holiness came to examine them, each painter having worked to merit this prize and the honour. Cosimo, who felt the inadequacy of his art and design, had sought to conceal this weak point by decorating his work with very delicate ultramarine and other lively colours and in giving great brilliance to his composition with a lot of gold, where there were neither trees nor grass, neither draperies nor clouds which were not thus rendered sparkling; he was convinced that he would thus obtain from the Pope, a poor connoisseur, the winning of the prize. The day of the presentation of the works, there was much laughter and liveliness among his colleagues, who all reacted by mockery rather than pity to turn him to ridicule. But they were themselves mocked because, as Cosimo had guessed, his colours dazzled the Pope's eyes who, though he had a great interest in these things, knew nothing about them. He estimated that Cosimo had created the best work of all. He had the prize given to him and ordered the others to put the finest blues possible in their compositions and to pick them out with gold so as to make them like those of Cosimo in vivacity and in richness of colour.

The unfortunate painters, in despair at having to comply with the poor artistic understanding of the Holy Father, then proceeded to spoil what they had done their best at. And Cosimo could laugh at those who had laughed at him.

This is an anecdote which one would love to be able to confirm. This story of a competition initiated by Sixtus IV for the best work is too calculated to be convincing; it sounds like a legend, but is none the less very characteristic. First, the state of mind of the commissioner. It is by no means improbable that, in his haste to get it completed, the Pope sought to stimulate the work of the various teams by giving prizes. Moreover, there is no doubt that Rosselli's style appeared trivial and rather heavy compared with Perugino at the top of his form, and both Botticelli and Signorelli who were able to give monumentality and elegance to their compositions. But the interesting point is the *technical* explanation of Rosselli's feebleness and his success. It is, in fact, the old technique of 'luxury' decoration, founded on a combination of the most expensive colours, which is presented as a procedure both easy and suited to seduce a clientele with poor taste. However, this search for a striking brilliance was not so much the work of Cosimo Rosselli as of the Umbrians, and of Perugino himself, when he got the chance; and above all of his pupil Pinturicchio, whose decorations in the Vatican were detested by the Tuscan artists. It all sounds as if Vasari had recorded about the Sistine Chapel a criticism which would be perfectly understandable for the apartments of Alexander VI of fifteen years later.

Not all the compartments of the decorations have the characteristics of which Vasari speaks, and nothing indicates that the Pope recommended a 'unity of style' based on the example of Cosimo. This story, recounted with eagerness by Vasari, was destined rather to account for the differences between the scenes and to minimize the historical importance of the cycle. Nothing is known of the origin of the story; it may have been born in Rome under Julius II, at a time when the systematic denigration of Quattrocento works, and especially those of Perugino, was made fashionable by the merciless Michelangelo.

The contract necessarily mentioned collaborators. They were customary for mural painting, all the more so when there was a need to hurry on the work. The result was that each of the Tuscan masters was accompanied by capable assistants. In this sense the experience of the Sistine Chapel was a unique instance of working together, as well as being at the same time the discovery of a new centre to discover the best that Tuscan art could achieve. With Cosimo Rosselli there was Piero di Cosimo, to whom Jacques Mesnil has suggested assigning some of the incongruous and amusing small details in the *Golden Calf* and the *Passage of the Red Sea*. Ghirlandaio was probably accompanied by his brother

David, and Botticelli no less probably by Filippino. It is reasonable to believe that this rather unusual company did not lack zest and was possibly not over-indulgent towards Roman circles, as the 'competition for the best fresco' rather suggests.

The organization of the double cycle is clear in its general lines, but obscure in its details. The structure is formed by the confrontation of the Life of Moses with that of Christ, in conformity with the typological reading of the Old Testament, which it explicates by the corresponding events in the New Testament. There is, therefore, an historic parallel: Moses appears as the biblical character who prefigures Christ. How ?

Moses appears here as priest and lawgiver, thaumaturge and head of state, a view which is not derived from the commentaries, where the parallel never has this continuous development. To achieve it, it was necessary to find in Jewish accounts episodes which are never even mentioned in the Bible. This relationship between Moses and Jesus was, however, the keynote of the thought of Philo Judaeus and above all was one of the strong points of Byzantine tradition. Transmitted, as has been shown, through the Octateuchs (including MS. Vat. Lat. 3550), this tradition foreshadows all the episodes in the chapel, including that of Moses in the desert or with the daughters of Jethro.

But this 'key' does not resolve all the meanings of the opposed parts of pictures. Certain symmetries are obvious: (I.) the two Nativities; (V.) the promulgation of the two Laws; (VII.) the final message. But others are obscure, for instance (II.) the *Journeys of Moses* contrasted with the *Baptism in the Jordan*, or (IV.) the *Passage of the Red Sea* facing the *Calling of the Apostles*. Historians have sought in vain for a satisfactory explanation and have concluded that there was a certain incoherence in the programme. This was not the case;

83   Sandro Botticelli. *The Life of Moses in Egypt*. Detail: *The Daughters of Jethro*. 1482. Fresco. Sistine Chapel, Vatican.
A well-known face and an elaborate coiffure, dear to the writers of the last century, to novelists and aesthetes.

84   Cosimo Rosselli. *The Last Supper.*
Detail: *The Capture of Christ.* 1482. Fresco.
Sistine Chapel, Vatican.
In Cosimo Rosselli's composition three
subsidiary themes, including the remarkable *Capture of Christ,* recall the biblical
episodes associated with the main subject,
and are seen through painted window-
openings.

85   Cosimo Rosselli and Piero di Cosimo.
Christ Preaching, and the Healing of the Leper.
Detail. 1482. Fresco. Sistine Chapel, Vatican.
In this group of Hebrews, represented in
modern costume there are several contemporary portraits, as throughout the whole
cycle in the chapel.

[ASSUMPTION]

I		[Moses Saved from the Waters]	[Nativity]
II	(1)	The Circumcision of the Sons of Moses (Perugino)	The Baptism of Christ (Perugino)
III	(2)	Moses in Egypt (Botticelli)	The Temptation of Christ (Botticelli)
IV	(3)	The Passage of the Red Sea (C. Rosselli)	The Calling of the Apostles (Ghirlandaio)
V	(4)	The Tables of the Law (C. Rosselli)	The Sermon on the Mount (C. Rosselli)
VI	(5)	The Punishment of Corah (Botticelli)	The Giving of the Keys (Perugino)
VII	(6)	The Testament of Moses (Signorelli)	The Last Supper (C. Rosselli)
VIII		The Death of Moses * (Signorelli)	The Resurrection * (Ghirlandaio)

Entrance Wall

*   works entirely repainted
[ ] lost works

it is even probable that this very carefully thought-out cycle was planned by the Pope himself. But the system on which it was organized could not have been divined without two sources of help. These were the discovery, only a few years ago, of the inscriptions or *tituli* crowning the frescoes, and the wording of a forgotten document.

1513: The 'Avviso' of the Conclave of 1513:   Doc. 6

[ ]	[ ]
1 Moses's Journey and the Circumcision of his Sons = *Observatio antique regenerationis per circoncisionem* = *Regeneratio*	The Baptism of Christ = *Institutio novae regenerationis*
2 Moses in Egypt = *Temptatio Moisi legis scriptae latoris* = *Temptatio*	The Temptation of Christ = *Temptatio Jesu Christi latoris Evangelicae legis*
3 The Passage of the Red Sea = *Congregatio populi a Moise Legem scriptam accepturi* = *Congretatio populi*	The Calling of the Apostles = *Congregatio populi legem evangelicam recepturi*
4 The Tables of the Law = *Promulgatio legis scriptae per Moisem* = *Promulgatio legis*	The Sermon on the Mount = *Promulgatio evangelice per Christum*
5 The Punishment of Corah = *Conturbatio Moisi legis latoris* = *Conturbatio legislatoris*	The Giving of the Keys = *Conturbatio Jesu Christi legislatoris*
6 The Testament of Moses = *Replicatio legis scriptae a Moise* = *Replicatio*	The Last Supper = *Replicatio legis evangelice a Christo*
7 The Death of Moses [ ]	The Resurrection = *Resurrectio et Ascensio Christi Evangelicae Christi legis latoris*

This document was a news-sheet, known from two examples, one in the British Museum, found by John Shearman; the other in the Vatican Library, found by D. Redig de Campos. It consists of two lists of the *tituli* corresponding to the Sistine frescoes with the names of the prelates who sat under each of them in the 1513 Conclave—the one which was to elect Leo X (the *titulus* of composition No. 7, on the left side, is missing). During the restoration work done from 1965 onwards, the inscriptions, painted in Roman capitals above each fresco, were found under the white stucco, and these correspond, except for a few details of spelling, to the programme given in the *avviso*.

This programme is too elaborate not to have been the work of a very learned theologian, which in fact the Pope himself was. Before the help given by the *tituli* no one had been able to work out the correlations between the two series of the Old and New Testaments; these are strict, but founded on partial and even on verbal correspondences. Nor was it possible to work out the sequence of the episodes. Sixtus's Chapel as reconstituted provides a lesson in religious iconography. The typology of the two Testaments is at the same time historical, since it follows the narrative, and dogmatic, in that it brings out the key ideas common to the *titulus* of each series, and is conceived so as to establish the teaching of the cycle:

1 *Regeneratio*	3 *Congregatio populi*	5 *Conturbatio*
2 *Temptatio*	4 *Promulgatio legis*	6 *Replicatio*

(the *tituli* of the histories on the altar wall and on the rear wall have disappeared.)

The most astonishing aspect is the frequent disagreement between the meaning and what actually appears in the picture. More precisely, the element which dominates the painted composition, the image, does not necessarily agree with the meaning given to it, and explained by the *titulus*. In the first scene from the Life of Moses, the Circumcision is mentioned by the *titulus* as corresponding to the Baptism of Christ, which is placed in full view, whereas the Circumcision is only a minor, almost insignificant, episode on the right-hand edge of the scene. In another instance, it is the totality of the idea that forms the link: the assembly of the people of God refers both to Israel at the Red Sea and to the Calling of the Apostles; the serene death of Moses and the Last Supper are both confirmations of the renewal of the Law. In the case of the *Punishment of the Rebels against Aaron* and the *Giving of the Keys* the idea of correlation has been abandoned: the only one that exists is the idea of the *conturbatio*, the defeat of the enemies of Faith employed in an inverse symmetry: the punishment of one group, the exaltation of the other, with secondary episodes: a few Jews jostled in front of the Temple, matching the impressive scene of the end of Corah, Dathan and Abiram.

86   Cosimo Rosselli and Piero di Cosimo. *Christ Preaching, and the Healing of the Leper.* Detail. 1482. Fresco. Sistine Chapel, Vatican.
Among Umbrian and Tuscan painters the open space of the sky almost always included flights of birds of prey: here there is also a conventional image of the wind.

An analysis can even explain these anomalies; the episodes given greatest weight are linked by a kind of continuous celebration of the authority, both civil and religious, of the lawgiver of the Old Testament, of the monarchic constitution of the Church, and of the choice of Rome; the two representations of the Arch of Constantine in the *Punishment of the Rebels* and the *Giving of the Keys*, placed opposite each other, is the best proof of this; or again, the representation of the façade of the Hospital of Santo Spirito in the *Temptation of Christ* with the Old Testament *Sacrifice of the Healed Leper*. The sequence of the thirty early Popes, from Peter to Marcellus, is placed between the windows as a pledge of the divine continuity of the Church, and the painted draperies in the lowest register, a damask with the tiara and the arms of the della Rovere, is a reminder of the continuing existence of the Papacy. The theme of the plenary sovereignty of the Papacy in Rome runs through and consolidates the whole scheme.

This insistence on the contemporaneity of the institution is displayed by a remarkable feature of the cycle: the large number of figures which are said to be portraits; it has been called a kind of *Who's Who* of Rome in 1482. The custom was by then widespread, but Rome lacked a gallery of personalities in the Curia, and the opportunity was not to be missed. In every, or almost every, scene characters from the Bible are shown next to bystanders from the contemporary world; they are juxtaposed so that the narrative is of the past and the present at the same time. Unfortunately most of the identifications rest only on fantasy. What is needed here is another journalistic *avviso* mentioning the portraits; unfortunately this practice did not then exist, and identification depends on such chance information as this:

> Portraits in the frescoes in the Sistine Chapel (from a letter by F. Orsini to Vincenzo Pinelli, *c.* 1560):   Doc. 7

> The portrait of Gaza, I don't know anyone who has it. But I remember having heard tell by the Cardinal di Sant'Angelo that Pope Paul III showed him in the Sistine Chapel in one of the panels by Cortona [Signorelli], Bessarion and five of his associates, among whom he named Argyropoulos, Gaza, Il Sipontino [Perotti]...; Gaza wore a hat...

This is proof that less attention was paid when visiting the chapel to the grand theological statements—which might well be taken for granted—than to the gallery of historical figures present in the frescoes and, so to speak, to Vatican history.

The first Mass was celebrated on 9 August 1483. After the departure of the Tuscan teams in the autumn of 1482, the completion of the decoration of the papal chapel had been hastened by confiding the last two scenes on the left-hand wall to Signorelli. There then remained the painting of the decoration of the curtains in the bottom register, with the arms of the Pope. Logically, the gallery of Popes which frame the windows above each of the frescoes must already have been painted; efforts have been made, for no good reason, to attribute them to Botticelli. But the painters had derived a great moral benefit from the Roman enterprise. Their summons to the Vatican had conferred upon them a new status, in some ways an international one.

A link can be discerned between Sixtus's enterprise and those which immediately followed in Tuscany. A competition emerges, all the more significant in that circumstances in Italy evolved quickly. The violent political crisis between Rome and Florence resulted in a firmer hold on power by the Medici, and in Lorenzo a certain care to affirm the authority of his city. The concatenation of events is not accidental; in a series of decorations undertaken by the Signoria and the Medici, the majority of the protagonists from the decoration of the Sistine Chapel are to be found, as if their time in Rome had been deliberately cut short.

Doc. 8   5 October 1482: Resolution of the governors of the works in the Palazzo Vecchio.

> The decision having been taken by the five black beans, they gave the order,
> according to the regulation in force, with the 31 August as the time for finishing, to
> the painter Domenico Tommaso del Ghirlandaio present and accepting... to paint
> the wall of the hall of the palace on the side of the Dogana, and to decorate the said
> palace with the image of St. Zenobius and other images [...]
>
> Also they gave the order, according to the regulation in force, to the painters
> Domenico and Sandro Marini [Botticelli] to paint and decorate the wall of the
> audience chamber of the palace.
>
> Also, they confided to the painters Pietro called il Perugino and to Blasio Antonio
> Tucci the wall of the hall of the palace on the side of the Piazza, that is to say of the
> window, to paint and decorate [...]
>
> Also they have confided the wall of the well of the same hall to the painter Piero
> Jacopo del Pollaiuolo.

The division of the works is fixed with precision. Piero Pollaiuolo is added to the team.
Thus an important official commission follows that of the Pope. But it was not executed.
Ghirlandaio was the only one to complete his programme.

In the following spring Lorenzo was to employ the same painters in the decoration of
the villa at Spedaletto, near Volterra; Botticelli and Perugino worked there side by side.
Ghirlandaio was missing, but he was very busy in Florence, and in September 1485 he was
to sign the contract—one of the most complete that exists—for the chapel of the choir of
Sta. Maria Novella, a famous cycle which was finished in 1490. Like the Sistine Chapel, it
includes an extraordinary gallery of portraits of notabilities.

Florence, in fact, had not only learned a political lesson from the events of the 1480s,
when a general conflict had been avoided thanks to the diplomacy of Lorenzo; the
spectacular undertaking of the Sistine Chapel added to its prestige. The proof is found in
a remarkable document which provides a picture of the artistic state of affairs, in 1484:

Doc. 9   *C. 1484: Letter from the Agent of Lodovico il Moro in Florence:*

> Sandro Botticelli, an excellent painter on panel and in fresco; his style has a virile
> quality and derives from an excellent understanding and perfect proportions.
>
> Filippino, son of Filippo [Lippi], the best disciple of the preceding and the son of
> the most original master of his time; his style has a softer quality and does not have,
> I think, the same artistic value.
>
> Perugino, a remarkable master, above all for mural fresco; his style has an angelic
> and very gentle character. Domenico Ghirlandaio, a good painter on panel and
> better in mural fresco; his style is very good; he is very active and very creative.
>
> All these masters, except Filippino, have demonstrated their abilities in the chapel
> of Pope Sixtus, then in the villa of Messire Lorenzo at Spedaletto; one does not
> know to whom to award the palm.

Sixtus IV died in Rome during the summer of 1484. As his successor, there was some talk
of the nephew of Calixtus III (*d.* 1458), Rodrigo de Borja, who when elected in 1492
would immediately undertake the decoration of the pontifical apartments in the
'luxurious' style decried by the Florentines. The new pontificate was that of the Genoese
Cibò, who became Innocent VIII, for whom an understanding with Florence was
fundamental; Piero Pollaiuolo was asked to make his tomb. The cultural centre of gravity
had returned to Florence, but no one forgot that the most striking demonstration of the
modern style had been in the chapel of Pope Sixtus. Its memory remained so vivid that it
was again to a Florentine that it fell, twenty years later, to decorate the ceiling, and half a
century after that to decorate the altar wall (where, as is well known, Michelangelo did not
hesitate to destroy Perugino's compositions).

Chapter 5
Mantegna's *Triumph of Caesar* (1490)

Before the Ovetari Chapel in the Eremitani in Padua, of 1449–50, no one had ever tried seriously to recreate figures *all' antica* or to place these figures in a setting *all' antica*. The precocity and the strength of the work are—or, rather, were, since it was almost totally destroyed in 1944—truly astonishing. Suddenly, a firmly based archaeological culture, able to marshal a mass of detail, appeared in that region of Italy which was, in fact, the best prepared to assimilate it. The interest in stelae, in epigraphy, in numismatics, in small bronzes, had for generations stimulated a world of amateurs and specialists, like Felice Feliciano, a friend of the young Mantegna.

In the following quarter-century, humanist erudition in the area of Verona, Padua and Mantua—the cities where Mantegna worked—developed a strictly archaeological character. Mantegna played a part in this through his collections, his studies and his travels in company with learned men, and by the systematic use which he made of their labours in themes, settings and costumes *all' antica*. In the Reggia at Mantua Mantegna began his great exposition with the medallions of emperors and the mythological scenes which gave to the ceiling of the Camera degli Sposi, finished in 1474, a characteristic flavour. He benefited from a steady protection, affectionate and patient, on the part of Lodovico Gonzaga, who bore with his recriminations, approved of his objectives, and satisfied all his exigencies. All the Gonzaga residences, at Cavriana, Marmirolo, Goito and elsewhere received fresco cycles (now lost), of which there is probably some echo in engravings. Engravings were one of Mantegna's most important discoveries, for the success of such prints cannot be exaggerated; through his copies of them (in 1494) Dürer achieved a new vision of fable and history. Mantegna was thus the mainspring of a sort of cultural laboratory protected by the Marquises of Mantua: Lodovico and, after 1478, Federico I, in parallel with what was being achieved in the more speculative and literary domain by Medici patronage in Florence.

There is clear evidence of this in an account by the young Cardinal Francesco, brother of the Marquis Federico:

23 February 1483: Letter from Cardinal Francesco Gonzaga to the Marquis Doc. 1 Federico, concerning the visit of Lorenzo il Magnifico to Mantua:

I notify to your Highness that the Magnificent Lorenzo yesterday visited the country. Today I accompanied him on foot to Mass at San Francesco. From there his Magnificence visited Andrea Mantegna where he looked with great pleasure at Andrea's paintings and at the sculptures of heads and other antique pieces, with which he seemed very pleased.

The house in Borgo San Giacomo, built after 1476, was still a modest one. The artist intended to build one which would be a museum for his collections and in a sense his mausoleum. Unfortunately nothing is known about the items in his collection. Eighteen

months later Mantegna wrote to Lorenzo de' Medici, putting himself under his protection and asking him for money. Why? Federico Gonzaga, who showed him the same affection and consideration as his father had done, had just died; of all Mantegna's protectors in Mantua, whose portraits he had painted in the Camera degli Sposi ten years earlier, none now remained: the Marchioness Barbara had died in 1481 and Cardinal Francesco in 1483. The new master of the principality, Marquis Francesco, was eighteen years old. Strikingly gifted for a military career, it was impossible to know if he would, like his ancestors, also be a Maecenas upon whom Mantegna could rely. Hence, in consequence of a moment of uncertainty, panic even, the petition to Lorenzo. The reflex is interesting, but the precaution was unnecessary; Francesco was his most faithful and trusting protector and Mantegna did not have to exile himself.

87 Andrea Mantegna. *Dormition of the Virgin.* Detail: *View of Mantua.* 1461. Tempera on panel. Prado, Madrid.
The religious scene opens on to a view across the lakes of the Mincio: 'after dinner, [the duke] embarked for a short rest on the lake... He disembarked at the port of the [Old] Court...' (Letter on the visit of Ercole d'Este to Mantua, August 1486.)

Doc. 2   6 November 1485: Letter from the Marquis Francesco to Mantegna, about a commission from the Duchess of Ferrara:

Most dear, The most illustrious Lady Duchess of Ferrara would like, in the letter

88 Pietro da Fano. *Lodovico Gonzaga*. About 1453. Medal. British Museum, London. Mantegna, summoned by Lodovico, remained in the service of the Marquises of Mantua.

89 Bartolo Talpa. *Federico Gonzaga*. About 1480. Medal. British Museum, London.

90 Savelli Sperandio. *Cardinal Francesco Gonzaga*. About 1480. Medal. Victoria and Albert Museum, London.

91a, 91b Bartolommeo Melioli. *Francesco II Gonzaga*. About 1480. Medal. Samuel H. Kress Collection, National Gallery of Art, Washington D.C. The most faithful and trusting of Mantegna's patrons.

which I send you herewith, so that you shall understand better her wish, which is, as you will see, to have a picture by you. We charge you to satisfy this lady; use all your diligence to complete it, using in it all your talent. We count on this. Do the best possible, that the said lady may have the pleasure of finding us full of zeal, which would add to your merit for my satisfaction.

Written in a friendly and almost deferential tone, this letter does not seek to conceal the diplomatic character of the undertaking. It is to be found in the rich Gonzaga archives. It is the first of a set of four sent in November and December, in which the young marquis uses all his authority over the painter to obtain the picture asked for by the wife of Ercole d'Este, Eleonora of Aragon. Mantegna worked slowly; the princess became impatient, the marquis urged the painter on, to the point of promising him a *manza*—a particular reward.

A picture of the Virgin surrounded by cherubim now in the Brera, Milan, mentioned in a Ferrarese inventory of 1493, has a good chance of being this work required by the Duchess; its theme and dimensions (allowing for its having been cut at the bottom) correspond to those of a picture for an oratory. The variations in the heads of the little singing angels give it an original character; the Christ Child has, as always in Mantegna, something powerful and grave which may well recall Donatello's types, and, through him, antique models.

Doc. 3   26 August 1486: Letter from Silvestro Calandra to the Marquis Francesco, about the visit of Ercole d'Este to Mantua:

Most illustrious Lord. Today the duke [Ercole] wanted to see the panelling, and then after lunch he went by boat to take some rest on the lake; he did not stay there long, for he is not accustomed to water, which made him ill. He disembarked at the port of the [Old] Courtyard to go and see the *Triumphs of Caesar* which Mantegna is painting; they pleased him greatly. He then returned by the covered way to the castle...

This letter from a chamberlain tells of a visit from a neighbour, Ercole d'Este, whose daughter Isabella was to marry the Marquis Francesco. After the customary outing on the Mantuan lakes—which was not a very happy one—he was taken to the Old Courtyard to see Mantua's new attraction. The *Triumphs* must have already been fairly far advanced to justify the visit; they may have been started in the spring of 1484, after the accession of Francesco.

If this were so, Mantegna's work, allowing for the interruption caused by his stay in Rome (1488–90), must have spread over some ten years. There is no reason to think that this monumental project could only have been conceived after the journey to Rome and the works in the Belvedere for Innocent VIII. Had not Mantegna already given striking proof of his archaeological knowledge in the Eremitani and in the panorama with figures behind the portraits of the Gonzaga in the Camera degli Sposi? It remains true that, since the work was restarted after 1490, its creation must have benefited from his Roman experience and, for example, from the detailed analysis of the military equipment and the pieces of booty which are to be seen on Trajan's column.

It seems that the destination of the work was not fixed in a positive way from the beginning. The sole fact of painting this *Triumph* on canvas—and not on the walls—is a remarkable novelty which introduces a new idea: the possibility of hanging them and removing them at will, like a tapestry. The canvases were used on a number of occasions to decorate the hall when there was to be a theatrical production, but this in no way implies a scenic function at the start of the work. They were also hung in castles like Cavriana.

It has recently become possible to say exactly how the cycle was installed in a new palace partly planned for it (as would be done in a modern museum) during the early years of the sixteenth century, soon after the artist's death. The humanist poet Equicola, a familiar of the Mantuan court, and accepted admirer of the Marchioness Isabella, has left notes and memoirs on the city, in which fortunately the fate of the now famous masterpiece is indicated.

Doc. 4   *C. 1508: Arrangement of a palace in Mantua for the reception of the Triumph of Caesar (from M. Equicola, 1521):*

In the furthest part of the city, near the church of San Sebastiano, a magnificent palace has been built so as to house permanently in a hall specially built for this

92   Andrea Mantegna. *Julius Caesar*. Ceiling of the Camera degli Sposi. 1474. Fresco. Palazzo Ducale, Mantua.

93   Andrea Mantegna. *Nero*. Ceiling of the Camera degli Sposi. 1474. Fresco. Palazzo Ducale, Mantua.
On the ceiling of the Camera degli Sposi, Mantegna inaugurated the type of decoration formed by medallions of emperors and mythological scenes.

94 Andrea Mantegna. Detail: *Head of an Old Man.* Camera degli Sposi. 1474. Fresco. Palazzo Ducale, Mantua.
The head of an old courtier, variously identified.

purpose, the *Triumph of Caesar*, on which Andrea Mantegna worked for many years. This *Triumph* appeared incomplete and unfinished, given the absence of the procession which followed the conqueror and the lack of spectators. Francesco provided it by summoning Lorenzo Costa, an excellent painter, and an amiable and esteemed courtier. Besides his other works, he was able with talent, art and knowledge to finish and complete this magnificent room.

Towards 1508 the series was definitively shown in a spacious palace. It then received two additions by Lorenzo Costa, but fortunately we have two important extra details on its presentation. A note by Sanudo in November 1515 says that the work was presented *da la spaliera in sù*, that is, above a fairly high wainscoting so that the bottom of the compositions would be level with the spectator (a foretaste of what Rosso would do at Fontainebleau twenty years later). This arrangement was all the more impressive in that the different episodes of the cycle were separated by pilasters which imposed a marked rhythm on the sequence of episodes. This is known from an observation by a visitor (Andreani) at the end of the century, and above all by the existence of engravings which in all probability show this original invention of Mantegna. The flat parts of these pilasters were actually decorated with trophies of arms. The formula was fashionable in northern Italy, in Urbino and even in Venice, and it came to have a remarkable development in Padua itself with the cycle by Parentino in the cloister of Sta. Giustina.

The importance of the *Triumph* does not seem to have been sufficiently appreciated. The recent restoration should permit a better grasp of the powerful originality of the work and, through the admiration which it aroused everywhere, its effect on art and culture.

C. 1490: The *Triumph of Caesar* (from Vasari, 1568):   Doc. 5

For the same Marquis [Mantegna] painted in a hall in the Palazzo S. Sebastiano in Mantua the *Triumph of Caesar*, which is the best thing he ever did. In this work can be seen arranged in a very beautiful order in the triumph, the beauty and ornamentation of the chariot, one who shouts insults at the conqueror, the family, the perfumes, the incense, the sacrifices, the priests, the crowned bulls for the sacrifice, the prisoners, the spoils taken by the soldiers, the order of the squadrons, the elephants, the booty, the victories, and the cities and fortresses symbolized on various chariots; with an infinity of trophies borne on spears, and various head and body armours, and head-dresses, ornaments and vases; and in the multitude of spectators a woman who holds a baby by the hand, who, having got a thorn in his foot, is crying and showing it to his mother in the most charming and natural manner.

He [the artist] used in this history a beautiful and excellent device: having placed the plane of the figures higher than eye-level, he set the feet of the front figures in profile and on the bottom line, making the others disappear more into the interior and losing sight of feet and legs, as was required by the necessity of vision; so also with the spoils, vases and other instruments and ornaments he made only the lower part to be seen and allowed the upper ones to disappear, as was proper for reasons of perspective.

Vasari's remarks bring out the two sensational characteristics of the cycle. Firstly, Mantegna's staggering archaeological knowledge, which assembles all that can be imagined in equipment, armaments, decorative pieces, costume, harness—all this was an unprecedented success, which, moreover, followed the major texts: the Triumph of Scipio recorded by Appian, and the Triumph of Caesar by Suetonius. The order of the procession is arranged fairly clearly according to Roman custom: 1, 2, 3, Bearers of pictures; 4,

95 Andrea Mantegna. *Madonna and Angels*. About 1485. Tempera on panel. Pinacoteca di Brera, Milan.
Mentioned in a Ferrarese inventory, this little panel has a good chance of being the work complained about by the Duchess of Ferrara in 1485.

Bearers of vases; 5, Elephants; 6, Bearers of armour; 7, Captives; 8, Musicians; 9, Caesar's chariot; 10, Senators [never executed].

The two extra pieces by Costa only fitted imperfectly into the programme: the *Sacrifice* (lost) was not in honour of Jupiter Capitolinus—as was the custom in Rome—but of Hercules, probably as an allusion to the family connections of the Marquis Francesco, whose portrait was included. The *Procession* was quite simply the triumph of Federico Gonzaga in the midst of horsemen and infantry. (The picture is now in Prague.)

All visitors recorded their astonishment and expressed their enthusiasm before this formidable cycle, which was a sort of pictorial encyclopaedia of antique military grandeur and archaeology. Vasari has clearly seen the pullulation of small details, like the dialogue of the two women to one of whom the baby turns. As he also recorded, the installation—almost certainly in accordance with the views of Mantegna himself (he died in September 1506, on the eve of the creation of the grand hall in the Palazzo S. Sebastiano)—was a success in the exploitation of perspective. This reaches its greatest

96 Andrea Mantegna. *Triumph of Caesar.* About 1490. Tempera on canvas. The Royal Collection, Hampton Court Palace.
1. *The Bearers of Pictures.*
2. *The Bearers of Trophies.*
3. *The Bearers of Trophies.*
4. *The Bearers of Vases.*
5. *The Elephants.*
6. *The Bearers of Armour.*
7. *The Captives.*
8. *The Musicians.*
9. *Caesar's Chariot.*

'In the southern part of the town, near the church of S. Sebastiano, a magnificent palace has been built to make a permanent home in a room specially built for the purpose, for the *Triumph of Caesar*...' (M. Equicola, *Commentarii Mantuani*, 1521.)

97 Andrea Mantegna. *Triumph of Caesar: The Bearers of Pictures*. About 1490. Tempera on canvas. The Royal Collection, Hampton Court Palace.

'... the *Triumph of Caesar*, on which Andrea Mantegna worked many years'. (M. Equicola, *Commentarii Mantuani*, 1521.)

power over the mind and eye when it arranges with precision forms seen from the bottom upwards; nothing is more suitable for a military parade, with the stamping of feet on the ground, nothing expresses better the formidable Roman power than an organized procession where the interminable filing past dominates the scene. Mantegna's work is not only a masterpiece without precedent in its amplitude and its humanist learning; it fulfills visually Mantegna's intimate thought by this impressive fusion of formal rigour, of the perspective effect and of Roman ideology.

Some idea of the admiration which it excited can be seen in the official document by which Mantegna, avid for honours and for hard cash, was solemnly rewarded by his lord.

98 Copy after Andrea Mantegna. *Triumph of Caesar: The Bearers of Trophies.* About 1500. Tempera on canvas. Pinacoteca Nazionale, Siena.
'...the *Triumph of Caesar* which is being painted, with figures as if they were living, which do not give the impression of a representation, but of an actual spectacle.' (Decree of the Marquis Francesco Gonzaga, 1492.)

99 Andrea Mantegna. *Triumph of Caesar: The Bearers of Vases.* Detail. About 1490. Tempera on canvas. The Royal Collection, Hampton Court Palace.
'The artist... had an excellent idea in this cycle... For the booty, the vases and the other ornamental objects, he showed only the lower parts, not allowing the upper ones to be seen...' (Vasari, *Life of Mantegna.*)

4 February 1492: Decree of the Marquis Francesco in favour of Mantegna: Doc. 6

[To honour merit is the glory of Princes.] For Hiero, king of Syracuse, the friendship of the great architect Archimedes was no mean illustration of his fame. Amid the great decisions of Alexander, he is above all glorious for not having wanted any other painter than Apelles, any other sculptor than Lysippus. Augustus derived glory and honour for having shown so much favour to Vitruvius, the architect of Verona, whom he raised from a base condition by ennobling him. In these circumstances what rank could we accord to Andrea Mantegna, this man of accomplished talent, without dispute the most remarkable of all those who profess painting through the diversity of his gifts? What rank should be accorded him? We have thought long on this subject. For we know the benefits he has received from us and from our ancestors, father and grandfather; we consider the remarkable works, so worthy of admiration, which he earlier painted in our chapel and in the room of our palace, and the *Triumph of Caesar* which he is now painting with figures so full of life and so animated that they give the impression not of a representation but of a living spectacle. The glory of the chapel which, with our consent and mandate, he has recently painted in the Vatican for the Pontiff Innocent VIII, has also reached our ears...

[There follows a series of donations of fiefs 'without any fiscal obligation or any charge and servitude'.]

The antique model served not only to nourish the imagination of the painter; it imposed itself equally on his master and protector. He was anxious to recall Hiero, Alexander and Augustus, all of them princes by whom it was proper to be inspired, before declaring the extraordinary merits of his painter, and to enumerate the masterpieces which he created for the Gonzaga family, in particular the cycle of the *Triumph*, which was the subject under discussion, without forgetting the flattering mention of the invitation to Rome. Important gifts sealed the privileged links between the painter and the Gonzaga.

Two years later, the invasion of Italy by Charles VIII of France disrupted the political life of the peninsula and led the Marquis to undertake a military campaign. In July 1495 he very nearly broke the French army at the crossing of the Taro near Fornovo (though it escaped to the north), and the day of the battle became a great date. One year later it was commemorated.

6 July 1496: Letter from Sigismond Gonzaga to the Marquis Francesco, on the   Doc. 7 commemoration of the victory at Fornovo:

My most illustrious and sole Lord. Having a continuing memory of the cruel and bitter passage of arms which took place a year ago in the Parmesan, in which the All-powerful God and His glorious Mother saved your Excellency from so many perils, after so many valorous and strenuous operations made by you for the death and destruction of the enemy, I have thought, together with my Illustrious Lady, for the creation of a durable memorial to the honour of God and His holy Mother. We have therefore organized a fine procession which took place solemnly this morning, with all the religious Orders of friars and priests, and was made in the following

100   After Andrea Mantegna. *Triumph of Caesar: The Bearers of Trophies.* About 1500. Engraving. Royal Library, Windsor.
The scene of the trophy-bearers, as shown here, includes the pilaster intended to separate it from the following scene.

101 Bernardino Parentino. *A Roman Triumphal Procession.* Fifteenth century. Drawing. Pierpont Morgan Library, New York.
This triumphal march may be considered as Parentino's own response to Mantegna's model.

102 Jacob of Strasbourg. *Triumph of Caesar.* About 1503. Engraving. Kupferstichkabinett, Staatliche Museen Preussischer Kulturbesitz, Berlin.
Twelve compositions entitled *Triumph of Caesar*, engraved from 1503 onwards, give a simplified rendering of the original.

103   Andrea Mantegna. *Triumph of Scipio.*
Detail: *The Drummer.* 1500. Tempera on
panel. National Gallery, London.
The man playing a flute and a drum,
formally marked with the sign SPQR,
opens the spectacle as a the symbol of a
whole art.

fashion: all the religious gathered at S. Sebastiano with the greater part of the people, where was exalted the image of the glorious Virgin created by m. Andrea Mantegna, on a large tribune richly and very solemnly decorated, and above the said image there was a young man dressed as God the Father, and two Prophets on either side, and on either side three little angels who sang hymns of praise, and in front were the Twelve Apostles. At the right moment, this tribune, which was carried by twenty porters, was raised and thus in procession the image was carried as far as [the church of] S. Simone, with such a concourse of people, men and women, the like of which number has never been seen in Mantua. A solemn altar had been prepared there in front of the choir of the new chapel, where a Solemn Mass was celebrated by m. Christhophoro Arrivabeno. But first Fra Petro da Naeto preached a fine sermon in the vulgar tongue to the people in praise of the glorious Virgin, exhorting the people to hold her in devotion, remembering that it was she who freed Your Excellency that day from so many perils [...]

   After dinner the image was placed in the appointed place, and had not been there three hours before there were placed before it images in wax and candles and other votive offerings, for which I believe that in a short time great devotion will accrue to it, and of all this good Your Excellency will have been the cause...

Your servitor...

The episode is remarkable for several reasons. The large panel painted by Mantegna celebrated the 'victory' of Francesco Gonzaga at Fornovo on the 6 July 1495; the work was therefore created with great speed. There is full information on the programme: originally, it was to have contained the whole princely family in adoration under a trellis, but eventually only the 'victor' was kept, flanked by Saints Michael, Andrew, Longinus and George. The picture was destined for the altar of a new chapel, called Sta. Maria della Vittoria, of which Mantegna himself provided the plans; but this chapel would eventually be built on the site of a house, of which the purchaser, a Mantuan Jew, had in 1493 obtained the authorization to remove an image of the Madonna painted on the exterior. Popular opinion was aroused. The procession, besides its political and military aspects in honour of the Marquis, gained an 'expiatory' character.

   Finally the popular procession in an order which involved all the people, shows that the customs of the thirteenth century had not disappeared. The devotion to Mary was always very strong; she was associated directly with the protection of the city, but this time a dynastic and personal flavour was added which naturally held the attention of the Marquis's agent. It may well be that, besides its traditional aspect, this manifestation was encouraged by the prestige attached to the idea of a triumph, furthered by Mantegna's huge painting. Panels and ensigns were part of the design in the first composition of the cycle.

While keeping things in their proper proportions, Francesco being no Caesar, nor Fornovo a grandiose victory, the festive transit of the holy image could well have appeared as the modern and real-life version of the antique parade.

The warrior saints Michael and George hold up the Virgin's mantle; St. Andrew and St. Longinus, the recognized protectors of Mantua, appear behind her. The Madonna, in a Leonardesque gesture, extends her protection over the Marquis in the armour of a great captain, and the Christ Child blesses him. The young St. John the Baptist, accompanied— why, is not clear—by St. Elizabeth, turns as is customary towards Jesus, who holds two red carnations. A coral branch for luck hangs from the strange pergola of leafy branches and fruit, a sort of bower of vegetation, where oranges, lemons and birds introduce a kind of scintillation of colours. A cameo, imitating bronze, inserts Adam and Eve, a reminder of Original Sin, on the base of the throne. It is one of the most minutely detailed, most acid, most metallic and sharp-cut of Mantegna's works.

In order to interpret correctly the increasing hardness of Andrea's art, it is essential to take into account the Roman cycle which required an implacable formal precision, and also the role played by copper engraving, which Mantegna used more and more as a means of expression. The *Triumph* was especially suitable for this treatment; the episode of the trophy-bearers was engraved together with a pilaster which was clearly destined to separate it from the following episode. A supplementary plate of the group of senators must be one of the missing scenes, and may have been engraved after the original *modello*.

A specific mention by a Paduan author points to the existence of a series of engravings from the beginning of the sixteenth century.

1504: Pomponius Gauricus, *De Sculptura*:   Doc. 8

Our friend Giulio [Campagnola] is to be congratulated on having reproduced so well [in engraving] the famous cohort by our dear Mantegna and his triumphs of Caesar.

Through these engravings, Mantegna's compositions would be used by all Western decorative artists either complete or in parts.

A Venetian, Benedetto Bordone, made twelve drawings for compositions called *Triumph of Caesar* which were engraved in 1503 by Jacob of Strasbourg. The order of the groups follows Appian's account, but the drawing is weak and the silhouettes lack imagination. Compared with Mantegna's series, they are dismal affairs, but this rather simplistic enterprise can be understood since it came at a time when Mantegna's own series was still unfinished. However, the Mantuan cycle created a great sensation, the echoes of which can be perceived in Parentino's studies (as evidenced by a curious drawing), and the vestiges of the decoration *all'antica* in the cloister of the Santo in Padua.

In the last year of his life Mantegna resisted commissions, but the pressures of the great families were strong. There is proof of this in a letter which constitutes a manoeuvre by Francesco Cornaro to obtain a work which he very much wanted.

New Year's Day, 1505/6: Letter from Pietro Bembo to the Marchioness of Mantua,   Doc. 9
about the commission to Mantegna from Francesco Cornaro:

[...] with Messer Francesco Cornelio, brother of the Most Reverend Cardinal, I am closely linked by family ties and with a relationship of an intimate familiar, as if I were in fact his blood-brother. To which must be added a great number of traits which make me honour him greatly and be desirous of giving him pleasure. For a long time ago, delighting in fine things as is usually the case with elevated and noble minds, he made an agreement with Messer Andrea Mantegna for the painting of

105 Andrea Mantegna. *Madonna of Victory*. 1496. Tempera on panel. Musée du Louvre, Paris.
'... the image of the glorious Virgin created by Andrea Mantegna was exalted by placing it on a grand tribune, richly decorated for the solemnity.' (Letter from Sigismondo Gonzaga, 1496.)

some canvases at the price of 150 ducats, giving him 25 in earnest money when sending him the measurements, Messer Andrea being agreeable to the work. I am now told that Messer Andrea refuses to do the work at this price and asks much more. This appears to Messer Francesco as really surprising and this is the general opinion, all the more in that Messer Francesco has the letter by which Messer Andrea confirms very precisely their agreement on the subject. Messer Andrea alleges that the work turns out to require more labour than he thought, and that he therefore wants a higher price. This is why I beg Your Excellency, if my services have any weight with you, that Your Ladyship will persuade Messer Andrea to heed the undertaking given to Messer Francesco and to address himself to this work, since it is more suitable for him than for any other to keep his promises, he who is called the 'Maintainer' of the world. [This is a pun on the verb *mantenere* and the name of Mantegna.] ...

[Messire Francesco does not mind about 100 or 200 ducats, but he does not wish to be treated in an off-hand manner, according to Bembo.]

The commissioner was simply forgetting the state of Mantegna's health; he was to die at the end of 1506. But there exists a panel which might well be the reduced version—or the *modello*—of a great frieze doubtless destined for the Palazzo Cornaro. This very beautiful grisaille panel forming a frieze is thus the last expression of the painter's desire to furnish, with images seen at ground level, an impressive reconstruction of public events. The Cornaro family had taken for their ancestor the legendary Scipio of the *gens* Cornelia. Scipio Nasica greets the statue of Cybele brought from Pergamon to Rome, in accordance with the Sibylline Books, to ensure the safety of the city against the Carthaginians. The extremely delicate chiaroscuro gives the composition a vivid and fresh rhythm, a sparkling clarity which enhances every detail. It is the perfection of a style which abandoned colour in order to find, as in engraving, in the resources of relief and in linear intensity, an epic quality exceptional in its day. In this learned work, Mantegna permits himself at most one very modern and light fantasy: the drummer inscribed 'S.P.Q.R.' who heads the procession is the symbol of a whole art.

Chapter 6
Perugino: A Master of Publicity (1490-1500)

106 Perugino. *The Giving of the Keys.* Detail: *Self-portrait.* 1481. Fresco. Sistine Chapel, Vatican.
'...two young [masters] of the same age, and same affection, Leonardo da Vinci and Pier della Pieve of Perugia, divine painter...' (Giovanni Santi, about 1485.)

No other painter of the fifteenth century enjoyed the same degree of favour as Perugino, above all after the Roman works of 1481–2. For twenty years he can be said to have reigned supreme in art, and his very advantageous contracts were the outcome of the flattering reputation which he contrived to maintain. Taste in courts, as well as that prevailing in monastic circles, turned towards him as to an uncontested leader in modern art. Historians have placed his sweet and tender style in the general framework of the more relaxed atmosphere which at that moment pervaded the West. But it is necessary to take account of a certain 'sentimentalism', basically not dissimilar from the notions of the Pre-Raphaelites who themselves praised Perugino to amateurs of painting as the master of a pure and delicate art. The documents give a clear picture of the manoeuvres of this artist-business man, whose purity of soul was probably not his chief characteristic. It is easy to understand how his success—which was incontestable—was largely due to a carefully orchestrated publicity, to an astonishing ability to attract clients and accumulate commissions. It is also possible to understand better the violent and contemptuous reaction which his 'soft manner' evoked among artists of the younger generation, with Michelangelo at their head.

Shortly after the brilliant enterprise in the Sistine Chapel, a provincial painter in the Marches who compiled a rhyming chronicle at the request of the Montefeltro mentioned him among the glories of art:

C. 1485: Giovanni Santi considers Perugino the equal of Leonardo: Doc. 1

... Two young [masters] of the same age, the same affection, Leonardo da Vinci and the Perugian
Pier della Pieve, divine painter.

It would be easier to understand the position in those years if it were known why Giovanni Santi put these two artists on the same plane. If he treated them as comrades, it was because they had been together in Verrocchio's workshop some eight or ten years earlier. When Perugino was summoned to Rome Leonardo went to Milan. Both were destined to have notable careers; both were experimenting with the most subtle techniques in painting, and were conversant with the Flemish use of oil-paint; both were adept at maintaining the interest of the public and charming their clientele. A typical document casts light on this point:

1488: Contract for the Altarpiece at Fano: Doc. 2 A

On 21 April 1488, in the VIth year of the Pontificate of Innocent VIII [...]
Master Pietro di Christoforo of Castillo, district of Perugia, and Master Joachim Blasio of Urbino, on the one part, and Pier Antonio a Lanceis and Matteo Martinetti

of Fano, syndics of the church of Sta. Maria Nuova, and Messer Pietro Antonio Galassi of Fano, as testamentary executors of Durante, called Giovanni Vianuzzi of Fano [...] on the other part have concluded the transaction, union, pact and agreement as follows: the said Master Joachim has promised solemnly to the aforementioned syndics and executors and has agreed with them that during the following three months, counting from now, and as soon as possible, he is to make and create, at his own expense and cost, an altarpiece for the high altar of the church of Sta. Maria Nuova of Fano, with its carved frame, ornamented and completed, according to the arrangement foreseen by the Apostolic Brief in the will of the said Durante, and according to the designs made by the said Master Joachim himself and drawn in colours on a paper which is to be given to the syndics and executors.

107 Perugino. *The Galitzin Triptych*. About 1490. Tempera on panel. National Gallery of Art, Washington D.C.
A typical Umbrian landscape with gentle curves and clear colours, and with a conventional arrangement of rocky screens in the wings.

108 Perugino. *The Fano Altarpiece*. 1497. Tempera on panel. Sta. Maria Nuova, Fano.
'In the [central] panel the image of the Blessed Virgin with her Son at her bosom, whom she piously adores... and with figures of appropriate size of St. John the Baptist, SS. Peter and Paul, St. Francis, St. Jerome, St. Louis, St. Michael Archangel and St. Mary Magdalen'. (Contract for the Fano Altarpiece, 1488.)

109 Perugino. *The Senigallia Altarpiece*. About 1500. Tempera on panel. Sta. Maria delle Grazie, Senigallia.
An exact repetition of the Fano Altarpiece in setting, architecture, accessories... except that the Magdalen at the right has been replaced by a local saint.

110 Perugino. *The Fano Altarpiece*. Panel from the predella, of the *Annunciation*. 1497. Tempera on panel. Galleria Nazionale delle Marche, Urbino.
'... to complete... the altarpiece, five scenes from the life of the Blessed Virgin: in the predella, her Nativity, her Presentation in the Temple, the Annunciation, the Purification...' (Contract for the Fano Altarpiece, 1488.)

The said Master Pietro has contracted and undertaken that in the time agreed upon and as soon as he can, he will paint and decorate at his own cost and expense for the gold, the fine colours and other elements indispensable for and to the quality of the painting of this altarpiece, the figures here below indicated: in the central panel the image of the Blessed Virgin with her Son at her breast, whom she piously adores, and also the representation and the figures according to suitable dimensions of St. John the Baptist, SS. Peter and Paul, St. Francis, St. Jerome, St. Louis, St. Michael Archangel and St. Mary Magdalen. Above, crowning the panel, he will paint the *Pietà* with the figures of the Blessed Mary and St. John the Evangelist on either side; and to complete the panel and the whole altarpiece, five scenes of the Life of the Blessed Virgin; in the predella her Nativity, her Presentation in the Temple, the Annunciation, the Purification and the Assumption. And to decorate all around this altarpiece and on the panel itself and everywhere possible, to decorate and enrich with gold, ultramarine blue and colours fine in quality and sufficiently in abundance, and in the other figures in such places as is suited to the panel [...]

Perugino was to receive 300 gold ducats for this work, of which the very precise description conforms to the norm of contracts, although all the scenes and all the figures are not always listed in such detail, as has been seen. The woodwork of the altarpiece, which was very important, was confided to a Master Joachim who was to receive eighty ducats; the design of this framework was laid down in a *modello* on paper. As to Perugino, he was given a programme of striking banality; his three-tiered altarpiece was to conform to hundreds of others. The insistence on the richness of the ornaments and the use of 'expensive' colours is in itself customary; it is a common clause right up to the sixteenth century, especially in the provinces. The document therefore has nothing unusual about it, except the unexpected compliment added to the text by the notary Pier Domenico Stati, in the form of a little poem of fourteen lines, which is no less than an inflated eulogy of the 'premier painter in the world' and of the frame-maker Joachim.

You, Peter, who art held to be the premier painter of all Italy,   Doc. 2F
And who art the first in the world,
And you, Joachim, who hath no equal
In wood-working and in the skill of your hand.
Another Parrhasius, another Lysippus, you who both
Triumph by the talent of the Ancients, and the art of the moderns,
Use and employ all your talent
To paint Mary. This is your task.
You know how to make beautiful likenesses of human images
And how to give one of Mary that will not be like any other;
Inscribe this double verse beneath your work:
Here is the finest work of the premier painter in the world, Pietro
And of the sculptor Joachim.

This extravagant puff, which associated the maker of the frame with that of the panels, betrayed a certain naivety in the emphasis of the eulogy. But it signified that, even in the eyes of the notary, Perugino knew how to shine and to make his merits known. The allusion to the Ancients (a painter and a sculptor) who are here surpassed was almost *de rigueur*. But Perugino was declared to be a particularly gifted painter of the Virgin; the image will be unlike any other.

The work was not finished until 1497, in the middle of a period of intense activity. The painter himself copied it exactly (with merely the substitution of one saint for another) in the altarpiece destined for another town in the Marches, Senigallia. Perugino's placid

classicism, rather sleepy and empty, is seen here in its most perfect equilibrium. The predella, of which the five scenes were specified in the contract, was beautifully executed, and was one of the really fine pieces from the workshop. It has been very carefully examined, because of an old hypothesis that Raphael collaborated on it. He entered the workshop at fourteen years of age, and he was quite capable of creating delicately modelled forms and of giving some animation to the rather flaccid figures of his master. It must be added that it was customary to hand over the small predella scenes to assistants who made their reputations with them.

111 Perugino. *The Fano Altarpiece*. Panel from the predella, of the *Birth of the Virgin*. 1497. Tempera on panel. Galleria Nazionale delle Marche, Urbino.

Doc. 3   8 March, 1494/5: Contract for the polyptych of St. Peter in Perugia:

The Reverend Father Dom Lactanzio di Giuliano, Florentine, abbot of the monastery of S. Pietro in Perugia, of the Order of St. Benedict, Congregation of Sta. Giustina, with Dom Benedict of Siena, Dom Daniele of Perugia of the same Order, the syndics and procurators of the said monastery, with the permission, agreement and will of the said Father Abbot present and approving, committing for themselves and their successors the possessions of the monastery, furniture, buildings, present and future, as guarantees, have ordered and granted to the eminent Master Pietro di Cristoforo of Castroplebis, excellent painter, here present, and agreeing for himself and his family, to paint and decorate the picture or *ancona* of the high altar of the said church of S. Pietro. To wit: in the central panel, the Ascension of Our Lord with the figure and representation of the Blessed Virgin Mary and the twelve Apostles with angels and such ornaments as shall be thought proper. In the lunette above, a figure representing God the Father Almighty, with two angels on either side supporting the mandorla. The predella at the foot of the said work is to be ornamented with narrative scenes, at the pleasure of the Father Abbot of the time. The pilasters, frames and all the decorative parts of the retable are to be ornamented with fine gold, ultramarine blue, and other fine colours as are suitable. That the said picture or ancona shall be well and carefully painted from top to bottom, decorated, gilded according to the manner of a good master, competent, regular and accomplished within less than two years [...] at the cost and expense of Master Pietro [...] All these articles the above-mentioned Master Pietro has promised to execute, follow, apply and observe to the said Lord Abbot acting for the said monastery, under pain of the measures later indicated and under the obligation of all his moveable and immoveable goods present and in the future [...] The Rev. Father Abbot has contracted and promised to pay the said Master Pietro, present, acting in his own name and that of his heirs, and to pay effectively for his painting, materials, colours, gold, and necessary ingredients for the perfect realization of the said painting and its ornaments of the said picture 500 large gold ducats to be paid over the next four years, starting from the day when the said picture shall have been begun, at the rate of one quarter per year.

The wooden frame of this huge altarpiece—difficult to reconstruct since it has been dismembered—had been ordered ten years earlier. As so often happens, the framing was the decisive element in the commission, which consisted of as many pieces as the framework required—a central panel, lunettes, side roundels and three elements for the predella, separated by four saints. Perugino obtained the commission with some payment in advance, and with a supplement for the high base, ornamented in 1496. The work is one of the most conventional altarpieces of the artist, who not only repeated over and over again his compositions, and the grouping and poses of his figures, but also left a large part of the execution to his collaborators. The documents give the names of Eusebio di Giacomo and Giovanni Francesco Ciambella, two young Perugian artists, as having been employed on this work. There was no question, on the other hand, of Raphael, whose

112 Perugino. *The Fano Altarpiece*. Panel from the predella of the *Marriage of the Virgin*. 1497. Tempera on panel. Galleria Nazionale delle Marche, Urbino.

113 Perugino. *The Fano Altarpiece*. Panel from the predella, of the *Presentation in the Temple*. 1497. Tempera on panel. Galleria Nazionale delle Marche, Urbino.
The predella is one of the best pieces to come from Perugino's shop: in the last two examples there is some reason to see the hand of the young Raphael.

114 Perugino. *An Antique Hero.* 1496.
Fresco. Collegio del Cambio, Perugia.
The inspiration came from a local humanist, Maturanzio, who placed Latin inscriptions—rather turgid—on the double
frescoes, evoking the Virtues in a gallery
of famous men of Antiquity, equipped in a
highly fantastic manner.

presence has been suggested, perhaps with some justification, in the painting of the Fano
Altarpiece. But these were the years when Raphael was working assiduously for the
insatiable impresario whom all the world hailed as the premier painter of Italy.

Somewhat unexpectedly, at the height of his reputation, Perugino seems to have been
sought by the Venetian authorities to come and work in the Doges' Palace.

1494: Perugino is invited to Venice: Doc. 4

Agreement with Maestro Pietro Perugino, painter, 1494, 9 August.

The Magnifici, Fantino Marcello and his colleagues, the noble Officers of the Salt,
on the command of the Most Serene Prince, have concluded a contract and are
agreed with Pietro Perugino, painter: he is charged with the painting of a panel in
the Sala del Gran Consiglio between two windows looking out towards S. Giorgio;
an allegory of Charity, and another panel or picture which he has undertaken to
paint between one window and another, and three and a half sections of vaulting [?]
in which he has to paint as many portraits of Doges as possible, and the scene of the
Pope driven out of Rome and the battle which followed, which he is to do over the
windows.

Moreover, the said Master Pietro shall be under the obligation to prepare
drawings of the work, and to remit them to the said officers, with the obligation of
painting the scene better than all the other works in the said Sala, as is suitable to a
place of such dignity. He is to make it richer than what was there before, the gold,
silver, blue and the colours and all that pertains to the craft of painting being at his
expense. The noble Officers of the Salt will supply him with the wood for the
support, and with canvas for the painting, scaffoldings and other accessories. The
said Master will receive in payment, according to the terms of the agreement, 400
gold ducats, that is ducats 400 [...]

From 1489–90, and very actively from 1492 onwards, work was continuing in the Sala
del Maggio Consiglio in the Doges' Palace in Venice. Together with Giovanni Bellini and
Alvise Vivarini at least half a dozen painters were working there, but they were not
concerned with the grand historical scenes. Among the most striking events of the
thirteenth century there was good reason to evoke the image of Pope Alexander III
pursued by Frederick Barbarossa and the battle of Legnano. The Doge Agostino
Barbarigo drew attention to this. The Office of the Salt—the wealthy office which was
bearing the cost of the enterprise—contracted with Perugino during the summer of 1494.
It would appear that the contract, in which the Council of Ten intervened as a third party,
stipulated a fee of 400 ducats, but was not legally registered as a result of new demands by
Perugino (if the interpretation of the letter of 1516, where Titian speaks of a salary of 'half
what was promised to Perugino', that is 400 ducats, is correct).* The fame of Perugino
must, therefore, have acquired a kind of national importance for the Doge to have
considered him. Perugino's financial exactions are not surprising. He was, in fact, in the
process of negotiating contracts on all sides: Milan (for the Certosa of Pavia) after Venice,
Perugia after Florence. In Perugia the local celebrity was treated with extreme
consideration: *Famosissimus in arte pittorum magister Petrus*, one reads in the contract for the
retable of the chapel of the Priors (6 March 1495). His triumph followed almost
immediately.

* The battle scene (destroyed in 1577) was
eventually given to Titian to paint, after
many arguments and intrigues, in 1516,
and delivered long afterwards, in 1552.

26 January 1496: Decision of the Collegio del Cambio at Perugia on the decoration   Doc. 5
of the Audience Chamber:

On 26 January 1496 the general and public assembly of the Jurists of the Arte del

115 Perugino. 1496. Audience Chamber of the Collegio del Cambio, Perugia.
'Cardus Cinaglia rose and spoke concerning the decoration of the audience chamber, saying that it was necessary to decorate it, to paint it, and to make it magnificent in some fashion.' (Decision of the Collegio del Cambio, concerning the decoration of the audience chamber, January 1496.)

116 Audience Chamber of the Collegio del Cambio. Diagram with the arrangement of the scenes:

A: Luna
B: Mercury
C: Apollo
D: Warriors on horseback
E: Warriors on horseback
F: Mars
G: Jupiter
H: Saturn
I: Venus
J: Cato
K: Prudence and Justice, with six Sages of Antiquity
L: Self-portrait and inscription
M: Fortitude and Temperance, with six Heroes of Antiquity
N: The Transfiguration
O: The Nativity
P: God the Father, Prophets and Sibyls

115

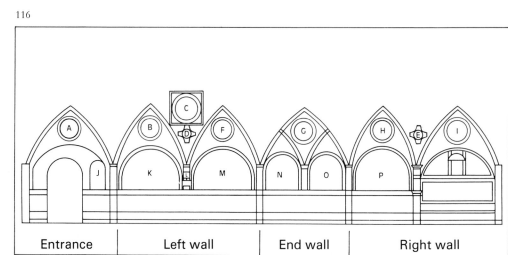

116

117 Pinturicchio. *Self-portrait*. 1501. Fresco. Baglioni Chapel, Sta. Maria Maggiore, Spello. ▷

117

118

Cambio were convoked and gathered together by the sound of the trumpet, by the voice of the herald, by summons by name [...] Before the Auditors the question was asked whether, to decorate the Audience Chamber with pictures, approaches should be made to Messer Pietro or to some other master [...] Cardus Cinaglia rose and said that, concerning the decoration of the Audience Chamber, it was essential to decorate it, to paint it and make it magnificent in some way or other. The advice and decision of the said [Auditors] was that it was necessary to choose those who could make an assignment, deliberation and positive decision with the said Auditors, as best suited them...

This document concerns the deliberations of the Auditors of the Cambio and is not precise about the terms of the contract. But enough is known about this enterprise to be able to affirm that it aroused the enthusiasm of the people of Perugia, and gave Pietro an

118 Perugino. *Self-portrait.* 1496. Fresco. Collegio del Cambio, Perugia.

'In an ornate frame, he made his own portrait... and below it the following inscription: "If the art of painting had been lost, he restored it".' (Vasari, *Life of Perugino.*)

Never had the self-glorification of the artist had such prominence. In the Baglioni Chapel at Spello, Pinturicchio, a brilliant disciple of Perugino, adopted the same formula, arranging the portrait inside an astonishing piece of still-life painting.

opportunity for a performance which was particularly enhancing to his reputation. His own education was not adequate for him alone to settle an original programme for the work. He was assisted by the local humanist Maturanzio, who prepared the Latin inscriptions beneath the two double frescoes of the Virtues, treated as a gallery of famous men of Antiquity. Two series, consisting of the same number of Prophets and Sybils, are on the wall opposite. The very banal iconographic cycle is as a whole fairly well adapted to a Judgement Chamber. The ceiling is more elaborate, with its planetary system set out in a series of small segments of vaulting accompanied by grotesques. The execution was relatively quick, but interrupted by strange comings and goings between Perugia and Florence. Perugino never gave up any projected commission and was determined to carry all before him. Also, the payments for the Cambio stretched out over ten years. On 3 March 1498, for example, the painter was in Perugia where he was paid for a panel destined for the Sala del Cambio; but on 2 June he rushed to Florence, where a son was born to him. He reappeared in 1499; regular payments continued. In 1500 on the right-hand wall of the Sala one of the panels bore that date and an inscription which Vasari copied out:

1500: Self-portrait and self-glorification of Perugino in the Cambio (from Vasari,   Doc. 6
1568):

In an ornamental frame he made his portrait which seems full of life, with underneath the following inscription:
   If the art of painting had disappeared,
   He restored it.
   If it had not been invented anywhere,
   He produced it.

This laudatory inscription placed in full view not only shows a remarkable gift for publicity; it constitutes, by the juxtaposition of a self-portrait in a setting of false perspective, a *trompe-l'œil*, an important innovation. This is not the first time that a painter represented himself within one of his compositions: the examples of Giotto and of the neo-Giottesques of 1390–1400 are very well known. Perugino represented himself in the right-hand group of the Apostles in the *Giving of the Keys*; his round face, his thick neck, his chin sinking into rolls of flesh, is the same image which is to be found here with less hair and ageing features which mark the passage of the twenty years between the works.

As has been noted by E. H. Gombrich, this arrangement of a portrait in *trompe-l'œil* in the form of a picture hanging from a pilaster must have made a sensation. Never had the self-glorification of the artist reached such a spectacular character and setting. The example was so well noted that in the following year, in the Baglioni Chapel at Spello, Pinturicchio, the only really brilliant pupil of Perugino (Raphael excepted) used the same formula, though placing the frame under a shelf bearing a Book of Hours which appeared to belong to the oratory of the Madonna. The inscription, more modest than the one in the Cambio, is surrounded by a rosary of large beads. In fact, no other examples of this ostentatious arrangement have been found; it is an original example in the history of self-portraits.

But why is it that in the Cambio the dominant impression is one of great monotony and slackness of style ? Vasari says:

1496: Perugino's pupils in the Cambio (*Life of Perugino*, 1550 and 1568):   Doc. 7

...Among Piero's pupils the best was Andrea Luigi of Assisi, called l'Ingegno ['Talented'], who in his youth competed with Raphael under Pietro's tutelage. He

employed him in all his major enterprises, for example in the Sala dell'Udienza of the Cambio in Perugia. [...]

But none of his pupils ever equalled the fluency of Pietro or the grace of colouring of his style, which enjoyed such fame in his own times that many came from France, Spain, Germany and other countries to learn it.

119 Perugino. *Venus*. Detail of the ceiling of the audience chamber in the Collegio del Cambio. 1496. Fresco. Collegio del Cambio, Perugia.
A medallion of one of the planets in a sharply delineated style, with ornamental ribbons and grotesques.

In the endless list of Perugino's assistants and pupils a few names stand out. That of Raphael naturally eclipses them all, because he managed to escape the clutches of a rather over-demanding master. The Andrea d'Assisi whom Vasari mentions would have been one of the assistants in the Sistine Chapel (where a large part of the *Baptism of Christ* is attributed to him by some art historians). But what is really noteworthy is the mention of this influx of foreigners. If Vasari is right—and there is every chance that he is—it has to be accepted that the international success of the 'soft and tender style' had become a distinctive feature of Western art. It is perhaps this art, so easily assimilable and of such facile charm, that furthered the real beginning of the osmosis between the styles of the north and those of the south.

Admiring declarations accompanied the stages of the artist's career up to this point without any hitches. In Rome Perugino's reputation remained intact, but people here only

120 Perugino. *The Assumption*. 1500.
Tempera on panel. Galleria degli Uffizi,
Florence.
The *Assumption* from Vallombrosa is typical of the industrialized output of the firm,
with its three stages, its repetitive types
and conventional ornament.

121 Perugino. *The Family of the Virgin*.
1502. Tempera on panel. Musée des
Beaux-Arts, Marseilles.
The family of the Madonna was stipulated
by the author of a will of 8 December,
1500, for a picture for his chapel in Sta.
Maria degli Angeli in Perugia. The inscribed haloes are an unexpected feature.

122 Perugino. *Allegorical Combat between Chastity and Voluptuousness.* Detail. 1503. Tempera on canvas. Musée du Louvre, Paris.
A detail from the episode of Daphne in the background of the moral allegory commissioned by Isabella d'Este: the elegance of the motif reminds one of the charming *Apollo and Marysas*, also in the Louvre.

knew his team, his school. Agostino Chigi wrote to his father, who was looking for a painter for his chapel in Sta. Maria del Popolo:

7 November 1500: Opinion of Agostino Chigi on Perugino: Doc. 8

... About your chapel, I know what you are thinking [....] You say you have spoken with a Messer Pietro Perugino; I tell you, if he is prepared to work on it with his own hand he is the finest master in Italy. And the one who is called Patorichio [Pinturicchio] is his pupil, but now he isn't here. Of other masters of any worth, there are none.

This is an interesting judgement, because it attests to the kind of void there was in Rome at the time of Alexander VI. These are the years during which the activity of the Perugino 'firm' became almost frantic. The polyptych for S. Pietro at Perugia was delivered, and the one for Pavia too; the *Assumption* at Vallombrosa, as insipid as it is huge, is dated 1500; the same date is inscribed on the self-portrait in the Cambio, finally completed. The advertising campaign was working splendidly, but Agostino Chigi's remark 'if he is

prepared to work on it with his own hand' betrays a certain uneasiness among his admirers.

His productivity during these years is truly extraordinary. It is the artisan practice of Neri di Bicci multiplied by ambition and the facile manner of a great master and a 'best seller'. A fairly second-rate work is a good instance of this.

123 Perugino. *Allegorical Combat between Chastity and Voluptuousness.* 1503. Tempera on canvas. Musée du Louvre, Paris.
'...it would have been more honourable for you, and more pleasing to us, to have painted it in oil...' (Letter from Isabella d'Este to Perugino, June 1505.)

Doc. 9   8 December 1500: The will of Ser Angelo di Tommaso Conti:

The eminent Messer Angelo di Tommaso Conti of Perugia by this present will [...] desired firstly that his body should be buried in the church of S. Domenico in Perugia [...] in his family sepulchre. He then decided, left and requested, etc., that his heirs mentioned below shall be held and obliged, in the year following the death of the testator, to have erected and constructed in the Church of Sta. Maria degli Angeli in Perugia [...] an altar for the celebration of Masses and divine offices, and that upon this altar shall be placed the retable ordered by the testator, and that there shall be

135

painted therein the images of St. Anne and her daughters, to wit the Glorious Virgin Mary with her Son Jesus Christ, St. Mary Cleophas, St. Mary Salome with her sons, and St. Joseph and St. Joachim, in the style and form set out in the model already prepared by the excellent painter Master Pietro Cristoforo of Castro Plebis, citizen of Perugia. And to pay for the picture 55 florins at the rate of 40 bolognese to the florin, as the remainder of 65 which was the price of this painting. The said Master Pietro has already received as earnest money and in part payment ten florins...

The family of the Madonna (or Holy Kinship) was therefore asked for by a will of 8 December 1500 for a chapel in Sta. Maria degli Angeli. Perugino's devoted admirer had previously ensured the painter's participation by paying him ten florins in earnest money. It only remained for his heirs to pay the remainder. But the unfortunate Angelo Conti was not very well served after his death. The panel is now in the Musée Longchamps in Marseilles. The feebleness of the execution is all too visible; the only interesting feature is the symmetry of the figures on either side of the vertical axis, where the enthroned Madonna has St. Anne standing behind her. The arrangement of the high base which raises the figures of the main group above the rest was already virtually an archaism at this date. Raphael, who was then probably working in Perugino's studio, quickly abandoned it. What should be remembered is the modern interpretation of the theme which Leonardo was advancing during these very years 1501–2. The parallelism between these two 'fraternal geniuses' imagined by Giovanni Santi fifteen years earlier is revealed as totally mistaken. Leonardo was now the painter furthest away from the graceful and popular art of his former fellow-pupil.

The continual stream of commissions for Perugino, coming from pious institutions and business men, had the fatal consequences which can readily be foreseen. Not only did the painter accept blithely commissions for works in which he could endlessly repeat his china figurines, but he was also tempted to strain his powers by undertaking work which involved an imaginative talent which he never had at any time possessed. This was the case with Isabella d'Este. Impelled by contemporary snobbery, the Marchioness of Mantua was determined to obtain Perugino's collaboration in the decoration of the *studiolo* which she was then creating. She succeeded. The text tells the story.

19 January 1503: Letter from Francesco Malatesta to the Marchioness Isabella: Doc. 10

I have to inform you that I have concluded the contract with Perugino for 100 gold ducats. I have paid out twenty, for the normal settlement of the legal document by Ser Pierfrancesco di Ser Macario de Macari.

This agreement had been hard to get. From 1497 onwards, not having been able to succeed with Giovanni Bellini, Isabella had successively requested Lorenzo da Pavia, an intarsia worker, then Giovanni da Montefeltro who lived at Senigallia, near Fano, where Perugino was then working, to negotiate with the painter. It finally required Francesco Malatesta, the diplomatic agent of the Gonzaga, to contrive a meeting with Perugino in October 1502 on his return to Florence and to negotiate the agreement of January 1503. These long negotiations may seem surprising. Perugino was clearly very reluctant to come to any agreement with the Marchioness. He spent two years on the creation of his picture, and the result was rather distressing.

The Marchioness's tyrannical character, the abstruse programmes which she imposed, and the pressure she exerted on her painters discouraged even the most willing among them. In fact, after signing the contract, Perugino did nothing about the *Allegorical Combat between Chastity and Voluptuousness*; he was at Castel di Pieve near Perugia, where he received the balance of his fee for the Cambio. But Isabella's agent seems to have seen quite clearly what the position was when he heard that the painter was always short of money, was on the look-out for quick and easy fees, and was ready 'to serve whomever would pay him hour by hour. According to unkind gossip—not necessarily false because it was unkind—Pietro was avaricious, bought goods, property and houses, and spent handsomely on a pretty wife whom he delighted to dress himself. Catastrophe loomed. After Mantegna's brilliant, and rather strained but strongly defined cycle, the Marchioness Isabella was asking Perugino to achieve in his delicate and tender style a work which could be compared with Mantegna's, on the abstruse themes which were so dear to her. Naturally he could not succeed, and his failure is one of the most interesting in the Renaissance. All the world witnessed it, and the final verdict of the Marchioness, although phrased ambiguously, was clearly unfavourable: an oil-painting would have been better.

Doc. 11   30 June 1505: Letter from Isabella d'Este to Perugino:

> ... Although executed with great care, since it has to be placed next to those by Mantegna which are in an extremely precise style, it would have been more to your honour and my satisfaction to have painted it in oils and it is to be regretted that Lorenzo Mantovano dissuaded you.

Pietro was now forced to face the hostility of other artists and the pitiless criticism of the younger generation to which, by his facile manner and his lack of seriousness, he had given only too many opportunities for indignation.

Doc. 12   *C. 1502–3: Perugino insulted by Michelangelo (from Vasari, 1550 and 1568):*

> Pietro had so much work to do and so much was commissioned from him that he endlessly repeated the same things. The principles of his art were so far reduced to a formula that he made all his figures look alike. When Michelangelo Buonarroti came on the scene, Pietro very much wanted to see his figures, because of the praises heaped on them by artists. And seeing the great reputation which he had acquired everywhere in his early years now overshadowed, he sought to offend working artists by bitter words. And for this reason he deserved, as well as some insults from them, that Michelangelo in public told him that he was a clown in art. But Pietro was unable to bear so great an insult; they both appeared before the Magistrate of the Eight, where Pietro did not come off to his advantage.

This anecdote is not confirmed by any police document or judicial record. But there is little reason to doubt it. It marks the entry of the young Michelangelo into artistic life, and fixes the moment when, in 1502–3, activity was picking up in Florence, official commissions were multiplying, and the critical spirit was naturally manifested at the expense of a fashionable painter and of a style typical of the 'manner' of the older generation. Once again, mockery and animosity reigned among painters in Florence, where Leonardo had recently returned from Milan. Nothing is known of what he may have said and thought of his old fellow-student; in his notes there is no mention of Perugino, but it is possible, without difficulty, to discover in his writings the elements of a radical criticism of an art without inventiveness or new approach. Twenty years after the triumph of the Sistine Chapel, the reputation of Pietro was attacked directly in Florence. No one had any further consideration for the splendid reputation which, a few years previously, had reached its culminating point in Siena and Perugia. After the high altar of the Servites (church of the Annunziata), which was finished by Perugino (who had taken the commission over after the death of Filippino Lippi) and unveiled in 1506, the painter counted for nothing in Florence. He was forced to return to his province, where in the end he had to accept contracts from mediocre convents for miserable fees.

Chronological Table 1500–1600

x	1500–1501	Perugia	Perugino, *Conti altarpiece* for Sta. Maria degli Angeli (Musée Longchamps, Marseilles)
x	1501	Spello	Pinturicchio, decoration of the Baglione Chapel
x	1501	Florence	Leonardo exhibits the cartoon for the *Virgin and Child with St. Anne* (National Gallery, London)
x	1501–1504	Florence	Michelangelo, *David* (Accademia, Florence)
	1502–1503	Perugia	Raphael, *Coronation of the Virgin (Oddi altarpiece)* for S. Francesco (Vatican Museum)
x	1503	Venice	Benedetto Bordone, *Triumph of Caesar*, engraved by Jacob de Strasbourg
x	1503–1505	Mantua	Perugino, *Allegorical Combat between Chastity and Voluptuousness* for the *studiolo* of Isabella d'Este (Louvre, Paris)
x	1503–1506	Florence	Leonardo *(Battle of Anghiari)*, and Michelangelo *(Battle of Cascina)* for the Palazzo della Signoria
x	1504	Florence	Michelangelo, *Holy Family (Doni tondo)* (Uffizi, Florence)
	C. 1504	Venice	Giorgione, altarpiece of S. Liberale (Castelfranco Veneto)
x	*C.* 1505	Mantua	Mantegna, *Introduction of the Cult of Cybele in Rome*, for Francesco Cornaro (National Gallery, London)
	1505	Monte Oliveto Maggiore	Sodoma, scenes from the cycle of the *Life of St. Benedict*
	1505–1509	Siena	Pinturicchio, *Life of Pope Paul II* in the Piccolomini Library
x	1506	Florence	Perugino, altarpiece for the Servites (various museums)
	1506	Venice	Dürer, *Feast of the Rose Garlands* for S. Bartolommeo, Venice (Prague)
	1506	Rome	Discovery of the *Laocöon*
	1506–1507	Florence	Raphael, *Madonna of the Goldfinch* (Uffizi, Florence) and *Belle Jardinière* (Louvre, Paris)
x	1507–1508	Venice	Giorgione and Titian, frescoes on the façade of the Fondaco dei Tedeschi
x	1508–1512	Rome	Michelangelo, Sistine Ceiling
	1508–1518	Rome	Raphael and his studio, decoration of the Stanze in the Vatican
x	*C.* 1510	Milan	Leonardo, *Virgin and Child with St. Anne* (Louvre, Paris)

	1511	Padua	Titian, frescoes in the Scuola del Santo
	1511	Florence	Fra Bartolommeo, *Marriage of St. Catherine* (Palazzo Pitti)
	1512	Rome	Raphael, fresco of *Galatea* in the Farnesina
	1513–1516	Rome	Michelangelo, *Moses* and the two *Slaves* for the Julius Tomb
	1514	Florence	Pontormo, *St. Veronica*, fresco in the Cappella del Papa, Sta. Maria Novella
	1514–1516	Rome	Raphael, cartoons for the tapestries of the *Acts of the Apostles*
x	1515–1516	Florence	Leonardo, projects for the new Medici palace
	1516	Rome	Raphael, directs the workshop of St. Peter's; *Santa Cecilia*
x	1516–1518	Florence	Michelangelo, projects for the façade of S. Lorenzo and for the new Medici Palace
	1517	Ferrara	Dosso Dossi, works in the Ducal Palace
	1517	Rome	Raphael studio, loggia of *Psyche* in the Farnesina
	1517–1519	Rome	Giovanni da Udine and the Raphael studio, decoration of the Vatican Loggie
	1518	Rome	Raphael, *St. Michael* and *The Holy Family* for Francis I
x	1518	Venice	Titian, *Assumption*, Frari
	1518–1519	Parma	Correggio, frescoes in the *Camera di S. Paolo*
	1518–1520	Rome	Raphael, *Transfiguration* (Vatican Museums)
	1519 (2 May)	Amboise	Death of Leonardo da Vinci
	1520 (6 April)	Rome	Death of Raphael
	1520–1533	Florence	Michelangelo, Medici tombs in S. Lorenzo
	1521	Bergamo	Lorenzo Lotto, *Polyptych of S. Bernardino*
	1520–1521	Parma	Correggio, dome fresco in S. Giovanni Evangelista
	1523	Florence	Rosso, *Marriage of the Virgin* in S. Lorenzo
	1525	Florence	Pontormo, frescoes in the Certosa di Galluzzo
C.	1525–1526	Rome	Rosso, *Lamentation over the Dead Christ* (Museum of Fine Arts, Boston)
x	1526	Venice	Titian, *Pesaro Madonna*, Frari
	1526	Florence	Pontormo, *Deposition*, Sta. Felicità
	1526–1527	Rome	Parmigianino, *Vision of St. Jerome* (National Gallery, London)
x	1527 et seq.	Venice	Pordenone, decoration of the choir of S. Rocco; decoration of the cloister of S. Stefano; *Corrieri Altarpiece* in S. Giovanni al Rialto
	1528	Parma	Correggio, *Education of Cupid* (National Gallery, London); *Jupiter and Antiope* (Louvre, Paris)
x	1528–1530	Venice	Titian, *Altarpiece of St. Peter Martyr* (lost)
x	1529	Venice	Lorenzo Lotto, Altarpiece for the Carmine

x	*C.* 1530	Venice	Pordenone, frescoes on the façade of the palace of Martino d'Anna
	C. 1530	Mantua	Giulio Romano, Palazzo del Te
	C. 1530	Parma	Parmigianino, *Self-portrait* (Vienna)
	C. 1530–1534	Parma	Correggio, *Danäe* (Rome, Borghese); *Io* and *Ganymede* (Vienna); *Leda* (Berlin)
	1530–1540	Genoa	Perino del Vaga, decoration of the Palazzo Doria
	1534–1536	Parma	Parmigianino, *Madonna del Collo Lungo* for Sta. Maria dei Servi (Uffizi, Florence)
	1534–1538	Venice	Titian, *Presentation of the Virgin* for the convent of the Carità (Accademia, Venice)
x	1534–1541	Rome	Michelangelo, *Last Judgement* in the Sistine Chapel
x	1537	Venice-Murano	Pordenone, work in the Doges' Palace; altarpiece of the *Annunciation* in Sta. Maria degli Angeli in Murano
x	*C.* 1540	Venice	Titian, lunettes in Santo Spirito in Isola (now Sta. Maria della Salute)
	1541	Rome	Titian, *Paul III and his Nephews* (Museo di Capodimonte, Naples)
x	*C.* 1545	Venice	Titian, altarpiece in S. Giovanni al Rialto
	1546	Rome	Vasari, decoration of the Palazzo della Cancelleria
	1547 (1 Jan)	Rome	Michelangelo, appointed to the direction of the works at St. Peter's
	1550	Florence	Vasari, first edition of the *Lives*
	1551	Venice	Veronese, *Sacra Conversazione*, S. Francesco della Vigna
	1552	Genoa	Alessi builds Sta. Maria di Carignano
	C. 1560	Maser	Veronese, decoration of the Villa Barbaro
	C. 1560–1563	Rome	Salviati and Sacchetti, decorations in the Palazzo Farnese
x	1562–1563	Venice	Veronese, *Marriage at Cana* for the convent of S. Giorgio Maggiore (Louvre, Paris)
	1562 et seq.	Caprarola	Taddeo Zuccaro and studio, decorations in the Palazzo Farnese
	1562–1566	Venice	Tintoretto, paintings in the Scuola Grande of S. Marco
	C. 1564	Florence	Bronzino, Chapel of Eleonora of Toledo in the Palazzo della Signoria
	1564 (18 Feb.)	Rome	Death of Michelangelo (solemn obsequies in Florence, 14 July)
x	*C.* 1565	Venice	Veronese, *Feast in the House of Simon* (Turin)
x	1566	Verona	Veronese, altarpiece of *St. George* in S. Giorgio in Braida
	1567	Milan	Tibaldi, architectural work on the Cathedral
	1568	Florence	Vasari, second edition of the *Lives*
	1569–1577	Rome	Federico Zuccaro, Marco Pino, etc., Oratory of Sta. Lucia del Gonfalon
	1570	Venice	Palladio, *Quattro Libri dell'Architettura*
x	1570–1572	Venice	Veronese, *Feast in the House of Simon* for the convent of S. Sebastiano (Brera, Milan); *Allegory of the Battle of Lepanto* (Accademia, Venice)

x	1572	Vicenza	Veronese, *Supper of St. Gregory*, Monte Berico
x	before 1573	Venice	Veronese, *Feast in the House of Simon*, for the Servites (Versailles)
	1573	Venice	Titian, *Pietà* (Accademia, Venice)
	1573	Florence	Vasari and studio, *studiolo* of Francesco de' Medici in the Palazzo della Signoria
	1573	Urbino	Barocci, *Rest on the Flight into Egypt* (Vatican Museums)
x	1573	Murano	Studio of Veronese, *Madonna of the Rosary* (Museum)
x	1573	Venice	Veronese, *Feast in the House of Levi* for the convent of SS. Giovanni e Paolo (Accademia, Venice)
	1573–1587	Venice	Tintoretto, decoration in the Doges' Palace; paintings in the Scuola Grande di San Rocco
	1576 (27 Aug)	Venice	Death of Titian
	1577 et seq.	Venice	Veronese, allegories in the Sala del Gran Consiglio in the Doges' Palace
	1580	Vicenza	Death of Palladio
	1580	Bassano	Jacopo Bassano, *Baptism of Sta. Lucilla* (Museum)
	1584	Milan	Lomazzo, *Trattato dell'Arte della Pittura*
C.	1584	Bologna	The Carracci, decorations in the Fava and Magnana Palaces
	1586	Venice	Scamozzi, Procurazie Nuove
	1590 et seq.	Rome	Taddeo Zuccaro, decoration of his own palace
	1597	Rome	Annibale Carracci, decoration of the Gallery in the Palazzo Farnese begun

Chapter 7
A Great Hostility: Leonardo and Michelangelo (1500-16)

From Vasari: *The Life of Leonardo da Vinci*, 1550 and 1568:

Doc. 1

There was a great dislike between Michelangelo Buonarroti and him [Leonardo]. Because of this, Michelangelo left Florence with the permission of Duke Giuliano, being summoned by the Pope for the façade of S. Lorenzo. When Leonardo heard this, he left and went to France where the king, who also knew of his work, was very fond of him and wanted him to paint the cartoon of St. Anne.

All historians have been struck by the first sentence of this text, which was written at a time when Michelangelo was still alive, but when Leonardo had died at Amboise more than thirty years before: a great hostility *(sdegno grandissimo)* between the two painters. This is one of the facts most taken for granted in the history of the Cinquecento which has more often been merely accepted rather than examined. The somewhat muddled explanation of Leonardo's departure for France goes back to the winter of 1516–17, and mentions a competition for the Medici project for the façade of S. Lorenzo, of which, as will be seen, all the circumstances are not easy to reconstruct despite the mention of Giuliano de' Medici, brother of Leo X. Vasari implies that this affair, which was unacceptable to Leonardo, was the last episode of an old rivalry. It must have begun about fifteen years before, almost at the turn of the century, when despite a considerable difference in their ages—Leonardo was born in 1452 and Michelangelo in 1475—they had plenty of opportunity to know each other and to detest each other. In fact a whole generation witnessed a kind of duel of geniuses, full of parries and lunges which suggest that it was essential to their natures.

During the years of Michelangelo's youth, Leonardo was in Milan in the service of Ludovico il Moro; he painted the *Last Supper* in Sta. Maria delle Grazie and prepared the casting of the giant statue of Francesco Sforza. All Italy talked about it. When the second French invasion took place in 1499, and Milan was taken by the army of Louis XII, Leonardo first fled to Venice, where he remainded only for a few weeks and then returned to Florence. His arrival in the spring of 1500, after seventeen years of feverish activity in Lombardy, was a kind of special event. The city, which had been shaken by the revolution of Savonarola (hanged and his dead body burned in May 1498), was still not prepared for the return of the Medici. The government of the Gonfalonier Soderini, formed of moderate aristocrats, advised by Machiavelli, was trying to recreate the unity of the Republic and to reanimate Florentine prestige. Leonardo was welcomed with great and flattering consideration. The authorities pressed important commissions on him.

The Affair of the *David*

A curious passage in Vasari concerns one of the Gonfalonier's first projects. The new Republic wanted a spectacular symbol of its strength and its civic sense. There existed in

124 Baldassare Lanci. *View of Florence* (sketch for stage set). About 1560. Drawing, pencil, pen and watercolour. Gabinetto dei Disegni, Uffizi, Florence.
The Palazzo della Signoria with its tower, on the right, aligned in perspective with the side of Sta. Maria del Fiore and the campanile (see Pl. 55).

the mason's yard of the Opera del Duomo—the body responsible for the maintenance of the cathedral—an enormous block of marble which several sculptors, including Agostino di Duccio (1464) and then Antonio Rossellino (1476) had failed to do anything with.

Suddenly, quite a series of discussions and intrigues can be imagined, leading to the inevitable conclusion which Vasari recounts:

Doc. 2   1501: Intrigues concerning the block of marble in the Opera del Duomo (from Vasari (1550 and 1568):

> Several of his friends wrote to him [Michelangelo] and said that he should come, because it was not impossible that he could get that marble which was in the Opera, spoilt; which Pier Soderini, then made the city's Gonfalonier for life, had several times declared that he would give to be worked by Leonardo da Vinci, and that he was at that moment on the point of giving it to Andrea Contucci da Monte Sansavino, an excellent sculptor, who was trying to obtain it...

An almost contemporary text indicates that Leonardo was very well thought of as a sculptor.

125 Michelangelo. *David*. Detail. 1501–4. Sculpture. Galleria dell'Accademia, Florence.
'... Master Michelangelo Buonarroti... with the task of creating... a figure in rough-hewn marble called the Giant...' (Commission for the *David* from Michelangelo, August 1501.)

1504: Judgement of Gauricus on Leonardo da Vinci: Doc. 3

A pupil of Verrocchio, Leonardo da Vinci, is well known from the great horse of Milan, which he was not allowed to complete, and by his painting of the *Last Supper*. He is a genius worthy of Archimedes.

Leonardo's name was indissolubly linked to the project for the colossal bronze equestrian statue for the Castello Sforzesco, which, on the eve of its casting, had been interrupted by the war in 1498. It was natural for Soderini to ask Leonardo's advice about the sculpture, a symbol of the new Florentine regime. It was perfectly reasonable that, as a bronze-caster and not a marble-worker, he would have declined the offer. Andrea Sansovino had just returned from Portugal, where he had been sent by Lorenzo de' Medici in 1491; his eagerness to get the commission is understandable.

The competition therefore took place in the spring of 1501. Michelangelo won. The contract for the *David* was signed in August.

Doc. 4   16 August 1501: Commission for the *David* from Michelangelo:

Their Excellencies the Consuls of the Arte de la Lana, gathered together in the Audience Chamber of the Opera, attentive to the interests as well as to the honour of the Opera, have designated as sculptor to the Opera the worthy master Michelangelo Buonarroti, Florentine citizen, with the mission of creating, finishing, and in all conscience achieving a marble figure in a partly worked block called the Giant, nine braccia high, actually on the premises of the Opera and formerly badly begun by Master Agostino da Firenze, within two years to be calculated from the next calends of September, with an indemnity and salary of six gold florins per month. Whatever the work entails, it must be executed within the premises of the Opera, which will do all it can to help him, and to furnish assistants, wood and all requirements. The work, that is to say the marble man, when finished, the consuls and overseers then in office will value if the work merits a supplement to the price; their judgement is final.

This document contains all the essentials; an enormous block which Agostino di Duccio had been unable to do anything with (he died in 1466); the dimensions which make it a giant, like Leonardo's unfinished horse; the advantageous terms, but a strict control. The execution lasted from September 1501 to the spring of 1504.

Doc. 5   1503: Michelangelo Works on the *David* (from Vasari, 1550 and 1568):

[He was commissioned to execute] as an emblem for the palace a young David with a sling in his hand to show that, as he had defended his people and governed it with justice, so those who held sway over the city should defend it energetically and govern it with justice. He began it in the Opera of Sta. Maria del Fiore, where he made an enclosure with the wall and with boards so as to surround the marble, and he continued to work on it so that no one could see him until he had brought it to perfection.

This secrecy, which accords well with the artist's nature, resulted in an effect of general surprise when the work was unveiled, but during the long months of waiting, it may also have induced a kind of nervous tension which could easily provoke an outburst of the mutual animosity between the two great men of the day.

Doc. 6   Between 1501 and 1505: Leonardo publicly insulted by Michelangelo (from the Anonimo Magliabecchiano, *c.* 1540):

Leonardo, together with Giovanni da Gavine, of Sta. Trinità, was going past the benches of the [Palazzo] Spini, where a group of worthy men were gathered to discuss a passage in Dante, and they called to Leonardo asking him to explain the passage. At that moment Michelangelo passed by, and, called to by one of them, Leonardo answered 'Michelangelo will explain it to you.' And as it appeared to Michelangelo that he had said this to make fun of him, he retorted angrily, 'You

126 Leonardo da Vinci. *David*. 1507. Drawing in pen and black chalk. Windsor 12591ʳ. Royal Library, Windsor.
Leonardo was a member of the jury which met on 25 January 1504, to decide on a site for the *David*. The drawing occurs on a sheet containing the plan and elevation of a palace with towers at the angles, and the sculpture seems to be treated as a project for a fountain.

127 Michelangelo. *Virgin and Child with St. Anne*. 1501. Pen drawing. Ashmolean Museum, Oxford.
A very different distribution of the three figures of the theme from that by Leonardo.

128 Cartoon of the *Madonna and Child with St. Anne*. About 1499. Black chalk heightened with white. National Gallery, London.
'...the Mother who seems in some way to rise from the lap of St. Anne, seizes the Child and pulls Him away from a little lamb, an innocent creature signifying the Passion... This study is unfinished...' (Letter from Fra Pietro da Novellara to Isabella d'Este, April 1501.)

explain it, who made a project for a horse to cast it in bronze and couldn't cast it, and to your shame just left it there.' And having said this he turned his back on them and went away, and Leonardo remained and became red-faced. And to embarrass him even more, Michelangelo added, 'And those fools of Milanese who believed in you.'

The story comes from a manuscript collection in the Biblioteca Nazionale of Florence, put together about 1540. The anonymous chronicler wanted to record a typical anecdote, which may well have been told by the Giovanni da Gavine, mentioned in the text. The scene is quite believable; the stone benches of the Palazzo Spini, facing the church of Sta.

Trinità at the exit from the thirteenth-century bridge (later to be rebuilt by Ammanati); Leonardo passes by. Everyone knows him. What are the loungers doing? They are arguing about a passage in the *Divine Comedy*, as doubtless often happened since about 1500 Dante's work was more than normally present in the minds of Florentines of all conditions. Why call on Leonardo? The poet's work abounds in scientific statements on geology, the stars, the phenomena of light. Everyone knew Leonardo's interest in cosmology, to which there are many references in Dante's works and in the commentaries on them. In a bibliographical note Leonardo had included a reference to a copy of Dante among the books of Archimedes (still unpublished) and scientific treatises.

But why did Leonardo turn to Michelangelo, whom a twist of fate had directed towards the little group? Much later on, Michelangelo wrote two sonnets in honour of Dante, where can be found the famous apostrophe:

Fuss'io pur lui—Had I only been him (meaning Dante) (*Rime* 248), and he wrote a long commentary (about 1540) on the place of Brutus in Inferno. It must be supposed that his predilection for the *Commedia*, read in the neo-Platonic Commentary of Landino (1481), was well known. Michelangelo had enjoyed the company of scholars in the circle of Lorenzo de' Medici. Leonardo, perhaps ironically, or even perhaps out of pure courtesy, referred the amateurs to the young artist, forgetting that his pride already made him forbidding.

His bitter retort is not inexplicable, above all in the context of the little competition for the 'block of marble'. Everyone knew that Leonardo had never had the time to do the casting, for all the meticulous preparation (as is proved by the MS. Madrid I, now

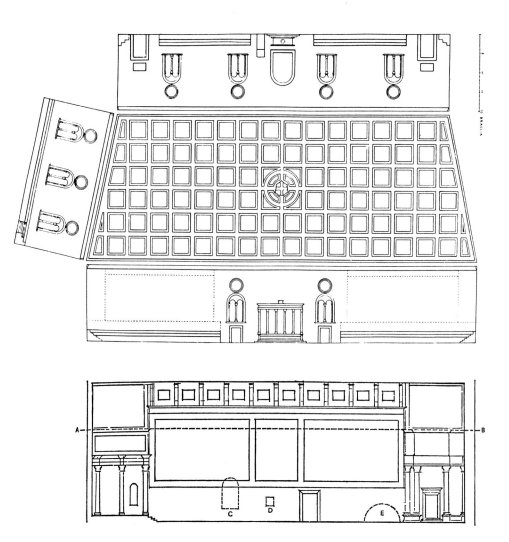

129a Palazzo Vecchio, Florence: reconstruction of the Sala del Gran Consiglio. (Diagram by J. Wilde.)
This vast room was sumptuously built and decorated with fine woods, a coffered ceiling and *spalliere* (seats with high backs set against the wall).

129b Palazzo Vecchio, Florence: reconstruction of the Sala del Gran Consiglio, east wall. (From C. Pedretti, *Leonardo, A Study in Chronology and Style*, London, 1973, p. 95.)
The probable position of the *Battle of Anghiari* (Leonardo da Vinci) and of the *Battle of Cascina* (Michelangelo). The line A-B marks the original level of the ceiling, before the transformation. C and D indicate old windows, E an arch that was filled in with bricks and stone.

rediscovered), for the giant horse; he had worked on it for seven or eight years in the Castello at Milan. Whether the scene took place in 1503, at the time when Soderini's commission fell to Michelangelo, during the two years when everyone was awaiting the result, or after the triumphal transportation of the *David*, reveals the undercurrent of conflict between the bronze-caster Leonardo and the marble-worker Michelangelo.

In January 1504 Michelangelo's work was sufficiently far advanced for discussions to take place on the best position for it. It was in truth a State matter.

Doc. 7   25 January 1504: Deliberation on the siting of the *David*:

Seeing that the statue of David is nearly finished, and wishing to place it so as to give it a site appropriate and suitable at the right moment for its installation, a site which must be stable and consolidated according to the instructions of Michelangelo, author of the said Giant, and the consuls of the Arte de la Lana, and wishing to have all useful advice for the realization indicated, [they] have decided to summon and to reunite for the purpose of taking a decision, masters, citizens and architects whose names (in common style) follow, and to record their declarations word for word:

Andrea della Robbia.	Lorenzo della Golpaia.
Giovanni Corniola.	The jeweller Salvestro.
The illuminator Attavanti.	The goldsmith Michelangelo
The Palace Herald.	Bandinelli.
The fife-player Giovanni.	Cosimo Rosselli.
Francesco Granacci.	Chimenti de Francesco Tassi.
The painter Biagio [Tucci].	The painter Sandro Botticelli.
The painter Piero di Cosimo.	Giuliano da Sangallo.
The jeweller Guaspare.	Antonio da Sangallo.
The jeweller and goldsmith	Andrea Sansovino, painter
Ludovico.	[in the margin, 'he is in Genoa'].
The goldsmith Andrea di Riccio.	Leonardo da Vinci.
The embroiderer Gallieno.	Pietro Perugino, painter at Borgo Pinti.
The painter David [Ghirlandaio].	The painter Lorenzo di Credi.
Simone Pollaiuolo.	The woodworker Bernardo della Cecca.
The painter Filippino Lippi.	

In Michelangelo's absence they all gave their views, some deciding for the zone of the cathedral, and more precisely on the steps; others for the Loggia dei Lanzi, where it would be better protected (this was Leonardo's opinion); others, fewer in number, for the platform outside the Palazzo della Signoria. The premier herald of the city being of this opinion, they decided in favour of the place where stood Donatello's *Judith*. On 14 May there took place, as a kind of triumphal procession, the transportation of the 'Giant' through the streets in a specially designed wooden crate.

Doc. 8   14 May 1504: The transportation of the *David* to the Piazza della Signoria (from the diary of Luca Landucci):

On 14 May 1504 the marble giant was transported from the Opera; it came out at 24 hours. It was necessary to break down the wall over the door so that it could be got out. That night stones were thrown at the Giant, so as to damage it; a night guard had to be put over it. It progressed very slowly, attached upright in such a way that it leaned without resting on its feet, with a very solid and ingenious wooden framework. It took four days work to get it to the Piazza, where it arrived on the

▷▷

130   Leonardo da Vinci. *The Battle of Anghiari*, reconstruction by C. Pedretti. 'First you must represent the smoke of artillery mingling in the air with the dust tossed up by the movement of horses and the combatants.' (Leonardo, MS. A, fo. 111ʳ–110ᵛ.)

131   Leonardo da Vinci. Study for the *Battle of Anghiari*. 1503. Pen drawing. Galleria dell'Accademia, Venice. '...the more the combatants are in this turmoil the less will they be seen, and the less contrast will there be in their lights and shadows.' (Leonardo, MS. A, fo. 111ʳ–110ᵛ.)

132   Leonardo da Vinci. Study for the *Battle of Anghiari*. 1503. Pen drawing. Galleria dell'Accademia, Venice. 'You must scatter arms of all sorts among the feet of the combatants... and you must show the dead, some half-covered with dust...' (Leonardo, MS. A, fo. 111ʳ–110ᵛ.)

133   Leonardo da Vinci. Study for the *Battle of Anghiari*. About 1503. Pen drawing. Royal Library, Windsor Castle. 'If you introduce horses galloping outside the crowd, make little clouds of dust...' (Leonardo, MS. A, fo. 111ʳ–110ᵛ.)

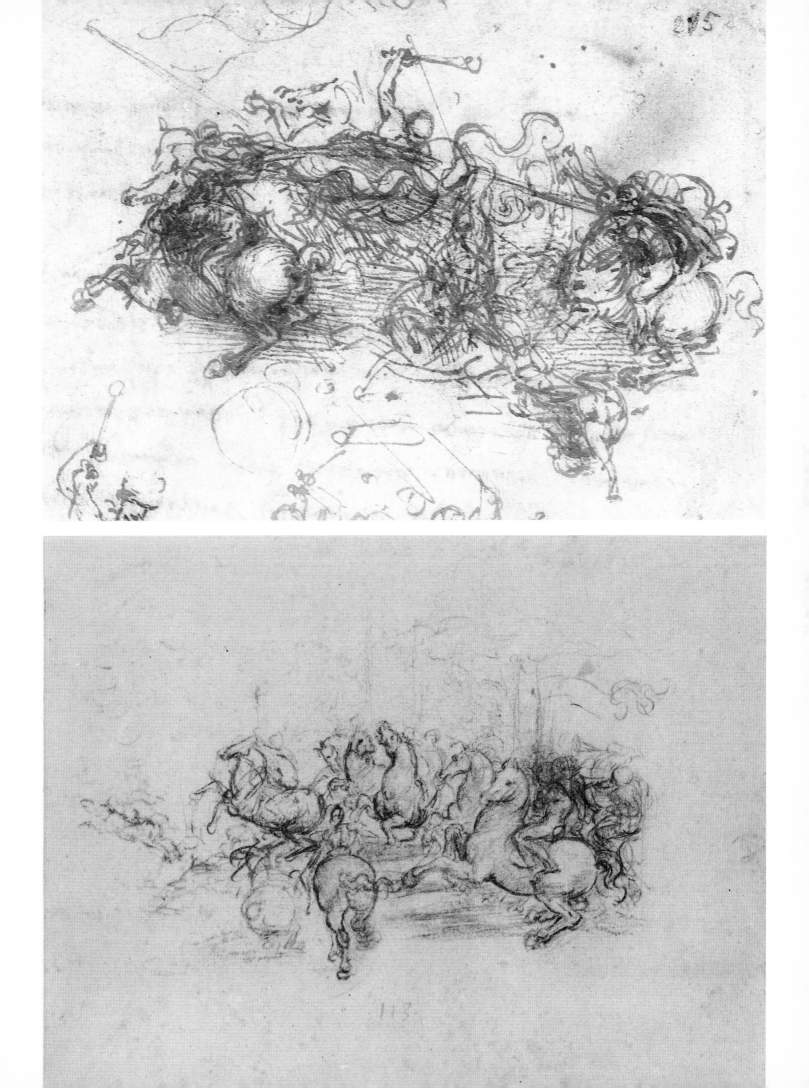

18th at 12 o'clock. More than forty men were employed in moving it, with underneath fourteen rollers covered with grease which were moved forward in alternation. Work continued until 8 June to place it on the terrace of the Judith, which has to be moved and taken into the palazzo. This Giant was the work of Michelangelo Buonarroti.

The hostile demonstration mentioned in passing proves that there was no unanimity among the Florentines about the initiatives taken by Soderini's government. The chronicler does not pursue the matter, as if these nasty actions were normal in a city where everything was a pretext for factional opposition. The details of the chariot recall the arrangements for processional vehicles for carnivals and festivities.

Two historic cartoons

To exploit the situation and to derive full benefit from the rivalry between the two artists, the Florentine Signoria decided to put them into direct competition in the most solemn public place: the Palazzo Vecchio. This time it was Leonardo who was first to receive the commission for a huge fresco, for which, after the popular success of the *David*, a counterpart was sought from Michelangelo.

During the early years of the new century the two artists were the star turns in the city, admired and courted by their fellow-citizens. Immediately after Leonardo's return he had received a commission for a retable for the high altar of the church of the Annunziata, and was also lodged by the Servites, whose church it was. Filippino Lippi, originally bespoken for this commission, immediately withdrew. But Leonardo never executed the work. On the other hand, in the spring he held a kind of private exhibition about which there is some information.

3 April 1501: Letter from Fra Pietro da Novellaro to Isabella d'Este: Doc. 9

Most illustrious and noble Lady.
I have received a letter from Your Excellency and I will act on your instructions with the greatest diligence, but, from what I hear, Leonardo's life is unstable and unpredictable; he appears to live from day to day. Since he came to Florence, he has only made a sketch, a cartoon representing the Child Jesus, aged about a year, jumping from the arms of His mother to seize a lamb, which He seems to be trying to reach. The mother, who rises in some way from the lap of St. Anne, seizes the Child to drag him from the little lamb, an innocent creature which signifies the Passion. One could say that St. Anne, rising slightly from her seat, wishes to prevent her daughter from separating the Child and the lamb; perhaps she signifies the Church which does not want to prevent Christ's Passion. The figures are life-size, but in a cartoon of small dimensions, since they are all sitting or leaning, each one sliding a little in front of the other towards the left. This study is unfinished...

This cartoon had perhaps been made in Milan and been brought to Florence by Leonardo. One may well ask if this might not be the work now in London. If it refers to another cartoon which has now disappeared, it has to be admitted that the picture in the Louvre, of about ten or so years later, reconstitutes the spirit and the marvellous ambiguity, the originality of which was stressed by Isabella d'Este's correspondent: it is a well thought-out pyramidal composition, with a kind of interlocked group of inclined figures with opposing movements, a *chiaroscuro* playing across fluid forms, without strong contours, giving the impression of being unfinished. There is a powerful theological symbolism in this curious family genre scene. A beautiful drawing by Michelangelo, now in Oxford, seems to derive from a critical reaction to the subtle composition, and proposes a quite different arrangement of the figures. But history has recorded the enthusiastic reaction of the public.

Doc. 10   1501: Public success of Leonardo's cartoon (from Vasari, 1550 and 1568):

> He painted finally a cartoon with Our Lady, St. Anne and Jesus, which was not only the admiration of all artists but, when the work was finished in the studio, there was a file of men and women, old and young, who came as to a solemn feast to see the prodigies of Leonardo, an object of popular admiration.

This type of nine days' wonder was not new in Tuscany, but around Leonardo, the 'new Archimedes', everything became larger than life. The trouble was that he became elusive. In 1502-3 he went to Romagna for some months to work as a military engineer in the service of Cesare Borgia, whose power failed to survive the sudden death of Pope Alexander VI (18 April 1503). In the spring of 1503, Leonardo became the inspector of engineering for the Florentine Republic in its fight with Pisa, and he worked unsuccessfully on the project to change the bed of the Arno. It was then, more or less to pin him down, that the great project of the Gonfalonier was thought up, in order to achieve one, then two works, to the glory of Florence and its troops, at the spectacular site of the Sala del Maggior Consiglio of the city, finished four years previously, on the second floor of the Palazzo Vecchio. The two rivals were therefore deliberately placed in competition in two neighbouring programmes. The sequence of events can be easily reconstructed: the commission to Leonardo in October 1503, followed by a contract in May 1504; the commission to Michelangelo given in July 1504, followed by a contract (which has now disappeared). Michelangelo's cartoon was ready by the beginning of 1505, Leonardo's in April. The extraordinary feat of having put the two rivals together in a double-barrelled programme had been successfully achieved. Leonardo was the only one, apparently, actually to begin work on the wall. But by autumn everything had been abandoned. The two artists left Florence, one for Milan to enter the service of the French (July 1506); the other for Rome to work for Julius II (March 1505). An extraordinary opportunity had been lost. But the 'battle of the cartoons' left a memory difficult to forget.

The project was, however, new—for Florence—and remarkable. The Medici government, swept out in 1494, had not refurbished the old sites of power; their palace sufficed. The Christian Republic of Savonarola had taken care to mark the return of popular government by arranging in the Palazzo Vecchio a new building which included an enormous hall built from 1495 onwards under the control of Cronaca. This huge hall had been conceived on the model of the Great Hall in the Doges' Palace in Venice. It was sumptuously built and given a decoration of fine woodwork, a coffered ceiling, and *spalliere* (benches and back rests) on the walls for which Cronaca was responsible, assisted by Antonio da Sangallo and Baccio d'Agnolo, and perhaps also by Michelangelo. The 'wise' government of Soderini, wanting a painted decoration, had desired scenes from Florentine history, from before the period of Medici rule. This naturally meant great victorious battles, different from those which had decorated the Medici palace in the Via Larga—the three episodes of the *Rout of San Romano*, painted by Uccello, which glorified Cosimo's friend, the *condottiere* Nicolo da Tolentino, honoured in 1456 by a commemorative monument in the cathedral.

It has been supposed, perhaps to make the episode more elegant, that Machiavelli, linked with Leonardo, played a part in the selection of the artist's theme. This was the battle of

Anghiari where, on 29 June 1440, the Florentines, allied to the papal forces, had repulsed the Milanese led by Piccinino. A long note—not autograph—preserved in the Cod. Atlanticus, 74ᵣ and ᵥ, contains the basic information on the episode—a narrative account from which Leonardo derived nothing. On the other hand, there had been, for a long time past, among his notes an incredibly detailed and autograph text on the manner of representing a battle.

1492: Leonardo MS. A, fo. 111ʳ - 110ᵛ: Doc. 11

First you must represent the smoke of artillery mingling in the air with the dust tossed up by the movement of horses and the combatants [...] This mixture of air, smoke and dust will look much lighter on the side where the light comes from than on the opposite side. The more the combatants are in this turmoil the less will they be seen, and the less contrast will there be in their lights and shadows. Their faces and figures and their appearance, and the musketeers as well as those near them you must redden. And this redness will diminish in proportion as it is remote from its cause. The figures which are between you and the light, if they be at a distance, will appear dark on a light background, and the lower part of their legs near the ground will be least visible, because there the dust is coarsest and densest.

And if you introduce horses galloping outside the crowd, make the little clouds of dust distant from each other in proportion to the strides made by the horses; and the clouds which are farthest removed from the horses should be least visible; make them high and spreading and thin, and the nearer ones will be more conspicuous and smaller and denser [...]

Make also a horse dragging the dead body of his master and leaving behind him, in the dust and mud, the track where the body was dragged along. You must make the conquered and beaten pale, their brows raised and knit, and the skin of their brows furrowed with pain, the sides of the nose with wrinkles going in an arch from the nostrils to the eyes, and make the nostrils drawn up—which is the cause of the lines of which I speak—and the lips arch upwards, revealing the upper teeth; and the teeth apart as with crying out in lamentation. And make someone shielding his terrified eyes with one hand, the palm towards the enemy, while the other rests on the ground to support his half-raised body. Represent others shouting, with their mouths open, and running away.

You must scatter arms of all sorts among the feet of the combatants, such as broken shields, lances, broken swords, and other such objects. And you must make the dead partly or entirely covered with dust...

The enveloping dust, the confused mêlée, the rictus of men and horses, the broken weapons, the scattered corpses, the strangeness and horror of postures and movements, a wildness of foam and blood: the description analyses all the possible aspects without involving the painter's concern with the emotive totality of the event. Leonardo had therefore long before grasped as an essential the conflict between detail and whole, between the definition of cruel gestures and the turbulence of a battle, which this huge painting would have made immediate as no literary discourse could.

In the *Last Supper*, all had been organized according to an order, a hierarchy and an equilibrium, at once dramatic and theological, which were suitable; in the *Anghiari*, it was a matter of orchestrating the fantastic turbulence of the 'most bestial of follies': war. And all this in a composition nearly twice the proportions of the *Last Supper* and at only a few paces away from a composition allocated to the young and dangerous Michelangelo.

In the dossier, there is a contract in good and due form with curiously precise clauses, designed to compel the painter to hold to his dates.

Doc. 12   4 May 1504: Contract with Leonardo for the *Battle of Anghiari*:

> The Magnificent and Noble Lords Priors of Liberty and Gonfalonier of Justice of
> the Florentine people: Given that Leonardo di Ser Piero da Vinci citizen of
> Florence, having several months ago agreed to paint a picture in the Sala del
> Consiglio Grande, having already begun the painting in a cartoon, and having even
> on this occasion received 35 gold florins, and the said Magnificent Lords desiring
> that the work shall be completed as soon as possible, and that to the said Leonardo
> shall be paid a certain sum now and again to that end, the said Magnificent Lords
> have decided that the said Leonardo da Vinci must finish all the painting of the said
> cartoon and bring it to its entire completion at the very latest by the month of
> February next of 1504 [1505 N.S.] without excuse or cavil, and that the said
> Leonardo da Vinci shall be paid 15 large gold florins every month, beginning on
> 20 April next.
>
> [If Leonardo does not complete the cartoon, he must make restitution of the
> money; if he begins the painting on the wall, a monthly salary is assured to him; if
> he does not begin it at once, it shall not be given to another painter to do without
> his agreement. The deed was made 'in the presence of Nicolo, son of Messer
> Bernardo Machiavelli, Chancellor of the said Signori'.]

Luck has had it that the excellent account-keeping of the Signoria has preserved the record
of numerous payments for materials and accessories; for example, on 30 June 1504, to a
baker: 'seven lire and five soldi for 84 pounds of sifted white flour delivered in two lots
to Leonardo da Vinci for glueing the cartoon', and later to a grocer for wax, sponge and
turpentine so as to obscure the windows.

On 13 March 1505 it is specified that a strict account should be kept of the deliveries
made for the Opera of Sta. Maria del Fiore for the *ponte* or scaffolding for the Great Hall.
The year 1505 was therefore decisive. Recently a striking note has appeared:

Doc. 13   6 June 1505: Leonardo, MS. Madrid II, fo. 1ʳ:

> Friday, 6 June 1505, on the stroke of the thirteenth hour, I began painting in the
> Palazzo. At the moment of taking up the brush, the weather broke, the bell rang out
> to warn the people, the cartoon tore, water spilled out and the basin which held the
> water broke. The weather suddenly became bad and heavy rain fell until nightfall,
> and the day became like night.

Contrary to what might be thought, there is no indication that Leonardo was recording a
bad omen; he was in the habit of noting anything that was surprising and the violence of
the storm was an event. But the chilly objectivity of the text gives it its dramatic overtone,
perhaps subconscious, of coincidence. Summer passed, but on the 31 October following
the payments ceased: the work was abandoned.

All this did not fail to excite attention, and many authors commented on this new
setback to the artist, this time in painting. Bad technique, bad drying. Leonardo had
thought to escape from the rules of traditional fresco painting, but he was wrong. The
Battle of Anghiari continued to preoccupy the administration. On 30 May 1506 Leonardo,
who wanted to go to Milan in the service of the French prince, had to sign an agreement
according to the terms of which he had to return to Florence after three months or else
would repay the money advanced up to the sum of 150 florins. The chanceries exchanged
letter after letter on the subject until the intervention of Charles d'Amboise, Governor of
the Milanese territories, in December 1506, and then that of Louis XII in person on
13 January 1507. The Signoria gave in to the king. Leonardo was even able to return to

134 Peter Paul Rubens, after Leonardo. *The Battle of Anghiari*. About 1600. Pen and watercolour. Cabinet des Dessins, Musée du Louvre, Paris.
'...someone shielding his terrified eyes with his hand... others shouting, with their mouths open...' (Leonardo, MS. A, fo. 111ʳ–110ᵛ.)

Florence in the spring of 1507 to settle personal affairs. On the wall of the Great Hall there remained a few traces of painting which slowly faded away.

The-left hand side of the wall, which was to have received Michelangelo's composition, remained empty. The contract signed by Soderini and the commissioners of the Palazzo Vecchio for the *Battle of Cascina*, almost certainly in the autumn of 1504, has not survived. In December Michelangelo was working on the cartoon; for him, too, the spring of 1505 was decisive, and he was even the first to abandon the work.

The choice of theme was unusual; an incident of the struggle against Pisa was wanted. In the Villani Chronicle the account was found of a clash which might well have been disastrous. In July 1364 the *condottiere* of the Florentine forces had established his camp near Pisa, as Soderini's mercenaries had done in 1504. The soldiers were bathing in the river when Mario Donati saw a suspect movement and gave the alarm. The theme was therefore of a troop of men getting out of the water, reaching for their arms in a state of agitation, a swarm of nude men in action, completed doubtless by the silhouettes of horsemen on the horizon. It has been suggested that scenes with horsemen were projected for either side of the central group. This seems unlikely. Just as Leonardo had concentrated his effect on the clash of cavalry, mixing men and beasts together, according to a formula which he had always studied, so Michelangelo, who had never carved a horse, quite probably wanted to deploy his repertory of *ignudi* which he had totally mastered.

In composing a kind of treasury of forms on a monumental scale consistent with his taste for the gigantic, it was a case of giving them sufficient robustness in order that they should compete adequately with the more refined forms, of varying sizes and less simply related to each other, which Leonardo was elaborating. The antagonism between the two artists led them to an even more vigorous affirmation of their own personalities, in that they had to stretch themselves so as to cover an incredibly vast area.

Leonardo's cartoon contained horsemen, Michelangelo's bathers. They have been defined as a homage: one to St. George, the other to St. John the Baptist, two of the patron saints of Florence. The enormous proportions of the Great Hall, still perceptible today, required that the two frescoes should cover two rectangles 7 metres high by 17½ metres wide, on either side of the altar on the east wall, *Anghiari* on the right, *Cascina* on the left.

In order to make the preparatory cartoons in these dimensions very large studios were required. Leonardo had his in a hall attached to the convent of Sta. Maria Novella, Michelangelo in a hall belonging to the Hospital of St. Onofrio (note the proximity to the hospital, which would have permitted anatomical studies). In February 1505 the cost of a 'mobile scaffolding' in the Sala del Consiglio Grande proves that Leonardo had begun working; the 663 pounds of plaster, 223 of linseed-oil, and 89 of Greek pitch correspond to the preparations of the wall. In November, as has been seen, everything stopped. It has been asked if, during the spring and summer of this same year, Michelangelo had not also

135   Unknown artist, after Leonardo da Vinci. *The Fight for the Standard*. Sixteenth century. Oil on panel. Private collection, Munich.

This panel, recently rediscovered, is perhaps a preliminary study—or a copy of it—for the central part of the *Battle of Anghiari*.

136 Reconstruction of the *Battle of Cascina* by Cecil Gould.
'The foreground was dominated by the bathers, in the background at the right was the battle, and, in the left background, troops on the alert.' (Cellini, *Autobiography*, 1558–9.)

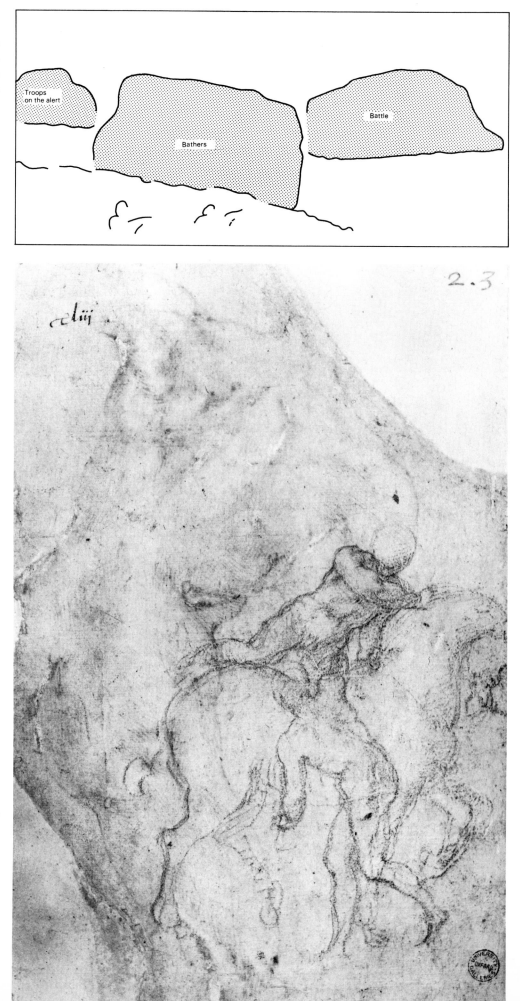

137 Michelangelo. Study for the *Battle of Cascina*. 1503–4. Black chalk. Ashmolean Museum, Oxford.
'In the´great hall of the Gran Consiglio, there are... the horsemen by Leonardo da Vinci and the drawings of Michelangelo.' (Albertini, *Memoriale*, 1510.)

138 Unknown artist. Sketch from memory after the *Battle of Cascina*. Sixteenth century. Pen drawing. Graphische Sammlung Albertina, Vienna.
'Michelangelo Buonarroti represented Florentine soldiers bathing in the Arno.' (Cellini, *Autobiography*, 1558–9.)

139 Michelangelo. Drawing for the *Battle of Cascina*. 1503–4. Pen and black chalk. Ashmolean Museum, Oxford.
'The gestures, poses and movements of these nude figures are such that neither ancients nor moderns have ever been able to produce anything so accomplished.' (Cellini, *Autobiography*, 1558–9.)

159

had his scaffolding next to that of his rival. This is unlikely; he knew that he had already been summoned to Rome by the new Pope. Did Leonardo and Michelangelo ever have an opportunity to discuss their two cartoons?

As a partisan of traditional fresco painting, Michelangelo could only have derision and contempt for Leonardo's claims to have rediscovered antique techniques, which led him to have fires lit so as to dry—unsuccessfully—his colours. The younger master, in his care for modelling and the breadth of treatment above all, could only have criticized the proliferation of ornament in the armour, the infinite multiplicity of details and attitudes, the swirling effect dominating Leonardo's composition. An expert in light colouring, of which the Doni *tondo* (1502) was a fine example, and of which the luminosity of the figures in the Sistine Ceiling was so soon to be a triumphant example—what could he have thought of a *sfumato* which drowns the contours?

Drawing, the great strength of the fresco painter, seems compromised, or at least complicated by a bizarre and disconcerting selectivity. This conflict—so new, so partisan—between the two manners led to such a serious reconsideration of the painter's art that it largely dominated the rest of the century in Rome and Tuscany.

As to Leonardo, everything had prepared him to repulse Michelangelo's insolence; according to him, sculpture must be subordinated to painting, whose subtleties it can never reproduce, in that nature, the diversity of objects, the discoloration imposed by air, the play of nearness and distance, are all unknown to it; this obliges one to ask what kind of landscape would have framed the mêlée of Anghiari, full of dust and the glitter of metal. The MS. Madrid I, which dates from exactly the same time as *Cascina*, contains an allusion to painters who are so passionately interested in anatomy that their figures resemble rather 'a sack of nuts than a human being'. The same criticism reappears in MS. E (1513–14), and must refer to the Sistine. Leonardo never let up. All that he might have had in common with the younger artist—the grasp of the whole and, in particular, of anatomy; the taste

140   Bastiano da Sangallo, after Michelangelo. Copy of the *Battle of Cascina*. 1542. Grisaille. Lord Leicester Collection, Holkham Hall.
In 1542 a reconstruction was made in grisaille by Bastiano da Sangallo, using existing fragments.

141 Peter Paul Rubens, after Leonardo da Vinci. *The Battle of Anghiari*. Detail. About 1600. Pen and watercolour. Cabinet des Dessins, Musée du Louvre, Paris.
'...the lips arch upwards, revealing the upper teeth; the jaws parted for a cry of pain.' (Leonardo, MS. A, fo. 111^r–110^v.)

142 Leonardo da Vinci. Study of a *Warrior* for the *Battle of Anghiari*. 1503–5. Black chalk. Museum of Fine Arts, Budapest.
An intensive study of the physiognomy of the horseman at the right in the *Battle for the Standard*.

143 Leonardo da Vinci. Study of horses for the *Battle of Anghiari*. 1503. Pen drawing. Royal Library, Windsor.
'You will show the dust enveloping... the rictus of men and horses.' (Leonardo, MS. A, fo. 111^r–110^v.)

161

for a careful, well thought out harmonious composition, the correspondence of forms, respect for human beauty, were probably cancelled out in his view by the fact that Michelangelo did not really look at nature and believed it possible to represent the passions and the diversities of the spirit without proceeding to a total analysis of the causative mechanisms.

In May 1506 Leonardo was sent for by the French authorities in Milan. But Michelangelo was unexpectedly back in Florence.

27 November 1506: Letter from Soderini: Doc. 14

> This excellent young man, unique in Italy in his profession, perhaps even in the world, [Michelangelo] has begun a composition destined for the Palazzo Pubblico, which will be something admirable.

It is necessary to know whether this information concerned the cartoon or the fresco. Historians are undecided; a payment of 280 lire as an advance, made on 28 February 1505, for the 'painting of the cartoon' is interpreted by some literally, by others as an indication that work on the painting after the cartoon was about to begin, and that therefore the drawing was ready. However, in his letters Michelangelo speaks only of the cartoon.

It is possible that during his quarrel with Julius II and his stay in Florence from May to November 1506, Michelangelo returned to his work with renewed interest, and thus restored the Gonfalonier's confidence. But the latter knew that the Pope, then in Bologna, was demanding his sculptor. He had to agree to lose him, as he had Leonardo. But the enterprise, though abandoned, was not forgotten. The earliest guide published on the monuments of Florence mentions it:

1510: Albertini's *Memoriale*:   Doc. 15

> In the great hall of the Maggior Consiglio is a picture by Fra Filippo Lippi, the horsemen of Leonardo da Vinci, and the drawings of Michelangelo.

The author of the guide therefore mentions, besides the traces left on the wall by Leonardo's work ('the horsemen'), the cartoon—but only the cartoon—by Michelangelo. The work had therefore been removed to the Sala del Gran Consiglio of the Signoria. But in 1512 there took place the revolution which restored the Medici: Giuliano re-entered Florence on 1 September and restored a pro-Medici administration.

December 1512: Transformation of the Sala del Maggior Consiglio (from Luca   Doc. 16
Landucci):

> [The new government] decided to transform the Sala del Maggior Consiglio, that is to say the wooden structure and the fine works made at such great expense, and the beautiful wall panels. Small rooms were made for soldiers and an entrance to the hall. This pained everyone, not the revolution, but the loss of this very valuable woodwork.

On 1 March 1513 grants were agreed and on 30 April a payment was made to a carpenter 'to place a framework round the pictures by Leonardo in the Great Hall to protect them'. The *Battle* was disappearing. Approximately fifty years later in 1557 it was finally covered up by Vasari's reworking of the Great Hall. What became of the cartoons?

Michelangelo's was deposited at Sta. Maria Novella in the room which was to become the Sala Papale, after the entry of Leo X on 30 November 1515. But the apartments were redecorated for this occasion and the cartoon was cut up into several pieces, and was taken to the Palazzo Medici. This was at the time of the illness of Giuliano, the Pope's brother. The artists allowed to come and make copies took advantage of the situation, rearranged the fragments, and even began to help themselves. Its dispersal was complete. In 1542 a reconstruction was made in grisaille, after the surviving elements, by Bastiano da Sangallo (now in the collection of Lord Leicester at Holkham). This must now suffice. According to Benedetto Varchi in 1564, fragments 'were preserved in Florence and elsewhere like relics'.

The two rivals were equally unlucky. Leonardo's cartoon, which had been elaborated with such care, remained *in situ*, that is, in Sta. Maria Novella. It is odd that Michelangelo's cartoon was for a time in the same place—that is, in Sta. Maria Novella, and perhaps even in the same room—in 1513. What is strange is that this same cartoon was broken up and removed in 1515 to the Medici Palace to be cut to pieces, bit by bit. Yet the *Anghiari* one, neither less famous nor less sought by copyists, was slowly destroyed in the room in Sta. Maria Novella where the artist had left it. A whole generation went there to learn. Cellini recounted an episode of his own youth: the visit of a former comrade of Michelangelo's.

Doc. 17   1518: Cellini copies the Michelangelo cartoon (from his *Memoirs*, 1558–9):

[Torrigiani] one day spoke about Michelangelo Buonarroti, the cause of which was a drawing which I had made after the cartoon of this divine Michelangelo. This cartoon was the first masterpiece in which Michelangelo displayed his marvellous genius and he did it in competition with Leonardo da Vinci, for both were destined for the Sala del Consiglio of the Palazzo della Signoria. Each one represented an episode from the war when Pisa was taken by the Florentines and the admirable Leonardo da Vinci had chosen to show a battle of horses with the capture of a banner, as divinely done as it is possible to imagine. Michelangelo Buonarroti in his showed a number of foot soldiers who, because it was summer, had gone to bathe in the Arno; and in that moment had shown that the alarm was given and the nude soldiers ran to arms, with such beautiful gestures that never either by the Ancients or other moderns were works seen which achieved such a high point; and as I have said, that of the great Leonardo was very beautiful and admirable. These two cartoons were one in the Palazzo de' Medici, the other in the Sala del Papa. And while they were there they were a school for the whole world.

144 Copy after Raphael. *Giuliano de' Medici*. 1513–14. Oil on canvas. Metropolitan Museum, New York.
Appointed *gonfaloniere* of Rome in 1513, Giuliano de' Medici, Duke of Nemours, is shown with a view of Castel Sant'Angelo. He was in Florence in 1515 and died there in March 1516.

Rivalry in the architectural projects of 1515

The explanation given by Vasari for the 'great hostility' is not to be dismissed. Though confused, it contains a kernel of truth. It covers with a ready-made formula the essential nature of the relations between the two rival artists, after the election of Giovanni de' Medici as Pope Leo X on 11 March 1513, which brought about a totally new situation in Florence and Rome.

Leonardo entered the service of the Pope's brother Giuliano, Duke of Nemours (1479–1516). This rather attractive and sensitive man was a poet and a perfect courtier; Castiglione, in the dialogues of the *Cortegiano*, portrays him as a cultured and gallant nobleman; he was, moreover, interested in the sciences and perfectly ready to play an important role as a patron of art and culture. Raphael painted his portrait in 1514. Nevertheless, the choice was not a happy one. Giuliano was a sick man. Solemnly received

145 Michelangelo. Tomb of Lorenzo de' Medici. Detail: *Il Penseroso*. 1525. Sculpture. S. Lorenzo, Florence.
Traditionally the figure of the *penseroso*, bowed in reverie, is identified with Lorenzo de' Medici.

in Rome and appointed as general of the papal armies, he was unable to lead his forces during the 1515 campaign. He died in Florence in March 1516. It was a disaster for the artist, who was now in his sixties, because Pope Leo neither liked nor understood Leonardo.

Giuliano was to have his tomb, carved by Michelangelo, in the New Sacristy of S. Lorenzo from 1524 onwards. Unless the identification of the two dukes in the New Sacristy is wrong, the figure of the *penseroso*, romantically bowed in a kind of dream, is traditionally accepted as Giuliano de' Medici. As he was the Captain of the Papal States, it is not absurd to wonder if Michelangelo, abandoning the expression of individual character, did not give him the proud air which would have corresponded to his official position under Leo X. In that case it would be necessary to abandon the usual identification, although there are good grounds for holding to the traditional view.

It was around S. Lorenzo that in 1515 or 1516 the last instance of the rivalry between the two men took place. After confronting each other in sculpture and in monumental painting, the two Florentine 'heroes' were opposed to each other in architecture. When the Medici recovered their palace in the Via Larga in 1515, they at once envisaged a new arrangement of the urban area in a very sensitive spot; that is, the zone which included the church of S. Lorenzo and their nearby palace.

In December 1515, after the battle of Marignano, when Leo X went to Bologna to negotiate with the King of France, he travelled through Florence where a ceremonial entry was arranged for him. The diary of a witness records the event in vivid terms.

Doc. 18 30 November 1515: Entry of Leo X into Florence (from Luca Landucci):

The 30 November, S. Andrew's Day, a Friday, the Pope made his entry into Florence, with such grand and triumphant honour, and such incredible expense, that it cannot properly be told. I will give a few details.

To meet him, there went forth all the notable citizens of the city, and among them about fifty young men, from the richest and most important families, all dressed in a livery of purple cloth, with collars and shoes of squirrel fur with gilded wands in their hands—a very fine sight. Then came a mounted cavalcade of citizens. And the Pope had many men on foot; among them was the Pope's guard of many German foot soldiers all wearing a coat of arms in the French fashion; and on horseback many crossbowmen and men armed with arquebuses which were his guard. And he was carried through the city by the Signoria under a rich baldaquin, and was borne to Sta. Maria del Fiore, and went down from there by a small gallery as far as the high altar, which in that church was so adorned with draperies and with a pavilion in the midst, with more steps than usual; and so many candles were lit that, besides the choir, the whole space was filled with them as far as the doors.

The nephew of Giuliano and of the Pope, Lorenzo di Piero de' Medici (who was also to die prematurely) had been elected Governor of Florence in May 1515. He must have been responsible for these highly political festivities. It was a kind of general mobilization. Temporary buildings, in the form of little temples, and triumphal arches, were scattered across the city. The great architects of the day—Sansovino, Antonio da Sangallo—worked on them. It has been assumed that Leonardo, who came specially from Rome, probably suggested the idea of a curious 'temple with eight façades'. But in any case this was the moment when he made projects for the new Palazzo Medici on the angle of the

146 Giorgio Vasari. *Triumphal Entry of Leo X into Florence.* 1546. Fresco. Sala di Leone X, Palazzo Vecchio, Florence.
'On the 30th November, St. Andrew's Day, a Friday, the Pope made his entry into Florence, with a triumph more grandiose, more honorific and rich, than one can express.' (L. Landucci, *Diario*, 1515.)

147 Michelangelo. Façade of S. Lorenzo. 1517. Pen drawing. Gabinetto dei Disegni, Galleria degli Uffizi, Florence.
Michelangelo, working as a sculptor, demonstrated in his sketch-models a knowledge of the orders and mouldings of ancient architecture more penetrating than that possessed by anyone else.

148 After a drawing by Michelangelo. Window at the angle of the loggia of the Palazzo Medici, Florence. 1517.
A monumental bay, crowned by a heavy pediment and supported on two strong consoles.

149 Leonardo da Vinci. Project for a church façade. 1490. Pen drawing. Galleria dell'Accademia, Venice.
An attempt at classical articulation, Albertian in spirit, with a clear rhythm and important volutes.

Via Larga and the Via de' Pucci, facing the old palace by Michelozzo. A drawing which has been found in the Cod. Atlan. 315^r (b) suggests that the whole area would have been reordered to create a perspective effect which would have enhanced the façade of S. Lorenzo.

The kind of jockeying for position which must have taken place in 1515–16 may easily be imagined, since it consists of suspicions and dislikes as much as of precise facts. Giuliano, Leonardo's patron, was in Florence in 1515 and Leonardo must then have conceived a grand project, with a new type of palace with towers on the four corners, as is shown in a sketch buried in a sheet of notes. This was certainly an 'idea' under discussion; but it would have required time to develop, because it once again drew attention to the Medicean centre of the city as against the Signoria. It would have been a kind of counterpoint to the Palazzo Vecchio, much desired by the new regime, which would have centred attention on S. Lorenzo, its tombs and its surroundings. It required Giuliano to impose it, but he died in the following March, and Leonardo returned to

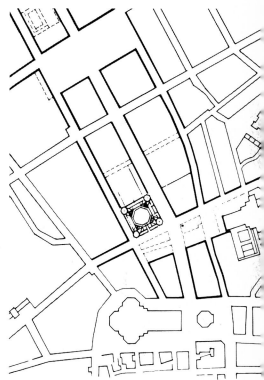

150 Leonardo da Vinci. Studies for a new Medici Palace in Florence. Detail. 1514–15. Pen drawing. Pinacoteca Ambrosiana (Codex Atl. fo. 315ʳ, b.), Milan. In the midst of a crowd of short notes on geometry or architecture there is a sketch for the plan of a palace with four towers (at the top left).

151 Plan of the Medicean quarter of Florence, according to Leonardo's project. The drawing in the Codex Atl. (fo. 315ʳ, b), Milan, can be interpreted to mean that the whole area would have been reconstructed to provide a perspective effect giving prominence to the façade of S. Lorenzo.

Rome before leaving Italy for good in the autumn of 1516. This is exactly the moment when Michelangelo was designing the monumental façade which S. Lorenzo still lacked. Here again the affair is difficult to elucidate. More than probably, the problem arose at the time of Leo X's visit in November 1515; the façade of the cathedral had been transformed for the entry by a gigantic false front constructed by Jacopo Sansovino and Andrea del Sarto, which the Pope liked. By contrast, the unfinished state of S. Lorenzo, the Pantheon of the Medici, must have been distressing. But, as was usual, the affair excited various initiatives and rivalries which Vasari records:

Doc. 19 1515–16: Rivalries for the project of the S. Lorenzo facade (from Vasari, 1550 and 1568):

For the architecture many architects in Rome competed before the Pope, and designs were made by Baccio d'Agnolo, Antonio da Sangallo, Andrea and Jacopo

Sansovino, the gracious Raphael, who was even brought to Florence during the Pope's visit for that reason. Whereupon Michelangelo decided to make a model, not wishing that any but himself should be in control or responsible for the architecture. But his not wishing to accept any help was the reason that neither he nor any other achieved anything and all the masters other than he returned to their own works.

This was a fine simplification of the new Florentine imbroglio. Nothing is known of the intervention of Raphael, but it had certainly been sought. All that can be said is that there already existed fine projects by Giuliano da Sangallo, who was to die in October 1516; Vasari erroneously cites his younger brother as being concerned with the project. On the other hand, Baccio d'Agnolo was entirely in Michelangelo's hands and when his project was accepted by the Pope in Rome in December 1516, Jacopo Sansovino, who had very much counted on the results of the grand entry of the preceding year, found himself eliminated from the programme of the sculpture as well as from the architectural programme. Furious, he wrote in June 1517 a very sharp letter to Michelangelo, who was already in Carrara, quarrying marble:

30 June 1517: Letter from Jacopo Sansovino in Florence to Michelangelo in Carrara: Doc. 20

Not having been able to speak to you before your departure, I have decided to let you know what I think of you. You know that in this place I knew very little about you. I have spoken with Jacopo Salviati and I understand that Bacino di Michelangelo is a man of great worth, the best that ever was. But Jacopo Salviati gave you a very good answer because he perfectly understood your character. Because of your praises Bacino believes he is going to get his share like any other. But I tell you this, the Pope, the Cardinal and Jacopo Salviati are men whose word is as good as a written contract. You measure them according to your own yardstick, you for whom neither contract nor word has any value and who change your mind just as it suits your convenience. Know that the Pope promised me the 'histories', and Jacopo also, and they are men who will keep them for me. I have done for you all that I could in your interest and for your fame. I had not then realized that you have never done any good to anyone; to think that you would begin with me, it's like wishing that water wouldn't wet. Moreover, you know well, we have very often talked together; may the time be damned when you said any good of anyone without reserve. I appeal to God. I will say no more. I have been very well informed; you will be too on your return. Enough.

The project was agreed in December 1516. Baccio was commissioned to make a model after Michelangelo's designs and was then eliminated. There was a clay model, then a second model in wood, and finally both were approved at the end of 1517, with the signature of the contract in January 1518; everything was to be abandoned in 1520 and Michelangelo's first architectural work came to nothing.

Michelangelo had known Giulio de' Medici since 1490, when they were together in the household of Lorenzo; he had certainly not viewed with any pleasure the favour which the young prince—Giuliano—showed to Leonardo, still less the grand projects for town planning in which the completion of S. Lorenzo would figure only as an element. All Michelangelo's efforts to gain control of the project seemed in some way to isolate it by ignoring the church and by treating the façade as a monument to the Medici and to Florence. In effect, the two concepts cancelled each other out and, as at the Palazzo Vecchio, only resulted in projects.

Michelangelo had conceived a powerful and very bold architectural complex, with a superb tension and formal rigour. Now, during these same years, Leonardo's notes contain numerous little designs for façades as if he were continuing to work on the theme which the Pope had finally commissioned from Michelangelo. A celebrated and very fine drawing in Venice illustrates the search for a classical organization and a rythmical clarity. In all his models Michelangelo, who worked as a sculptor, gave proof of his possessing a deeper knowledge than anyone else of the Orders and profiles of Antiquity. The fervour with which he worked on his projects for S. Lorenzo may perhaps have been partly inspired by his anxiety to surpass his absent rival. The events recounted by Vasari were to lead to a new confrontation in Florence during the winter of 1515–16, when Giuliano de' Medici was still alive. They could not bear to be associated in the same project either from near or from afar. If Michelangelo needed the Duke's permission to leave Florence, it was so as to break up the desired collaboration. On their return, the Medici had, like Soderini in the Palazzo Vecchio, wanted to marry incompatibles. As in the Great Hall of the Signoria, the idea of this association was fatal to the planned urban reconstruction. Nevertheless, in 1517, Michelangelo made the designs for a monumental window which was to enclose the loggia at the back of the Medici Palace on the corner of the Piazza S. Lorenzo.

Michelangelo never let his guard down. The memory of Leonardo remained odious to him for the whole of his life, and not for anything in the world would he have admitted that he might owe anything to him. The proof of this hostility towards one who may be regarded as a fundamental adversary is to be found in the reply given by Michelangelo many years later, in 1546, in the course of an enquiry on what was called the *paragone*—that is, the hierarchy to be established between painting and sculpture. After having declared that good painting is that which tends towards an effect of relief, which is natural to sculpture, Michelangelo concludes:

oc. 21   1546: Letter from Michelangelo to Benedetto Varchi:

> He who has written that painting is more noble than sculpture, if he has properly understood what he has been discussing, my housemaid would have expressed it better than he has.

There is no doubt whom he has in his sights; the sarcastic allusion to his writings does not allow of any hesitation, nor does the sharp and disdainful tone, which even after forty years Michelangelo could not depart from when commenting on the object of his *grandissimo sdegno*.

Chapter 8
Rivalries in Venice: The Competition for the
St. Peter Martyr (1528-30)

About 1525–30, several painters who had until then been active chiefly on the mainland, sought and found work in Venice itself. Lorenzo Lotto arrived at the end of December 1525 and lodged in the Dominican monastery of SS. Giovanni e Paolo. He still had some difficult matters to settle, in particular the question of the choir-stalls at Bergamo for which he had to send designs. But he remained in Venice, which he would only leave for the Marches at the end of 1531 or in 1532. At about the same time, the energetic Pordenone, who was at the height of his powers (he was just over forty), seems to have achieved his penetration into Venice rather more successfully. For him it was the decisive moment when, twenty years after Giorgione's death, he revived the idea of grand painted façades; he had created a sensation with a house in the S. Benedetto quarter:

C. 1530: Pordenone paints the façade of a Venetian palace (from Vasari, 1568):   Doc. 1

He decorated the front of the palace of Martin d'Anna on the Grand Canal with a number of compositions, including a Marcus Curtius on horseback, painted with a foreshortening which made it appear in volume and in relief; and also a Mercury flying through the air on either side, among all sorts of ingenious novelties. This work greatly pleased the whole city of Venice, and Pordenone received more compliments that any artist who had ever worked in the city.

An illusionistic façade on a notable site on the Grand Canal indicated an extraordinary will to succeed. The palace was that of Martino d'Anna, a Flemish merchant who thus obtained an excellent piece of publicity. But as with all the decorations, this one could not resist either the *tramontana* or the sea air. A century later, it was mentioned as javing totally vanished, but the chronicler who recorded this added an odd note:

1529: Michelangelo an admirer of Pordenone (from Ridolfi, 1648):   Doc. 2

It is said that the famous Michelangelo, attracted by the fame of this noble work and passing through Venice, said that in fact Fame was not lying and had not vainly sung the praises of the author.

152   Titian. *The Ancona Altarpiece.* Detail: *View of Venice.* 1520. Oil on panel. Pinacoteca Civica, Ancona.
The view of the twilit lagoon spreads a melancholy veil across the composition, in which the branches of the fig-tree take their place as a Marian symbol.

Michelangelo, in flight from the siege of Florence, had in fact taken refuge in Venice at the end of the summer of 1529; he stayed for several weeks, avoiding, so it is said, curiosity-mongers. It seems remarkable that he found time to praise the merits of Pordenone, but this tradition should not be doubted. It supplies one point to be remembered. Very powerful painting, with violent and exaggerated effects was unusual in Venice; a horse leaping across the void towards the spectator became the symbol of a pictorial revolution.

153   Titian. *The Ancona Altarpiece*. 1520.
Oil on panel. Pinacoteca Civica, Ancona.
The whole composition revolves around
the poses and glances of the figures.

One may well ask what Titian thought of all this. He had collaborated with Giorgione in 1507–8 on the famous *Fondaco dei Tedeschi*, which was a sensational model for new, ambitous and showy façade decorations. But he had never again done a façade decoration, and his art, which had never ceased to gain in solemnity, in power, rejected *tours de force* of this type.

Titian had just finished the huge *Pesaro Madonna* in the Frari, which was inaugurated on 8 December 1526. Since the *Assumption*, unveiled in 1518 in the same church, he had worked for Alfonso d'Este and had painted numerous portraits which went to the courts of Italy; but he was far from achieving an uncontested primacy in Venice itself. He endeavoured to attract official commissions, such as the mural decoration of the chapel in the Doges' Palace, which was visited by Doge Andrea Gritti in December 1523. But all was not yet won. After all, Lotto, experienced in many fields, and a landscape-painter of deep and subtle ability, believed that he still stood a chance. On the other hand, the powerful temperament of Pordenone was interesting because of the movement which he imparted to his figures. It was he who seemed to offer the greatest danger to the beginnings of Titian's reign. The writers of the period have reiterated it. The episode of the *St. Peter Martyr* was to show that he knew, and knew well, how to defend himself.

154 Pordenone. Study for the façade of the Palazzo d'Anna. About 1530. Pen drawing. Victoria and Albert Museum, London.
'He decorated the front of the Palazzo Martino d'Anna on the Grand Canal with numerous compositions, including one of Curtius on his horse...' (Vasari, *Life of Pordenone*.)

173

1527 ff.: Rivalry between Titian and Pordenone (from Vasari, 1568):   Doc. 3

But among the reasons which caused [Pordenone] to give incredible study to his works was rivalry with the most excellent Titian [...] He was commissioned by the superintendents of S. Rocco to paint frescoes in the chapel and tribune of that church [...] And because he was always competing with Titian he tried to paint in the same places as Titian had already worked in; and in S. Giovanni in Rialto he made a S. Giovanni Elemosinario, giving alms to the poor [...] Many people, out of malignity rather than truth, praised Giovanni Antonio [Pordenone]. He also painted in the cloister of S. Stefano many stories in fresco from the Old Testament, and one from the New, separated by figures of Virtues; in which he demonstrated tremendous foreshortenings of figures: which was something he always delighted in doing, seeking to place them in all his works in the most difficult poses, adorning them better than any other painter.

This testimony is important. The Florentine historian was well aware of current events when he visited Venice in 1540. As he carefully noted, Venetian malice had sedulously envenomed the situation. The competition between the two artists then occupied everyone's attention, Pordenone seeking to conquer by exploiting his famous 'foreshortenings' and Titian by his mastery of deep and brilliantly managed colour. The cloister of S. Stefano has, unfortunately, lost its decoration and at S. Rocco it has only partially survived. It is possible only to imagine the astonishing effects used by Pordenone to achieve supremacy. In his account, Vasari has made a mistake by citing the *St. John Giving Alms* (a work by Titian painted at least ten years later) as one of Pordenone's works. The Venetian Ridolfi corrected the error:

1527 ff.: Pordenone fears for his life (from Ridolfi, 1648):

In the church of S. Rocco he was allotted the choir, where he produced a   Doc. 4

155   Pordenone. *SS. Martin and Christopher*. About 1527. Oil on panel. S. Rocco, Venice.
'The *operai* of S. Rocco commissioned him to paint in fresco the chapel and the choir... There he displayed striking foreshortenings...' (Vasari, *Life of Pordenone*.)

Transfiguration with, at the sides, a ring of columns, with putti between them, holding the hat, staff and scrip of the pilgrim-saint[...]

At about the same time he painted a fresco in the cloister of S. Stefano, above a colonnade, twelve scenes from the Old and New Testaments [...]

It is said that, while he was working on this he kept his sword and buckler handy, because of Titian's enmity arising from their rivalry. In consequence of that rivalry he painted for the altarpiece of the Corrieri in S. Giovanni di Rialto a St. Catherine, St. Sebastian and S. Rocco, a superb composition, but which did not lower Titian's reputation, who had painted the S. Giovanni Elemosinario for the High Altar there.

156   Lorenzo Lotto. *St. Nicholas of Bari.* Detail. 1529. Oil on panel. I Carmini, Venice.
'For the Carmelite brothers he also made a panel of St. Nicholas floating in the clouds... with a very fine landscape below, full of small figures of people and animals...' (Vasari, *Life of Lotto.*)

The chronicle is now more precise and more significant. The competition has become a merciless struggle, in which there is even a danger of death. A Shakespearean climate invests the whole affair. The Rialto picture is correctly cited, but Titian's picture, painted about 1545, has rather to be understood as his response to his rival. But this work, glowing in its warm colour, poses a problem. During and after the 1530s, the figure of a saintly bishop, shimmering in his priestly vestments, standing out against a heavenly glory and occupying almost all the picture space, had become a major theme. Pordenone had realized its importance; Lotto, during these same years, had provided one grand example in the

157 Lorenzo Lotto. *St. Nicholas of Bari.*
1529. Oil on panel. I Carmini, Venice.
'Of bad colouring, it seems to me that one
can see a notable example in an altarpiece
by Lorenzo Lotto which is in the church of
the Carmini in Venice...' (Dolce, *Dialogo
della Pittura*, 1557.)

158 Cigoli, after Titian. *St. Peter Martyr*. About 1580–90. Oil on canvas. Fitzwilliam Museum, Cambridge.
'... Titian's merit gained the day...' (Ridolfi, *Le Maraviglie*, 1648) and the copies or imitations are the proof of this success.

Carmine. The brilliance of the gold tones and the glitter of the silk embroideries created a motif perfectly adapted to mosaic. A few years later, precisely dated to 1545, in the central dome of the atrium of the basilica, the Zuccato brothers executed in mosaic a large figure of St. Mark, as priest. Who did the cartoon for this? According to Ridolfi it was Titian who was the supplier for the workshops of the mosaicists. But it has been suggested, that it may have been by Lotto, or in any case after him, as a fine work, painted for one of the city's churches, might induce one to believe.

159 Martino Rota, after Titian. *St. Peter Martyr*. Detail: *The Cherubs*. 1558. Engraving.
'Descending from heavenly glory, two charming little angels hold out to the martyr the palm of triumph which awaits him in Heaven.' (Ridolfi, *Le Maraviglie*, 1648.) *See* Pl. 161.

160 Titian. *Study for the Altarpiece of St. Peter Martyr*. Detail. 1528. Pen drawing. Wicar Collection, Musée des Beaux-Arts, Lille.
'...the saint... fallen to the ground and attacked with fury by a swordsman.' (Vasari, *Life of Titian*.)

178

161 Titian. *Study for the Altarpiece of St. Peter Martyr.* 1528. Pen drawing. Wicar Collection, Musée des Beaux-Arts, Lille.
'He drew them, it has been said, from a cast of Cupid, a work by Phidias.' (Ridolfi, *Le Maraviglie*, 1648). *See* Pl. 159.

162 Pordenone. *Study for St. Peter Martyr.* 1527. Black chalk drawing. Devonshire Collection, Chatsworth.
Pordenone's study gives a more massive and forceful version of the murder than Titian's sketch.

163   Martino Rota, after Titian. *St. Peter Martyr.* 1558. Engraving.
'The crime is shown taking place at the edge of a thick wood of oak-trees... The saint lying on the ground is dominated by the impious assassin.' (Ridolfı, *Le Maraviglie*, 1648.)

1529: The *pala* for the Carmelites painted by Lotto (from Vasari, 1568):   Doc. 5

For the Carmelites he [Lotto] painted a panel of St. Nicholas floating in the air, dressed in pontifical vestments, accompanied by three angels and with Sta. Lucia and St. John at his feet. At the top are clouds, and below there is a most beautiful landscape with many small figures and animals in various places: on one side St. George on horseback is killing the dragon, and not far off is the damsel, with a city nearby and a stretch of sea.

This altarpiece, still to be seen in the church of the Carmine in Venice, bore the date 1529 next to the now vanished signature. It was one of the few public commissions given to Lotto during his stay. It is also one of his most successful works: the chasuble with its golden reflections accentuates the hieratic character of the image, frontal and rigid as if under the effect of the beatific vision, which seems to be shared by the symmetrically placed saints. The three angels introduce a countervailing movement to the three figures in the heavenly zone, separated by the firm horizon of the sea from the deep and dense landscape which fills the bottom of the panel with the breadth of a predella. A tiny scene of St. George on the right side, and other narrative scenes of a hagiographic character on the left can also be seen. In this general context it is easier to understand the information, gathered together a century later, about the *St. Peter Martyr* in the Dominican church.

Doc. 6   *C.* 1527: Competition for the *St. Peter Martyr* (from Ridolfi, 1648):

> It is said that there was a competition for the commission for this work, in which Pordenone and Palma Vecchio took part, Palma's small *modello* being preserved in Casa Contarina at San Samuello; but the merit of Titian prevailed, since the fame of his worth was so widespread that Heaven and men together were inspired in his favour.

This remark about the 'competition' in the church of SS. Giovanni e Paolo does not appear to have attracted all the notice it deserves. It is not surprising that Pordenone pushed himself forward, nor should the participation of Palma cause surprise. However, the altarpiece of *St. Peter Martyr* which is now at Alzano Lombardo, near Bergamo, and which is by Palma, was long attributed to Lotto before being restored to Palma. Lotto may also have considered entering the competition but have allowed his friend to do so instead. The links between the two painters were sufficiently close to justify this. Their more fluid art, their tenuous composition and softer contours were not really suitable for this dramatic theme.

Why was this altarpiece painted, anyway? St. Peter Martyr was a Dominican inquisitor who was assassinated by heretics in 1252 between Milan and Como. His cult, propagated by the Order of Preachers, became important from time to time during periods of struggle for the integrity of dogma. It is easy to understand that at the end of 1525 the confraternity of St. Peter Martyr established at SS. Giovanni e Paolo in Venice began negotiations. Precedents were not lacking in Lombardy: after Foppa, who at Sant'Eustorgio in Milan transformed the preacher's martyrdom into a commonplace drama, like an assassination by marauders in a bit of woodland, the next were an artist who has wrongly been believed to be Lotto, but who must have been Palma the Elder (about 1515), and then Bonvicino Moretto, both of whom gave the subject the scale of an altarpiece.

On 27 April 1530 the work was installed on the altar of the confraternity. But Titian, as usual very careful about his best interests, had great difficulty in obtaining a proper settlement and ended by making a formal complaint:

Doc. 7   16 May 1531: Declaration by Titian during the lawsuit brought by him against the Confraternity of S. Pietro Martire:

> *Petitio:* There is a proverb which I, Tician de Vecelis, have found by experience to be very true—that a great service is usually repaid by great ingratitude. Having painted the *pala* of *St. Peter Martyr* for the Confraternity of the said Saint in the church of SS. Giovanni e Paolo, I did not wish to let the members of the said Confraternity have it until it was paid for, but, to please Ser Jacomo da Pergo, and to do him a favour, he being the president of the Confraternity, I allowed myself to

be persuaded by him to place the said altarpiece in the said church. This was done on the promise and word of the said Ser Jacomo, that I should receive from the brothers of the Confraternity, for my work, from legacies or gifts, at least 100 ducats and if possible more...

[The president and Confraternity not having kept their word, Titian demanded a payment, either direct or by transfer from legacies. He obtained little satisfaction, as an addition shows] *Additio petitionis.* I, Titian de Vecellis, having made a complaint against Ser Jacomo da Pergo for the sum of 100 ducats, and having received since then a piece of cheese worth 4 ducats, *vel prout iustificabitur; item* 9 ducats in money, which makes 13 ducats in all, errors excepted, and *ideo* I deduct 13 ducats from my demand and ask *solum* for 60 ducats [*sic*] to be placed to my account *cum reservatione residui, etc.*

1528–30: Aretino's arrival in Venice and the *pala* of *St. Peter Martyr* (from Vasari, 1568): Doc. 8

Having left Rome before the Sack to go to live in Venice, Pietro Aretino, the most famous poet of our time, there became very friendly with Titian and Sansovino: which was very honourable and useful to Titian, whose name he made known wherever his pen reached [...] To turn to the works of Titian, he made the altarpiece of S. Pietro Martire in the church of SS. Giovanni e Paolo, over life-size, the said saint in a glade of very large trees, fallen to the ground and attacked by a furious soldier who has wounded the saint in the head, so that he is barely alive, and one sees in his face the horror of death; while in another friar, who is fleeing, we see terror and the fear of death: in the air are two nude angels emerging from a beam of heavenly light, which also gives light to the landscape, which is very beautiful, and to the whole composition. It is the most finished, most celebrated, the largest and best understood of all his works, and not surpassed by any of his later works.

Since the work disappeared in an accident in 1877, one is grateful to Vasari for his enthusiastic description, in which it is important to note the stress he puts on the exceptional 'dynamism' of the composition. Instead of a noble and hieratic representation, like those of episcopal figures, a powerful dramatic action filled with violent intensity takes place under storm-wracked trees. The flash of lightning which rends the sky signifies both the shattering of nature, designed to accentuate the impression of a terrifying upheaval by the swirling of the air, and also the celestial intervention which already crowns the martyrdom of the inquisitor-saint. The evocation was so powerful that it constituted a kind of model. When Ridolfi in his turn started a local history of painting, he had to use all his talent (more down to earth than that of his Tuscan model) to describe the same picture:

1528–30: The *pala* of *St. Peter Martyr* (from Ridolfi, 1648): Doc. 9

Let us now consider the famous altarpiece of *St. Peter Martyr* in the church of SS. Giovanni e Paolo, in which it is generally agreed that the painter achieved a manner neither falling below nor exceeding that finish, which is required by art and by the situation, and in which he arrived by rarest art at emulation of nature itself.

The event is represented at the opening of a thick clump of oaks and other trees and plants, which form with their branches a shady curtain, mantling the sun. Here the saint, fallen to the ground, is attacked by the impious murderer, who seizes the edge of his cloak and redoubles his blows [...] In a celestial glory there descend two splendid young angels, who hold out to the martyr the palm of glory prepared for

164 Palma Vecchio. *St. Peter Martyr*.
About 1530. Oil on panel. S. Martino,
Alzano Lombardo.
This altarpiece, long attributed to Lotto, is
perhaps the competition piece painted by
Palma (see doc. 6). The feebleness of the
composition is striking.

165 Giacomo Piccini, after Pordenone.
David and Goliath. Mid-sixteenth century.
Engraving.

him in Heaven. They are so beautiful they seem like Sons of Heaven. They were taken from a cast of Cupid, said to be the work of Phidias; and it is universally believed that it would not be possible to compose better, since he set himself to imitate the celebrated works of Antiquity (which he understood very well, and Vasari erred in saying that Titian did not make such studies), these children being not only marvellously coloured, but also marvellously drawn.

Titian's composition is known from a copy—attributed to Niccolò Cassana—in the church itself, and from an engraving by Rota which ensured that it was known all over

Europe. Never had the branches of trees played a more important role in a narrative scene: the oblique lines of the tree trunks control the composition, the frightened gesture of the fleeing monk extends their movement, those of the assassin concentrate it. The effect of light filtering through the leaves must have been extraordinary. This was Titian's first great demonstration of his ability to recreate a dramatic event in terms of sublime tragedy. It may well be asked if it would have been as grandiose without the pressure exerted by

166   Titian. *David and Goliath*. 1542–4. Oil on canvas, attached to the ceiling. Sta. Maria della Salute, Venice.
The similarity with the subjects painted by Pordenone stresses the way in which Titian has taken over the motives used by his rival in the way he has composed the *David and Goliath*.

the competition with Pordenone, a painter of expression and movement. Ridolfi—hunting for an original observation—mentions the motif of the little angels. A sheet of drawings confirms that Titian took a great deal of trouble with the winged figures which descend from Heaven upon the leafy branches to enliven and illumine the upper parts of the composition. It is interesting to note that the historian found it necessary to insist on a 'quotation' from the antique for something which was in effect a commonplace in all Venetian painting. Vasari is expressly taken to task on this point. It was a way of insisting that Venice could dip into humanist culture just as well as Rome, and, in particular, Titian could.

The most serious threat to Titian was the opening to official commissions which public enthusiasm had afforded to Pordenone. Vasari has recorded that once again the latter was invited to decorate a *concorrenza di Tiziano* the great rooms of the Doges' palace. In November 1537 he was asked to work in the Sala del Maggior Consiglio. All these works disappeared in the great fire of 1577. The decade of 1530–40 was effectively dominated by Titian's struggle with Pordenone. The letter sent by the heads of the Council of Ten to the Officials of the Salt Office states exactly that, while commissions to Titian should be given, others should be given to his rival.

1537: Letter from the Council of Ten to the Ufficio al Sal: Doc. 10

> In the said Sala giving to the excellent painter Zuon Antonio Pordanon those other positions and canvases as shall seem good, since it is not necessary to add others to those already begun by the said Titian.

It is no accident that Vasari links the names of Titian and Aretino; their friendship began at this time. Aretino became the painter's recognized publicist, and it was he who extolled the picture in the Dominican church as a formidable, incomparable masterpiece:

29 October 1537: Letter from Aretino to the sculptor Tribolo: Doc. 11

> The architect Sebastiano [Serlio] indulgent of my great pleasure in, but mediocre judgement of, sculpture, has made me understand by words how the folds ornament the draperies of the Virgin which your talent is creating for me. He has also spoken to me of the languid fall of the limbs of the dead Christ, artistically disposed on her lap. I have understood the grief of the mother and the pitiable state of the Son, even before I have seen it. But while he was recounting to me the miracle which is being born from your industry, behold the author of the *St. Peter Martyr*, which would petrify you and Benvenuto were you to see it. Fix your eyes and the light of your intellect on that work and you will understand all the vivid terror of death and all the sorrows of life in the face and flesh of the man fallen to the ground, marvelling at the livid coldness of the point of his nose and his extremities. You will be unable to restrain your voice, crying out as you contemplate his companion in flight, in whom you will recognize the whiteness of cowardice and the pallor of fear. Truly you would do no more than justice to say that there is no finer picture in Italy. What a marvellous group of *putti* in the air, standing out from the trunks and foliage of the spreading trees; what natural simplicity of the landscape, what mossy rocks dripping with water, water which gushes from the source opened by the brush of the divine Titian! Whose modest benignity warmly salutes you and puts himself entirely at your service, swearing that he has no equal in his desire for your fame. Nor can one express his desire to see the two figures which, as I have already said, you have freely decided to send me, a gift that will not be met with silence and ingratitude.

Aretino cleverly linked a letter of encouragement to the sculptor Tribolo—from whom he expected to extract a present and whose praises he sang on trust because of what their common friend Serlio had said of him—and the praise of Titian's recent picture, presented as a model of perfection. The exalted tone serves to heighten the purely 'naturalist' account by the writer, interested only in stressing the astonishing aspects of truthfulness, the signs of death, the gestures of terror, the wild movement of the branches; nothing is said on the true grandeur of the scene and the heavenly commotion which ennobles the martyr. But the advertising formula, the 'most beautiful work in Italy', has been set in train.

These spectacular declarations mark the true end of the episode. About 1540 the dominant position which Titian had not yet attained in 1530 was now achieved. Lotto, invited to Jesi and elsewhere, had resumed after 1532–3 his erratic course towards the Marches, and he left Venice for good in 1538; he is then found in Ancona, weary and worried, beginning to compile the strange *Libro delle spese* which becomes the chronicle of his distress. Pordenone, who left for Ferrara at the same date, died suddenly in the employ of Alfonso d'Este the following year, and 'there was no lack of persons who thought for several months that he had been poisoned' (Vasari). The field, one might say, was clearing. There was also—other than Aretino's extravagant letters—a certain number of indications which confirmed the renewal of Titian's control of the situation. About 1540 he had occasion to paint certain themes of the Old Testament previously painted by Pordenone in S. Stefano. This work was done in the Augustinian convent of Santo Spirito in Isola. The church was demolished in 1656, but three of the pictures which decorated it were placed in the sacristy of Sta. Maria della Salute, where they may still be seen. Never had Titian created such impressive perspective effects of *di sotto in sù* as in these works. Their closeness to the corresponding episodes treated by Pordenone is not without interest: the assimilation of the motifs treated by his rival in the composition of the *Sacrifice of Isaac*, the *Cain and Abel*, the *David and Goliath* is perfect with, it must be admitted, something of deeper understanding, of greater inspiration than Pordenone's *brio*.

Lotto's fate—if it may be called that—had been settled long since. Venetian glory was not for him. Nevertheless, Titian's dedicated publicists never forgot that his memory had finally to be obliterated. An astonishing passage in Dolce is proof of this:

Doc. 12   1557: Lotto's works as seen by Dolce:

> It seems to me that we have a notable example of these bad colours in the altarpiece by Lorenzo Loto which is in the Carmelite church here in Venice...

A criticism of cold colours and the overworked tonal values by Lotto is not surprising in one who was a spokesman for Aretino. The elegiac genius of Lotto, like the 'martial' vigour of Pordenone, had to disappear before Titian.

168   Giorgio Vasari. *The Splendours of the Farnese Family.* Detail: *Portrait of Michelangelo.* About 1540. Fresco. Sala dei Cento Giorni, Palazzo della Cancelleria, Rome.

⊳

169   Michelangelo. *The Last Judgement.* Detail: *St. Bartholomew.* 1534–41. Fresco. Sistine Chapel, Vatican.
'[*The Last Judgement*] contains a thousand heresies, and above all that skin of St. Bartholomew without his beard; it is the flayed man who has the beard, which proves that this skin is not his...' (Letter from Don Miniato Pitti of Montoliveto to Vasari, May 1545.) It is a fact that Michelangelo inserted his own portrait into the shapeless skin.

⊳⊳

170   Michelangelo. *The Last Judgement.* Detail: *The Damned.* 1534–41. Fresco. Sistine Chapel, Vatican.
'... not only a refusal to observe the decency proper for martyrs and virgins, but even to the extent of the gesture of [a damned man] being seized by his genitals...' (Letter from Aretino to Michelangelo, November 1545.)

condemnation of the 'indecency' of the work. These were the cardinals known as the Theatines (from S. Gaetano of Thiene, their founder) grouped around Giampiero Carafa (the future Paul IV), J. Sadoleto, G. Contarini, M. Cervini and Reginald Pole. These reformers were members of a circle of 'spirituals' who were supported by Vittoria Colonna, and were now convinced that only a doctrinal regeneration could save the Church.

However, Michelangelo had for a number of years been associated with their opinions, through Vittoria Colonna, who shared their anxieties. The criticisms emanated, therefore, from members of the Curia to whom Michelangelo was far from being an unknown person. On the other hand, Cardinal Francesco Corner (Cornaro), a Venetian, had for a long time been an open admirer of the artist. His enthusiasm is not surprising. The Farnese Pope also believed in Michelangelo, and he expressed the opinion of many Romans, intrigued and excited by the enormous undertaking. He supported him without weakening and entrusted to him all the main enterprises in Rome, where he was striving to revive pontifical authority after the drama of the Sack of Rome in 1527. He asked in vain for his coat of arms to replace those of Julius II between the Ceiling and the *Last Judgement;* he remained indifferent to the strong criticisms of his Master of Ceremonies, Biagio Martinelli da Cesena, criticisms which in fact antedated those of the Theatines. The affair was only at its beginning. This is proved by the remarks made several years later by a friend to Vasari when he was in Naples.

1 May 1545: Letter from Don Miniato Pitti of Montoliveto to Giorgio Vasari: Doc.

Messer Giorgio Amantissimo, salute,
Several days have passed without my writing to you, as I was prevented by domestic affairs and the monks; and I have a heap of things to tell you, such as: that I am well, and would like to hear the same of you; and that I have had a letter of yours, which said that I was held to be clownish at Naples because in Rome I preferred the ceiling [of the Sistine Chapel] to the wall *[Last Judgement]:* because in it there are a thousand heresies, especially in the beardless skin of St. Bartholomew, while the flayed one has a beard, which shows that it is not his own skin, etc.

Don Miniato Pitti was, it appears, a long-standing collaborator of Vasari, a conventual full of good humour who took it upon himself to keep Vasari informed. Before treating matters of common interest, he replies to his friend by making a mocking allusion to the criticisms levelled at the *Last Judgement.* A good indication that the details of the work were discussed in conversation is in the St. Bartholomew holding in his hands the flayed skin which is his symbol. This kind of discussion was to be heard everywhere, as in the virulent attack which Aretino launched—or rather tried to launch—in an abominable letter frequently quoted, but which possibly did not immediately become public.

6 November 1545: Letter from Aretino to Michelangelo: Doc.

On seeing the complete sketch of the whole of your Day of Judgement, I was able to perceive the noble grace of Raphael in the lovely beauty of its invention. Nevertheless, I, as one baptized, am ashamed of the licence, so harmful to the spirit, which you have adopted in the expression of the concepts where is set out the end to which every sense of our supremely truthful faith aspires. So; that Michelangelo so stupendous in fame, that Michelangelo so outstanding in wisdom, that Michelangelo whom we admire for his conduct, has been willing to show to people no less impiety of irreligion than perfection of painting? Is it possible that you, who as a divine being do not condescend to the society of men, should have done such

a thing in the foremost temple of God? Above the main altar of Jesus? In the most important chapel in the world, where the great cardinals of the Church, where the reverend priests, where the Vicar of Christ with Catholic devotions, with sacred rites, and with holy prayers, bear witness to, contemplate, and adore His body, His blood, and His flesh?

If it were not a wicked thing to make such a comparison, I would boast of the judgement shown in the *Treatise on Nanna*, preferring the wisdom of my discernment to your faulty conscience, since I in lascivious and immodest subject-matter not only use restrained and polite words, but tell my story in pure and blameless language. But you, in a subject-matter of such exalted history, show angels and saints, the former without any of the decency proper to this world, and the latter lacking any of the loveliness of Heaven.

Remember that pagans in their statues—I don't say of Diana clothed, but in the naked Venus—made them cover with their hands the parts which should not be revealed; and one who is a Christian, because he values art more than the Faith, displays as a genuine spectacle not only absence of decorum in the martyrs and virgins, but also the gesture of the man dragged away by his genital organs, a sight

171   Michelangelo. *The Raising of Lazarus*. 1518–19. Red chalk drawing. British Museum, London.
A study for the picture by Sebastiano del Piombo, *The Raising of Lazarus* (National Gallery, London), which was painted in competition with Raphael's *Transfiguration*. These large nude figures will be used again in the *Last Judgement*.

172   Michelangelo. *Study of a Nude Man*. 1504–5. Pen drawing. British Museum, London.
Drawings of nude figures, like this one, originally made for the *Battle of Cascina*, were reused for the *Last Judgement*.

One of the early sketches for the agitated composition in which the major lines of direction are already fixed and in which the role of the nude is decided upon. 'It is indecent to see these bodies in a state of nudity on the altars and in the churches of God.' (A. Caterino, *Commentaria*, 1551.)

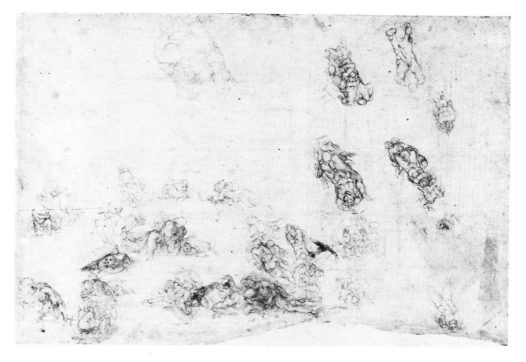

to which eyes would be shut tight even in a brothel. What you have done would be appropriate in a voluptuous whore-house, not in a supreme choir. Hence it would be a lesser vice if you were an unbeliever, rather than that, believing in such a manner, you diminished the belief of others.

But even here the excellence of such outrageous marvels should not remain unpunished, since the miracle of their being is the death of your fame. But you could revive your good name by making the flames of fire cover the shame of the damned, and that of the blessed with the rays of the sun, or imitate Florentine modesty which under a few gilded leaves covered that of its beautiful colossus; and this stands in a public square, not in a sacred place. So thus may God forgive you, as I do not say this because of the contempt which I have for the things I desire; because satisfying what you undertook to send me should be attended to by you with all dispatch, since in such an act you would silence envy, which says that only Gherardi and Tomai can dispose of them. But if the treasure which Julius left you so that you should place his remains in the receptacle of your carving was not sufficient to make you keep the promise, what hope then can I have? Though not your ingratitude, nor your avarice, great painter, but the grace and merit of that great Pastor is the reason for it; although God wills that his eternal fame shall live simply in having been himself, and not in a proud machine of sculpture created by your art. In this matter your failure to honour your debt is attributed to you as a theft. For our hearts have more need of the feeling of devotion than of the liveliness of art; may God inspire the Holiness of Paul as it inspired the Blessedness of Gregory, who wished at first to strip Rome of the superb statues of idols which took, by their beauty, reverence from humble images of saints. To end, if you had accepted the advice, in composing the Universe, the Abyss, and Paradise, with the glory, the honour and the terror sketched out for you from the instruction, the example, and the wisdom of my letter, which the century has read, I dare to say that then Nature and every benign influence would not repent of your having been given so clear an intellect that today your supreme ability has made you into a simulacrum of the marvellous, but the providence of the One who rules everything will take account of such a work, without making use of His own laws in governing the hemispheres.

From Venice, November 1545.

Your servant Aretino.

P. S. Now that I have somewhat given vent to my anger against the cruelty with which you repay my devotion, and having, it appears to me, made you see that, if you are divine, I am not made of water, tear this up, just as I have reduced it to bits, and remember that I am such that even kings and emperors reply to my letters.

The original of this letter was found in the Medici archives. With certain changes in wording and corrections which make it somewhat less confused, it appeared in a collection of Aretino's letters in 1550, as a letter addressed to Alessandro Corvino in July

174 Michelangelo. *The Last Judgement* (first version). 1534–5. Drawing in black chalk, with the outlines reinforced in ink by another hand. Casa Buonarroti, Florence.

'... one can see that he has striven to create strange figures in varied poses.' (Letter from Nicolo Sernini to Cardinal Ercole Gonzaga, November 1541.)

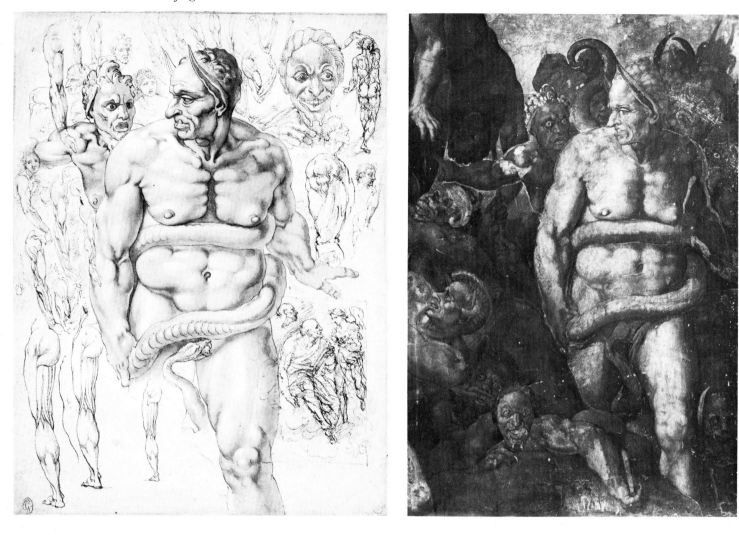

175 Ambrogio Figino. *Copy of the Figure of Minos in Michelangelo's Last Judgement.* About 1560. Pen, brown wash, with traces of red chalk. Metropolitan Museum of Art, New York.
A drawing done before the restoration by Daniele da Volterra.

176 Michelangelo. *The Last Judgement.* Detail: *Minos.* 1534–41. Fresco. Sistine Chapel, Vatican.
According to Vasari, the figure of Minos may be identified with Biagio da Cesena.

177 Marcello Venusti. *Copy of Michelangelo's Last Judgement.* About 1549. Museo e Galleria Nazionale di Capodimonte, Naples.
Marcello Venusti's copy in Naples has the merit of showing the state of the fresco *before* the reworkings of 1565; it also includes a God the Father and the dove of the Holy Spirit above the figure of Christ, as if to confirm the orthodoxy of the work.

1547, the direct interpellations having been suppressed. This little bit of camouflage, characteristic of the author, has led to the erroneous conclusion that the letter was never sent. Aretino simply found it more expedient to let Michelangelo know about his personal griefs in the midst of reproaches concerning his work, and to publish only the latter, as if it were his considered opinion on a regrettable scandal.

It is a masterpiece of intelligent perfidy. Michelangelo never replied to the invitations and to the letters of the critic who wanted to obtain the 'drawings of the divine Buonarroti'; he was wrong to forget that Aretino was the correspondent of kings. For the rest, all is there: the profound immorality of an art which does not shrink from exhibiting nudities in the papal chapel (Aretino had evidently not been to Rome; he speaks only from a knowledge of the accounts and the commentaries which were then current); on this point his general remarks echo very strangely the comments made at the time of Hadrian VI (1524) about the *ignudi* on the ceiling. There follow allusions to the favours conferred upon young friends of the artist, and above all the accusation of having accepted huge sums from Julius II for a tomb which had never been made. The nastiest part, without doubt, is the threat at the end; it is just to destroy impious works, as Pope Gregory did with pagan idols. Rather should the artist entrust himself to the direction of a pious counsellor, whose identity is easy to guess.

The cynicism of this inflated and rascally letter is not in doubt. But it is not possible to reduce an attack so well-founded to the sole plane of a vindictive personal feud. It was intended to signify that Michelangelo was wrong to believe that all was permitted him. It

178 Jacopo Vivo. *Interpretation of the Frescoes in the Sistine Chapel.* About 1570. Engraving. Biblioteca Apostolica, Vatican. A popular interpretation of the work of Michelangelo with the *Last Judgement* in the middle, the elongated format giving greater importance to the lower zone of the damned.

179 Martino Rota, after Michelangelo. *The Last Judgement*. About 1570. Engraving.
The composition, reorganized in a simplified and artifical form, is surmounted by a bust of the artist.

cannot even be excluded that the letter may have been partly inspired by a sudden access of devotional scruple; Aretino had just suffered the loss of his mistress Pierina. He was also aspiring, it appears, to the dignity of a cardinalate. He was the author of Christian poems dedicated to the strictest theologians. He was perfectly able to have suddenly suffered an attack of prudery, or at least to share seriously in the preoccupations of the Roman censors. A few years later, in 1550, the new Pope Julius III would make him a Knight of St. Peter. In this context it would appear that Aretino was not alone in taking the initiative, but that, like many others, while protesting his admiration for Michelangelo, he entertained serious doubts; he certainly displayed a more spirited nastiness, mixed with a vulgar resentment about advances repulsed. His prudish comments are embarrassing through their repetitiveness. He says nothing about the extraordinary energy of the huge picture; he only cites the bits that could scandalize. But scandal is his business, and he was to return to it.

He could also be dangerous because of his intervention, which tended to favour the 'corrected' portions of the work.

January 1546: Letter from Aretino to Enea Vico: Doc. 4

The *Day of Judgement* which Bazzacco, one of the most gifted artists of design, has conscientiously drawn from the composition by Buonarroti can never fully satisfy all the requirements of the graver, with the clearest, firmest and softest strokes, delicately and lightly traced on the copper accurately and exactly. However, the existence of such a work, apart from copies of it elsewhere, is no service to the decorum appropriate to the religion it embodies. By Divine command, the end of the world will take place and it is fitting that all the world should participate in this tremendous and triumphal event. For this reason I am certain that our merit in such a work will obtain a reward from Christ the Highest, and a useful one from the Grand Duke of Florence. Take care to finish this holy and praiseworthy enterprise, so that the scandal which might be caused by the licence of Michelangelo's art among the Lutherans on account of the small respect paid to natural shame disclosed by the figures in the abyss and in Heaven may be avoided—but this is in no way to diminish the honour due to you for having been the cause of everyone's delight.

As with all Aretino's writings, which are extravagant and in inflated language, it is impossible to give an idea of this letter by more than an approximate translation. But the meaning is clear enough. The Grand Duke wanted a print of the work of which the whole world was talking. He commissioned it from Enea Vico. The problem of a good reproduction was a serious one. The famous publisher Salamanca had produced in 1543 a print which was unsuccessful, as Giulio Bonasone's was in 1546. This was known. To create a copper-plate engraving of this immense composition with more than 300 figures in a surging mêlée required enormous technical skill; above all, it required a careful interpretation of certain details. And there was always the stumbling block of the arbitrary use of the nude and of ambiguous gestures, without taking into account what some found to be obtrusive iconographic additions. Few celebrated compositions have been so often distorted as was the *Last Judgement*. Even the painted copy by Marcello Venusti (Naples), which has the merit of showing the state of the fresco before the retouches done in 1565, etc., includes a God the Father and the dove of the Holy Spirit above Christ. Cosimo de' Medici's anxieties are therefore understandable. But at this point Aretino, in the full flood of his polemic, decided to intervene with Vico, whom he knew well. He praised the undertaking, with the ludicrous comment that the Last Day merited a wide publicity, but he warned the engraver against the doubtful implications and the 'Lutheran' novelties—that is, unorthodox (the term 'Lutheran' had already acquired this sense in common usage)—such as the total nudity of the figures. He also proposed the use of the amended version by a certain Battista Bazzacco. The project was not proceeded with. But it can be seen that Aretino's relentlessness was concentrated on a concern for religious propriety or at least that he never abandoned this theme. The affair had reached a point where a reply was essential; it came from the two biographers and commentators of Michelangelo: Vasari in 1550, Condivi in 1553.

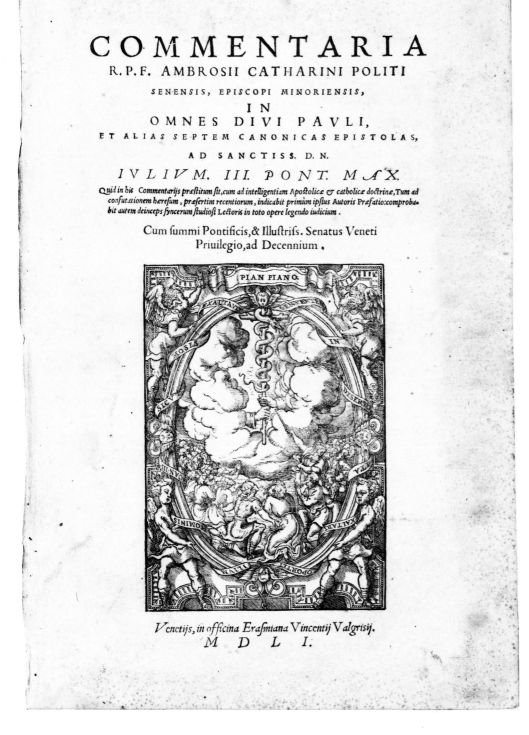

COMMENTARIA
R.P.F. AMBROSII CATHARINI POLITI
SENENSIS, EPISCOPI MINORIENSIS,
IN
OMNES DIVI PAVLI,
ET ALIAS SEPTEM CANONICAS EPISTOLAS,
AD SANCTISS. D.N.
IVLIVM. III. PONT. MAX.

Quid in his Commentarijs praestitum sit, cum ad intelligentiam Apostolicae & catholicae doctrinae, Tum ad
confutationem haeresum, praesertim recentiorum, indicabit primùm ipsius Autoris Praefatio:comproba-
bit autem deinceps syncerum studiosi Lectoris in toto opere legendo iudicium.

Cum summi Pontificis, & Illustriss. Senatus Veneti
Priuilegio,ad Decennium.

Venetijs, in officina Erasmiana Vincentij Valgrisij.
M D L I.

180 Caterino. *Commentaria*, frontispiece.
1551.
The first severe criticism of Michelangelo's art, made in a pamphlet dedicated
to Julius III. The frontispiece has the
emblem of the brazen serpent.

Doc. 5   1550: Vasari's *apologia* for the *Last Judgement*:

And in truth, the multitude of figures, the *terribilità* and the greatness of the work
are such that it is impossible to describe them, since it is full of all possible human
emotions, all marvellously expressed. There are the proud, the jealous, the avaricious,
the luxurious, and the others, all easily recognizable by the informed spectator, since
he observed every necessary convention of expression, attitude and every other
natural circumstance in representing them; so that however marvellous and huge it

is, it was not impossible to him, who was always learned and wise, with wide experience of men, and having acquired that wisdom from the knowledge of the world that philosophers get from their speculation and writings.

In the arrangement of the *Vite* published in 1550 the Life of Michelangelo was the last chapter, which summed up the whole history of modern art. The *Last Judgement* was only one episode in the extraordinary panorama of the career and works of the artist. But Vasari, it may well be thought, inspired perhaps by Michelangelo's own words, has used the most persuasive arguments not only to render the formidable audacity of the *Last Judgement* acceptable, but also to cancel out in advance any complaints on account of the nudes and their consequences by an interpretation at the deepest level. The body has become the symbol of the affections and the passions, the index of the emotions. This is a demonstration of a knowledge which is displayed in its totality in the handling and the play of forms, and which could not be done in any other way, which justifies the artist's thought, and which, at the same time, renders useless all references to an occult 'philosophy'. But in one sense it was too late. Ten years after the unveiling of the work strict Roman circles, far from being disarmed, were still worried over its success.

1551: A. Caterino, on the errors of painters: Doc. 6

> There is an outstanding painter and sculptor of our times, by name Michelangelo, who is admirable in depicting the naked bodies of men and their *pudenda*. I praise his art for this fact, but the fact itself I blame vehemently and detest, for it is most indecent to see all these nudities everywhere, on the altars and in the chapels of God. Truly these and many other great abuses sully the Church of God, the Bride of Christ. For my present purpose, what I wish to say is that Michelangelo's absolute perfection in the painting of nude bodies with their obscene parts—which even Nature veils in us—is not that of the Apostle, when he denounces and depicts with the living brush of the Spirit the shameful nakedness of heretics.

This text is taken from a series of essays on St. Paul's Epistles, published by a Dominican, Ambrogio Politi, known as Caterino. He knew Michelangelo well, because the painter, in company with Vittoria Colonna, had just followed the lectures on the Apostle to the Gentiles given privately about 1540 in the garden of S. Silvestro al Quirinale. The admiration of the preacher did not prevent him from denouncing the 'abuses' of which the artist was guilty, and the brief allusion which he makes to the controversy over the *Last Judgement* ends by regretting that so great a talent had been so ill employed.

Quite unlike Aretino, the theologian never sought to harm. He was, it appears, sincerely pained by what he considered to be a grave deviation (the allusion to heretics is not very illuminating), but nothing irremediable. It is the idea of impropriety which recurs. So many nudes, so many *pudenda*, above the altar ! This appeared something intolerable. It is still the same reaction of the Theatines as was first registered in November 1541. It sought, as an inevitable consequence, to have the offending images destroyed or, alternatively, to have the indecent details effaced. At the end of the reign of Paul III the matter was raised officially. Injunctions of this kind were never to end. But fifteen years were to pass before anything of the kind was undertaken, and it required no less than a decree of the Council of Trent to effect the 'corrections'.

It may be thought that the protests of the bigots had yet another aim: that of finally obtaining legislation about images in churches; that is, the definition of what was licit and appropriate, and the establishment of rules for the guidance of prelates in their dioceses. As is known, these demands were formulated under pressure from virulent critics among the Reformers and in particular by Calvinist iconoclasts. It is strange, yet finally not untypical, that Counter-Reformation circles were led to dub as 'Lutheran' any illegitimate or wrong-headed traits in church art. In any case the term acquired great power from the moment when the struggle with the Reformed Church began. It was necessary to work through the Council in order to try to save the unity of the Church. And the Council, which Paul III finally convoked, had to face the difficult problem of images.

This is the background to the monotonous accusations and the impassioned protests to which the *Last Judgement* gave rise in the middle of the sixteenth century. But it is impossible to understand either the sudden bitter turn taken by these discussions, or the deliberate risk assumed by the artist in conceiving his *Last Judgement* as a spectacle of nudities, if one overlooks one simple fact—which is the key to the whole question.

As a result of the criticisms of humanists (Erasmus) and Reformers (Zwingli, Calvin) the Curial theologians came to realize that the Church had never, in fact, established any definite rules concerning images. Since the Council of Nicaea, which had re-established their use, everything had evolved, or had developed without the Latin Church—in contradistinction to the Greek Orthodox—ever finding it necessary to codify its practices. In certain dioceses, rules existed, though they had more often than not fallen into disuse. Practices varied; the rule was based on the usages of devotion or, to use the theologians' vague term, on 'tradition'. The point had now been reached when too many new ideas, an art of excessive brilliance and overpowering personalities, had led to ideas which were more and more disputable, and were now being contested. The non-existent norm had to be defined. By denouncing Michelangelo's abuses, the critics stressed the urgency of this matter. But everything was made more complicated by the fact that Michelangelo was quite definitely not a personality like any other.

Doc. 7   1552: Luca Gauricus draws up Michelangelo's horoscope:

> Mercury in the morning, at 27 degrees from the Sun, in the House of Saturn, bathed by Venus in an elementary irradiation. The consequence: the exceptional painter and sculptor Michelangelo, more illustrious than Phidias and Praxiteles, with abundant riches. This success seems to be confirmed by Jupiter residing in the second House, according to the elementary horoscope calculation, and favourably touched by Venus. The gifts of his genius have caused him to be showered with great riches and high honours by the Princes of the Church.

The publication by Paul III's astrologer is a sort of treatise of famous men, seen from a 'scientific' angle. The portrait of each one is given from the standpoint of the relations between the planetary divinities, here Mercury, Saturn, Jupiter and Venus. The remarks about the artist's wealth and the favour of pontiffs, whether or not they were based on the stars, echoed an opinion widespread throughout Christendom. How could such a person be censured?

Besides the problem of the nudes, the interpretation of the fresco was also a source of perplexity. The diversity of the attitudes did not make up for the absence of explicit attributes. This was said everywhere, even in Venice. In any discussion about the higher aims of painting, it was inevitable that the discussion finally turned on Michelangelo's *Last Judgement*.

Doc. 8   1557: Dialogue on the *Last Judgement* from L. Dolce's *L'Aretino*:

> Fabrini: 'I have heard it said that in the stupendous composition of the *Judgement* there are concealed allegorical senses, very recondite and accessible only to a few.'
> Aretino: [...] 'I would willingly believe that, were it not that one sees ridiculous things in that same *Judgement*.'
> Fabrini: 'Such as?'

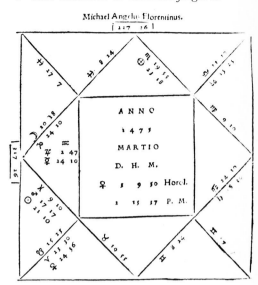

181   Luca Gauricus. *Michelangelo's Horoscope.* (*Tractatus Astrologicus*, Venice 1552.) Mercury—which stands for practical gifts is in the House of Saturn; the faculty of contemplation—watched over by Venus—the aspiration to beauty, and supported by Jupiter, which promised the favour of the great.

182 Federico·Zuccaro. *Taddeo Zuccaro Copying the Last Judgement.* About 1546. Drawing and watercolour. Gabinetto dei Disegni, Galleria degli Uffizi, Florence.
This drawing is evidence of the interest of the younger generation of Roman artists in Michelangelo's masterpiece. Taddeo Zuccaro (born in 1529) arrived in Rome in 1543, and was immediately employed as a copyist.

Aretino: 'Is it not ridiculous to have imagined, in Heaven, among the crowd of the Blessed, certain of them tenderly kissing each other? They should be intent on higher things, with their minds raised to divine contemplation and the future judgement [...] Again, what mystical sense is there in having represented Christ without a beard? Or the sight of a devil pulling down by his testicles a large figure who bites his fingers in pain? Do not oblige me to go on—I do not wish to seem to speak ill of a man who is otherwise divine.'

Fabrini: 'I repeat that his inventions are most ingenious and understood by few.'

Aretino: [...] 'If Michelangelo wishes that his ideas should be understood only by the learned few, then I, who am not one of them, leave his thoughts to him.'

The intervention of the Venetians is explained by the presence of Aretino, who became the dominating interpreter of culture, and by the prestige of Titian, which also required to be supported by a constant critical activity. Dolce's compilation answered this double requirement. The thesis is simple: Michelangelo's strength lay, certainly, in his drawing, but 'whoever has seen one of his figures has seen them all.' Raphael, on the other hand, shows a greater diversity in nudes as in everything else; he adds a delicacy unknown to Michelangelo, but both of them are surpassed by Titian.

The passage about the *Last Judgement* is less simplistic than usual. To the details denounced by everyone—easily characterized by the allusion to the *pudenda* of the man damned for lechery—follow criticisms which would be repeated more and more often: the beardless Christ, the saved embracing one another. The author seems to believe that Michelangelo has betrayed the tradition; but he merely says that the artist's intentions remain obscure. The argument of hermeticism is, in one sense, less distressing, but for the Venetians it indicated a unacceptable pretentiousness inadmissible in sacred art.

The saddest moment in this long polemic was reached when theologians echoed the doubts insinuated by their reproaches into the mind of the ageing artist. This cannot be doubted in view of the letter addressed by a correspondent of Carlo Borromeo exactly twenty years after the unveiling of the *Last Judgement*.

6 September 1561: Letter from Scipione Saurolo to Cardinal Borromeo: Doc. 9

...I respectfully beg Your Illustrious and Reverend Lordship to be pleased to read this discourse of mine on the painting in His Holiness's Chapel and to give it the attention due to a matter of such importance and so worthy of consideration. It greatly displeased Pope Paul III, of blessed memory, and, had he lived, he would have dealt with it, as I have been told by Cardinal Santa Croce, later Pope Marcellus, and the Cardinal of Carpi, and Veralli, of good memory. And I know that the Cardinal Alessandrino [Michele Bonelli] said to me that Paul III wished to deal with it by enlarging the chapel on the side of the Sacristy, after I had complained to everybody. I know that in the last year of Paul IV Michelangelo said that he wished to arrange it, since it was a matter of conscience to leave such a thing behind...

The threats against this 'scandalous' work made during the pontificate of Paul IV Carafa (1555–9) continued to be expressed. A young Lombard writer, in a collection of 'dialogues of the dead' which long remained unpublished, ascribed to Leonardo a vengeful description, addressed to... Phidias!

C. 1563: Comment on the *Last Judgement* attributed to Leonardo by Lomazzo: Doc. 10

It is said that his idea was to make on this wall a cage or crew of porters and mountebanks who would leap up and down, noting the impropriety of those all too evident members and testicles, not only in the devils and imaginary creatures, but in

the Saints as well; and that he was not far short of doing so in the case of Christ, or showing the nature of St. Catherine, whose pose suggests more lustful thoughts in the spectator (together with the attitudes of many other women), rather than the trembling which so awful a day ought to engender. It is also said that those kisses which are offered and received are not proper, and are more suited to marriages and brothels. And there are many other criticisms, if one forgets or ignores the fact that this work is the true splendour of all Italy and of artists, who come from the Hyperborean ends of the earth to see and draw it. Only a few months or years ago, Pope Paul IV, called the Theatine, wished to throw it to the ground, saying that it was not right that in St. Peter's there should be such wicked exhibition of nakedness and buffooneries.

183 Michelangelo. *The Last Judgement*. Detail: *The Elect Embracing*. 1534–41. Fresco. Sistine Chapel, Vatican.
In the upper part of the composition... 'he did not show this exchange of embraces among the saved without an elevated judgement and significance.' (Comanini, *Il Figino*, 1591.)

Lomazzo—who perhaps never even went to Rome—becomes merely the echo of what was said in Rome and elsewhere over the previous twenty years, with the crude words which have already been encountered. But he adds a mention of the destruction of an inconvenient masterpiece desired by the preceding Pope. A delicate situation since, as the writer observes, the whole world passes respectfully before this work which has become the most famous in the world. This is what now would render the affair insoluble.

Then occurred what could be expected: a treatise entirely consecrated to Michelangelo's works in the Sistine Chapel and above all to the *Last Judgement*. Fate willed that this opusculum appeared a few months after the artist's death.

> I do not believe that there is any artist, however clumsy, who does not know or think that Michelangelo was more concerned with art than with historical truth, and that this did not proceed from ignorance on his part, but from the desire to demonstrate to posterity the excellence of his own genius, and the excellence of the art in him [...]
> I hold that artist to be much more ingenious who adapts his art to the truth of the subject rather than to artistic ends.

The author, a cultured theologian, calm and severe, conscious of the importance of the debate, adopts from the start a lofty tone, full of reverence for the illustrious artist and sincerely pained by his fantasies, his bizarre liberties, his errors. All the old objections are rehashed: the nudes, the *pudenda*, a too attractive St. Catherine, angels without wings, Charon from mythology... Numerous comments are made in passing on the way in which artists can arrange scenes as they think fit. The argument is set out straight off: Horace's maxim *quidlibet audendi potestas* has been admissible up to now; it no longer is. It expresses a situation no longer valid.

That is what the preface of the book sets out. As far as Michelangelo is concerned, his genius sets him apart, but he has truly been the victim of a fallacious principle. He has been concerned to give greater expression to the development of his art, to the power of forms, than to the truth of the theme; that is, to the theological content.

This conclusion leaves far behind accusations of heresy, and no one now speaks of 'Lutheran' inventions. Very adroitly, the problem has now shifted towards the proclivity of the exceptional artist no longer to recognize limits, even those of religious authority (this is now the accusation of pride). In a sense, Gilio seems to express a conclusion which many visitors must have come to. From it came a powerful appeal to the authorities to set out the doctrine of the Church in face of artistic imprudence. This was, in fact, the aim of the book. But the relative absolution granted to Michelangelo was only obtained at the expense of a refusal to give him the essential homage which his fame merited. The power of the *Last Judgement* derived from the fact that it was not a series of formal inventions, but the figurative exposition of a kind of personal theology, the extent of which was now being circumscribed.

The affair of the *Last Judgement* had acquired the value of a symbol. It had been sustained by the virulent criticism of the 'rigorists', who at their worst clamoured for the destruction of the work, and under Paul IV were very close to achieving it. But it was also necessary that the moment be seized to ask the great question of the Church's control over artistic activity, at least in churches. It was the question of *sacred art* which was being formulated and quite naturally so, at the Council of Trent.

The twenty-fourth session of the Council was a hasty one. It took place from 11 November to 3 December 1563, immediately before the Council closed. The affair of the *Last Judgement* was raised there, the 'scandal' taken seriously, and measures were decided. At the beginning of 1564 a commission sat to define them; it included Carlo Borromeo, Cardinal Morone, close to the Theatines, and three other prelates. It was this commission that took the decision to appoint Daniele da Volterra. A financial document after the death of the painter (1566) fixes without doubt his responsibility.

C. 1566: Payment to the heirs of Daniele da Volterra: Doc. 12

> ... the sum of 60 scudi due to the late master Daniele, painter, in payment for the work done by him in 1565 in covering the pudenda of the figures in the Chapel of Pope Sixtus...

The quantity of the interventions made to 'correct' the nudities were, to judge from the salary received by the 'breeches-maker', considerable; loin-cloths, the green robe of St. Catherine—whose pose, considered equivocal, was even reversed, constituted what may be called a respectful attack. The work survived, but so did the critics and the difficulties of interpretation.

By the end of the century, its importance for all the schools of painting had become such that a reticent or denigratory attitude was no longer possible. Theological commentary ended by treating Michelangelo as a doctor of the Church who could not contradict Holy Writ.

Doc. 13   1591: Dialogue on the *Last Judgement* from Comanini's *Il Figino ovvero della Fine della Pittura* (Mantua):

Figino: 'It has been said that Michelangelo wrongly painted Christ as almost beardless in the representation of the *Last Judgement*, while theologians teach that men will be resurrected with beards, to be formed again at the mature age of the Saviour, from which it is deduced that Buonarroti in this matter departed from the truth; for, to speak like a theologian, if the Resurrection of Christ is an example for that of men, who will rise bearded, it is very plain that he should not have painted our Redeemer with an almost beardless chin. And the kissing which this same painter has represented between some of the Saints in Heaven, troubles the grave censors of the arts, who say that he has indubitably fallen into indecorum in this matter, it not being likely that the elect should conduct themselves in this manner after they have received their bodies again, since in their reciprocal love each will glory in the beatitude of the other.'

Martinengo: 'Is there any way in which to free Michelangelo from this calumny of indecorum? I think him so great a man that I cannot imagine him representing kissing among the crowds of the Blessed without good reason and judgement...
[The works of painters must be defended as Aristotle defended the images of poets, which are often improbable, by affirming the sense of an allegory above and beyond the literal sense.] The Bride in the *Song of Songs* says to the Bridegroom 'Let him kiss me with the kisses of his mouth'; and how can the Church ask for a kiss from her Divine spouse? What connection is there between the amorous actions of men and the Divine love? But by allegory the mists of indecorum are dissipated, since this kiss, so ardently desired by the Bride, is to be understood as the Incarnation of the Word, combining the two Natures, divine and human, making a communication between the two, as in a kiss the two mouths are united and the two breaths combined...'

Thus, after a half-century of bitter public argument the controversy died down in high-minded meditation: the theological extensions of the work of art were now to be trusted. The censure finally ended. The severe rules which the *Last Judgement* had helped to inspire in the Doctors of the Council of Trent, would now be either followed or disregarded, according to countries and dioceses. In other words, things would continue as before.

Chapter 10
Arguments with the Inquisition (1573)

On 4 February 1571 a fire in the refectory of the convent of SS. Giovanni e Paolo in Venice destroyed the large *Last Supper* which Titian had painted about 1555. To replace it the fathers approached Veronese who, with Tintoretto, was then the most fashionable painter and the one to whom commissions of importance were most readily given. Titian was now very old (he was to die five years later) and could no longer undertake work on this scale; approaches were made to the most brilliant of his heirs. Paolo Caliari was forty-three years old. There was no doubt about his standing with the authorities, as is shown by the part he played in the public celebrations of what was, in fact, the major event of the age: the naval victory of Lepanto over the Turks on 7 October 1571.

It is almost impossible to exaggerate the importance, for Italy and for the whole of Christendom and above all for Venice, of the success of the allied fleets of Spain and the Serenissima against this terrible foe. The action of the allied powers was commemorated in the picture of the *Virgin of the Rosary* (1573, Museum, Murano) which was executed by Veronese's studio, showing the group of the princes invoking the protection of the Madonna. The 'miraculous' salvation was more directly celebrated by a very large and involved allegory which the artist probably painted himself in 1571 or 1572 (now in the Accademia). It represents a huge and confused battle scene where warships clash in a mêlée shot through with rays of light and shadow. Above the clouds is a group of saints attended by angels: SS. Peter, Rocco, Giustina and Mark present the figure of Venice veiled in white to the Madonna floating above them in a golden glory. To these traditional intercessors the city thus expressed its pious gratitude. A period of peace and prosperity began for the Republic. In this climate of recovered confidence Veronese's light and brilliant painting, with its large orchestrations of Venetian life, could develop a new dimension.

This is what was indicated three quarters of a century later in Ridolfi's remarks on Veronese's grand compositions:

1562–73: The *Feasts* painted by Veronese (from Ridolfi, 1648): Doc. 1

Paolo's fame was greatly increased by the four large canvases of *Feasts* painted for churches in the city, in which, with various inventions, he represented the sumptuous appurtenances of regal banquets.

The first was the one in the refectory of S. Giorgio Maggiore, of the *Marriage at Cana* [...]

The second, the one in San Sebastiano, of 1570, of the *Feast in the House of Simon* [...]

The third is in SS. Giovanni e Paolo, painted in 1573, from the account given in St. Luke of the feast in the house of Levi, which was painted to replace a *Last Supper* by Titian which had been burnt in a fire. Fra Andrea de' Buoni, being anxious to replace that picture, offered Paolo a sum of money, alms and penitence offerings; an amount which probably no man of the present time would accept to prime so large

184 Veronese. *Allegory of the Battle of Lepanto.* 1573. Oil on canvas. Galleria dell'Accademia, Venice.
The battle of Lepanto, 7 October 1571, is represented as a seascape, where the vessels and their sails are locked together, surmounted by a symbolic ceremony showing the reception of the victorious Venice in Heaven, presented by the city's patron saints.

a canvas. The poor friar could raise no larger sum, but his entreaties persuaded Paolo finally to agree to so large a task, more from desire of glory than of profit.

The scene is represented as taking place beneath a grand loggia of three arcades, through which one sees beautiful palaces which charm the eye. In the centre is the Saviour, near Him is Levi, clad in purple, and around them there is a crowd of Publicans and others, mingled with the Apostles, forming a remarkable gallery of heads of varying character, and among these admirable figures is Fra Andrea in a corner, with a napkin over his shoulder: for this one portrait one might have asked the price paid for the whole.

Among the admirable details is the figure of the host, leaning on a pedestal, where everything indicates the precise quality of the personage. He is painted with such fresh flesh-colours that he seems alive; next to him is an Ethiopian slave, dressed in Moroccan fashion, holding a pannier and with a laughing air which causes the spectator to laugh also.

In short, the whole work is managed with all the skill possible in this genre, for Paolo did not wish to have on his conscience the idea that Fra Andrea might have occasion to regret the use of his money.

The fourth is in the refectory of the Servites, another *Feast in the House of Simon* [...]

Ridolfi's compilation (which made use of the recollections of Palma Giovane) sought to provide for Venetians, whose activities Vasari was only partially able to record, a work which would play the same role as the great Florentine's. It records very exactly that, ten years after the immense *Marriage at Cana* of 1562–3 (6.66×9.9 m, now in the Louvre) Veronese painted one after the other, three variations, on the theme, including the *Feast in the House of Levi* (5.55×12.8 m, now in the Accademia). Why such insistence on portraying grand Venetian gatherings, giving a grandiose treatment to fairly rare themes like the *Feast in the House of Simon* or the *Feast in the House of Levi*? It is difficult not to see in them a kind of self-celebration of Venice so soon before and after the events of 1571.

It was customary to depict the *Last Supper* in monastic refectories, as was often done in Florence and also, by the famous Leonardo, in Milan. As has been well observed concerning Leonardo's great work in Sta. Maria delle Grazie, the moment which dominates the composition may be either the dramatic declaration 'one of you shall betray me', or the eucharistic miracle. In any case, the Apostles as a group manifest astonishment, caused by fear or by wonder. A rich study of expressions was thus necessarily a part of the theme. But the rule was not absolute; it was possible to use the *Marriage at Cana*, which presented fewer problems and, while it proclaimed the sacramental nature of marriage—and its festive setting—by the presence of Christ, implied a eucharistic reference by the miracle of the wine.

Veronese has established exactly in the centre of his canvas of the *Marriage at Cana* a vertical axis of symbolic values: the lamb being cut up on the balustrade; the frontal image of Christ working the miracle; the hour-glass which serves as a moral warning; and finally the group of musicians whose profane orchestra takes the place of the angels who usually celebrate the divine act.

185 Veronese. *Allegory of Venice*. 1575–7. Oil on canvas. Audience Chamber, Palazzo Ducale, Venice.
Amid the customary symbols of grandeur, Peace and Justice, accompanied by their emblems, come before the throne where they are dominated by the Queen of the Seas.

C. 1565: The Feast in the House of Simon in S. Nazzaro (from Vasari, 1568):   Doc. 2

In Verona, in the refectory of the Black Monks, he painted a large picture of the feast made by Simon the leper for the Lord, when the adulteress threw herself at His feet, with many figures, drawn from life, and with most rare perspectives, and under the table there are two dogs, so fine that they seem living and natural, and further off there are some cripples, excellently painted.

186 Andrea Palladio. Refectory of S. Giorgio Maggiore, showing the original position of the *Marriage at Cana*. Monastery of S. Giorgio Maggiore, Venice.
The Marriage at Cana, painted in 1563, for the refectory of the convent, was the first of the biblical banquets mentioned in Ridolfi (*Le Maraviglie*, 1648). The reconstruction shows how it was adapted to the architectural setting.

In this passage from Vasari, which points to another grand 'banquet' scene by Veronese, the principal characteristics of his art are clearly defined: a grand architectural decoration, filled with incident and with beautiful details for connoisseurs, but with the canonical element given due importance; here the gesture of the Magdalen, the occasion for the famous words which the Evangelist puts into Christ's mouth on the validity of extravagant expense done in His honour (Luke 7: 37 et seq.). The import of this text should perhaps not be forgotten since, through its justification of liturgical luxury, it legitimated the deployment of *magnificentia* in painting. Only a short while before painting the picture destined for the Dominican monastery of SS. Giovanni e Paolo, Veronese painted the *Feast of S. Gregorio Magno* for the sanctuary at Monte Berico near Vicenza. It has been suggested quite reasonably that Palladio had a hand in this work. In a high framework of Corinthian columns, which form a baldachin, the central group shows Christ intervening miraculously next to the saintly Doctor. There too, in a work for the monks' refectory, the picture shows a spectacular banquet.

187 Veronese. *The Marriage at Cana*. Detail. 1562–3. Oil on canvas. Musée du Louvre, Paris.
It has often been said, on the strength of Zanetti's remarks (1771) that the three musicians represent Titian, Veronese and Tintoretto. This is probably a guide's fantasy.

The composition for SS. Giovanni e Paolo combines grand structures forming a portico seen frontally with glimpses of sky beyond—a typical formula of Veronese ever since his great exemplars of 1563 and thereafter. Nothing could be more propitious to the play of light and shade or to the shimmer of the costumes. The central group is not without links with the picture by Titian (known from a copy), but it remains a puzzle to determine the exact theme of this work and why, alone among this large group of representations of banquet scenes for refectories, it was the object of an enquiry by the Inquisition, which followed soon after its completion.

188 Veronese. *The Feast in the House of Levi.* 1573. Oil on canvas. Galleria dell'Accademia, Venice.
'That which, above all, increased Paolo's fame were four large canvases of Banquets for the churches of the city.' (Ridolfi, *Le Maraviglie*, 1648.) This was probably the most important of them.

This picture is dated 20 April 1573 from the inscription on the top pillar of the staircase. Another inscription reads FECIT D. COVI. MAGNU. LEVI—LUCAE CAP V ('There was a great banquet at the house of Levi—Luke ch. 5'.) The Gospel reference is uncommon. All the banquet scenes include in their profane setting a Christian lesson, but here this does not appear and, moreover, the theme itself does not appear before Veronese. There is therefore reason to believe that the inscription was added as an afterthought; it is a response to the conclusion of the judgement, which required that the painting should be duly 'corrected'. But this injunction can only be understood if the composition represented a *Last Supper* which, for reasons to be given later, had aroused the anxieties of the Council. Ridolfi said nothing about Veronese's difficulties with the justiciars of religion. Fortified by his experience of ten years, during which he had treated these scenes from the Gospels in a Palladian setting, Paolo believed that he could adapt this brilliant formula to the *Last Supper* itself. At the convent of the Dominicans, traditionally linked with the Inquisition, there were clearly second thoughts, and the affair gave rise to a debate which, however, does not appear to have had much publicity. Very fortunately, the records of the enquiry by the Holy Office have survived. A critical edition of them has been made, and it is now possible to work on this text, which opens exceptional perspectives on the problems of the Counter-Reformation.

18 July 1573: Memorandum on the appearance of Paolo Veronese before the Inquisition: Doc. 3

Called before the Holy Office, in front of the sacred tribunal Paulus Caliarius Veronensis, living in the parish of S. Samuele, asked about his name and Christian name, and replied as follows.
  Asked about his profession:
  A. 'I paint and make figures.'
  Q. 'Do you know why you have been summoned here?'
  A. 'No.'
  Q. 'Can you imagine what the reasons might be?'
  A. 'I can well imagine them.'

189 Veronese. *The Feast in the House of Levi.* Detail. 1573. Oil on canvas. Galleria dell'Accademia, Venice.
'What is the meaning of these men-at-arms dressed in the German fashion, holding a halbard?' (Enquiry by the Holy Office, 18 July 1573.)

Q. 'Tell us what you think they are.'

A. 'I think it is on account of what has been said to me by the Reverend Fathers, or, rather, by the Prior of the monastery of SS. Giovanni e Paolo (whose name I do not know), who told me that he had been here and that Your Illustrious Lordships had told him to have a figure of the Magdalen substituted for a dog in the picture, and I said to him that I would do anything willingly that was for my own honour and that of the picture, but that I could not imagine how the figure of the Magdalen could be well contrived, for a number of reasons which I will state if given the opportunity.'

Q. 'What is the picture which you have just spoken about ?'

A. 'It is a picture representing the Last Supper of Jesus Christ with His Apostles in the house of Simon.'

Q. 'Where is this picture ?'

A. 'In the refectory of SS. Giovanni e Paolo.'

Q. 'Is it a fresco, on wood or on canvas ?'

A. 'It is on canvas.'

Q. 'How many feet high is it ?'

A. 'It might be 17 feet.'

Q. 'And in width ?'

A. 'About 39.'

Q. 'In this Last Supper of Our Lord did you paint attendant figures?'

A. 'Yes.'

Q. 'How many did you represent, and what is the office of each ?'

A. 'First of all the inn-keeper, Simon, and then below him a servant whom I supposed to have come out of interest and to see how the table was being prepared. There are many other figures that I cannot now recall at all, since I painted that picture a long time ago.'

Q. 'Have you painted other *Suppers* than that one ?'

A. 'Yes.'

Q. 'How many have you painted, and where are they ?'

A. 'I made one for Verona, for the reverend monks of S. Lazzaro: it is in their refectory. Another is in the refectory of the reverend fathers, of S. Giorgio here in Venice.'

Q. 'But that is not a *Supper*, and it is not called the *Last Supper* of Our Lord.'

A. 'I have made another one in the refectory of S. Sebastiano in Venice, another in Padua for the fathers of the Maddalena. I cannot remember having painted any others.'

Q. 'In the *Supper* which you painted for SS. Giovanni e Paolo what is the significance of the figure whose nose is bleeding ?'

A. 'It is a servant whose nose has been made to bleed by some accident or other.'

Q. 'What is the significance of those armed men and those dressed in the German fashion, holding halberds ?'

A. 'Here I have to say a few words.'

Q. 'Say on.'

A. 'We painters, like poets and fools claim licence, and I represented these halberdiers, one drinking and one eating at the bottom of a staircase, standing by in case they are wanted, because it seemed to me reasonable and possible that the master of the house, who, so I have been told, was rich and grand, would have servants of that kind.'

Q. 'And the man dressed as a buffoon, with a parrot on his wrist ? Why did you represent him in the picture ?'

A. 'He is there as an ornament, as is usual.'

Q. 'Who are those at the table of Our Lord ?'

191 Veronese. Study for a *Feast in the House of Simon*. About 1587. Pen and wash. Staatliche Kunstsammlungen, Schloss Wilhelmshöhe, Kassel.
Study for a *Feast in the House of Simon*, where the perspective effect stresses the most telling element of the composition, which places the kneeling sinner in the centre.

A. 'The twelve Apostles.'

Q. 'What is St. Peter doing, who is the first ?'

A. 'He is carving the lamb, to pass it down the table.'

Q. 'What is the one next to him doing ?'

A. 'He holds a plate to receive whatever St. Peter will give him.'

Q. 'Tell us what the third man is doing.'

A. 'He is picking his teeth with a little fork.'

Q. 'Who do you think were really there at the Last Supper ?'

A. 'I believe that there were only Christ and His Apostles, but, since there remains some space in a picture I fill it with figures of my invention.'

Q. 'Did someone commission you to paint Germans, buffoons and similar things in this picture ?'

A. 'No. I was commissioned to ornament it as I thought fit; in any case, it is large and can contain a lot of figures.'

Q. 'Are the ornaments which you, as a painter, are accustomed to introduce into pictures not appropriate and relevant to the subject, or are they just left to your imagination without reason and discretion ?'

A. 'I make pictures with all the considerations that seem to me appropriate and as far as my intellect allows.'

Q. 'Does it seem to you appropriate, in the Last Supper of Our Lord, to represent buffoons, drunken Germans, dwarfs and other scurrilities?'

A. 'No.'

Q. 'Then why did you do so?'

A. 'I supposed that all these people were outside the place where the actual Supper took place.'

Q. 'Do you not know that in Germany and other places infected with heresy they are accustomed, with paintings full of scurrilities, to vilify and ridicule the things of Holy Church, so as to teach false doctrine to ignorant or stupid people?'

A. 'Yes, it is bad; but I must repeat what I have already said, that I have a duty to follow the example of my predecessors.'

Q. 'What have your predecessors done? Similar things?'

A. 'Michelangelo in Rome, in the Papal Chapel, painted Our Lord, his Mother, St. John, St. Peter and the Celestial Court and represented them all nude, including the Virgin Mary and in various attitudes that do not conform to reverence.'

Q. 'Do you not know that in representing the Last Judgement one would hardly

192 After Titian. *The Last Supper. C.* 1560 Titian painted a *Last Supper* for Philip II of Spain. The original (in the Escorial) has been cut down, but this copy in the Brera, Milan, may preserve the original design.

193 H. Lautensack. *Papist Supper*. Lutheran caricature. 1556. Engraving.
Example of the 'paintings [= prints] full of stupidities [so as] to vilify and turn to ridicule the things of Holy Church...', coming from Lutheran countries.

expect clothing and it would not be right to do so; and in these figures there is nothing that is not of the Spirit—no buffoons, no dogs, no weapons, no other foolishness? Taking this and other things into account do you think you did well to paint your picture in that way and would you defend it as good and decent?'

A. 'Illustrious Lords, I do not wish to defend it: but I did think I had done it well. I did not take so many things into consideration. I was far from imagining such a great disorder, especially as I had placed these buffoons outside the place where Our Saviour is.'

These things having been said, the judges pronounced that the said Paolo should be held responsible to correct and amend his picture within the space of three months from the date of the reprimand, according to the judgement and decision of the sacred tribunal and all to be at the expense of the said Paolo. *Et ita decreverunt omni melius modo.*

The tone of this extraordinary interview may seem strangely objective and relaxed. Paolo, who had just painted, or was about to paint, the official commemorations of Lepanto, could not be treated as an ordinary man. The Inquisitor displays great circumspection, his curiosity is shown by questions to which the answers appear casual, sometimes even amusing. But no one could say that this was a kind of comedy. For the interrogation is carefully directed: all the questions bring to light point by point the immense part played by the free invention and fantasy of the painter in these enormous compositions where obviously it was unavoidable. To add to this, Veronese insists several times that there exists an implicit convention which completely justifies him. This is the distinction between the central theme and the marginal episodes ('outside the place where the Saviour is') where one may embroider more freely. But the really important moment is when Paolo invokes an ancient principle in art, restated in every generation from the time of Horace's maxim *quidlibet audendi potestas*. Veronese propounds this law, which has nothing original

194 Veronese. *Martyrdom of St. George.* 1566. Oil on canvas. Church of S. Giorgio in Braida, Verona.
'...the one who went the furthest is M. Polo Caliari in the altarpiece of St. George...' (Cristoforo Sorte, *Osservazioni nella Pittura*, 1580.)

or provocative about it: 'we painters, we take the same licence as is taken by poets and fools.' In adding 'fools' he perhaps overstates his case, but behind the words *i poeti e i matti* there is the doctrine of the privileges claimed by inspiration, which were certainly not displeasing to Venetians. An old debate is being renewed here, but in front of the tribunal did he really run any risk? What were they aiming at?

The interview becomes really serious when, at the end, the allusion to satirical pictures—or rather to prints—emanating from the Reformers confirms that in Venice they were well aware of the anti-papal arguments and the virulent satires which had been incessant over the last half century. Could Paolo's fantasies give the impression of a buffoonery calculated to ridicule the image of the Saviour? They might well appear in this light to ill-conditioned minds, and some foreign visitor may even have publicly remarked on it. The time was now past when one could accumulate haphazardly in religious cycles a mass of accessories or anecdotal figures. This was clearly the intention of the interrogator.

195 Veronese. *Madonna and Angels.* About 1575. Gouache. Cabinet des Dessins, Musée du Louvre, Paris.
'I would paint the baby in the cradle, surrounded by angels... some of them accompanying with their singing the Child's sleep...' (Statement by Veronese, from Ridolfi, *Le Maraviglie*, 1648.)

Paolo's defence is very revealing: he appeals to Michelangelo, and deliberately invokes the argument, already a quarter-century old, but ever ready to be revived, of the painter's *licentia* as regards iconography. The discussion becomes sharper and the judge quite correctly amends Paolo's claims. He is then forced to recognize that with such a luxurious and unrestrained composition he has somewhat lost sight of *convenienza*, propriety. He does not dare to add that in representing the *Last Supper* as a banquet in a princely house—which in itself is not improper—he intended a celebration of its grandeur. He admitted that this led to a multiplication of gratuitous and even trifling details.

By requiring him to explain himself the judge never showed any intention of bullying him. Venice never allowed the Inquisition to act in its territories. The archbishop G. B. Dei presided over the tribunal; a Roman by origin, he was the natural exponent of the hard line. But the second president was the patriarch F. Trevisani, a notorious supporter of Venetian privileges in matters of ecclesiastical jurisdiction. It was out of the question to risk a conflict of jurisdiction in this matter. As a result of a complaint or of a direct criticism which we now know nothing about, an opportunity was provided for a reminder that it was not possible indefinitely to ignore the resolutions of the Council of Trent. The tendency, now general, for Catholic authorities to give a new, more carefully considered, character to religious art was bound also to bear upon Venetian art. Behind the Inquisitor's questions can be heard the disciplined and commanding thought of Cardinal G. Paleotti, the most influential theologian of art of the sixteenth century. The critical question, asked quite bluntly, 'Did anyone command you to paint those four Germans and the jesters and all the other things?' came towards the end. What is being sought is precisely whether there was an advisor who might have led the painter, either unwittingly or deliberately, to include suspect ideas. Suspect of what? Of heresy, certainly, and more precisely still a 'Lutheran' mocking of the Eucharist. Hence the closer, more aggressive questions: 'Why those *Todeschi*?' Was the intention to mix in with the crowd of the faithful, Lutherans full of mockery for the solemnity of the rite in which they no longer believed? And, concerning the consecration of bread and wine, is it not possible to see behind the array of victuals, and worse even, in the servant with the nose-bleed, an odious mockery of the Sacred Species, the bread and wine which Christ is about to transmute into flesh and blood?

In the *Marriage at Cana* the servants distribute bread and pour wine, and prefiguration of the communion has always been understood. In this *Last Supper* profane exuberance drowns this aspect of the situation. Hence the suspicion that it was desired to minimize it, to blot it out.

The painter's defence was that he could have sinned by imprudence. He had treated the sacred theme with a certain sense of decorum which was agreeable to his religious commissioners. After all, he had to have a spacious composition since the picture, which was going to be placed in a huge refectory, required a large number of figures. It was truly the most extravagantly grandiose work ever, but the essential was there, in conformity with the tradition and the practice of Veronese, to respect all the elements of the iconographical definition of the *Last Supper*. A penetrating analysis, figure by figure, eventually discerns in all the Apostles, as in the Leonardo, a different pose which can be interpreted as a reaction to Christ's words, 'One of you shall betray me.' The sombre Judas, embarrassed, turns away; St. John on Christ's left is struck with consternation and extends his open hand as if to interrogate Christ, who turns towards him.

This is where, in fact, the detailing of the scene is unclear; what exactly is Christ's gesture? No one knows. Peter on his right appears more concerned to help himself to lamb than to think, unless a suddenly interrupted gesture is imagined, but his face is not that of a man shaken with shock. And so on. The impression is that the painter has thought up all the necessary diversity in poses according to Christ's words and actions, but that he has only too thoroughly confounded them with the normal variety of gestures and movements at a banquet. It was not the references to the traditional signs of the sacred composition which were lacking; it was the unity of purpose, the co-ordination which should have dominated the spectacle and guided the spectator. Without the evidence of this unity the religious value vanishes. The superb language brought to such perfection by Leonardo and preserved in Titian's work, cannot survive this gross amplification; the parade of magnificence destroys it. The Inquisitor's questions turn around this essential point without actually expressing it, but the point has become a delicate one since the Council had broached the problem of the legitimacy of images for the first time in eight centuries. It is therefore an error to believe that the interrogation was just a comedy to satisfy a rather unsympathetic Roman injunction, just as it would be wrong to believe that Veronese was an incurably casual and light-minded artist, the thoughtlessly impious man which Ruskin believed him to be.

The nudes in Michelangelo's *Last Judgement* had just been covered over on the Pope's orders. The most precise kind of practical recommendations abounded about 1570.

Doc. 4   1570: J. Molanus, *On Sacred Paintings and Images*:

> Scenes from profane history are not to be painted in churches, a pagan custom that
> is to be repudiated by Christians, not imitated.

In its last session of 1563 (XXV, tit. 2) the Council of Trent maintained solemnly, against
Lutheran and above all Calvinist criticisms, the legitimacy of images on the altar, as it had
been defined by the Second Synod of Nicaea. Nevertheless, it was recommended that a
careful watch should be kept on their value as incitements to piety and theological
instruction so as to forbid any casualness and any irresponsible fantasy, of which, over the
centuries, artists had only too often shown themselves capable, and this particularly in
modern times. It was the duty of ecclesiastical authorities to remind them of the rules of
convenienza and decorum.

A little before the affair of the Holy Office, on 28 February 1573, the Cavaliere Vitali
of Verona wrote to a learned man, Cristoforo Sorte, inviting him to write an account of
his observations on colours in painting. The work includes a series of practical suggestions
on the choice of colours appropriate to particular types, allegories such as those of the
Seasons, and so on. His hero is his compatriot Veronese, for reasons of local fame,
precisely because he is a master of the appropriate use of colour. In compositions there are
delicate instances, such as the representation of the Holy Spirit, and without any doubt it
was then necessary to submit oneself to the advice of the authorities of the Holy Catholic
Church.

Doc. 5   1580: Cristoforo Sorte's judgement on Veronese:

> Among all the many paintings I remember having seen, the one that stood out most

196, 197   Veronese. *Dialectic, or Industry.*
1575–7. Oil on canvas. Palazzo Ducale,
Venice.
The emblem of the spider's web is suitable
for either of the allegories, since it is a
model of patient activity. Here it is used to
extol the capacity for initiative and
subtlety characteristic of the city.

was M. Paolo Caliari's altarpiece of S. Giorgio here in Verona, which Your Excellency and I saw together. For to the figures in the clouds he has marvellously given their *decorum*, both in painting them in tender colours and in illuminating them divinely with supernatural light, and also in having understood the perspective of distance, both in distant figures and in those which are represented near, as it were naturally, well understood and executed with perfect rightness.

This appreciation would remain that of the classic age. The orthodoxy of Veronese was never questioned. The only thing that mattered was his organization of scenes, a mastery the more admired in that his subjects required more and more often a large number of persons in complex relationships. There is no question of any reproaches to the artist. Must it be understood that the episode of the Inquisition was useless ? The chronicles of the period are silent about this. But one bit of information which it would appear has not up to now received sufficient notice, suggests that Veronese should be accorded a certain importance.

Veronese's iconographical illustrations (from Ridolfi, 1648):   Doc. 6

In addition to the paintings these gentlemen [the Muselli brothers] also possess some drawings on tinted paper, heightened with white. It would be tedious to record all the inventions, but we will mention only certain spirited ideas, which he noted with his own hand on the reverse of some of them, sending them to those who had asked for them, and we list them in the actual order [...] Fourth painting: There is an infinite number of forms and poses for pictures that have been made of the Virgin, who was almost always represented by Dürer in the same way, with the Child on her arm, He being always nude. The Greeks [Byzantines] all made Him wrapped in draperies, since they did not have experience in representing bodies. Nevertheless, every figure of the Child may be represented nude or clothed. Michelangelo made the Child asleep, with His Mother reading a book; but I have never seen her by the cot, dressing the Saviour. I would make the Child in the cradle, with angels around, holding panniers of fruit, with flowers in their hands, or playing various instruments, some singing to the sleeping Child, with the Virgin watching over Him, accompanied by St. Anne [...]

Sixth painting: If I had the time I would represent a sumptuous table beneath a splendid loggia, with the Virgin, the Saviour, and Joseph; and I would make them served by the most magnificent troop of Angels imaginable, who would present to them on plates of gold and silver an offering of foods and an abundance of superb fruits. Others would be engaged in providing precious victuals on crystal plates or in gilded cups, to show the services offered by the Blessed to their God; as will be explained more fully at the end of this volume, for the information of painters and for the delight of amateurs; and of this invention I have seen a remarkable drawing.

The old historian provided this information with an interesting precision, and he takes the trouble to stress that he had seen the principal examples of this 'new' sacred iconography defined by Veronese. It would be fascinating to be able to affirm that this little work came to the painter's mind after the trial of 1573. It is permissible to suppose so, while regretting that the whole is not completely known to us, and that the *Libro* mentioned has not yet turned up. The drawings which survive, having gone through the hands of Mariette, are now in the Louvre, and illumine perfectly the spirit of those efforts to create pious compositions which were carefully thought out and presented. The double preoccupation with orthodoxy and with the ennoblement of the subject shown here was in perfect agreement with the Counter-Reformation. The session of June 1573 had therefore been to some extent profitable for Paolo. It encouraged him to revise his formulas and to abandon a certain casualness in the subsidiary motifs which only played a distant part in the general orchestration of the theme. But the *magnificentia* is not abandoned for all that. Paolo again returned to his old habits, although he took care to justify his treatment of the narrative by making a group of angels act the roles of the servants and musicians around the *Virgin of the Nativity*. Even more, the dream of a 'celestial banquet' keeps to the arrangement of the 'noble loggia', the luxurious table appointments and the elegant dishes for the benefit of the Holy Family.

Must it be accepted that Paolo, cut to the quick, afterwards found this perfect defence for his sumptuous art? The painter in all sincerity strove to retain the qualities proper to his *maniera*, and the profane pleasures of his art, as if he were thus trying to reinsure himself against an uncertain future. It seems more reasonable to believe that Paolo was deeply aware of the new movement in religious art. The debate with the Inquisition was intended as a warning to artists to be careful. It came from Rome, and thus was not given great weight in Venice. Veronese did not tremble for his art. But at least the Council made its weight felt; a new style of 'reasoned compositions' was to gain favour. For the first time iconography became officially a problem for painters. And it was in this way that Veronese found it useful to compose a repertory all his own.

Is it far-fetched to think that in his *Dialettica* in the Doges' Palace two years later Veronese set out to demonstrate this capacity for initiative, subtlety and sometimes craftiness for which his city was celebrated?

Epilogue

The old Tuscan historian, who did virtually all the research on which his often vitally important body of information was based, triumphantly entitled his book in 1550:...*from Cimabue to our own times*. He sought to record growth and progress through an orderly sequence of artists. There is nothing like the fund of documentary sources accumulated by Vasari, and his work remains indispensable, though his statements should always be treated with caution. But the doctrine of the progress of art towards perfection, towards a model style, an absolute achievement, which he did so much to propound, must be totally distrusted. Despite the continuous reassessment of all those aspects of this history which have been brushed aside—the unrecognized artist, the forgotten families—the text-book treatment which delimits the classic summit by an energetic rise and an inevitable decline is far from having been eradicated from men's minds. One of the aims of this book has been to eliminate it. An exposition in the form of a chronicle recreates 'situations' in which no finalistic interpretation can subordinate one element to another. Every element is valid in its own right.

The decision to concentrate on the sources has led to a down-to-earth and fragmented discussion. This experience seems to answer to an actual need, as is borne out by a remark by a British colleague: 'We have all read history books where the notes at the bottom of the page were infinitely more amusing than the text; why then not have a book composed of footnotes?' (*T.L.S.*, 5 August 1983, p. 826). This challenge has been taken up here. But, nevertheless, these ten significant 'situations' remain an arbitrary selection. If a summary chronological grid were established for painting alone to cover the three centuries, with perhaps two stages in 1400 and 1500, the same treatment is perfectly conceivable for every point in the series. If this experience is valid, it opens up an entirely new system, and perhaps even creates a new kind of history of art. This overturns the optimistic statement made in the introduction: the history of Italian painting, if it is subjected to these critical exigencies, appears less and less easy to write.

The temperature becomes cooler and the horizon changes once there is no further recourse to the customary framework: mediaeval and Gothic, pre-Renaissance, classic Renaissance, Mannerism and so on. In some instances, the terms may be evoked by the evidence or the documents themselves; but the customary conceptual apparatus neither appears nor dominates. Once the convenience of taking an overall view is abandoned, the concrete facts are spread out beneath one's gaze with all their pleasant and unpleasant surprises: the slowness of developments, the hazards besetting careers, the importance of established forms and, in the conflict of competition, the sudden bursts of inventiveness, followed by opposition and criticism. But in concentrating one's attention exclusively on the actual 'moment' of artistic production in the place where it occurred and at the time when it came about, one deprives oneself of two important facilities, which the history of the arts—as also the history of culture generally—have used and abused for a long time; reference to the state of society, and the imposition of style cease to be simple explanatory principles. These two notions are strongly entrenched in the more popular forms of art history, where they have achieved the status of received opinions. The interest of a limited study is to return them to a neutral role, to the usefulness of a mnemonic process. All works of art are bound to the society in which they were created, and imply a stylistic truth, but here an effort has been made to treat these two kinds of evidence as the supports for an analysis designed to isolate all the possible factors, the synthesis resolving itself into a general relationship of all its elements.

Each one of the detailed analyses which have been presented here have their starting-point in ascertainable facts, so as to re-establish the activity of the artists in their proper milieu. In an affair like the cycle in the Sistine Chapel, the politics of religion and ordinary political concerns set in train an enterprise which rather presupposes a 'modernist' pope. Superficially, everything seems easy to explain. But once one enters into the actual work, new elements appear, of which one would have had no idea at all without the evidence provided by the work itself, and the light thrown upon it by learned discoveries, in particular the unexpected—and on the whole fairly artificial—theological framework of the cycle. These given facts suggest that the character of the pontificate which presided over its creation should be interpreted more subtly. The picture of the period and the ambience in Rome becomes more complex, the more it is subjected to a stricter analysis. One has to take into consideration forces and preoccupations of which history was either not aware or had misunderstood.

One should therefore avoid saying that art is the *product* of society since this activity operating within a given group helps to mould it and to form it—and when it is a question of the Trecento and the Quattrocento this is no small matter. Knowledge acquired by looking at architecture and painting, etc., is far deeper and more meaningful than any other kind. This knowledge is more or less explicit in any idea which one forms of that society, and it therefore cannot properly be used to explain that which, in fact, serves to throw light upon it. The conjuction of communal zeal, the Marian cult, and the *Maestà*, form something like a common force in which many aspects can be observed. But the need was not extinguished by the multiplication of grandiose altarpieces. Quite the contrary. New examples of the *Maestà* appear. Art engenders art, and the city, which sets great store by it, adjusts its conduct and its customs as a result.

The same reasoning seems true of all the episodes. The organization of the cities keeps power in princely or bourgeois hands, and the mass of the people observe them, submit to them, accompany them while retaining far more of the attentions of their rulers than one would believe. Political authority, basically rather unstable, has to be unremitting in its efforts to improve its image; in some ways this is a duty incumbent upon it. Also it must know how to rise to the occasion; the attitude of the Medici at the time of the Council of Florence was one of extreme prudence. That of Federico Gonzaga twenty years later was very different; who was he trying to impress when he accepted Mantegna's astonishing projects? A very delicate analysis becomes essential. There will never be too much information to account for the permutations of motivation. Why did so many abbots, bishops, princes, chase so eagerly after Perugino? The role of the 'public image' in the static and dynamic aspects of society has to be sought in new ways. It is no longer sufficient to say with the naïve brand of sociology that this is all propaganda. There is present a phenomenon of acceleration or, perhaps better, of inflation, which may be considered as a characteristic of the central moment of the Renaissance. The prestige attached to artistic luxury is a trap. Rulers plunge into it because they are fascinated and in a sense constrained by it. Then yet another competing ruler follows suit. The great beneficiary is, finally, the class of artists which has meanwhile organized itself, with its ambition and even sometimes with arrogance. The multiplicity of biblical scenes which Veronese portrayed as sumptuous banquets marks, in Venice, the summit of pictorial 'inflation'; the attitude of the painter displays the supreme point of self-assurance. No matter what kind of censure he incurred, he knew that he brought to his city what it needed.

Whether it is Sta. Maria del Fiore or the Mantuan lakes, compositions gain that much more by being brought closer to their site of origin in that this symbolically represented townscape or landscape appears as the bearer of the style, the power of which is found in the works themselves. Thus all seems to form a system. But a new problem keeps arising within the record. The beautiful model of a highly 'compressed' townscape, repeated five times in Duccio's *Temptation*, is an instance of a series of variations on an urban stereotype, the importance of which has been proved by recent studies. The marvellous view of the Venetian lagoon at sunset in the altarpiece in Ancona (*Madonna and Child Appearing to SS. Francis, Aloysius and a Donor*) offers a completely 'Titianized' landscape of a kind which continued to nourish the painter's imagination. This type of harmony is possible all through the history of Italian art only because of the powerful impact of representation on the collective conscience and the important place it occupied in the collective imagination. The tighter the links are drawn between the paintings and the social realities of the time, the more they tell us about the mixture of fixity and mobility which characterize them. Initiative and constraint are constant yoke-fellows, with periods of slackening which contrast with moments of excitement or of conflict, responding to changes in personnel, power, or government. Ultimately, it is impossible to enclose art within the definition of a past age—though one may well wonder why this 'product' can still interest people today—nor can all these manifestations be packaged up in the single envelope of autonomous style and its appropriate dialectic, only then to be surprised that they respond so closely to the general vicissitudes of history.

One of the phenomena which is revealed in an exceptional manner by the abundance of documentation is the attention paid to the role of artists in the cities and, in parallel, the authority, even the overweening conceit of some masters. Giotto's fame, prolonged during the whole of the Trecento, and the new departures to which it gave rise, are all the more typical in that here literature intervened forcefully. The ambitious artist then had to achieve a similar fame by means of a *maniera*, a style, which would be immediately recognizable. As the movement intensified, great figures like Leonardo and Michelangelo, or simply strikingly successful ones like Perugino, became possible. For a long time this development was not to have any equivalent in the West. It supplied a guide-line, but since personalities had now entered the lists, it requires an even closer examination of the manner in which are combined the fortuitous and the inevitable or, as has been said in a different context, accident and necessity.

These great reputations only create in legend the figure of the omniscient artist, superior to all circumstances and all constraints. The episode of Leonardo and Michelangelo suggests that a degree of caution is necessary. One of the frequent and naïve errors of historians during the last century, and often even now of learned scholars, was to credit artists with the total responsibility for the works they created. There is a tendency to speak of the 'Mariology' of Duccio, of Piero's historical learning, of Perugino's hagiography… But these artists all treated themes which they never had to invent, based on schemes of composition which they did not have to devise, and linked to a programme which they themselves never defined. Only a thorough and delicate process of thought can cast light on the relationship between what was specified with the commission and what the artist made of it.

The matter is made more complicated by the fact that the greatest are precisely those whose conduct falls outside the customary; they dare to overthrow *at the same time* the formal properties and iconographic convention, thus leaving in their wake a degree of uneasiness. Two striking examples have been discussed: Mantegna and his cycle of the *Triumph*, and Michelangelo with his novel arrangement of the *Last Judgement*. It now occasions no surprise that the first had the reputation of being an archaeologist, and the second that of being a theologian. The problem, which is a far from simple one, becomes that of grasping the relationship which exists between this 'knowledge' which is being constituted, and the exigencies of their art which develop in parallel.

These important new developments are illuminating through their exceptional character. Usually everything happened on a less exalted plane, defined by the current type of works: altarpieces, political and moral allegories, etc. Not only does the kind of picture control the programme and, to a certain degree, the 'manner', but the destination of the work—church or palace, religious or civic building—brings to the enterprise specifications which it is essential to know about. The biblical and Gospel 'cycle' destined for the Sistine Chapel had to include, given its pontifical and Roman character, a certain number of allusions to Antiquity and to the personalities in the Curia. Nothing of the sort is to be found in the *Last Judgement*. Mantegna's archaeological and military 'cycle' does not appear to include a single portrait; it is projected in a vision of pure history, just as the *da sotto in sù* perspective excludes the ground on which the spectator stands. But in the Gonzaga thank-offering altarpiece everything is made closer to actuality. The painter's hard style is given full rein in both cases, but with a calm inflection and a kind of pictorial pietism.

The minutiae of the documents show very clearly the importance attached to the *craft*. The texts of contracts, the comments of contemporaries, are continual reminders of this by the way technical considerations are included in the contract: how much gold was to be used, or the criticism of the meretricious glitter in the Sistine Chapel, or the reproaches made to Perugino for having neglected to paint in oils, etc. In the Sienese episode, the artistic unity is the altarpiece, now transformed into an assemblage of panels to serve a liturgical function. The painter has to fit in with the carpenter, who sometimes takes precedence over him; the creator of the framework of an altarpiece is as much praised as Perugino himself. It is one of the grave weaknesses of the traditional history of styles that the succession of personal styles is described without taking into account these set conditions, which are so vividly present in the chronicles. Perhaps in this way it is possible to see more clearly exactly what was the painter's contribution. This swung powerfully between two poles; one was concerned with craft, with fidelity to the pattern, with the stereotype; the other was aesthetic, the display of the painter's individual style. The latter was particularly important in the choice of the accessories, the secondary figures, or in the *parerga* of which ancient writers spoke and which in fact allowed a lot of latitude. The Sistine Chapel cycle is a good example of the freedom allowed to the painters in a narrative cycle; Veronese extended the principle to a sacred scene, and his panoramic work, in which the theme was submerged in the *parerga*, met with the well-known objections. Discovering why this evolution was possible is yet another problem.

The interest of the 'sources' is thus to force one to consider in a new way works which may well be famous, and even familiar. One is constantly forced to work within the gaps, sometimes discouraging, which exist between the documents. But it is more stimulating than stultifying to recognize what one does not know. Why did Dante give so much weight to Giotto's *grido* ? Did Duccio really go to Paris ? Did Michelangelo and Leonardo ever speak to each other in the Palazzo Vecchio ? Why the scandalous contempt for Lotto among Titian and his friends ? These unanswered questions arouse curiosity.

Paintings, around which is arrayed the tightly drawn net of increasingly strict and ingenious historical criticism, are not materials like any others. Their power to supply information on the mental and social structures of the past is considerable, because they affect us differently from the documents which concern them. These indicate in particular, where historical analysis would lead one to forget, the emotional impact of these works; all the accounts record a general public overwhelmed with admiration, fascinated intellectuals, clerics and laymen alike dazzled by them. One obviously allows for the sometimes ridiculous exaggerations of praise, and even for the mutability of tastes. But no criticism should ever try to cancel out the evidence of the emotive resources contained within these representations. Here is to be found the record of the moving nuances, of poetic aspirations, of all the richness of feeling enclosed in patiently elaborated forms. In short, an authentic record which one cannot always identify.

A doctor once said that if the subjective history of every individual coincided with his exterior history, if what he told himself coincided with what one knew about him, psychotherapy would be useless. If what can be communicated openly or covertly by works which interest one could be grasped and easily aligned with the known facts of chronology and historical science, a specific discipline would not be necessary. But the two histories never merge, and that which can revive the warmth of the living past is above rubies. It is just that it concerns pictures composed in precise circumstances for which there are now no equivalents. It is not unlike those convex mirrors which were then becoming more common; they have a refractory curvature so that it is necessary to interpret the image. Without these instruments, the space would appear lifeless and the dwelling shadowy. The Renaissance is now far away, but it would be pointless for the modern world to deprive itself of these inhabited mirrors.

Texts and Documents

Texts and Documents—Introduction

On the historiography of Italian art:
J. von SCHLOSSER, *Die Kunstliteratur*, Vienna, 1924; Italian edition (revised) as J. SCHLOSSER-MAGNINO, *La letteratura artistica*, Florence, 1964, reprinted 1977.

Vasari:
The edition by G. Milanesi in 9 volumes, Florence, 1878–85, reprinted 1906 and 1973–7, remains fundamental. There is an almost complete English translation by G. du C. de Vere in 10 volumes, without annotation, London, 1912–15. It has been reprinted. A major new Italian edition, ed. by P. Barocchi and R. Bettarini, Florence, 1966– (in progress), has reached 7 volumes and contains the text of both the 1550 and 1568 editions.

On Italian scholarship:
G. PREVITALI, *La fortuna dei primitivi, dal Vasari ai neoclassici*, Turin, 1961.

On the culture of the age:
Several summaries in the Essays in Honour of E. Garin, *Il Rinascimento. Interpretazioni e problemi*, Bari, 1979.

On the organization of workshops and the art market:
H. LERNER-LEHMKUHL, *Zur Struktur und Geschichte des florentinischen Kunstmarktes im 15. Jahrhundert*, Wattenscheid, 1936;
M. WACKERNAGEL, *Der Lebensraum des Künstlers in der florentinischen Renaissance*, Leipzig, 1938. An English edition, *The World of the Florentine Renaissance Artist*, ed. and trans. by A. Luchs, was published by Princeton University Press in 1981.
E. CAMESASCA, *Artisti in bottega*, Milan, 1966.

On the documents:
The fundamental work on contracts is now: H. GLASSER, *Artists' Contracts of the Early Renaissance* (a dissertation of 1965), New York, 1977.
For the criticism of archival documents, see the studies by U. PROCACCI, references to which are given in his article 'Le *catasto* florentin et les artistes', *Revue de l'Art*, no. 54, 1981; also 'Sources and Documents Series', ed. H. Janson: C. GILBERT, *Italian Art, 1400–1500*, New Jersey, 1980, and R. KLEIN and H. ZERNER, *Italian Art, 1500–1600*, New Jersey, 1966.

Various texts:
G. GAYE, *Carteggio inedito d'artisti dei secoli XIV, XV, XVI*, 3 vols., Florence, 1839–40, reprinted Turin, 1961.
P. BAROCCHI, *Trattati d'arte del Cinquecento. Fra Manierismo e Contro-Riforma*, 3 vols., Bari, 1960–2, and *Scritti d'arte del Cinquecento* (arranged by themes), 3 vols., Milan, 1970–7.

On the sociological aspects:
M. BAXANDALL, *Painting and Experience in Fifteenth Century Italy*, London, 1972.
P. BURKE, *Culture and Society in Renaissance Italy*, London, 1972.
D. S. CHAMBERS, *Patrons and Artists in the Italian Renaissance*, London, 1970 (127 documents of various kinds, of which 23 are contracts).

On sumptuary expenditure:
P. VEYNE, *Le Pain et le Cirque. Sociologie historique d'un pluralisme politique*, Paris, 1976.

J. BURCKHARDT, *Civilisation de la Renaissance en Italie*, French translation with notes and Introduction by R. Klein, 3 vols., Paris, 1966. The standard English translation is that by S. Middlemore, 1878 and numerous later editions.

On the artists' claims to independence:
A. CHASTEL, 'Le *dictum Horatii: "quidlibet audendi potestas"*' 1977, reprinted in *Fables, Formes, Figures*, no. 17, vol. I, Paris, 1978, pp. 363 ff.

On invention and the role of the painter:
The works of E. H. GOMBRICH, especially *Norm and Form: Studies in the Art of the Renaissance*, London, 1966; *The Heritage of Apelles*, London, 1976; and M. MEISS, *The Painter's Choice: Problems in the Interpretation of Renaissance Art*, New York, 1976; R. LONGHI, *Da Cimabue a Morandi* (an anthology selected by G. E. Contini), Milan, 1973.

Doc. 1

NERI DI BICCI, *Le Ricordanze*, fo. 44ᵛ:

Mercholedì a dì 13 di dicenbre 1458
Tavola da Mosc[i]ano tolsi a dipigniere e fare di legniame
Richordo a me Neri di Bicci dipintore chome el sopradetto dì ò tolto a fare fare di legniame e a dipigniere da G[i]ano di Simone da Mosc[i]ano chamarlingho della Chonpagnia di Santa Maria che · ssi rauna nella chiesa di Santa [*sic*] Andrea a Mosc[i]ano e da Checho d'Antonio maestro di murare e da Orlandino di Lionardo, tuti da Mosc[i]ano, la quale tavola ò fare a tute mia ispese di legniame e d'oro e d'azuro e d'ogni altro cholore e chosa cher per detta tavola bisogniassi, fatta e formata in quello propio modo e forma che quella feci a Bernardo Ghera[r]di e Ormanozo Detti in nella chiesa di Sa[n] Romeo di Firenze, chon un'Anunziata drentovi chome in quella e chosì fatta e ornata chome istà quella e quasi di quella misura e grandeza o incircha; piutosto dìsono e' sopradetti uomini volélla alquanto minore: e' sopradetti G[i]ano, Ant[oni]o e Orlandino mi debono dare per legniame, oro e cholori e maeistero per detta tavola f. ventiotto, c[i]oè f. 28 di sugello in questo modo, c[i]oè per tuto el presente mese di dicenbre 1458 f. 5 e per tuto genaio prosimo f. 9: per tuto f. 14 che fia la metà di f. 28; e[l] resto mi debono dare per tuto (nove) ottobre 1459 e chosì fatto d'achordo cho' sopradetti Giuliano, Franc[esch]o e Orlandino el sopradetto dì.

B. Santi (ed.), Pisa, 1976, p. 106.

Doc. 2

Contract of 14 January 1454:

Pro Nardo Angeli et Teodosio
Die XIIII dicti mensis (gennaio 1454) actum in appotecha abbatie residentia mey notary, presentibus Christoforo Viterbucy et Antonio et Angelo Franceschj testibus ad hoc vocatis et rogatis.
Cum hoc sit quod Petrus Benedicti Petri de Burgo habuerit certam quantitatem denariorum pro facienda et edificanda tabula Societatis Sancte Marie de Misericordia prout dixerunt apparere manibus Ser Mary et scriptum signatum manibus dicti Petri et Benedicti quod est penes Nardum Angeli de Pichis id circha Benedictus pater dicti Petri presens sit et convenit Nardo predicto et Teodosio domini Christofori de Pichis eorum nominibus et ceterorum suorum heredum in unum quo si dictus Petrus non rederet ad dictam terram Burgi ad faciendam dictam tabulam per totam quadragesimam proximam futuram predictus Benedictus teneretur reddere dictam quantitatem in dicto scripto contentam et ecc. et pro predictis omnibus observandis obligavit se suos heredes in bona presentia et futura.et ecc. renumptiantem et ecc. quarum precepi et ecc.

E. BATTISTI, *Piero della Francesca*, 2 vols., Milan, 1971, II, doc. XXXIV.

198   Duccio. *Maestà*. Detail of the predella panel: *The Temptation in the Temple*.
1311. Tempera on panel. Museo dell'
Opera Metropolitana, Siena.
Spatial composition, showing the interior
of the cathedral, exploiting the richness of
a double effect.

Doc. 1

G. VASARI, *Life of Giovanni Cimabue*, ed. Milanesi, I, p. 254:

Fece poi per la chiesa di Santa Maria Novella la tovola di Nostra Donna, che è posta in alto fra la
cappella de' Rucellai e quella de' Bardi da Vernio: la qual opera fu di maggior grandezza, che figura
che fusse stata fatta insin a quel tempo; ed alcuni Angeli che le sono intorno, mostrano, ancor
ch'egli avesse la maniera greca, che s'andò accostando in parte al lineamento e modo della
moderna: onde fu quest'opera di tanta maraviglia ne' popoli di quell'età, per non si essere veduto
insino allora meglio, che da casa di Cimabue fu con molta festa e con le trombe alla chiesa portata
con solennissima processione, ed egli perciò molto premiato ed onorato.

On the *Rucellai Madonna*:
P. TOESCA, *Il Trecento*, Turin, 1951, p. 512.
J. H. STUBBLEBINE, *Duccio di Buoninsegna and his School*, Princeton, 1980, I, pp. 21·ff.

Doc. 2

Contract for the *Madonna dei Laudesi* (Archivio di Stato, Florence):

Lapus quondam Ugolini populi sancte Marie Novelle et Guido magister quondam Spigliati populi sancti Laurentii rectores sotietatis sancte Marie Virginis ecclesie sancte Marie Novelle et Corsus magister quondam Bonagiunte et Dinus quondam Benivieni populi sancte Marie predicte operarii ut asseruerunt electi de voluntate sotietatis predicte ad infrascriptum opus fieri faciendum pro sotietate predicte rectorio et operario nomine pro sotietate predicte locaverunt ad pingendum de pulcerima pictura quandam tabulam magnam ordinatam fieri pro sotietate predicta ad honorem beate et gloriose Virginis Marie Duccio quondam Boninsengne pictori de Senis. Promictentes et convenientes eidem Duccio operario et rectorio nomine ut dictum est dare et solvere eidem et eius heredibus aut cui dederit et concesserit pro pretio et nomine pretii picture dicte tabule ab eo infrascripto modo pingende et fiende et in termino quo picta et completa fuerit libras centum quinquaginta florenorum parvarum. [...] Et versa vice dictus Duccius conducens dictam tabulam ad pingendum a predictis rectoribus et operariis locantibus ut dictum est promisit et convenit eisdem recipientibus pro se et sotietate predicta dictam tabulam pingere et ornare de figura beate Marie Virginis et eius omnipotentis Filii et aliarum figurarum ad voluntatem et placimentum dictorum locatorum et deaurare et omnia et singula facere que ad pulcritudinem dicte tabule spectabunt suis omnibus sumtibus et expensis. Hoc videlicet pacto et condictione habitis inter eos quod si dicta tabula non erit picta pulcra et laborata ad voluntatem et placibilitatem eorundem locatorum quod ad dictum pretium nec ad aliquam partem ei persolvendum nullatenus teneantur et ad nullam refectionem aliquarum expensarum ab eo in eadem tabula factarum set ad ipsum Duccius ipsa tabula remaneat. [...]

G. MILANESI, *Documenti per la storia dell'arte senese*, I, Siena, 1854, no. 16.
J. H. STUBBLEBINE, op. cit., app. no. 5, pp. 192 ff.

Doc. 3.

G. VASARI, *Life of Giovanni Cimabue*, ed. Milanesi, I, pp. 254–5:

Dicesi, ed in certi ricordi di vecchi pittori si legge, che mentre Cimabue la detta tavola dipigneva in certi orti appresso porta San Piero, passo il re Carlo il vecchio d'Angiò per Firenze; e che, fra le molte accoglienze fattegli dagli uomini di questa città, lo condussero a vedere la tavola di Cimabue; e che per non essere ancora stata veduta da nessuno, nel mostrarsi al re vi concorsero tutti gli uomini e tutte le donne di Firenze, con grandissima festa e con la maggiore calca del mondo. Laonde per l'allegrezza che n'ebbero i vicini, chiamarono quel luogo Borgo Allegri; il quale, col tempo messo fra le mura della città, ha poi sempre ritenuto il medesimo nome.

On Duccio's career:
E. CARLI, *Duccio*, Milan, 1952.
E. CARLI, *Dipinti senesi della Maremma e del contado*, Milan, 1955.
See also C. VOLPE, 'Preistoria di Duccio', in *Paragone*, no. 49, 1954.

On Duccio and Florence:
R. LONGHI, 'Giudizio sul Duecento', in *Proporzioni*, II, 1948, pp. 5 ff. (on the *Rucellai Madonna*), reprinted in *Opere complete*, vol. VII, Florence, 1974, pp. 32 ff.

Doc. 4

Fine levied on 5 June, 1294 (Biccherna registers):

Item xiii solidos iiij denarios die dicta a Duccio pictore pro una condempnatione facta de eo in x solidos et pro tertio pluri quia non juravit ad capitaneum populi tempore domine Baronis fo li.

J. H. STUBBLEBINE, op. cit., app. no. 19.

On Duccio's condemnations:
J. H. STUBBLEBINE, op. cit., app. nos 3, 4, 10, 11, 30, 31, 34, 35, 36.

On Duccio in Paris:
K. MICHAELSSON, 'Le livre de la taille de Paris, l'an 1296', in *Arsskrift, Acta Universitatis Gotheburgensis*, LXIV, 1958, p. 269; and '...l'an 1297', ibid., LXVII, 1961, p. 421. See also J. H. STUBBLEBINE, op. cit., app. nos 27, 28.

Doc. 5

Contract for Duccio's *Maestà* (Florence, Archivio Diplomatico):

Anno domini *mccviij* indictione *vij* die *viiij* mensis octubris. Appareat omnibus evidenter quod dominus Jacobus quondam domini Giliberti de Mariscottis de Senis operarius operis sancte Marie civitatis Senarum nomine et vice dicti operis et pro ipso opere ex una parte et Duccius pictor olim Boninsegne civis senensis ex altera parte cum ipse Duccius accepisset a dicto operario ad pingendum quandam tabulam ponendam supra maiori altari maioris ecclesie sancte Marie de Senis comuniter et concorditer fecerunt inter se pacta et conventiones infrascripta et infrasciptas et pepigerunt et promiserunt sibi invicem inter se occasione laborerii dicte tabule faciendi et complendi pro ut inferius continetur. In primus videlicet quod dictus Duccius promisit et convenit dicto domino Jacoppo operario recipienti et stipulanti pro dicto opere sancte Marie et eius nomine pingere et facere dictam tabulam quam melius poterit et sciverit et Dominus sibi largietur et laborare continue in dicta tabula temporibus quibus laborari poterit in eadem et non accipere vel recipere aliquod aliud laborerium ad faciendum donec dicta tabula completa et facta fuerit. Dictus autem dominus Jacoppus operarius nomine dicti operis et pro eo dare et solvere promisit dicto Duccio pro suo salario dicti operis et laborerii sedecim sol den sen pro quolibet die quo dictus Duccius laborabit suis manibus in dicta tabula salvo quod si perderet aliquam doctam diei debeat exconputari de dicto salario pro rata docte sive temporis perditi. Quod quidem salarium idem operarius nomine quo supra dare teneatur et promisit dicto Duccio hoc modo videlicet quolibet mense quo dictus Duccius laborabit in dicta tabula dare eidem Duccio decem libras denariorum in pecunia numerata et residuum dicti salarii exconputare in denaris quos idem Duccius dare tenetur operi sancte Marie supradicto. Item promisit dictus operarius nomine supradicto furnire et dare omnia que necesse erunt pro dicta tabula laboranda ita quod dictus Duccius nihil in ea mictere teneatur nisi suam personam et suum laborem. [...]

G. MILANESI, op. cit., no. 22.
J. H. STUBBLEBINE, op. cit., app. no. 38, p. 202.
J. POPE-HENNESSY, 'A Misfit Master', in *New York Review of Books*, 20 November 1980, pp. 45 ff.

For the detailed measurements of the panel:
J. WHITE, *Duccio: Tuscan Art and the Medieval Workshop*, London, 1979.

On the restoration:
C. BRANDI, *Il Restauro della Maestà di Duccio*, Rome, 1959.

Doc. 6

Anonymous Sienese Chronicle, 1202–1391 (MS in the University Library, Siena):

... e anco nel detto tempo, e della signoria predetta si forni di fare la tavola dell'altare maggiore, e funne levata quella, la quale stà oggi all'altare di S. Bonifatio, la qualle si chiama la Madonna degli occhi grossi, e Madonna delle grazie, E questa Madonna fù quella, la qualle esaudì il populo di Siena quando furo rotti e Fiorentini a monte aperto, e in questo modo fù promutata la detta tavola, perchè fù fatta quella nuova, la quale è molto più bella, e divota e magiore, ed è da latto di dietro el testamento vecchio, e nuovo. E in quello dì, chesi portò al Duomo si serrero le buttighe, e ordinò il Vescovo una magnia, e divotta compagnia di Preti, e Frati con una solenne pricisione accompagnatto da Signori Nove, e tutti e gl'Uffizialli del comuno, e tutti e popolari, e di mano in mano tutti e più degni erano appresso a la detta tavolla co' lumi accesi in mano, e poi erano di dietro le donne, e fanciulli con molta divozione, e accompagniorno la detta tavola per infino al duomo facendo la intorno al chanppo, come s' usa, sonando le chanpane tutte a gloria per divozione di tanta nobille tavola, quanto è questa. La qual tavola fece Duccio di Nicolò dipentore, e fecesi in chasa de' Mucatti di fuore della porta a' stalloregi. E tutto quello di sistette a orazione

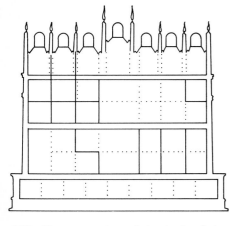

199   Reconstruction of the back of the *Maestà*.

con molte limosine, le quali si fecero a povare persone, preghando Idio, e la sua madre, la qualle è nostra Avochata e ci difenda per la sua infinita misericordia da ogni aversità, e ogni malle e ghuardici da mani di traditori, e nimici di Siena.

G. DELLA VALLE, *Lettere sanesi sopra le Belle Arti*, Rome, 1785, II, pp. 67–8.

Doc. 7

History of Siena by Sigismond Tizio:

Die interea mercurii quae mensis nona fuit [1311] tabula imaginis Mariae Virginis a Laterini vico in quo fuit depicta... ingenti honore ac religione... in aram majorem aedis sacrae translata est. Eam namque tabulam Duccius Senensis inter ejusdem opificii artifices ea tempestate primarius pinxerat ex cujus officina veluti ex equo trojano pictores egregii prodierunt.

G. DELLA VALLE, ibid., II, p. 68.

Doc. 8

Li angelichi fiorecti rose e gigli	(Responsio Verginis ad dicta Sanctorum):
Onde s'adorna lo celeste prato	Diletti miei ponete nelle menti
Non mi diletta più che i buon consigli.	Che li devoti vostri preghi onesti
Ma talor veggio chi per proprio stato	Come vorrete voi farò contenti
Disprezza me e la mie tera inganna	Ma se i potenti a debili fien molesti
E quando parla peggio è più lodato	Le vostre orazion non son per questi
Guardi ciascun cui questo dir condanna.	Ne' per qualunque la mia terra inganni.

Inscriptions on the *Maestà* by Simone Martini in the Palazzo Pubblico, Siena:

G. MAZZONI, 'Influssi danteschi nella *Maestà* di Simone Martini', in *Archivio storico italiano*, IV, 1936, pp. 144 ff.
N. RUBINSTEIN, 'Political Ideas in Sienese Art', *Journal of the Warburg and Courtauld Institutes*, XXI, 1958, p. 172.
E. BORSOOK, *The Mural Paintings of Tuscany, from Cimabue to Andrea del Sarto*, 2nd ed., Oxford, 1980, pp. 19 ff.

200 Giotto and his studio. *The Verification of the Stigmata*. Detail. About 1300. Fresco in the Upper Church, Basilica of S. Francesco, Assisi.
'In the cycle in the Upper Church at Assisi, a large hanging icon gives some idea of the devotional picture which was treasured by Petrarch.' (G. Previtali.)

Doc. 1

Dante, *Purgatorio*, XI, vv. 94–6:

> ... Credette Cimabue nella pintura
> tener lo campo, e ora ha Giotto il grido,
> si che la fama di colui è scura.

This passage has been the subject of innumerable commentaries, in particular:
J. von SCHLOSSER, 'Zur Geschichte der Kunsthistoriographie. 1. Die florentinische Künstleranekdote. 2. Filippo Villanis Kapitel über die Kunst in Florenz. 3. "Gotik"' (1896), reprinted in *Präludien*, Berlin, 1927, pp. 248 ff.
R. SALVINI, *Giotto Bibliografia*, Rome, 1938.
M. MEISS, *Painting in Florence and Siena after the Black Death*, Princeton, 1951, pp. 5 ff.
P. MURRAY, 'Notes on Some Early Giotto Sources', *Journal of the Warburg and Courtauld Institutes*, XVI, 1953, pp. 58 ff.
E. FALASCHI, 'Giotto: the literary legend', in *Italian Studies*, XXVII, 1972, pp. 9 ff.
See also: E. BATTISTI, 'Giotto nel Trecento', in *Rinascimento e Barocco*, Turin, 1960, ch. 2.

The immediate success of Giotto's manner can be illustrated by the connections between Giotto's *Dormition* (Berlin) and the panel by Jacopo del Casentino. The *Dormitio Virginis* comes from Ognissanti (*c.* 1315), which seems to be confirmed by its having served as a model for Jacopo (*c.* 1320).
G. PREVITALI, *Giotto e la sua bottega*, Milan, 1967, pp. 109 ff.

Doc. 2

Nomination of Giotto:

Domini Priores artium et Vexillifer iustitie una cum offitio Duodecim honorum virorum, cupientes ut laboreria que fiunt et fieri expedit in civitate Florentie pro comuni Florentie honorifice et decore procedant, quod esse commode perfecte nequit nisi aliquis expertus et famosus vir preficiatur et preponatur in magistrum huiusmodi laboreriorum, et in universo orbe non reperiri dicatur quemquam qui sufficientior sit in hiis et aliis multis magistro Giotto Bondonis de Florentia pittore, et accipiendus sit in patria sua velut magnus magister et carus reputandus in civitate predicta...

C. GUASTI, *Santa Maria del Fiore*, Florence, 1887, pp. 43–4.
W. PAATZ, 'Die Gestalt Giottos im Spiegel einer zeitgenössischen Urkunde', in *Eine Gabe der Freunde für Carl Georg Heise*, Berlin, 1950, pp. 85–102.

Doc. 3

Lorenzo GHIBERTI, *I Commentari*:

Fu dignissimo in tutta l'arte, ancora nella arte statuaria. Le prime storie sono nello edificio il quale dallui fu edificato, del campanile di sancta Reparata furono di sua mano scolpite et disegnate; nella mia età vidi provedimenti di sua mano di dette istorie egregiissimamente disegnati.

J. von Schlosser (ed.), *Lorenzo Ghibertis Denkwürdigkeiten (I Commentari)*, I, Berlin, 1912, p. 37.

Doc. 4

Antonio Pucci, *Centiloquio*, canto LXXIX, vv. 84–6:

Per maestro Giotto, dipintor sottile,
Il qual condusse tanto il lavorio
Ch'è primi intagli fe' con bello stile

Cited by E.H. GOMBRICH, 'Giotto's Portrait of Dante?', *Burlington Magazine*, CXXI, 1979, p. 477.

On the Campanile reliefs:
J. POPE-HENNESSY, *Italian Gothic Sculpture*, London, 1955.
M. TRACHTENBERG, *The Campanile of Florence Cathedral*, New York, 1971. According to an interesting interpretation, the relief of *The Painter*, on its left side, belonged to the cycle by Andrea Pisano, but this medallion would have been moved from its original position (near the early, eastern, door) and enlarged so that it could be replaced on the north wall *c.* 1439.

Doc. 5

BOCCACCIO, *Il Decamerone*, 6th day, 5th novella:

E per ciò, avendo egli quella arte ritornata in luce, che molti secoli sotto gli error d'alcuni che più a dilettar gli occhi degl'ignoranti che a compiacere allo'ntelletto de' savi dipignendo era stata sepulta, meritamente una delle luci della fiorentina gloria dirsi puote; e tanto più, quanto con maggiore umiltà, maestro degli altri in ciò vivendo, quella acquistò, sempre rifiutando d'esser chiamato maestro; il qual titolo rifiutato da lui tanto più in lui risplendeva, quanto con maggior disidero da quegli che men sapevan di lui o da' suoi discepoli era cupidamente usurpato.

V. Branca (ed.), *Opere*, Milan, 1976, IV, pp. 550–1.

For the relations of Petrarch and Boccaccio with Giotto, see C. GILBERT, 'The fresco of Giotto in Milan', *Arte Lombarda*, 47/48, 1977, pp. 31 ff.

Doc. 6

Testament de Pétrarque:

Dimitto tabulam meam sive iconam Beatae Virginis Mariae, opus Jotti pictoris egregii, quae mihi ab amico meo Michaele Vannis de Florentia missa est, cujus pulchritudinem ignorantes non intelligunt, magistri autem artis stupent. Hanc iconam ipsi magnifico domino lego, ut ipsa Virgo benedicta sit sibi propitia ad filium suum Jesum Christum.

T. E. MOMMSEN, *Petrarch's Testament*, Ithaca (New York), 1957, p. 22.

In the fresco cycle in the Upper Church at Assisi—where not all historians recognize the presence of Giotto, but where, at least, the great 'Giottesque' style took shape—one of the scenes contains a representation of a great suspended icon, which gives an idea of the devotional picture dear to Petrarch. See G. PREVITALI, op. cit., Milan, 1967, p. 193.

Doc. 7

BENVENUTO DA IMOLA, *Commentarium super Dantis Aligherii Comoediam*:

Et hic nota quod aliqui mirantur hic ex ignorantia, et dicunt: quare Dantes nominavit hic homines ignoti nominis et bassae artis, cum potuisset dignius facere mentionem de viris excellentissimis qui pulcra et nobilia opera fecerunt avidissimi gloriae? Sed certe poeta fecit hoc cum magna arte et jure optimo, quia per hoc dat tacite intelligi, quod appetitus gloriae ita indifferrenter occupat omnes, quod etiam parvi artifices sunt solliciti circa illam acquirendam, sicut videmus quod pictores apponunt nomina operibus [...]
   Et hic nota, lector, quod poeta noster merito fecit commendationem Giotti, ratione civitatis, ratione virtutis, ratione familiaritatis [...]

Giottus adhuc tenet campum, quia nondum venit alius eo subtilior, cum tamen fecerit aliquando magnos errores in picturis suis, ut audivi a magnis ingeniis...

J. P. Lacaïta (ed.), Florence, 1887, III, pp. 310, 312, 313.

No attempt is made here to study the question of 'copies' after Giotto; as an example we give *The Visitation*, a drawing after Giotto (Uffizi). This drawing on parchment belonged to Vasari's personal collection. The composition is close to that of one of the scenes in the right transept of the Lower Church at Assisi, which was the work of a first generation Giottesque. It is presumed to be a copy of an original by Giotto. See L. GRASSI, *I disegni italiani del Trecento e del Quattrocento*, Venice, n.d. (1960 ?), no. 2.

Doc. 8

F. VILLANI, *De origine civitatis Florentiae*:

Vetustissimi, qui res gestas conspicue descripsere, pictores optimos atque imaginum statuarumque sculptores cum aliis famosis viris in suis voluminibus miscuerunt. [...] Michi quoque eorum exemplo fas sit hoc loco, irridentium pace dixerim, egregios pictores florentinos inserere, qui artem exanguem et pene extinctam suscitaverunt. Inter quos primus Johannes, cui cognomento Cimabue dictus est, antiquatam picturam et a nature similitudine quasi lascivam et vagantem longius arte et ingenio revocavit. Siquidem ante istum grecam latinamque picturam per multa secula sub crasso peritie ministerio iacuisset, ut plane ostendunt figure et imagines que in tabellis parietibusque cernuntur sanctorum ecclesias adornare. Post hunc, strata iam in novis via [*MS.* nivibus], Giottus, non solum illustris fame decore antiquis pictoribus comparandus, sed arte et ingenio preferendus, in pristinam dignitatem nomenque maximum picturam restituit. Huius enim figurate radio imagines ita liniamentis nature conveniunt, ut vivere et aerem spirare contuentibus videantur, exemplares etiam actus gestusque conficere adeo proprie, ut loqui, flere, letari et alia agere, non sine delectatione contuentis et laudantis ingenium manumque artificis prospectentur: extimantibus multis, nec stulte quidem, pictores non inferioris ingenii his, quos liberales artes fecere magistros, cum illi artium precepta scripturis demandata studio atque doctrina percipiant, hii solum ab alto ingenio tenacique memoria, que in arte sentiant, exigant. Fuit sane Giottus, arte picture seposita, magni vir consilii et qui multarum usum habuerit. Historiarum insuper notitiam plenam habens, ita poesis extitit emulator, ut ipse pingere que illi fingere subtiliter considerantibus perpendatur. Fuit etiam, ut virum decuit prudentissimum, fame potius quam lucri cupidus. Unde ampliandi nominis amore per omnes ferme Italie civitates famosas spectabilibus locis aliquid pinxerit, Romeque presertim arce pre basilica sancti Petri ex musivo periclitantes navi apostolos artificiosissime figuravit, ut orbi terrarum ad urbem confluenti arte vique [*MS.* urbeque] sua spectaculum faceret. Pinxit insuper speculorum suffragio semet ipsum eique contemporaneum Dantem Allagherii poetam in pariete capelle palatii potestatis. Ab hoc laudabili valde viro, velut a fonte sincero abundantissimoque, rivuli picture nitidissimi defluxerunt...

The text from MS. Ash. 942 (British Museum) and MS. Gadd. 89 inf. 23 (Bib. Laurenziana) in C. FREY, *Il Libro di Antonio Billi*, Berlin, 1892, pp. 73–5; from MS. Barb. Lat. 2610 (Vatican Library) in M. BAXENDALL, *Giotto and the Orators*, Oxford, 1971, pp. 146–7.

There are some variations in the MSS., the oldest being of *c.* 1381 and the most recent, with corrections, of 1395–6. In this latter there is no longer any mention of an altarpiece, but of a mural painting in the Bargello: *in pariete*. See P. BRIEGER, M. MEISS and C. SINGLETON, *Illuminated Manuscripts of the 'Divine Comedy'*, Princeton, 1969, vol. I, p. 40.

J. von SCHLOSSER, *art. cit.*, 1896, reprinted in *Präludien*, 1927, pp. 261 ff.
P. L. RAMBALDI, 'Dante e Giotto nella letteratura artistica', *Rivista d'Arte*, IX, 1937, pp. 286 ff.
A. CHASTEL, 'Giotto coetaneo di Dante' (1963), reprinted in *Fables, Formes, Figures*, Paris, 1978, vol. I, p. 378.
E. H. GOMBRICH, *art. cit.*, *Burlington Magazine.*, pp. 471 ff.
R. HOLBROOK, *Portraits of Dante*, London 1911, pp. 73 ff.

On the hypothesis of the three grouped portraits: A. PARRONCHI, 'Il più vero ritratto di Dante', *Bolletino del museo civico di Padova*, LII, 1963, pp. 4 ff.

The Paduan, mentioned by Dante (Inferno, XVII, 64 ff.) in the circle of the usurers, has often been identified as Reginaldo, Enrico's father:

> E un che d'una scrofa azzurra e grossa
> Segnato avea lo suo sacchetto bianco...
> (And one who with a fat blue sow
> Had marked his little white bag...)

If this were the case, it might be thought that the son would have been unwilling to agree to honouring the poet in the fresco of the *Last Judgement*, as is maintained by E. BORSOOK, *The Mural Paintings of Tuscany from Cimabue to Andrea del Sarto*, 2nd ed., Oxford, 1980, no. 33, p. 13. But the idea may well have emanated from the painter.

On the *Navicella* and the Spanish Chapel: M. MEISS, *Painting in Florence and Siena after the Black Death. The Arts, Religion and Society in the Mid-Fourteenth Century*, Princeton, 1951, ch. IV.

Doc. 9

FRANCO SACCHETTI, *Novella* CXXXVI:

Nella città di Firenze, che sempre di nuovi uomeni è stata doviziosa, furono già certi dipintori e altri maestri, li quali essendo a un luogo fuori della città, che si chiama San Miniato a Monte, per alcuna dipintura e lavorìo, che alla chiesa si dovea fare; quando ebbono desinato con l'Abate, e ben pasciuti e bene avvinazzati, cominciorono a questionare; e fra l'altre questione mosse uno, che avea nome l'Orcagna, il quale fu capo maestro dell'oratorio nobile di Nostra Donna d'Orto San Michele: – Qual fu il maggior maestro di dipignere, che altro, che sia stato da Giotto in fuori ? – Chi dicea che fu Cimabue, chi Stefano, chi Bernardo, e chi Buffalmacco, chi uno e chi un altro. Taddeo Gaddi, che era nella brigata, disse:

– Per certo assai valentri dipintori sono stati, e che hanno dipinto per forma, ch'è impossibile a natura úmana poterlo fare; – ma questa arte è venuta e viene mancando tutto dì. –

Disse uno, che avea nome maestro Alberto, che era gran maestro d'intagli di marmo:

– E' mi pare che voi siate forte errati, però che certo vi mosterrò che mai la natura non fu tanto sottile quant'ella è oggi, e spezialmente nel dipignere, e ancora del fabbricare intagli incarnati. –

Li maestri tutti, udendo costui, rideano, come se fossi fuora della memoria. [...]

Il Trecento novelle, ed. Sansoni, Florence, 1946, p. 192.

Doc. 10

Cino RINUCCINI, *Responsiva alla inventiva di Messer Antonio Lusco*:

Ora nell'ultimo non è da dimenticare lo ingegnoso Giotto, il quale dei nostri maggiori sì le naturali effigie rappresenta, che continuo pungente alle virtù ci sospigne, e che non solo Cimabue moderno, ma gli antichi Scopa, Policleto, e Prassitele avanza.

Published by D. Moreni following the *Invectiva Lini Coluccii Salutati... in Antonium Luschum Vicentinum de eadem republica male sentientem*, Florence, 1826, p. 246.

Doc. 11

Letter from P. P. Vergerio:

Faciendum est igitur quod etatis nostre pictores qui, cum ceterorum claras imagines sedulo spectent, solius tamen Ioti exemplaria sequuntur...

Epistolario, ed. L. Smith, Rome, 1934, p. 177; quoted by E. PANOFSKY, *Renaissance and Renascences in Western Art*, 2nd ed., London, 1965, p. 13, n. 2 (dating the letter in 1396).

Doc. 12

Cennino CENNINI, *Libro dell'Arte*, capit. 1:

Sì come piccolo membro essercitante nell'arte di dipintoria, Cennino d'Andrea Cennini da Colle di Valdelsa nato, fui informato nella detta arte XII anni da Agnolo di Taddeo da Firenze mio maestro, il quale imparò la detta arte di Taddeo suo padre; il quale suo padre fu battezzato da Giotto e fu suo discepolo anni XXIIII. Il quale Giotto rimutò l'arte del dipignere di greco in latino e ridusse al moderno; ed ebbe l'arte più compiuta che avessi mai più nessuno.

Ed. with commentary by F. Brunelli and preface by L. Magagnato, Vicenza, 1971, pp. 4–5.

We do not know the date of compilation of the precious collection of technical recipes known as the *Libro dell'Arte*, but there is reason to believe that it was put together about the end of the Trecento, in the wake of the Giottesque revival. It circulated in MS (there are several examples), but was not printed until the nineteenth century.

On the 'return to Giotto' *c.* 1380:
M. BOSKOVITS, *Pittura fiorentina alla vigilia del Rinascimento*, Florence, 1975.

Doc. 13

G. VASARI, *Life of Agnolo Gaddi*, ed. Milanesi, I, p. 646:

Il ritratto d'Agnolo, fatto da lui medesimo, si vede nella cappella degli Alberti in Santa Croce, nella storia dove Eraclio imperatore porta la croce, allato a una porta, dipinto in profilo, con un poco di barbetta e con un cappuccio rosato in capo, secondo l'uso di que' tempi.

Texts and Documents—Chapter 3

Doc. 1

L. B. ALBERTI, *De Pictura* (1436), Dedication to Filippo Brunelleschi:

Ma poi che io dal lungo essilio in quale siamo noi Alberti invecchiati, qui fui in questa nostra sopra l'altre ornatissima patria ridutto, compresi in molti ma prima in te, Filippo, e in quel nostro amicissimo Donato scultore e in quegli altri Nencio e Luca e Masaccio, essere a ogni lodata cosa ingegno da non posporli a qual si sia stato antiquo e famoso in queste arti.

C. Grayson (ed.), Bari, 1973, p. 7.

The abundant literature on the subject of Alberti's little work does not, perhaps, adequately take into account the circumstances created by the arrival of Pope Eugenius IV in Florence immediately after the return of Cosimo de' Medici. In the episode quoted the general feeling of the pictures is in accordance with the precepts of *De Pictura*; but, with the arrival of Domenico Veneziano, other considerations began to make themselves felt. Alberti sought to give a theoretical, even scientific, basis to the art then being practised; beyond that, he arranged his treatise on the model of the rhetoricians, a humanist exercise in itself, and the consequences in studio practice ought not to be exaggerated. In any case, in the following years Alberti turned his attention to other matters. Between 1434 and 1438 he wrote the ironical and bitter dialogues *Intercoenales*. One of them, *Uxoria*, bears a dedication, dated 2 December 1438, to Piero de' Medici. See C. GRAYSON, 'Una intercenale inedita di L. B. Alberti', *Italia medioevale e umanistica*, III, 1960, pp. 291 ff.

Doc. 2

Leonardo BRUNI, *Rerum suo tempore gestarum commentarius*:

Per hoc ipsum fere tempus basilica Florentina ab Eugenio Papa solemniter dedicata fuit. Cuius rei causa pons ligneus incredibili celeritate ac mirabili opere aedificatus est ab Ecclesia praedicatorum, ubi Pontifex habitabat, ad ipsam basilicam, quae erat dedicanda. Is vero pons non solum ad magnificentiam pertinuit, verum etiam ad necessitatem. Tantus enim in ipsa dedicationis die concursus hominum fuit ex agro, ac finitimis oppidis, et ex ipsa multitudine urbana, ut complerentur omnes aditus, omnesque viae, nec Pontifex cum suis Cardinalibus et Praelatis transire unquam prae nimia turba potuisset, nisi pons ad hoc ipsum superiniectus viam eis praebuisset. [...]

E. Santini and C. di Pierro (eds.), Città di Castello, 1926 (*Rerum Italicarum Scriptores*, XIX, 3), p. 453.

W. and E. PAATZ, *Die Kirchen von Florenz*, III, Frankfurt, 1952, p. 462.

Doc. 3

Letter from Domenico Veneziano to Piero de' Medici, 1 April 1438:

Spectabilis et generose vir. Dopo le debite rechomandacione. Avisovi per la dio gracia Io essere sanno, desideroso vedervi sanno e lieto. Più e più volte ho dimandato de vui, e mai non o saputo nula, salvo chio dimandato manno donati, el quale me dise, vui esere in ferara, e sanisimo. Hone

201 Adimari Wedding Master. *Marriage Procession in Florence.* Detail. Mid-fifteenth century. Tempera on panel. Galleria dell' Accademia, Florence.

ricenta gran chonsolacione; e avendo saputo prima dove fosti stato, vaverei schrito per mia chonsolacione e debito; avenga dio che la mia bassa chondicione non merita schrivere a la vostra gientileza; ma solamente el perfecto e buono amorer chio porto a vui, e a tuti i vostri, me dà soma audacia de potervi schrivere, chonsiderando quanto io ve sono tenuto et hublighato.

Hora al presente ho sentito che chossimo à deliberato de far fare, cio dipinghiere una tavola daltare, et vole un magnificho lavorio. La quale chosa molto me piace, et più mi piacerebe se posibile fuse per vostra megianità chio la dipingiese, e se cio aviene, ho speranza in dio farvi vedere chose meravigliose, avengna che ce sia di bon maestri chome fra Filipo et fra Giovane, i quali anno di molto lavorio a fare, e spetialmente fra Filipo à una tavola che va in santo Spirito, la quale lavorando lui di e noto, non la farà in cinquani, si è gran lavoro. Ma che se sia, el grande e buono animo chio desservirvi, me fa prusuntuoso per oferendome, che si io facese mancho bene che niuno che ce sia, voglio essere hoblichato ad ogni meritoria choricione, a farne che hogni pruova a farne hogni pruova *(sic)* che bisognia honorando hogni uno. E se pure el lavorio fuse si grande, che chossimo deliberase darlo a più maestri, hoveramente più a uno che a un altro, prieghovi, quanto è possibile a servo pregare signiore, chelvi piacia adoperare le vertù vostre in versomi favorevole e agliutatore in fare chionabia qualche particela. Che se vuï sapessi el desiderio chio ho de fare qualche famoso lavorio, et spicialmente a vui, me saristi in cio favorevole. Son certo che per nui non remarà. Prieghovi fatene el posibole, chiovi prometo ne reveverete honore de fatti miei [...]

E. GAYE, *Carteggio inedito d'artisti dei secoli XIV, XV, XVI,* Florence, 1840–, I, no. XLIX, pp. 136–7.

E. H. GOMBRICH, 'The Early Medici as Patrons of Art' (1960), reprinted in *Norm and Form,* London, 1966, pp. 35 ff.

On the tondo of the *Adoration of the Magi:*
F. AMES-LEWIS, 'Domenico Veneziano and the Medici', *Jahrbuch der Berliner Museen,* XXI, 1979, pp. 67 ff.

Doc. 4

VESPASIANO DA BISTICCI, *Vita di Eugenio IV P.P.*:

[...] pensò papa Eugenio volere fargli passare in Italia alle sue ispese, a fine che s'unissino colla Chiesa romana. Passò lo 'nperadore di Gostantinopoli et il patriarca e tutti e' prelati degni aveva quella natione. Venono a Ferrara tutti alle spese del papa, grandissimo numero. Cominciando il morbo a Ferrara, el papa se ne venne a Firenze, et quivi aparechiò il luoghi pe' Greci, et ordinò la provisione loro mese per mese. [...] si fece in Sancta Maria Novella uno bellissimo aparato di panche et luoghi da sedere, et chiamorollo in concilio de' Greci [...]

Venono in questo tempo Iacopiti et Etiopi, et dal Presto Giovanni mandati al pontefice romano, et a tutti faceva il papa le spese. Fece venire papa Eugenio tutti e' dotti uomini erano in Italia et fuori d'Italia. [...]

Et un dì solenne venne il pontefice con tutta la corte di Roma et collo imperadore de' Greci, et tutti e' vescovi et prelati latini in Sancta Maria del Fiore, dov'era fatto un degno aparato, ed ordinato il modo ch'aveva a istare a sedere i prelati de l'una Chiesa e dell'altra. [...] Il papa era parato in pontificale, e tutti e' cardinali co' piviali, et i vescovi cardinali colle mitere di domaschino bianco, e tutti e' vescovi così greci come latini colle mitere del bocaccino bianco et parati, e' vescovi latini co' piviali, e' Greci con abiti di seta al modo greco molto richi, et la maniera degli abiti greci pareva assai più grave et più degna che quella de' prelati latini. [...]

Il luogo dell'imperadore [era] in questa solennità dove si canta la pistola a l'altare magiore, et da quelo medesimo luogo, com'è detto, erano tutti i prelati greci. Eravi concorso tutto il mondo in Firenze, per vedere questo atto si' degno. Era una sedia al dirimpeto a quella del papa da l'altro lato, ornata di drappo di seta, et lo 'mperadore cor una vesta alla greca di brocato domaschino molto rica, cor uno capeletto alla greca, che v'era in su la punta una bellissima gioia; era uno bellissimo uomo colla barba al modo greco.

Le Vite, ed. A. Greco, Florence, 1970, I, pp. 16 ff. (English trans. by W. G. & E. Waters, London, 1926 and later reprints). The memoirs of the great Florentine bookseller are very full concerning Eugenius IV and Florence.

The celebrated *cassone* panel by the Adimari Wedding Master (Accademia, Florence) shows such a procession on a dais and beneath an awning, in front of the Baptistry, but, it is true, on a secular occasion.

Doc. 5

G. VASARI, *Life of Andrea del Castagno and Domenico Veneziano*, ed. Milanesi, II, pp. 676–7:

Fece Maestro Domenico, a olio, Gioacchino che visita Sant'Anna suo consorte; e di sotto, il nascere di Nostra Donna, fingendovi una camera molto ornata, ed un putto che batte col martello l'uscio di detta camera con molto buona grazia. Di sotto fece lo Sposalizio d'essa Vergine, con buon numero di ritratti di naturale: fra i quali è messer Bernardetto de' Medici, conestabile de' Fiorentini, con un berrettone rosso; Bernardo Guadagni, che era gonfaloniere: Folco Portinari, ed altri di quella famiglia. Vi fece anco un nano che rompe una mazza, molto vivace; ed alcune femmine con abiti indosso, vaghi e graziosi fuor di modo, secondo che si usavano in que'tempi. Ma quest'opera rimase imperfetta...

W. and E. PAATZ, *Die Kirchen von Florenz*, IV, Frankfurt, 1952, pp. 24, 49–51.

Recent documentation in:
H. WOHL, 'Domenico Veneziano Studies: the Sant' Egidio and Parenti Documents', *Burlington Magazine*, CXIII, 1971, pp. 635 ff.

On the remains of the Sant' Egidio frescoes:
M. SALMI, 'Ricerche intorno a un perduto ciclo pittorico del Rinascimento', in *Atti e Memorie dell'Accademia fiorentina... La Colombaria*, N.S. I, 1943–6, pp. 421–32.
L. BECHERUCCI, Notice concerning the work of M. Salmi, in *Rivista d'Arte*, XXVI, 1950, pp. 223 ff.

Doc. 6

Payment of September 1439, from Sant' Egidio:

Maestro Domenicho di Bartolommeo da Vinezia che dipignie la Chappella Maggiore di Santo Gidio, de' dare adi XII di Settembre f. quarantaquattro, posto de' avere al quaderno segnato DDC. 185 [...]
    E de' dare adi XII di Settembre f. due S. XV a oro, porto Pietro di Benedetto dal Borgho a San Sepolchro sta cho'llui assieme Fiorini 2 lire 3 soldi 3.

The complete documentation is in E. WOHL, art. cit. (and now also in his *Domenico Veneziano*, London, 1980).

On the Prato Master:
M. SALMI, 'Paolo Uccello, Domenico Veneziano, Piero della Francesca e gli affreschi del Duomo di Prato', *Bollettino d'Arte*, XXVIII, 1934, pp. 1–27.
R. LONGHI, 'Il maestro di Pratovecchio' (1952), reprinted in *Opere complete*, VIII, I, Florence, 1975, pp. 99 ff.

Doc. 7

Letter from Filippo Lippi to Piero di Cosimo de' Medici, 13 August 1439:

Per risposta duna vi mandai orriceuta de Voi, chè penata tredici dì avella, chennò auto danno assai. Voi mi rispondete in choncrusione cheddella tavola nè altro partito ne potete pilgliare, e chio vela chonservi, che per dio ò male el modo sio mi parto, eppiù non mi potete dare uno quatrino. Io di questo ò aunto grande dolore per più rispetti; e questo è uno di quelli, edè chiaro essere uno de più poveri Frati, che sia in Firenze, sono Io, ed àmi laciato dio chon sei nipote fanculle da marito, e infermi e disutili, e quello pocho è assai di bene alloro sono io. Seppotessi farmi dare a chasa vostra uno pocho di grano e di vino, che mi vendete, mi sarà grande letizia, ponedolo a mio chonto. Io vene gravo cholle lagrime alliochi, che sio mi parto Io lasci a questi poveri fanculli. [...] Io vi priegho non vi sia grave due versi allui a Ser Antonio, chio li sia rachomandato. Ella risposta vostra sia subito partirmi l'altro di; che sono chiaro sio cistò otto di, Io sono morto; tanto èlla paura. Persio rispondete a chasa vostra, che chosì lado, acciò non nintervengha chome dellaltra.
                                   Frate Filippo dipintore in Firenze.

E. GAYE, op. cit. I, no. LII, pp. 141–2: English translation in D. CHAMBERS, op. cit., pp. 91–3.

On Cosimo de' Medici's tolerance towards Fra Filippo: C. GUTKIND, *Cosimo de' Medici il Vecchio*, Florence, 1949.

Doc. 8

Agreement on the Barbadori Altar, 8 March 1436 (O.S.), i.e. 1437: *(Deliberazioni e Stanziamenti dei Capitani della Compagnia di Or San Michele)*:

1436, die VIII Martii, Jacobus Phylippi aurifex populi Sancti Nicholai de Florentia promisit quod frater Phylippus Tomaxii ordinis Sancte Marie del Carmine consignabit bonum computum de florenis quadraginta, quos habere debet a dicta Societate pro pinctura tabule altaris cappelle gherardi de Barbadoris, sin autem de suo proprio consignabit: et ea propter promixit et obligavit et renuntiavit pro guaranrigia, presente dicto frate Philippo et promittente ut supra et Maso Pieri et Marcho testibus.

I. B. SUPINO, *Fra Filippo Lippi*, Florence, 1902, p. 56.
G. MARCHINI, *Filippo Lippi*, Milan, 1975.

Doc. 9

G. VASARI, *Life of Fra Giovanni da Fiesole* (Angelico), ed. Milanesi, II, pp. 508–9:

Ma particolarmente è bella a maraviglia la tavola dell'altar maggiore di quella chiesa: perchè, oltre che la Madonna muove a divozione chi la guarda per la semplicita sua, e che i Santi che le sono intorno, sono simili a lei; la predella, nella quale sono storie del martirio di San Cosimo e Damiano e degli altri, è tanto ben fatta, che non è possibile immaginarsi di poter veder mai cosa fatta con più diligenza, nè le più delicate o meglio intese figurine di quelle.

R. BORGHINI, *Il Riposo*, Florence, 1584, p. 620.
T. BODKIN, 'A Fra Angelico predella', *Burlington Magazine*, LVIII, 1931, pp. 183 ff.
J. POPE-HENNESSY, *Fra Angelico*, London, 1952, 2nd ed., 1974.

Doc. 10

Letter from Matteo de' Pasti to Piero di Cosimo de' Medici, 1441:

Di Venezia di 24 del [no month given] 1441.

Spetabillis ac maior honorande. Per questa mia vi fo noto come io ho inparato da' poi ch'io son a Vinesa cossa che al vostro lavoro non poria essere cossa più singulare, come sarano; e questa cossa è oro masinato, ch'io lo dipingho come ogni altro collore, e ivi cominciato ad ornare questi, che son fatti per modo che non vedisti mai si fatta cossa. Quelle verdure son tutte tochate d'oro masinato ch'o fatto mille ricamuci a quelle damiselle. Si che caramente vi priegho, che vui mi vogliate mandare la fantasia degli altri, a cio ch'io ue li conpischa; e s'el vi piace ch'io vi mandi questi, io velli mandero, si comandatime quello vi piace ch'io facia, ch'io son pronto a ubedirvi in qualunque cossa a vui sia grata. [...] s'el vi paze, mandatime ch'io facia quello della Fama, perch'io ho la fantasia, salvo non so, se quella dona che sede, la volete in camora [gamurra] di piciolato o pur in manto, come a me piacesse: el resto so tutto quello va andare, cioè el caro tira 4 lionfanti: e si non so se vui volete scudieri e damiselle driedo, o pur omeni famosi vechi: si che avisatime di tutto, perch'io faro una bella cossa, per modo che sarete contento. E perdonareteme tutto, e valerà più un di questi ch'io faro hora che non valle tutti queste che son fatti...

G. MILANESI, 'Lettere d'artisti italiani dei secoli XIV, XV', in *Il Buonarroti*, IV, 1869, pp. 78–9. English translation in D. CHAMBERS, op. cit., no. 48, pp. 94–5.

E. H. GOMBRICH, 'The Early Medici...', art. cit., p. 47 (partial quotation of the text of the letter), illustrating the mention of 'Triumphs' by a *cassone* panel. The work which occupied Matteo has been interpreted as a panel and a connection has been suggested with the four curved panels, parts of a piece of furniture, with rounded angles (Uffizi). They have been attributed to a specialist in this decoration, but he cannot have been Matteo. See P. SCHUBRING, *Cassoni*, Berlin, 1912, nos 208–11; G. CARANDENTE, *I Trionfi del primo Rinascimento*, Turin, 1961, no. 132, pp. 128–9.

In the letter the reference is probably to the work of a miniaturist, since Matteo began as an illuminator (Breviary for Lionello d'Este, 1446), before he became a celebrated medallist and adviser to Sigismondo Malatesta at Rimini.

In a Florentine MS of 1440/50 the miniature of the *Triumph of Fame* shows a chariot, oddly seen from the front, drawn by two horses instead of two elephants. See D. SCHORR, 'Some Notes on the Iconography of Petrarch's *Triumph of Fame*', *Art Bulletin*, XX, 1938, p. 107.

Doc. 11

Bull *Laetentur caeli* of 6 July, 1439:

Diffinimus insuper explicationem verborum illorum *filioque*, veritatis declarandae gratia, et imminente tunc necessitate, licite ac rationabiliter symbolo fuisse appositam.

J. GILL, *The Council of Florence*, Cambridge, 1959, pp. 413–4.
The connection between the *Baptism* and the Council has often been proposed:
K. CLARK, *Piero della Francesca*, cit., p. 24.
A. CHASTEL, *Annuaire du Collège de France*, 1979–80, pp. 733 ff. and recently by
A. GINZBURG, *Problemi di Piero della Francesca*, Turin, 1981.

202 Melozzo da Forlì. *Sixtus IV Inaugurating the Vatican Library.* 1474. Fresco. Pinacoteca, Vatican.

Doc. 1

G. VASARI, *Life of Pietro Perugino*, ed. Milanesi, III, pp. 578–9:

Per che talmente si sparse la fama di Pietro per Italia e fuori, che e' fu da Sisto IIII pontefice con molta sua gloria condotto a Roma a lavorare nella cappella in compagnia degli altri artefici eccellenti; dove fece la storia di Cristo quando dà le chiavi a S. Pietro, in compagnia di don Bartolomeo della Gatta abate di S. Clemente di Arezzo, e similmente la natività e il battesimo di Cristo, et il nascimento di Mosè, quando dalla figliuola di Faraone è ripescato nella cestella; e nella medesima faccia dove è l'altare fece la tavola in muro con l'assunzione della Madonna, dove ginocchioni ritrasse papa Sisto.

On the pontificate of Sixtus IV:
L. von PASTOR, *History of the Popes*, IV, London, 1900.

On the papal finances and the budget of 1480–1:
C. BAUER, 'Studi per la storia delle finanze papali...', *Archivio della R. Società romana di storia patria*, I, 1927, pp. 319 ff.
P. PARTNER, 'The "budget" of the Roman Church in the Renaissance period', in *Italian Renaissance Studies*, ed. E. F. Jacob, London, 1960, pp. 156 ff.

On urbanism in Rome in the time of Sixtus IV (1471–84): V. GOLZIO and G. ZANDER, *L'Arte in Roma nel secolo XV*, Bologna, 1968, ch. X.

On the *She-Wolf* and the other Roman remains as the basis of the Capitoline Museum:
W. HECKSCHER, *Sixtus IIII aeneas insignes statuas populo romano restituendas censuit*, The Hague, 1955.

On the votive church of Sta. Maria della Pace:
G. URBAN, 'Die Kirchenbaukunst des Quattrocento in Rom', *Römisches Jahrbuch für Kunstgeschichte*, IX/X, 1961/2, pp. 176 ff.

Doc. 2

Contract of 27 October 1481 (Vatican Archives):

Locatio picture capelle magne nove palacii apostolici sive
  deputacio ad ipsam depingendam.

Die xxvii Octobris 1481. Rome in camera apostolica pontificatus sanctissimi in christo patris et domini nostri domini Sixti pape iiii anno undecimo Rome in palacio apostolico honorabilis vir dominus Johannes Petri de Dulcibus de Florencia habitator Rome superstans sive commissarius fabrice palacii apostolici agens ut dixit de mandato et ex commissione sanctissimi domini nostri pape sibi facta presentibus me notario publico et testibus infrascriptis gratis etc. conduxit sive locavit ac conducit sive locat providis viris Cosmo Laurentii Phylippi Rosselli, Alexandro Mariani, et Dominico Thomasii Corradi de Florentia, et Petro Christofori Castri Plebis Perusin. diocesis depictoribus Rome comorantibus picturam capelle magne nove dicti palacii apostolici a capite altaris inferius, videlicet decem istorias testamenti antiqui et novi cum cortinis inferius ad depingendum bene diligenter et fideliter melius quo poterunt per ipsos et eorum quemlibet et familiares suos prout inceptum est. Et convenerunt ac promiserunt ipsi depictores eidem domino Johanni Petri superstanti locatori nomine dicti sanctissimi domini nostri pape dictas decem istorias cum earum cortinis ut predicitur depingere et finire hinc ad quintamdecimam diem mensis marcii proxime futuri, cum precio solutionis et extimationis ad quam seu quod extimabuntur istorie iam facte in dicta capella per eosdem depictores, sub pena quinquaginta ducatorum auri de camera pro quolibet eorundem contrafaciente, quam penam sponte sibi imposuerunt et ad quam si contrafacient incidi voluerunt et volunt, que pena aplicari debeat fabrice dicte capelle etc. Et pro predictis omnibus et singulis ipsi depictores obligarunt se et omnia eorum et cuiuslibet ipsorum bona presentia et futura et quilibet eorum tenetur pro alio contrafaciente et predicta non observante sive observantibus etc. in meliori et strictiori forma camere etc. Submiserunt se etc. Renunciarunt etc. Constituerunt procuratores etc. Et iuraverunt etc. Fiat in ampliori forma etc. Et etiam ex pacto fuerunt concordes quod quedam obligacio per dictos depictores alias facta dicto Johanni Petri superstanti super pecuniis per eos receptis et recipiendis ratione dicte depicture maneat in suo valore et robore etc. Presentibus venerabilibus viris dominis Marino de Monte alto et Baptista de Spello camere apostolice notariis pro testibus et me Johanne Gerones eiusdem camere notario rogato.

L. D. ETTLINGER, *The Sistine Chapel before Michelangelo. Religious Imagery and Papal Primacy,* Oxford, 1965, App. A, pp. 120–1.

On the Sistine Chapel:
R. LIGHTBOWN, *Sandro Botticelli*, 2 vols., London, 1978, ch. 6.

203 Ghirlandaio. *St. Zenobius in Glory.* 1483. Fresco. Palazzo Vecchio, Florence. 'By the decision of five black beans, they gave the order... to the painter Domenico Tommaso del Ghirlandaio... to paint the wall of the room in the palace next to the Dogana, and to decorate the said palace with an image of St. Zenobius...' (Resolution of the Governors, October 1482.)

The builder of the Sistine Chapel may have been the Giovannino de' Dolci who was a signatory of the October 1481 contract. If Dolci was not the architect who conceived this unusually enormous space, manifestly destined to receive painted decoration, the author may have been Baccio Pontelli, to whom Vasari attributes everything important built in Rome under Sixtus IV. See G. URBAN, art. cit., p. 170, and V. GOLZIO and G. ZANDER, op. cit., p. 382.

E. BATTISTI, 'Roma Apocalittica e Re Salomone' (1957), reprinted in *Rinascimento e Barocco*, Turin, 1960, ch. III, established a particularly interesting connection with the Temple of Solomon, often invoked from the time of Nicholas V to justify monumental building by the Church: the rectangular plan, the proportions (60×20 cubits), and the division into three by cornices [...] correspond well.

Doc. 3

JACOPO DA VOLTERRA, *Diarium Romanum*:

Nondum sacellum majus est absolutum continua enim emblemate et pictura ornatur.

E. Carùsi (ed.), Città di Castello, 1904, pp. 83–4; quoted by L. D. ETTLINGER, op. cit., p. 26.

Doc. 4

G. VASARI, *Life of Sandro Botticelli*, ed. Milanesi, III, pp. 316–7:

... papa Sisto IIII, avendo fatto fabricare la cappella in palazzo di Roma e volendola dipignere, ordinò ch'egli ne divenisse capo; onde in quella fece di sua mano le infrascritte storie, cioè quando Cristo è tentato dal Diavolo, quando Mosè amazza lo Egizzio e che riceve bere da le figlie di Ietro Madianite, similmente quando, sacrificando i figliuoli di Aron, venne fuoco dal cielo, et alcuni Santi Papi nelle nicchie di sopra alle storie.

Laonde acquistato fra' molti concorrenti che seco lavorarono, e fiorentini e di altre città, fama e nome maggiore, ebbe dal Papa buona somma di danari; i quali ad un tempo destrutti e consumati tutti nella stanza di Roma per vivere a caso come era il solito suo, e finita insieme quella parte che e'gli era stata allogata e scopertala, se ne tornò subitamente a Fiorenza.

On the Tuscans in Rome:
J. MESNIL, 'Botticelli à Rome', *Rivista d'Arte*, III, 1905, pp. 112 ff.

The account given by Vasari of Botticelli's frivolity and his sudden departure from Rome has been contested. The four artists may have returned to Rome because their payments were not regularly met: in December 1483 Botticelli asked one of his nephews to collect money owing to him in Rome. D. COVI, 'Botticelli and Pope Sixtus IV', *Burlington Magazine*, CXI, 1969, p. 616; R. LIGHTBOWN, op. cit., Doc. 20.

On the frieze-like composition of *cassoni* panels:
In the Latin epic poem *Carliades* (1480) by Ugolino Verino there is an imaginative description of a fresco-cycle by 'Alexander' (i.e. Sandro Botticelli) which has been reasonably compared to the continuous representation of narratives on *cassone* panels.
See E. H. GOMBRICH, 'Apollonio di Giovanni...' (1955), reprinted in his *Norm and Form*, London, 1966, pp. 11 ff.

On the Triumphal Arch in the fresco of the *Punishment of Corah*...:
F. MAGI, 'Il coronamento dell'arco di Costantino', in *Rendiconti della Pontificia Accademia romana di Archeologia*, XXIX, 1958, pp. 83 ff.

Observations on the portraits in the Sistine Chapel:
J. POPE-HENNESSY, *The Portrait in the Renaissance*, London, 1966.

Doc. 5

G. VASARI, *Life of Cosimo Rosselli* (1568), ed. Milanesi, III, pp. 187–9:

Chiamato poi con gl'altri pittori all'opera che fece Sisto Quarto pontefice nella cappella del palazzo, in compagnia di Sandro Botticello, di Domenico Ghirlandaio, dell'Abbate di S. Clemente, di Luca da Cortona e di Piero Perugino, vi dipinse di sua mano tre storie, nelle quali fece la sommersione di Faraone nel mar Rosso, la predica di Cristo ai popoli lungo il mare di Tiberiade e l'ultima cena degl'Apostoli col Salvatore; nella quale fece una tavola a otto facce tirate in prospettiva, e sopra quella, in otto facce simili, il palco che gira in otto angoli, dove molto bene scortando mostrò d'intendere quanto gl'altri quest'arte.

Dicesi che il Papa aveva ordinato un premio, il quale si aveva a dar a chi meglio in quelle pitture avesse a giudizion d'esso Pontefice operato. Finite dunque le storie, andò Sua Santità a vederle quando ciascuno de' pittori si era ingegnato di far sì che meritasse il detto premio e l'onore. Aveva Cosimo, sentendosi debole d'invenzione e di disegno, cercato di occultare il suo deffetto con far coperta all'opera di finissimi az[z]urri oltramarini e d'altri vivaci colori, e con molto oro illuminata la storia, onde né albero, né erba, né panno, né nuvolo vi era che lumeggiato non fusse, facendosi a credere che il Papa, come poco di quell'arte intendente, dovesse perciò dare a lui il premio della vittoria. Venuto il giorno che si dovevano l'opera di tutti scoprire, fu veduta anco la sua, e con molte risa e motti da tutti gl'altri artefici schernita e beffata, uccellandolo tutti in cambio d'avergli compassione. Ma gli scherniti finalmente furono essi, perciò che que' colori, sì come si era Cosimo imaginato, a un tratto così abbagliarono gl'occhi del Papa, che non molto s'intendeva di simili cose ancora che se ne dilettasse assai, che giudicò Cosimo avere molto meglio che tutti gl'altri operato. E così fattogli dare il premio, commandò agl'altri che tutti coprissero le loro pitture dei migliori az[z]urri che si trovassero e le toccassino d'oro, acciò che fussero simili a quelle di Cosimo nel colorito e nell'essere ricche. Laonde i poveri pittori disperati d'avere a sodisfare alla poca intelligenza del Padre Santo, si diedero a guastare quanto avevano fatto di buono; onde Cosimo si rise di coloro che poco inanzi si erano riso del fatto suo.

Doc. 6

D. REDIG DE CAMPOS, 'I "tituli" degli affreschi del Quattrocento nella Cappella Sistina', in *Rendiconti della Pontificia Accademia romana di Archeologia*, XLII, 1969/70, pp. 299 ff.;
D. REDIG DE CAMPOS, 'I "tituli" degli affreschi del Quattrocento nella Cappella Sistina', in *Studi di Storia dell'Arte in Onore di V. Mariani*, Naples, 1971, p. 113 ff.
R. SALVINI, 'The Sistine Chapel: Ideology and Architecture', in *Art History*, 3, 1980, pp. 144 ff.

Doc. 7

Letter from F. Orsini to V. Pinelli:

Quanto al ritratto del Gaza, io non conosco persona che l'habbia. Ben me ricordo havere inteso del Card. S. Agnolo che Papa Paolo III li mostrava nella cappella di Sixto IV uno di quei quadroni di mano del Cortone, dove era il Bessarione con cinque de suoi, fra quali nominava l'Argyropulo, il Gaza, il Sipontino, etc., e che il Gaza haveva un capello in testa.

P. de NOLHAC, *La Bibliothèque de Fulvio Orsini*, Paris, 1887, p. 166.

Doc. 8

Resolution of the Operai of the Palazzo Vecchio, 1482:

Supradicti operarii, – obtento partito per quinque fabas nigras secundum ordinem, dederunt et locaverunt, vigore legis propterea edite per oportuna consilia, die 31 mensis Augusti proxime preteriti pro finali conclusione Dominicho Tomasi del Grillandaio, pictori, presenti et recipienti etc., faciam sale palatii populi florent. versus doanam ad faciendam et pingendam immaginem Sci. Zenobii et aliarum immaginum pro ornando dicti palatii etc.
D.D.
Item dederunt et locaverunt vigore dictae legis Dominicho et Sandro Marini, pictoribus, faciam sale audientie dominorum dicti palatii ad pingendum et ornandum pro ornamento dicti palatii.

Item locaverunt Pietro, vocato Perugino, et Blaxio Antonii Tucci, pictoribus, faciam sale palatii dictorum dominorum, versus plateam, videlicet faciam fenestrae, ad faciendum et pingendum; solvendum salarium ut in deliberatione de Dominicho del Grillandaio continetur.

Item locaverunt faciam putei dicte sale Piero Iacobi del Pollaiuolo pictori etc.

G. GAYE, *Carteggio inedito d'artisti dei secoli XIV, XV, XVI*, vol. I, Florence, 1839, p. 578.
J. MESNIL, art. cit. (1905), p. 43.
R. LIGHTBOWN, op. cit., no. 19.
The circumstances dictating the cancellations and changes of programme are not clear.

Doc. 9

Letter from Lodovico il Moro's agent (Archivio di Stato, Milan):

Sandro de Botticello pictore Excellen^mo in tauola · et in muro · le cose sue hano aria virile ·
   et sono cum optima ragione · et integra proportione.
Philippino di Frati Philippo optimo · Discipulo del sopra dicto · et figliolo del piu singulare
   maestro di tempo suoi · le sue cose hano aria piu dolce · non credo habiano tanta arte ·
El Perusino Maestro singulare; et maxime in muro · le sue cose hano aria angelica, et
   molto dolce.
Dominico de Grilandaio bono maestro in tauola · et piu in muro · le cosse sue hano bona
   aria, et e homo expeditiuo, et che conduce assai Lauoro ·
Tutti questi predicti maestri hano facto proua di loro ne la capella di papa syxto excepto
   che philippino · Ma tutti poi allospedaletto del M^co · Laur^o · et la palma e · quasi ambigua ·

P. MÜLLER-WALDE, 'Beiträge zur Kenntnis des Leonardo da Vinci', in *Jahrbuch der preussischen
Kunstsammlungen*, XVIII, 1897, p. 113.
H. HORNE, *Botticelli*, London, 1908, doc. XXIV (and reprinted Princeton, 1980).
R. LIGHTBOWN, op. cit., doc. 30.

Doc. 1

Letter from Cardinal Francesco Gonzaga to his father, the Marchese Federico:

Ceterum significo a la Celsitudine vestra come il Magnifico Lorenzo di Medici andó heri vedando la terra. Et hogj laccompagnai a messa a Sancto Francisco a pede. De li la sua Magnificentia se drició a casa de Andrea Mantegna, dove la vite cum grande piacere alcune picture desso Andrea et certe teste di relevo cum molte altre cose antique, che pare molto se ne deletti. Se ne venimo poi a la corte...
 Mantue xxiii Febrij 1483.

Ill^{me} D. V. Filius et servitor,
Franciscus de Gonzaga
cum Racc.

204   Andrea Mantegna. *Madonna of Victory*. Detail: Francesco Gonzaga. 1496. Tempera on panel. Musée du Louvre, Paris.

P. KRISTELLER, *Mantegna*, London, 1901, no. 39, p. 481.

On the situation peculiar to the north of Italy and the character of the 'archaeological' humanism which developed there:
A. CHASTEL, *La Renaissance méridionale*, Paris, 1965, pp. 132 ff.

Doc. 2

Letter from Marchese Francesco to Mantegna, 6 November 1485:

Andree Mantinee,
 Carissime noster La Illustrissima Madonna duchessa de Ferrara nostra per sue littere: quale te mandiamo qui incluse, ad cio che melio intendi lo volere suo, haveria caro: come vederai de havere uno certo quadro de la mano tua. Comittemoti per satisffare a quella madonna: che usi ogni diligentia per finirlo interponendoli lo ingegno tuo: come ne confidamo debbi fare: et piu presto sia possibile: adcio che la prefata Ill. Madonna sia compiaciuta del che nui siamo studiossimi [*sic*] Concurreralli e li effecti e la virtu tua et precipuo contento nostro.
 Godij vj Nobris. 1485.

P. KRISTELLER, op. cit., no. 42, p. 482.

The picture for Eleonora of Aragon:
Un quadro de legno depincto cum nostra donna et figliolo cum serafini de mano del sopra dicto Mantegna (Inventory of the Estense Guardaroba, 1493):
G. CAMPORI, *Raccolta di Cataloghi*, Modena, 1870, p. 1.
P. KRISTELLER, op. cit., no. 1, p. 306.

The picture in the Brera Gallery, Milan (89×71 cm):
A. MARTINDALE and N. GARAVIGLIA, *Mantegna*, London, 1971 (Milan, 1967), no. 62.

Doc. 3

Letter from Silvestro Calandra to the Marchese Francesco, 26 August 1486:

Ill. S. mio... Hozi lo Ill. Duca [Ercole di Ferrara] ha voluto vedere la spalera et doppo disnare montò inbarcha per andar un poco a solazo per il laco, dove stette poco spacio, perche laqua li facea male per non gli essere consueto: et smonto al porto de Corte per andare avedere li Trionphi de Cesare che dipinge il Mantegna: li quali molto li piaqueno; poi se ne venne per la via coperta in castello.

Mantue xxvi. Augusti 1486.

Ill^me D. V. Fidelis servus
Silvestro Calandra.

Ill. princ. et Ex. dno meo sing. Francisco Marchioni Mantue etc.

P. KRISTELLER, op. cit., no. 46, p. 483.

On the *Triumphs*:
A. MARTINDALE, *The Triumphs of Caesar by Andrea Mantegna in the Collection of H. M. the Queen at Hampton Court*, London, 1979.

Doc. 4

M. EQUICOLA, *Commentarii Mantuani*, 1521, Bk. IV:

Nel ultima parte de la cita, propinquo alla chiesa di san sebastiano palazo superbissimo, edeficio e bello, per sicuramente collocare in una salla ad solo questo effecto fabricata, lo triumpho de C. Iulio Cesare fatiga de molti anni di misser Andrea Mantegna, parea dicto triumpho tranco e mutilato per non vi essere quella pompa che sequir solea il triumphante. Mancavanovi li spectatori al che provede Francesco prudentemente chiamando alla sua liberalita Lorenzo Costa, homo non solamente in pictura excellentissimo, ma amabile e honorato cortegiano. Questo, oltra le altre laudate opere, con ingegno, arte, e scienta, de dicta bellissima sala il capo e fine adorna.

Text in A. MARTINDALE, op. cit., doc. 26, p. 185.

Mario Equicola (*c.* 1470–1525), was a pupil of Ficino and a member of the Este Court, and later of that of Isabella d'Este at Mantua. He wrote *De natura de Amore* (Venice, 1525) and *Istitutioni al comporre in ogni sorte di rima della lingua volgare con un eruditissimo discorso della pittura...* (Milan, 1541). See D. SANTORO, *Della vita e delle opere di Mario Equicola*, Chieti, 1906.

Doc. 5

G. VASARI, *Life of Mantegna*, ed. Milanesi, III, pp. 396 ff.

Al medesimo marchese dipinse, nel palazzo di San Sebastiano in Mantoa, in una sala, il trionfo di Cesare; che è la miglior cosa che lavorasse mai. In questa opera si vede con ordine bellissimo situato nel trionfo la bellezza e l'ornamento del carro, colui che vitupera il trionfante, i parenti, i profumi, gl'incensi, i sacrifizi, i sacerdoti, i tori pel sacrificio coronati, e' prigioni, le prede fatte da' soldati, l'ordinanza delle squadre, i liofanti, le spoglie, le vittorie, e le città e le ròcche in vari carri contraffatte, con una infinità di trofei in sull'aste, e varie armi per testa e per indosso, acconciature, ornamenti e vasi infiniti; e tra la moltitudine degli spettatori, una donna che ha per la mano un putto, al qual essendosi fitto una spina in un piè, lo mostra egli piangendo alla madre con modo grazioso e molto naturale. Costui [...] ebbe in questa istoria una bella e buona avvertenza; che avendo situato il piano, dove posavano le figure, più alto che la veduta dell'occhio, fermò i piedi dinanzi in sul primo profilo e linea del piano, facendo sfuggire gli altri più a dentro di mano in mano, e perder della veduta dei piedi e gambe, quanto richiedeva la ragione della veduta; e cosi delle spoglie, vasi ed altri istrumenti ed ornamenti fece veder sola la parte di sotto e perder quella di sopra, come di ragione di prospettiva si conveniva di fare.

All the relevant documents are assembled by A. MARTINDALE, op. cit.

Doc. 6

Decree from the Marchese Francesco on behalf of Mantegna:

[...] Hieronis namque Syracusarum regis phamam illustravit non mediocriter Archimedis summi architecti familiaritas. Inter praeclara Alexandri edicta illud maxime celebratur quo ab alio quam ab Appelle pingi ab alio quam a Lysippo fingi se vetuit. Magno etiam decori fuit et glorie Augusto quod Vitruvium Veronensem architectem suum tanta liberalitate persequutus sit, ut ex... [?] et ignobili fecerit clarissimum. Quae cum ita sint quid officij conferre possemus in Andream mantiniam consumatissime virtutis virum: ex omnibus sine controversia qui picturam profitentur: quadam ingenij diversitate excellentem conferre possemus. Diu multumque cogitavimus: Nam cum nec inscij essemus de nobis et de maioribus patre atque avo benemeritum esse: et cum intueremus eius opera praeclara et admiratione digna que in sacello et camera nostre arcis quondam pinxerit, et que modo Iulij Cesaris triumphum prope vivis et spirantibus adhuc imaginibus nobis pingit adeo ut nec repraesentari: sed fieri res videatur: Cum et ad aures nostras pervenerit phama illius nobilissimi delubri: quod consensu ac mandato nostro nuper Innocentio VIII. Pont. Max. depinxit in vaticano [...]

P. KRISTELLER, op. cit., no. 52, pp. 486.

Doc. 7

Letter from Sigismondo Gonzaga to the Marchese Francesco, 6 July 1496:

Illmo S. mio Unico. Havendo io a continua memoria il dì crudele et acerrimo del facto d'arme che hozi è un anno se fece in Parmesana, nel quale il summo Dio e sua gloriosa matre salvò da tanti periculi V. Ex. doppo molte valorose e strenue operatione facte per lei a morte e destructione de li nemici, ho pensato insieme cum la mia Illma Madonna in questo dì fare qualche laudabile memoria a laude de Dio e de sua gloriosa matre. Et cossi havemo ordinato una bella processione, la quale questa matina solemnemente cum tutte le regole de frati e preti s'è facta in questo modo: Tutti li religiosi si adunoreno a San Sebastiano cum la mazor parte del populo, dove era exaltata la Imagine di la gloriosa Verzene che ha fornita m. Andrea Mantinea suso uno tribunale grande adornato molto solemnemente, et sopra ad essa imagine gli era uno zovene vestito da Dio Patre et dui propheti da ogni canto, da li ladi tri anzoletti che cantavano certe laude e per contra gli erano li xii apostoli. Quando fue el tempo, se levò questo tribunale che era portato da xx fachini et cossì processionaliter se portò questa imagine fin a San Simone cum tanto numero de persone maschij e femine che mai non ne fu viste tante in Mantua. Quivi era aparechiato uno solemne altare suso il cantone de la nova Capella, dove celebrò una solemne messa m. Christhophoro Arrivabeno. Ma prima frate Petro da Caneto fece una bella oratione vulgare al populo in laude de la Verzene gloriosa, in exhortárli ad haverla in devotione, ricordandoli che l'era stata quella che havea liberata V. Ex. in simile dì da tanti periculi [...]

Il doppo disnare essa imagine fu collocata al loco deputato, dove non stete tre hore che ge furono presantate alcune imagine de cera e doperi et altri voti, per il che credo che in breve tempo gli acrescerà grandissima devotione e de tutto questo bene V. Ex. ne serà stata causa...

Mantue 6 Julij 1496.   Servitor
                                                                                    Sigismundus de Gonzaga

P. KRISTELLER, op. cit., no. 60, pp. 490.

On the circumstances of 1495/6:
A. LUZIO, 'La Madonna della Vittoria del Mantegna', *Emporium*, X (1894), pp. 358 ff.

On Mantegna and engraving:
In a letter to Gian Francesco Gonzaga of 21 December 1491 Mantegna mentions engravings:
'Having heard that Your Excellency has sent the small painting to Milan, I am sending another, since I have the prints *(stampe)* to produce others in honour of the Virgin Mary, to whom I am indebted for more graces than I have deserved.'

This letter is one of the first mentions of engraving as a kind of *aide-mémoire* allowing the repetition of a composition. It has been suggested that the *stampa* which came in so useful was the engraving B8, which represents the Virgin and Child seated, of the type known as the Virgin of Humility. See E. TIETZE-CONRAT, *Mantegna*, London, 1955, p. 241.

On Jacob of Strasburg's suite:
J. M. MASSING, 'Jacobus Argentoratensis. Etude préliminaire', *Arte Veneta*, XXXI, 1977, pp. 42–52.

On the drawing by Parentino (Scholz Collection, New York) representing an agitated and confused triumphal procession, with a collection of arms and trophies carried by elephants and oxen, which has been thought to be an original response by Parentino to Mantegna's model, see C. GILBERT, *Drawings of the Italian Renaissance from the Janos Scholz Collection*, Bloomington, Ind., 1958, no. 6, and E. J. OLSZEWSKI, *The Draftsman's Eye*, Cleveland, Ohio, 1981, no. 117, pp. 142 ff.

Doc. 8

1504: Pomponius Gauricus, *De Sculptura* fo. 5^v:
Laudatur Julius noster quod Palladiam illam Mantenii nostri turbam, Caesareusque triumphos tam bellissime sit imitatus.
A. Chastel and R. Klein (eds.), Geneva–Paris 1969, p. 101. The identification of *Julius noster* with Giulio Campagnola is almost certain, given his links with Gauricus, and the friendship of Giulio's father Girolamo with Leonico Tomeo. The fame of the composition did not escape the notice of French noblemen. Cardinal Georges d'Amboise had it carved on the reverse of the entrance doors to the lower court at Gaillon, as is attested by a very detailed correspondence:
'… gli è sculpito tutto il triumpho de Julio Cesare ne le forme ch'el famoso Mantinia lo dipinse…'
R. WEISS, 'The Castle of Gaillon in 1509–1510', in *Journal of the Warburg and Courtauld Institutes*, XVI, 1953, p. 6.

Doc. 9

Letter from Pietro Bembo to the Marchesa of Mantua, on the first day of 1505:

[…] Con Mess. Francesco Cornelio fratello del Rmo cardinale io servo e stretto parentado et molto cara et famigliare domestichezza non meno che se io li fussi carnal fratello. Aggiungonsi a questo molte sue singularissime parti che fanno che io infinitamente lo onoro et desidero di piacerli. Esso già buon tempo, siccome vaghissimo delle rare cose, il che sogliono essere per lo più tutti li spiriti elevati e gentili, convenne con mess. Andrea Mantegna che li dipingesse alcuni telari per prezzo di ducati 150, et diedeneli per caparra 25 avendoli prima mandate le misure, et ben veduto per mess. Andrea l'opera che ci andava. Ora mi si dice che esso mes. Andrea ricusa di voler più fare detta opera per quel prezzo, e ne dimanda molto più. Il che è paruto a Mess. Francesco la più nuova cosa del mondo et pare a chiunque la ode dire, massimamente avendo mes. Francesco lettera di Mes. Andrea, per le quali esso particolarmente conferma il patto detto di sopra tra loro. Allega mes. Andrea che l'opera riesce maggiore che esso non istimava, et però ne vuole più mercede. Il perche priego e supplico V.E., se la mia servitù è in alcun conto appresso Lei, che V.S., persuada Mes. Andrea ad attendere alla fede data e mes. Francesco et a dar principio alla tolta impresa delle sue pitture, massimamente richiedendosi a lui più che a veruno altro il mantenere delle promesse, che è chiamato il Mantegna del mondo. […]

C. D'ARCO, *Delle Arti e degli Artefici di Mantova*, Mantua, 1857, II, no. 68, p. 57.

On the Cornaro 'frieze' (National Gallery, 73.5×268 cm):
A. BRAHAM, 'A Reappraisal of the "Introduction of the Cult of Cybele at Rome" by Mantegna', *Burlington Magazine*, CXV, 1973, pp. 457–63.
M. DAVIES, *Early Italian Schools* (Catalogue of the National Gallery, London), 2nd. ed., 1961, pp. 330–4.

Doc. 1

Giovanni SANTI, *Cronaca*, XXII, 96, vv. 125–7:

> ... Dui giovin par detate e par damori
> Leonardo da Vinci el Perusino
> Pier dalla Pieve che un divin pictore...

H. Holtzinger (ed.), Stuttgart, 1893.

Perugino's career was the subject of a fundamental but now outdated study by W. BOMBE, *Geschichte der peruginer Malerei bis zu Perugino und Pinturicchio*, Berlin, 1912.

F. CANUTI, *Il Perugino*, 2 vols., Perugia, 1931, from which I have borrowed extensively, remains indispensable.

In this chapter I have been influenced by the severe judgement of G. VASARI, *Life of Pietro Perugino*, ed. Milanesi, III, pp. 565 ff., on his vulgarity, greed, and unscrupulousness.

The catalogue by E. CAMESASCA, *Perugino*, in the series Classici dell'Arte, Milan, 1969 (French trans., Paris, 1969) is particularly useful.

The problem of the early works has still to be tackled. Penetrating observations in F. ZERI, 'Il Maestro dell'Annunciazione Gardner', *Bollettino d'Arte*, XXXVIII, 1953, pp. 191 ff.

205   Perugino. *The Fano Altarpiece.* 1497. Tempera on panel. Sta. Maria Nuova, Fano.

Doc. 2

A

Contract for the Fano Altarpiece (Archivio notarile, Fano):

Dictis millesimo [1488], indictione [sexta], tempore pontificatus [S.mi in Christo Pontificis et Domini nostri Domini Innocentij Divina Providentia Papae Octavi], et die XXI dicti mensis aprilis [...]

Magister Petrus olim Christofori de Castro Plebis districtus Perusii, et Magister Jovachinus Blasii de Urbino ex una parte et Petrus Antonius a Lanceis et Matheus de Martinotiis de Fano sindici ecclesiae Sanctae Mariae Novae et Ser Petrus Antonius de Galassis de Fano videlicet: dictus Matheus etiam et Ser Petrus Antonius tamquam ambo fideicommissarii et executores testamenti Durantis olim Joannis Vianutii de Fano, scripti et apparentis ut dicitur publice manu Ser Francisci Damiani de Monte Maiori civis Fani et notarii publici ex alia parte, ad infrascriptam transactionem unionem pactum et concordiam devenerunt videlicet: quod dictus Magister Jovachinus promisit et convenit solemni stipulatione prefatis Sindicis et executoribus hinc ad semestre proxime futuri incoando impresentiarum et quam citius fieri potuit in dicto semestri suis proprijs lignaminibus sumptibus et expensis conficere laborare et fabricare et construere unam iconam pro altari magno ipsius ecclesiae Sanctae Mariae Novae de Fano iuxta dispositionem factam per breve apostolicum super testamento dicti Durantis iuxta et secundum designia facta per ipsum Magistrum Jovachinum et designata et picta in quadam charta et dimissa apud ipsos Sindicos et executores bene sculptam et ornatam ac aptam.

Dictus vero Magister Petrus promisit et se obligavit etiam infra dictum tempus de quo supra et quod citius fieri potuit etiam in dicto tempore pingere ornate omnibus eius sumptibus et espensis auri colorum finorum et aliorum necessariorum et convenientium in ipsa icona pingenda perpulchre infrascriptas figuras videlicet: in quadro imaginem Beate Virginis cum eius filio in gremio devote adorantis eum nec non imaginem et figuras secundum proportiones earum congruas Sancti Johanni Baptiste Sanctorum Petri et Pauli Sancti Francisci Sancti Hieronymj Sancti Ludovici Sancti Micaelis Arcangeli et Sanctae Mariae Magdalene. Sursum vero in summitate et altitudine quadri ipsius pingere pietatem cum imaginibus Beatae Mariae et Sancti Johannis Evangeliste a lateribus: et in fine quadri et totius tabulae festa Beate Virginis in quinque quadris, videlicet: in pratella Nativitatem Beatae Virginis, presentationem factam in templo, annuntiationem, purificationem et assumpionem, et circum circa dictam iconam ornare et etiam in ipsa tabula tota et omnibus eius locis ornare et redimire suis convenientis, auro, azurro tramerino et omnibus coloribus finis pulcre et ornate et sufficienter copiose, et aliis figuris in locis opportunis secundum convenientiam quadri ipsius. [...]

B

Poem by the notary Pier Domenico Stati:

Pictor in Italia tota qui primus haberis
    Petreque qui primus pictor in orbe manes
Et Jovachine pares tibi qui non invenis ullos
    In tabulis caesis artificique manu
Alter Parrhasius alter Lysippus et ambo
    Qui ingenio priscos vincitis arte novos
Ponite et ingenium vestrum hic intendite totum
    Pingenda in Maria: Vester enim hic labor est
Effigies hominum similes pulchrasque potestis
    Vos alia similem non dare sed Mariae
Haec duo vos operi subscribite Carmina vos iam
    Autores operis artifices operibus
Optimus et primus pictor iam Petrus in orbe
    Hoc dedit incisor et Joavachinus opus.

F. BATTISTELLI, 'Notizie e Documenti sull'attività del Perugino a Fano', *Antichità viva*, XIII, 1974, no. 5, p. 67.

The work was executed only between 1493 and 1497 and is signed and dated in that year. On its history see the exhibition catalogue, *Lorenzo Lotto nelle Marche*, Ancona, 1981, no. 2.

On the predella: R. LONGHI, 'Percorso di Raffaello Giovine', *Paragone*, no. 65, 1955, and the Lotto catalogue cit., no. 3.

Doc. 3

Contract for the polyptych of S. Pietro, Perugia (Archives of S. Pietro, Perugia):

Magistri Petri pittoris locatio Ancone altaris majoris monasterii. [...]
    Reverendus in Cristo Pater Dopnus Lactantius Juliani de Florentia, Abbas monasterii Santi Petri de Perusia, ordinis sancti Benedicti Congregationis sanctae Justinae, nec non dopnus Benedictus de Senis, et Dopnus Daniel de Perusio eiusdem ordinis, Sindici et procuratores dicti monasterii, de licentia, consensu, et voluntate dicti domini Abbatis, praesentis, et consentientis, et quilibet eorum per eos et eorum successores obligando res et bona dicti monasterii, mobilia, stabilia, praesentia et futura, pro ipsorum omnium observatione conduxerunt et locaverunt spectabili viro *Magistro Petro Cristofori de Castro Plebis, pictori excellentissimo*, praesenti, et acceptanti pro se et suis, ad depingendum et ornandum tabulam sive Anconam majoris altaris dictae ecclesiae S. Petri, hoc modo, videlicet: In campo sive quadro ipsius Tabulae Ascentionem D. N. J. C. cum figura et Imagine gloriosissimae Virginis Mariae et XII Apostolorum cum aliquibus angelis et aliis ornamentis, secundum quod in facto cognoverit opportunum. In circulo vero superiori pingatur figura sive Imago Dei Patris omnipotentis cum duobus angelis ad latus sustinentibus circulum. Predulam autem ad pedes historiatam, pictam, et ornatam ad voluntatem domini abbatis pro tempore existentis Colupnae (Columnae) autem et cornices et totum aliud ornamentum ipsius tabulae ornari debeant ad aurum finum, et azurrum ultramarinum finum, et alios finos colores secundum quod magis convenerit. Ita quod ditta tabula sive Ancona a capite usque ad pedes sit bene ac diligenter depicta, ornata, deaurata ut supra, ad usum boni sufficientis et legalis ac perfecti magistri, infra tempus duorum annorum [...], omnibus ipsius *Magistri Petri* sumptibus et expensis,

etc. Quae omnia et singula praefatus *Magister Petrus* facere, tenere, attendere et observare promisit dicto domino abbati pro dicto monasterio recipienti, sub poenis infrascriptis et obligatione omnium suorum bonorum mobilium et stabilium, praesentium, et futurorum. [...] praefatus Reverendus Pater Abbas, per se, etc., obligando dictum monasterium et eius bona ut supra, promisit et convenit eidem *Magistro Petro*, praesenti, stipulanti, et recipienti pro se et suis haeredibus, solvere et cum effectu numerare pro sua pictura, mercede, coloribus auro, et aliis necessariis et opportunis ad perfectionem dictae picturae, ornamentorum dictae tabulae, ducatos auri largos quingentos, solvendos infra quatuor annos, incipiendo a die, quo inceperit dictam picturam, videlicet anno quolibet quartam partem [...]

F. CANUTI, op. cit., II, pp. 176–7, doc. no. 224.

The panels of this polyptych are now dispersed between:
Musée, Lyons, central panel (280×216 cm), lunette (114×230 cm); Musée, Nantes, *tondi* of *Jeremiah* (diam. 127 cm) and *Isaiah* (diam. 127 cm); Musée, Rouen, predelle—1. *Epiphany*, 2. *Baptism*, 3. *Resurrection* (all 31×59 cm); S. Pietro, Perugia, four small panels (32×37,5 cm); Vatican Museum, four small figures (35.5×26 cm).

206 Perugino. *Polyptych of S. Pietro.* (1496; reconstruction.)
'That the said picture or ancona shall be well and carefully painted from top to bottom, decorated, gilded according the manner of a good master... at the cost and expense of Maestro Pietro.' (Contract for the polyptych for S. Pietro in Perugia, 1494–5.)

Doc. 4

Agreement between Perugino and the Provveditori al Sal of Venice, 9 August 1494:

Marcado de *M. Piero Peroxin* depentor.
   1494, di 9 Augusti.
   I Magnifici Signori M. Fantin Marcello et compagni, dignissimi Provvedadori al Sal, de comandamento dil Ser.mo Principe, hano fato marchado, et sono rimasti dacordo cum *M. Piero Peroxin depentor*, el qual ha tolto a depenzer ne la sala del gran Conseio, uno campo tra una fenestra et l'altra in ver S. Zorzi, tra el qual campo de la historia de la charitade è uno altro campo, over quadro, il qual campo ha tolto a depenzer, si è (cioè) da una fenestra à l'altra; et sono tre volti compidi (?) e mezo; nel qual dié depenzer i tanti doxi quanti achaderà, et quela historia quando il Papa scampò da Roma, et la bataia seguita di soto, havendo a compir quela cossa achadrà in cima di le fenestre oltra la mitade.
   Ittem el dicto *M. piero* sarà obligato far tuor in desegno l'opera, et al presente, et quella darà ai prefati magnifici signori provvedadori, essendo obligado far essa historia piue presto miorar, ch'altramente de li altri lavori facti nela ditta sala, sì come si conviene a quelo degno loco, dovendo far dicta opera più richa de la prima, a tutte soe spexe de oro, arzento, azuro, et colori, et de tutte quelle cosse appartien a l'arte del depentor; et li magnifici S.ri provvedidori li farano far il teller de legnami et de telle da depenzer suxo, et i soleri (palchi) et altri inzegni azò depenzer possi. Harà dito maistro per suo pagamento del ditto lavor, chum li muodi dichiaradi di sopra ducati quatrocento doro, zoè duc. 400.

F. CANUTI, op. cit., II, pp. 165–6, doc. no. 198, from GAYE, *Carteggio*, II, pp. 69–70. It has been doubted whether the 'Piero Peroxin' of the document really was Pietro Perugino, but Canuti (pp. 96 ff.) has no difficulty in elucidating the problem.

Doc. 5

Resolution of the Collegio del Cambio, Perugia (Archives of the Cambio, Perugia):

Anno Domini MCCCCLXXXXVI, die XXVI Januari. Convocata et congregata et cohadunata publica et generali adunantia Hominum et Juratorum Artis Cambi, sono tubae, voceque preconis, bapnita et praeconizata [...]
   Coram quibus Auditores proposuerunt ornamentum Audientiae, utrum debeat ornari per totum aliquibus picturis, per manum M. Petri, vel alterius Magistri [...]
   Cardus Cinaglia surgens dixit idem. Circa ornamentum Audientiae dixit, quod Audientia debeat ornari, pingere, aut quovis alio modo pulcherrima fieri. Judicio et adiudicatione dictorum, eligendi homines, qui una cum dictis Auditoribus arbitrium habeant... locandi, et deliberandi, et expresse dandi, prout eis videbitur et placebit...

F. CANUTI, op. cit., II, pp. 159–60, no. 256.
The contract was signed in the presence of the notary to the Cambio.

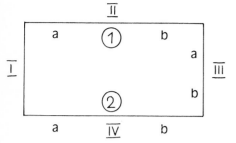

DIAGRAM

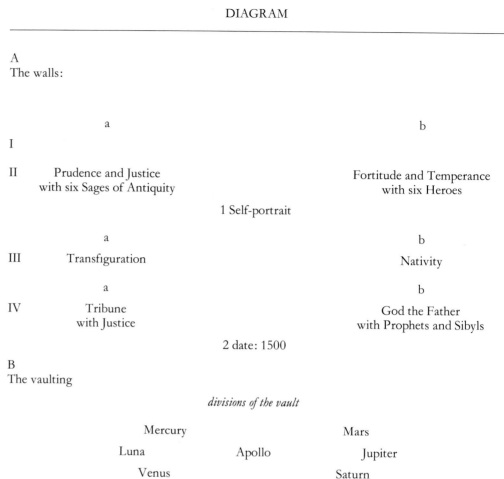

A
The walls:

	a	b
I		
II	Prudence and Justice with six Sages of Antiquity	Fortitude and Temperance with six Heroes

1 Self-portrait

III	a Transfiguration	b Nativity
IV	a Tribune with Justice	b God the Father with Prophets and Sibyls

2 date: 1500

B
The vaulting

divisions of the vault

Mercury		Mars
Luna	Apollo	Jupiter
Venus		Saturn

Doc. 6

G. VASARI, *Life of Pietro Perugino*, ed. Milanesi, III, p. 582:

Ed in uno ornamento fece il suo ritratto, che pare vivissimo; scrivendovi sotto il nome suo in questo modo:

PETRUS PERUSINUS EGREGIUS PICTOR. / PERDITA SI FUERAT PINGENDI: / HIC RETTULIT ARTEM. / SI NUSQUAM INVENTA EST / HACTENUS: IPSE DEDIT.

E. H. GOMBRICH, 'Tradition and Expression in Western Still Life', (1959), reprinted in *Meditations on a Hobby Horse, and Other Essays...*, London, 1963, p. 102.

Doc. 7

G. VASARI, *Life of Pietro Perugino*, ed. Milanesi, III, pp. 595, 598:

... Fra i detti discepoli di Pietro miglior maestro di tutti fu Andrea Luigi d'Ascesi, chiamato l'Ingegno, il quale nella sua prima giovenezza concorse con Raffaello da Urbino sotto la disciplina di esso Pietro; il quale l'adoperò sempre nelle più importanti pitture che facesse, come fu nell'Udienza del Cambio di Perugia [...]
Ma nessuno di tanti discepoli paragonò mai la diligenza di Pietro nè la grazia che ebbe nel colorire in quella sua maniera, la quale tanto piacque al suo tempo, che vennero molti di Francia, di Spagna, d'Alemagna et d'altre provincie per impararla.

On Andrea da Assisi (documented 1484–1516) and his participation in the work of the 'firm':
U. GNOLI, *Pittori e Miniatori nell'Umbria*, Spoleto, 1923.

A. VENTURI, *Storia dell'Arte italiana*, vol. VII, 2, Milan, 1913, thinks he may already have been working for Perugino on the Sistine frescoes.

Doc. 8

Sopra la Cappella vostra ho visto l'intentione vostra [...] che voi dite haver parlato a Mr. Pietro Perugino, vi dico, che volendo fare di sua mano, Lui è il meglio Mastro d'Italia. E questo che si chiama Patorichio è stato suo discepolo, il quale al presente non è qui. Altri mastri non ci sono che vaglino.

Letter from Agostino Chigi to his father, 7 November 1500:

A. CUGNONI, 'Agostino Chigi il Magnifico', in *Archivio della Società romana di Storia patria*, 2, 1879, p. 481.

On the Lombard interest in Perugino:
F. MALAGUZZI-VALERI, 'Il Perugino e la Certosa di Pavia', in *Repertorium für Kunstwissenschaft*, XXVI, 1903, pp. 372–81: letters from the Duke to Venice, Florence and Perugia to obtain for himself works by Perugino.

Doc. 9

Will of Ser Angelo di Tommaso Conti, 8 December, 1500 (Archivio notarile, Perugia):

Anno Domini, Millesimo quingentesimo die VIII mensis Decem.
    Egregius vir Ser Angelus Thomae Contis, de Perusio P. Heburnee, Parochiae S. Savini, etc. per hoc presens testamentum [...]
    In primis quidem etc. corpus suum sepeliri voluit apud Ecclesiam S. Dominici de Perusio, P. S. Petri, in sepultura suorum Parentium (omissis). Item iudicavit et reliquit, voluit, etc. quod infrascripti eius heredes teneantur, et debeant infra unum annum, a die mortis ipsius testatoris, erigi facere et construi in Ecclesia S. Marie Angelorum de Perusio [...] unum altare pro missis et divinis offitiis celebrandis, et super eodem altari ponatur tabula, quam ipse testator iam fieri fecit, et in eadem tabula pingantur immagines S. Anne et filiarum eius, videlicet Gloriosissime Virginis Marie cum filio suo, Ieshu Cripsto, S. Marie Cleofe, S. Marie Salome, cum filiis eius et S. Ioseph et S. Iohachim eo modo et forma prout coeptum et designatum est in ea, per *excellentissimum pictorem Mag. Petrus Cristofori de Castro Plebis, civem perusinum*; et solvere pro pictura florenos quinquaginta quinque, ad rationem quadraginta bolonenorum pro flor., pro residuo sexaginta quinque, quod fuit pretium dicte picture; de quibus sexaginta quinque florenis dictus *Mag. Petrus* iam habuit pro arra, et parte pretii, florenes decem ad dictam rat...

F. CANUTI, op. cit., II, pp. 197–8, doc. no. 280.

Doc. 10

Letter from F. Malatesta to the Marchesa Isabella:

1503, 19 gennaio, Firenze.
    Fr. Malatesta alla marchesa Isabella.
    Le notifico di aver conchiuso il contratto al Perugino in cento ducati d'oro, e di averne sborsati venti, giusto strumento rogato da Ser Pierfrancesco di Ser Macario de Macari.

W. BRAGHIROLLI, 'Notizie e Documenti inediti intorno a Pietro Vannucci', *Giornale di Erudizione artistica*, II, 1873, pp. 73 ff.

On the *studiolo* of Isabella d'Este:
E. VERHEYEN, *The Paintings in the 'Studiolo' of Isabella d'Este at Mantua*, New York, 1971.
Le Studiolo d'Isabelle d'Este (Dossiers du département des peintures, ed. S. Béguin, 10), Paris, 1975.

Doc. 11

Letter from Isabella d'Este to Perugino, 30 June 1505:

... Ma quando fusse stato finito con magior diligenzia havendo a stare appresso quelli di Mantinea che sono summamenti netti seria stato magior honore vostro et più nostra satisfactione et rincrescene che quello Lorenzo mantovano vi dissuadesse da colorirlo ad olio.

W. BRAGHIROLLI, art. cit., and W. BOMBE, op. cit., doc. LII, p. 376.

Doc. 12

G. VASARI, *Life of Pietro Perugino*, ed. Milanesi, III, p. 585:

Aveva Pietro tanto lavorato e tanto gli abbondava sempre da lavorare che e' metteva in opera bene spesso le medesime cose; ed era talmente la dottrina dell'arte sua ridotta a maniera, ch' é faceva a tutte le figure un' aria medesima. Perché, essendo venuto già Michelagnolo Buonarroti al suo tempo, desiderava grandemente Pietro vedere le figure di quello, per lo grido che gli davano gli artefici. E vedendosi occultare la grandezza di quel nome che con si gran principio per tutto aveva acquistato, cercava molto con mordaci parole offendere quelli che operavano. E per questo meritò, oltre alcune brutture fattegli dagli artefici, che Michelagnolo in pubblico gli decesse ch' egli era un goffo nell' arte. Ma non potendo Pietro comportare tanta infamia, ne furono al magistrato degli otto tutti due dove ne rimase Pietro con assai poco onore.

207 Anonymous. *Piazza della Signoria.* Sixteenth century. Galleria Corsini, Florence.
The Piazza del Palazzo Vecchio, with the Loggia on the right side of the palace, seen in a schematic view of the execution of Savonarola.

Doc. 1

G. VASARI, *Life of Leonardo da Vinci*, ed. Milanesi, IV, pp. 47–8:

Era sdegno grandissimo fra Michelagnolo Buonarroti e lui: per il che partì di Fiorenza Michelagnolo per la concorrenza, con la scusa del duca Giuliano, essendo chiamato dal papa per la facciata di San Lorenzo. Lionardo intendendo ciò, partì ed andò in Francia, dove il re avendo avuto opere sue, gli era molto affezionato, e desiderava che colorisse il cartone della Sant'Anna.

After this chapter was completed I learned that the 21st *Lettura vinciana* had been delivered, on 25 April 1981, by Romeo de Maio, on the theme *Leonardo e Michelangelo nel mito della rivalità.*

Doc. 2

G. VASARI, *Life of Michelangelo*, ed. Milanesi, VII, pp. 152–3:

Gli fu scritto di Fiorenza da alcuni amici suoi che venisse, perchè non era fuor di proposito aver quel marmo, che era nell'Opera, guasto; il quale, Pier Soderini, fatto gonfaloniere a vita allora di quella città, aveva avuto ragionamento molte volte di farlo condurre a Lionardo da Vinci, ed era allora in pratica di darlo a maestro Andrea Contucci dal Monte Sansavino, eccellente scultore, che cervaca di averlo.

On the waiting block: C. SEYMOUR Jr., *Michelangelo's David, a Search for Identity*, Pittsburg, 1967.

Doc. 3

P. GAURICUS, *De Sculptura: 'De claris sculptoribus'*:

Postremo et ipse Alverochii discipulus Leonardus Vincius, Equo illo quem ei perficere non licuit, in Bois maximo, pictura Symposii, nec minus et Archimedaeo ingenio notissimus.

A. Chastel and R. Klein (eds.), Geneva-Paris, 1969, p. 261.

Doc. 4

Michelangelo's commission for the *David*, 16 August 1501:

Spectabiles viri consules artis lane una cum dominis operariis adunati in audientia dicte opere, attendentes ad utilitatem et honorem dicte opere, elegerunt in sculptorem dicte opere dignum magistrum Michelangelum Lodovici Bonarroti, civem florentinum, ad faciendum et perficiendum et pro fede finiendum quendam hominem vocato Gigante abozatum brachiorum 9 ex marmore, existentem in dicta opera, olim abozatum per magistrum Augustinum grande (?) de Florentia, et male abozatum, pro tempore et termino annorum duorum proxime futurorum, incipiendorum kalendis Settembris proxime futuri et cum salario et mercede quolibet mense fl. vi au. latorum de moneta; et quicquid opus esset eidem circa dictum edificium faciendum, opera teneatur eidem prestare et commodare et homines dicte opere et lignamina et omnia quecomque alia quibus indigeret; et finito dicto opere et dicto homine marmoreo, tunc consules et operarii qui tunc erunt, iudicabunt an mereatur maius pretium; remictentes hoc eorum conscientiis [...]

C. SEYMOUR, op. cit., App. II, p. 136, no. 37, completing C. de TOLNAY, *Michelangelo*, vol. I, Princeton, 1947.

Doc. 5

G. VASARI, *Life of Michelangelo*, ed. Milanesi, VII, p. 154:

[...] per la insegna del palazzo, un Davit giovane con una frombola in mano; acciochè, sì come egli aveva difeso il suo popolo, e governatolo con giustizia, così chi governava quella città dovesse animosamente difenderla e giustamente governarla: e le cominciò nell'Opera di Santa Maria del Fiore, nella quale fece una turata fra muro e tavole, ed il marmo circondato, e quello di continuo lavorando, senza che nessuno il vedesse, a ultima perfezione lo condusse.

Doc. 6

Anonimo Magliabecchiano:

E passando ditto Lionardo, insieme con Giovanni da Gavine, da santa Trinita, dalla pancaccia delli Spini, dove era una ragunata d'uomini da bene, e dove si disputava un passo di Dante, chiamaro detto Lionardo dicendogli che dichiarasse loro quel passo. E a caso appunto passò di qui Michele Agnolo, e chiamato da un di loro, rispose Lionardo: Michele Agnolo ve lo dichiarerà egli. Di che parendo a Michelagnolo l'avesse detto per sbeffarlo, con ira gli rispose: «dichiaralo pur tu che facesti un disegno di uno cavallo per gittarlo di bronzo e non lo potesti gittare, e per vergogna lo lasciasti stare.» E detto questo voltò loro le rene e andò via, dove rimase Lionardo che per le dette parole diventò rosso. E ancora Michele Agnolo volendo mordere Lionardo gli disse: 'E che t'era creduto da que' capponi de' Melanesi'.

A. M. Ficarra (ed.), Naples, 1968, pp. 122–3, 125.

Doc. 7

Deliberations over the siting of the *David*, 25 January 1504:

MDIII. Die 25 mensis Ianuarii

Viso qualiter statua seu David est quasi finita, et desiderantes eam locare et eidem dare locum conmodum et congruum, et tale *(sic)* locum tempore, quo debet micti et mictenda est in tali loco, esse debere locum solidum et resolidatum ex relatu Michelangeli, magistri dicti gigantis, et consulum artis lane, et desiderantes tale consilium mitti ad effectum et modum predictum etc., deliberaverunt convocari et coadunari ad hoc eligendum magistros, homines et architectores, quorum nomina sunt vulgariter notata, et eorum dicta adnotari de verbo ad verbum:

> Andrea della Robbia
> Giovanni Cornuola
> Vante miniatore
> Laraldo di palazzo
> Giovanni piffero
> Francesco d'Andrea Granacci
> Biagio pittore
> Piero di Cosimo pittore
> Guasparre orafo
> Ludovico orafo e maestro di gietti
> El Riccio orafo
> Gallieno richiamatore
> Davit dipintore
> Simone del Pollaiuolo
> Philippo di Philippo dipintore
> Lorenzo dalla Golpaia
> Salvestro gioiellieri
> Michelangelo orafo
> Cosimo Roselli
> Chimenti del Tasso
> Sandro di Botticello pittore
> Giovanni alias vero Giuliano
> et Antonio da Sco. Gallo
> Andrea da Monte a Sco. Savino
>   pittore (*in margine*: e a Genova)
> Lionardo da Vinci
> Pietro Perugino in pinti pittore
> Lorenzo di Credi pittore
> Bernardo della Ciecha legnaiuolo [...]

E. GAYE, *Carteggio*, II, 455; cited by C. SEYMOUR, op. cit., App. II, pp. 140–1. On the siting: ibid., pp. 59 ff.

Doc. 8

Luca LANDUCCI, *Diario fiorentino*:

E a dì 14 di maggio 1504, si trasse dell'Opera el gigante di marmo; uscì fuori alle 24 ore, e ruppono el muro sopra la porta tanto che ne potessi uscire. E in questa notte fu gittato certi sassi al gigante per far male; bisognò fare la guardia la notte: e andava molto adagio, così ritto legato che ispenzolava, che non toccava co' piedi; con fortissimi legni, e con grande ingegno; e penò 4 dì a giugnere in Piazza, giunse a dì 18 in su la Piazza a ore 12: aveva più di 40 uomini a farlo andare: aveva sotto 14 legni unti, e quali si mutavano di mano in mano; e penossi insino a dì 8 di giugno 1504 a posarlo in su la ringhiera, dov'era la Giuditta, la quale s'ebbe a levare e porre in Palagio in terra. El detto gigante aveva fatto Michelagnolo Buonarroti.

I. del Badia (ed.), Florence, 1883, p. 268.

The fact that the *Gigante* had stones thrown at it during its journey can hardly be explained except by the symbolism associated with David—anti-Medicean, or, more precisely, republican. Originally ordered by the Opera del Duomo, it was transferred to the Palazzo Vecchio, like the marble *David* by Donatello in 1416. It has been suggested that the decision to place it at the entrance to the Palazzo must have been taken even before the meeting of 25 January 1504, which would have been little more than a public relations exercise to obtain approval of the work by the citizens: S. LEVINE, 'The Location of Michelangelo's David and the Meeting of January 25, 1504', *Art Bulletin*, LXI, 1974, pp. 31 ff., and contradicted by R. PARKS, 'The Placement of Michelangelo's David: a review of the Documents, ibid. LXII, 1975, pp. 560 ff.

Doc. 9

Letter from Fra Pietro da Novellara to Isabella d'Este 3 April 1501:

1501, 3 aprile.
Ill.ma et Ex.ma D.na etc. Hora ho havuta di V.a Exa. et farò cum omni celerità et diligencia quanto quella me scrive: ma per quanto me occorre, la vita di Leonardo è varia et indeterminata forte, sì che pare vivere a giornata. Ha facto solo dopoi che è ad Firenci uno schizo in uno cartone: finge uno Christo bambino de età cerca uno anno che uscendo quasi de bracci ad la mamma, piglia uno agnello et pare che lo stringa. La mamma quasi levandose de grembo ad S.ta Anna, piglia el bambino per spiccarlo da lo agnellino (animale immolatile) che significa la Passione. Santa Anna alquanto levandose da sedere, pare che voglia ritenere la figliola che non spicca el bambino da lo agnellino, che forsi vole figurare le Chiesa che non vorrebbe fussi impedita la passione di Christo. Et sono queste figure grande al naturale, ma stano in piccolo cartone, perchè tutte o sedeno o stano curve et una stae alquanto dinanci al l'altra verso la man sinistra: et questo schizo ancora non è finito.

L. BELTRAMI, *Documenti e memorie riguardanti la vita e le opere di Leonardo da Vinci*, Milan, 1919, no. 107, pp. 65–6.

Doc. 10

G. VASARI, *Life of Leonardo da Vinci*, ed. Milanesi, IV, p. 38:

Finalmente fece un cartone dentrovi una Nostra Donna ed una Sant'Anna con un Cristo, la quale non pure fece maravigliare tutti gli artefici, ma finita ch'ella fu, nella stanza durarono due giorni d'andare a vederla gli uomini e le donne, i giovani ed i vecchi, come si va alle feste solenni; per veder le maraviglie di Lionardo, che fecero stupire tutto quel popolo.

Doc. 11

Leonardo da Vinci, MS. A, fo. 110 ʳ–111 ᵛ:

... Dalla parte che viene il lume parrà questa mistione d'aria, fumo e polvere molto più lucida che dalla opposita parte; i combattitori quanto più fieno infra detta turbolenzia meno si vederanno e meno differenzia fia dai loro lumi alle loro ombre.

Farai rosseggiare i volti e le persone e l'aria e li scoppettieri insieme co' vicini, e detto rossore quanto più si parte dalla sua cagione più si perda; e le figure, che sono in fra te e 'l lume, essendo lontane, parranno scure in campo chiaro, e le loro gambe quanto più s'appresseran alla terra men fieno vedute, perchè la polvere è lì più grossa e più spessa.

E se farai cavalli correnti fori della turba, fa li nuboletti di polvere distanti l'uno dall'altro quanto pò essere lo 'ntervallo de' salti fatti dal cavallo, e quello nuvolo ch'è più lontano da detto cavallo men si vegga, anzi sia alto, sparso e raro, e 'l più presso sia più evidente e minore e più denso. [...]

Farai alcun cavallo stracinare morto il suo signiore, e dirieto a quello lasciare per la polvere e fango il segnio dello stracinato corpo.

Farai li vinti e battuti pallidi, colle ciglia alte nella lor congionzione, e la carne, che resta sopra loro, sia abbondante di dolente crespe. Le fauci del naso sieno con alquanto grinze partite in arco dalle anarise e terminate nel prencipio dell'occhio; le anarise alte, cagion di dette pieghe; le labbra arcate scoprino in denti di sopra, i denti spartiti in modo di gridare con lamento, l'una delle mani faccia scudo ai paurosi occhi, voltando il dentro inverso il nimico, l'altra stia a terra a sostenere il levato busto.

Altri farai gridanti colla bocca isbarrata e fuggenti: fara' molte sorte d'arme in fra i piedi de' combattitori come scudi rotti, lance, spade rotte e altre simili cose; farai omini morti, alcuni ricoperti mezzi dalla polvere, altri tutti.

J. P. RICHTER, *The Literary Works of Leonardo da Vinci*, London, 1939, I, nos 601–2.

G. FUMAGALLI, *Leonardo omo sanza lettere*, Florence, 1952, pp. 167–8.

These texts, which were put together in the *Trattato della Pittura*, compiled by Melzi (cf. the edition by McMahon, Princeton, 1956, p. 266), are of various dates; those from MS A are *c.* 1490/2, the later ones *c.* 1510. Other notes date from the same time as the painting. On this point see C. PEDRETTI, in the commentary to the 1971 London edition of Richter, p. 353. See also K. CLARK, *Leonardo da Vinci*, Cambridge, 1952, pp. 133 ff. C. GOULD, 'Leonardo's great battle-piece. A conjectural reconstruction', *Art Bulletin*, XXXVI, 1954, p. 122.
A. CHASTEL, *Léonard de Vinci, La Peinture*, Paris, 1964, pp. 59–61.

There has been much speculation on the placing of the two scenes and their composition. In the first instance, there is some agreement that the east wall of the Sala del Gran Consiglio was the one chosen (it was later much reworked by Vasari)—e.g. the proposed reconstruction by J. WILDE, 'The Hall of the Great Council of Florence', *Journal of the Warburg and Courtauld Institutes*, VII, 1944, pp. 65–81, with supplemantary observations by the same author in 'Michelangelo and Leonardo', *Burlington Magazine*, XCV, 1953, pp. 65–77. A quite different solution has been advanced by C. A. ISERMEYER, 'Die Arbeiten Leonardos und Michelangelos für den grossen Ratssaal in Florenz', *Festschrift für L. H. Heydenreich*, Munich, 1964, p. 83 ff.; according to the arrangements made in 1504 three frescoes were to be painted on each of the major walls, east and west, and Leonardo and Michelangelo were to have worked on opposite walls. He argues that the quantity of paper allocated to Leonardo was much greater than that to Michelangelo, which may indicate that Leonardo was originally entrusted with the whole wall. The most likely place for the two compositions remains the east wall, with the two central windows separating the two slightly unequal scenes. On the Hall of the Great Council see also: C. PEDRETTI, *Leonardo da Vinci inedito. Tre saggi*, Florence, 1968, II. *Nuovi documenti riguardanti la Battaglia d'Anghiari*. The two projects are unknown in their entirety, and one can only guess at their arrangement from drawings and from copies made before they were destroyed. The question of the *Battle of Anghiari* is very difficult: the bravura fragment of the *Battle of the Standard* is known from the magnificent Rubens drawing.

For Michelangelo, Gould has ingeniously suggested that the nearest painting to *Cascina* in time is the *Deluge* of the Sistine, which was the first to be painted on the ceiling, in 1508. There one sees the groups distributed in three planes, suggesting a remarkable arrangement with the *Bathers* in the foreground, the battle in the middle distance to the right, and, in the background to the left, troops on the alert.
C. GOULD, *Battle of Cascina*, Newcastle-upon-Tyne, 1966.

Doc. 12

Resolution of the Signoria, 4 May 1504 (Archives of the Signoria):

Atteso e magnifici et excelsi Signori Signori Priori di Libertà et Gonfaloniere di Giustitia del popolo Fiorentino, come havendo più mesi fa Lionardo di Ser Piero da Vinci, cittadino Fiorentino, tolto a dipignere uno quadro della Sala del Consiglio grande, et sendoci già per detto Lionardo cominciata tal pictura in sur un cartone, et havendo etiam per tal cagione presi fior. XXXV lar. doro in ore, et desiderando e prefati magnifici Signori, che tale opera si conducha quanto più presto si può al suo desiderato fine, et che a detto Leonardo si paghi per tal conto di tempo in tempo qualche somma di denari; però e prefati magnifici Signori... deliberorono etc. che il detto Lionardo da Vinci debba havere interamente finito di dipignere el detto cartone et rechatolo alla sua intera perfectione per infino a tutto el mese di Febbrajo proxime futuro de 1504 [1505] ogni exeptione et gavillatione rimossa: et che al detto Lionardo si dia et paghi fior. XV lar. doro in oro, per ciascuno mese a buon conto, intendendosi cominciato el primo mese addi XX del mese d'Aprile proximo passato. [...]

A. DE RINALDIS, *Storia dell'opera pittorica di Leonardo da Vinci*, Bologna, 1926, pp. 194–5.

Doc. 13

Leonardo da Vinci, MS Madrid II, fo. 1ʳ:

Addì 6 di giugno 1505 in venerdi, al toco
delle 13 ore, cominciai a colorire in
palazo. Nel qual punto del posare il
pennello, si guastò il tenpo e ssonò a ban-

co, richiedendo li omini a ragione. Il
cartone si stracciò, l'acqua si versò, e ru-
pesi il vaso dell' acqua che ssi portava.
E subito si guastò il tenpo e ppiove
insino a ssera acqua grandissima.
E stette il tenpo come notte.

The Madrid Codices, ed. L. Reti, vol. 5, New York, 1974, p. 1.

Doc. 14

Letter from Pier Soderini to the Cardinal of Volterra, Florence, 27 November 1506:

... Noi certifichiamo la S.V. lui essere bravo giovane, et nel mestieri suo l'unico in Italia, forse etiam in universo [...] Significando alla S.V. che ha principiato una storia per il pubblico che sarà cosa admiranda...

E. GAYE, op. cit., II. p. 92.

Doc. 15

Francesco ALBERTINI, 1510:

Nella sala grande nuova del consiglio maiore lunga brac. 104. larga 40. e una tavola di fra Philippo, li cavalli di Leonar. Vinci, et li disegni di Michelangelo.

Memoriale di molte statue et Picture sono nella inclyta Cipta di Florentia Per mano di Sculptori et Pictori excellenti Moderni et Antiqui, Florence, 1510, fo. a vi.

A. DE RINALDIS, op. cit., p. 207.

Doc. 16

Luca LANDUCCI, *Diario fiorentino*:

E in questo tenpo piacque a questo governo nuovo di guastare la sala del Consiglio maggiore, cioè el legniame e tante belle cose, ch'erano fatte con tanta grande spesa, e tante belle spalliere; e murorono certe camerette per soldati e feciono una entrata dal Sale; la qual cosa dolse a tutto Firenze, non la mutazione dello Stato, ma quella bella opera del legniame di tanta spesa.

I. del Badia (ed.), Florence, 1883, p. 333.
A. DE RINALDIS, op. cit., p. 208.

Doc. 17

B. CELLINI, *La Vita*, I, 12:

In questo proposito cadde in sul ragionar di Michelagnolo Buonarroti; che ne fu causa un disegno che io avevo fatto, ritratto da un cartone del divinissimo Michelagnolo. Questo cartone fu la prima bella opera che Michelagnolo mostrò delle maravigliose sue virtù, e lo fece a gara con uno altro che lo faceva, con Lionardo da Vinci, che avevano a servire per la sala del Consiglio del palazzo della Signoria. Rappresentavano quando Pisa fu presa da' fiorentini, e il mirabil Lionardo da Vinci aveva preso per elezione di mostrare una battaglia di cavagli con certa presura di bandiere, tanto divinamente fatti quanto immaginar si possa. Michelagnolo Buonarroti in nel suo dimostrava una quantità di fanterie che per essere di state s'erano missi a bagnare in Arno; e in questo istante dimostra che e' si dia allarme, e quelle fanterie ignude corrono all'arme, e con tanti bei gesti che mai né delli antichi né d'altri moderni non si vide opera che arrivassi a così alto segno; e sì come io ho detto, quello del gran Lionardo era bellissimo e mirabile. Stetteno questi dua cartoni, uno in nel palazzo de' Medici, e uno alla sala del papa. In mentre che gli stetteno in piè, furno la scuola del mondo.

G. D. Bonico (ed.), Turin, 1973, p. 32.

In the *Life of Bandinelli*, Vasari recounts how Bandinelli, as early as 1512, had arranged to cut the cartoon to pieces (ed. Milanesi, VI, p. 138), but the whole affair is unclear. See C. de TOLNAY, op. cit., I, p. 209.

Doc. 18

Luca LANDUCCI, *Diario fiorentino*:

E a dì 30 di novenbre 1515, el dì di Santo Andrea, in venerdì, entrò el Papa in Firenze con tanto grandissimo e trionfante onore, e incredibile spesa, che dire non si può. Direnne qualche particina.

Andogli incontro tutta la città di cittadini principali, e in fra l'altre, circa 50 giovani, pure de' più ricchi e principali, tutti vestiti a una livrea di veste di drappi pagonazze, con vai al collo, a piede, con certe asticciuole in mano darientate, molto bella cosa; poi grandissima cavalleria di cittadini. E el Papa aveva molta giente appiede, e fra l'altre aveva la guardia del Papa, moltissimi fanti Tedeschi a una divisa che portavano tutte manare alla franciosa; e a cavallo molti balestrieri e scoppettieri tutti alla sua guardia. E lui fu portato per tutta la città dalla Signoria con ricco baldacchino, e fu posato a Santa Maria del Fiore, e andò su per palchetto insino a l'altare maggiore, nella qual chiesa era tanta adorna di drappelloni con un padiglione nel mezzo, con più gradi che non s'usa: e fu accese tante falcole, che, oltre al coro, erano pieno tutto l'andito primo insino alle porte.

I. Del Badia (ed.), Florence, 1883, p. 352.

On the Entry into Florence of Leo X:
J. SHEARMAN, 'The Florentine *Entrata* of Leo X, 1515', *Journal of the Warburg and Courtauld Institutes*, XXXVIII, 1975, pp. 136–54.

Doc. 19

G. VASARI, *Life of Michelangelo*, ed. Milanesi, VII, pp. 188–9:

[...] per l'architettura concorsero molti artefici a Roma al papa, e fecero disegni Baccio d'Agnolo, Antonio da San Gallo, Andrea e Iacopo Sansovino, il grazioso Raffaello da Urbino, il quale nella venuta del papa fu poi condotto a Fiorenzo per tale effetto. Laonde Michelagnolo si risolse di fare un modello, e non volere altro che lui in tal cosa superiore o guida dell'architettura. Ma questo non volere aiuto fu cagione che nè egli nè altri operasse, e que'maestri disperati ai loro soliti esercizi si ritornassero.

On this complicated affair:
J. S. ACKERMAN, *The Architecture of Michelangelo*, 2 vols., London, 1961, Catalogue, p. 3 ff.

Doc. 20

Letter from Jacopo Sansovino to Michelangelo, 30 June 1517:

Non v'avendo possuto parlare inanzi la partita vostra, mi sono messo a farvi intendere lo animo mio verso di voi. Sapiate che da voi a me, di qua, fu pocha dotta. E parlai con Iachopo Salviati, e intesi come Bacino di Michelagniolo era così valente uomo, el meglio che ci fussi. Ma Iachopo Salviati vi rispose assai bene a proposito, perchè à conosciuto la natura vostra a punto. E per questo vostro lodarlo, Bacino fa stima d'averne la parte sua come uno altro. E più vi dico che el Papa, el Cardinale e Iachopo Salviati sono uomini che quando dicano uno sì è una carta e uno contratto, con ciò sia sono verili e non sono come voi dite. Ma voi misurate loro colla cana vostra, che non vale con esso voi né contratti né fede, e a ogni ora dite no e sì come vi venga bene e utile. E sapiate c[h]'el Papa mi promesse le storie, e Iachopo anchora; e sono uomini che me le manterano. E ò fatto inverso di voi tanto quanto io ò potuto, di cosa vi sia utile e onore. E non mi ero avisto anchora che voi non faciesti mai bene a nessuno; e che, cominciando a me, sarebe volere che.ll'acqua none inmollassi. E massimo sapete siamo stati insieme a molti ragionamenti, e maladetta quella volta che voi dicessi mai bene di nessuno universalemente. Or sia con Dio. Non dirò altro. Sono stato raguagliato assai bene; el simile sarete voi alla vostra tornata. E basta.

Il Carteggio di Michelangelo, ed. G. Poggi, vol. I, Florence, 1965, p. 291.
The meaning of the second sentence is obscure.

Doc. 21

Letter from Michelangelo to Benedetto Varchi (probably April/June, 1547):

Colui che scrisse che la pictura era più nobile della scultura, se gli avessi così bene intese l'altre cose che gli à scricte, l'arebbe meglio scricte la mie fante.

Il Carteggio di Michelangelo, ed. G. Poggi, vol. IV, Florence, 1979, p. 266.

Doc. 1

G. VASARI, *Life of Pordenone*, ed. Milanesi, V, p. 115:

Fece anco in sul detto Canal Grande nella facciata della Casa di Martin d'Anna molte storie a fresco, ed in particolare un Curzio a cavallo in iscorto, che pare tutto tondo e di rilievo; siccome è anco un Mercurio che vola in aria, per ogni lato, oltre a molte altre cose tutte ingegnose; la quale opera piacque sopra modo a tutta la città di Venezia e fu perciò Pordenone più lodato che altro uomo che mai in quella città avesse insino allora lavorato.

Information on these epoch-making decorations is very scanty: see L. FOSCARI, *Affreschi esterni di Venezia*, Milan, 1936.
On Pordenone's presence in Venice and the dating of his works, see the recent summary by C. FURLAN in the catalogue of the exhibition *Da Tiziano al Greco*, Venice, 1981, pp. 71 ff., which takes account of recent research.

Doc. 2

C. RIDOLFI, *Le Maraviglie...* (1648):

Dicesi ancora che il famoso Michel'Angelo tratto dalla fama di si nobile fatica se ne passo a Venezia, ove vide in effetto che la Fama non era stata menzognera né vanamente haveva decantata le lodi dell'autore.

D. von Hadeln (ed.), I, p. 120.

Whether true or not, this anecdote confirms the original position of Pordenone during these years, and the privileged relationship between him and the 'Roman' style. In 1536 L. Dolce speaks of the grandeur of Michelangelo's draughtsmanship *à propos* of Pordenone in the introduction to a romance, *Il primo libro di Sacripante*.

Doc. 3

G. VASARI, *Life of Pordenone*, ed. Milanesi, V, pp. 115 ff.:

Ma, fra l'altre cose che fecero a costui mettere incredibile studio in tutte le sue opere, fu la concorrenza dell'eccellentissimo Tiziano; [...] gli fu dai soprastanti di San Rocco data a dipignere in fresco la cappella di quella chiesa con tutta la tribuna. [...]

E perchè gareggiando cercò sempre di far opere in luoghi, dove avesse lavorato Tiziano, fece in San Giovanni in Rialto un San Giovanni Elemosinario, che a' poveri dona danari; ed a un altare pose un quadro di San Bastiano e San Rocco ed altri Santi, che fu cosa bella, ma non però eguale all'opera di Tiziano, se bene molti, più per malignità che per dire il vero, lodarono quella di Giovan Antonio. Fece il medesimo, nel chiostro di San Stefano, molte storie in fresco del Testamento vecchio; ed una del nuovo, tramezzate da diverse Virtù; nelle quali mostrò scorti terribili di figure: del qual modo di fare si dilettò sempre, e cercò di porne in ogni suo componimento e difficilissime, adornandole meglio che alcun altro pittore.

The question posed by the *S. Giovanni Elemosinario* presents difficulties: one has the impression that Vasari was attributing to Pordenone by mistake the famous picture by Titian. But there is a

208　Pordenone. *Study for the Façade of the Palazzo d'Anna*. Detail. About 1530. Pen drawing. Victoria and Albert Museum, London.
A great façade decorator, the artist never hesitated to make use of astonishing feats of *trompe l'œil*, like that of the leaping horse. (Marcus Curtius?)

drawing by Pordenone at Windsor, *St Augustine*, which may preserve some record of the frescoes in the cupola of S. Giovanni Elemosinario, painted *c.* 1528–9. See C. FURLAN in the catalogue of the exhibition *Il Pordenone e L'Amalteo*, Pordenone, 1980, p. 45.

The Santo Stefano cycle was summarily described by Vasari (1550) and in more detail by Ridolfi (1648). The few surviving fragments (*Adam and Eve Expelled from Paradise, Christ and the Magdalen, Christ and the Woman of Samaria*) are preserved in the Ca' d'Oro. The engravings by Piccini (17th century) give some idea of other scenes. These strongly constructed compositions—'difficult', as Vasari called them, by which he meant skilfully foreshortened—mark the entry into Venice of the Roman Grand Manner. They seem to date from around 1532. See *Da Tiziano al Greco*, op. cit., nos 2, 3.

Doc. 4

C. RIDOLFI, *Le Maraviglie dell'Arte…* (1648):

Nella Chiesa di San Rocco gli fù locata la maggior Cappella, nella quale diede a vedere Christo trasfigurato nel Tabor; ne' fianchi dell'Altare compose un giro di colonne, frammettendovi alcuni putti, che tengono il cappello, il bordone e la tasca del Santo Pellegrino [...]

Circa lo stesso tempo fece a fresco nel Chiostro di Santo Stefano sopra à colonnati dodeci sacre historie del vecchio e nuovo Testamento [...]

Dicesi, che mentre Gio. Antonio stava occupato in quel lavoro tenesse à canto la spada e la rotella, per l'inimistà contratta con Titiano per la gara, che trà di lor passava; onde alla di lui concorrenza fece nell'altare de' Corrieri in San Giovanni di Rialto la tavola con Santa Caterina, San Sebastiano e San Rocco veramente figura rarissima, mà non puote già abbassare la fama di Titiano, che fatto haveva il San Giovanni Elemosinario nell'Altar maggiore.

D. von Hadeln (ed.), op. cit., I, pp. 120, 121, 123.

The works in the choir being scarcely recognizable now, the principal survivors are the two paintings on the Sacristy presses, *St. Martin* and *St. Christopher*, which are notably powerful. They date from 1528–9, according to a correction made by J. Schulz, 'Pordenone's Cupolas', *Studies in Renaissance and Baroque Art Presented to Anthony Blunt*, London, 1967, p. 46. See also C. GOULD, 'The Cinquecento at Venice, IV, Pordenone versus Titian', in *Apollo*, 1972.

Doc. 5

G. VASARI, *Life of Jacomo Palma and Lorenzo Lotto*, ed. Milanesi, V, p. 250:

Ne' frati Carmelitani fece il medesimo in una tavola San Niccolò sospeso in aria ed in abito pontificale, con tre Angeli; ed a' piedi Santa Lucia e San Giovanni; in alto certe nuvole, ed a basso un paese bellissimo con molte figurette ed animali in vari luoghi: da un lato è San Giorgio a cavallo, che amazza il serpente; e poco lontana la donzella con una città appresso ed un pezzo di mare.

On Lotto and Venetian painting:
B. BERENSON, *Lotto*. 2nd ed., London, 1956, p. 76.

Doc. 6

C. RIDOLFI, *Le Maraviglie dell'Arte…* (1648):

Dicesi che nella dispositione di quell'opera vi concorressero il Pordenone e'l Palma vecchio, di cui conservasi in casa Contarina di San Samuello un picciolo modello; nondimeno prevalse il merito di Titiano, essendo che il grido del suo valore estendevasi per ogni parte spirando a suo favore il Cielo e gli huomini insieme.

D. von Hadeln (ed.), op. cit., I, p. 167.

On the *pala* in the Collegiata at Alzano (Bergamo):
A. BIANTI and A. BOSCHETTO, *Lorenzo Lotto*, Florence, 1955, p. 105.
G. MASCHERPO, *Lorenzo Lotto a Bergamo*, Milan, 1971, pp. 22 ff.

The *pala* of S. Pietro Martire (290×190 cm) at Alzano Lombardo (Bergamo) poses a double problem, difficult to resolve. The work has such evidently Lottesque characteristics—the gestures, the woodcutters in the forest, the celestial group—that all the older writers from F. M. Tassi (1793) onward attributed it to Lotto and dated it within the period of his work for Bergamo, from 1524 to 1532. After the cleaning by Pellicioli about 1920, Longhi (1926) mentioned Palma and since then writers have cited it as his, with the exception, to my mind justified, of G. Mariacher in *I Pittori bergamaschi*, Bergamo, 1975, vol. I, p. 206, no. 2. The presence of two hands cannot be excluded. As for the date, if one retains the Palma attribution it must be before 1529, when he died, but it is difficult to place it within the period 1510–15 proposed by Mariacher. The connection between the work and the competition of 1528 is, therefore, still to be established; but it is not improbable.

Doc. 7

Declaration by Titian during the lawsuit against the Confraternity of S. Pietro Martire:

Petitio: El se dice uno proverbio et certo essendo acaduto a mi Tician de Vecelis trovo esser verissimo: qual è che uno gran servicio si suol satisfar de una grande ingratitudine. Imperho che havendo io depinto una palla de s. Piero martire ala scuola del ditto santo in la giexia de s. Zuanne polo, non volendo io dar ditta palla a quelli di ditta scuola se non era satisfatto, per far cosa grata et compiacer a ser Jacomo da Pergo, el qual era gastaldo de ditta fraternità mi lassai persuader a exaudir quello a poner ditta palla in la giexia predicta da S. Zuannepolo et cusi fu portada con pacto et promissione perho chel ditto ser Jacomo mi promesse di operar che io haveria tra da li fratelli de ditta fragia et legati overamente lassi facti per altri per il far de dita palla ducati cento et in più si potrà haver qual più etiam sia mio. [...]

Additio petitionis. Havendo io Titian de Vecellis produto una domanda contra ser Jacomo da Pergo per la qual rechiedo chel sia sententià in ducati cento et havendo da poi havuto una peza di formagio de valuta de ducati 4 vel prout iustificabitur; item ducati 9 de contanti che sono in tutto ducati 13 salvo errore calculi, et ideo mi removo dala mia dimanda de diti ducati 13 et dimando chel sia sententià solum in ducati 60 (*sic*) per poner a bon conto del mio credito cum reservatione residui etc.

G. GIOMO, 'San Pietro martire e Tiziano', *Nuovo Archivio Veneto*, 1903, pp. 66–7.

Doc. 8

G. VASARI, *Life of Titian*, ed. Milanesi, VII, pp. 438–9:

Essendo innanzi al sacco di Roma andato a stare a Vinezia Pietro Aretino, poeta celeberrimo de'tempi nostri, divenne amicissimo di Tiziano e del Sansovino: il che fu di molto onore e utile a esso Tiziano, perciochè lo fece conoscere tanto lontano quanto si distese la sua penna, [...] Per tornare all'opere di Tiziano, egli fece la tavola all'altare di San Piero Martire nella chiesa di San Giovanni e Polo, facendovi maggior del vivo il detto santo martire dentro a una boscaglia d'alberi grandissimi, cascato in terra ed assalito dalla fierezza d'un soldato, che l'ha in modo ferito nella testa, che, essendo semivivo, se gli vede nel viso l'orrore della morte; mentre in un altro frate, che va innanzi fuggendo, si scorge lo spavento e timore della morte: in aria sono due angeli nudi, che vengono da un lampo di cielo, il quale dà lume al paese, che è bellissimo, ed a tutta l'opera insieme; la quale è la più compiuta, la più celebrata, e la maggiore e meglio intesa e condotta che altra, la quale in tutta la sua vita Tiziano abbia fatto ancor mai.

R. PALLUCHINI, *Tiziano*, 2 vols., Florence, 1969, I, p. 388.
H. E. WETHEY, *The Paintings of Titian*, vol. I, *The Religious Paintings*, London, 1969.

Doc. 9

C. RIDOLFI, *Le Maraviglie dell'Arte...* (1648):

Hor consideriamo la famosa tavola di S. Pietro Martire, posta nella Chiesa de' Santi Giovanni et Paolo, nella quale si tiene, che l'autore componesse una maniera non eccedente nè mancante di quel finimento, che richiede l'arte e la qualità del sito, e ove gionse ad emulare con arte rarissima la natura [...]

Lo avvenimento è rappresentato nel principio di folto bosco d'annose quercie e d'altre piante ripieno, che formano de' rami loro ombrosa cortina per riparo del Sole. Quivi il Santo caduto a terra è soprafatto dall'empio homicida, che afferandogli il lembo della cappa, radoppia fieramente il colpo [...] Scendono da celeste splendore due vezzosi Angeletti, che arrecano al Martire generoso la palma del trionfo preparatogli nel Cielo; e così belli sono, che sembrano germi di Paradiso; quali ritrasse da un getto di Cupidine, che si crede opera di Fidia, e si tiene dall'universale, che non si possino meglio comporre, proponendosi egli tal' hora l'imitazione delle cose celebri antiche, molto bene da lui conosciute, errando in questo luogo il Vasari, che da Titiano non fossero tali studi praticati, essendo que' bambini condotti nel colorito non solo, mà nel disegno à termini di maraviglia.

D. von Hadeln (ed.), op. cit., I, pp. 167–8.

On the motif of the *putti* by Phidias (or Praxiteles):
P. BUCCARELLI, 'I troni degli dei e l'arte veneta del Rinascimento', in *Historia*, Milan-Rome, XII, 1934, pp. 630 ff.
O. BRENDEL, 'Borrowings from Ancient art in Titian', *Art Bulletin*, XXXVII, 1955.

Doc. 10

Letter from the heads of the Council of Ten to the Provveditori al Sal:

... Deputando nella ditta Sala al Exellente pittor Zuon Antonio da Pordanon quelli altri lochi et quadri come vi parara non essendo conveniente nelli quadri principiati per el ditto Titian altri se ne habbia ad impazar.

'Archivalistische Beiträge zur Geschichte der venezianischen Kunst', *Italienische Forschungen des kunsthistorischen Instituts in Florenz*, I, 1911, p. 134.

See the note by C. FURLAN, cat. cit., p. 72.
W. FRIEDLÄNDER, 'Titian and Pordenone', *Art Bulletin*, XLVII, 1965. Discussion of the dates in C. GOULD, 'The Cinquecento at Venice...', art. cit.

Doc. 11

Letter from Aretino to the sculptor Tribolo, 29 October 1537:

Messer Sebastiano architettore, con piacere del molto diletto e del mediocre giudizio ch'io ho de la scultura, m'ha fatto vedere con le parole in che modo le pieghe facili ornano il panno de la Vergine che l'ingegno vostro mosso da la sua volontade lavora a mio nome. Hammi detto ancora come languidamente caschino le membra del Cristo che morto le avete posto in grembo con l'attitudine de l'arte: onde io ho veduto l'afflizione de la madre e la miseria del figliuolo prima ch'io l'abbia vista. Ma ecco nel raccontarmi egli il miracolo, che nasce da lo stile de la vostra industria, l'autore di quel *San Pietro martire*, che nel guardarlo converse e voi e Benvenuto ne l'imagine de lo stupore; e, fermati gli occhi del viso e le luci de l'intelletto in cotal opra, comprendeste tutti i vivi terrori de la morte e tutti i veri dolori de la vita ne la fronte e ne le carni del caduto in terra, maravigliandovi del freddo e del livido che gli appare ne la punta del naso e ne l'estremità del corpo, né potendo ritener la voce, lasciaste esclamarla, quando nel contemplar del compagno che fugge, gli scorgeste ne la sembianza il bianco de la viltà e il pallido de la paura. Veramente voi deste dritta sentenza al merito de la gran tavola nel dirmi che non era la più bella cosa in Italia. Che mirabil groppo di bambini è ne l'aria, che si dispicca dagli arbori, che la spargono dei tronchi e de le foglie loro; che paese raccolto ne la semplicità del suo naturale, che sassi erbosi bagna la acqua, che ivi fa corrente la vena uscita dal pennello del divin Tiziano! La modesta benignità del quale caldissimamente vi saluta, e offerisce sé e ogni sua cosa giurando che non ha pari l'amore che la sua affezione porta à la vostra fama. Né si potria dire con quanto desiderio egli aspetti di vedere le due figure che, sì come dico di sopra, per elezion di voi medesimo deliberate mandarmi, dono che non passarà con silenzio né con ingratitudine.

Di Venezia, il 29 di ottobre 1537.

PIETRO ARETINO, *Lettere sull'arte*, ed. E. Camesasca, I, Milan, 1957, pp. 73-74.

Doc. 12

L. DOLCE, *Dialogo della Pittura*, Venice, 1557:

Fabrini: 'Di queste cattive tinte parmi, che si vegga assai notabile esempio in una tavola di Lorenzo Loto, che è qui in Vinegia nella Chiesa de' Carmini.'

P. Barocchi (ed.), *Trattati d'Arte del Cinquecento*, I, Bari, 1960, p. 184.
M. W. Roskill (ed.), New York, 1968, p. 154 (with English translation).

209   Federico Zuccaro. *Taddeo Zuccaro Painting the Façade of the Palazzo Mattei*. About 1590. Black chalk, pen and wash. Albertina, Vienna.
Michelangelo riding through the streets of Rome passing in front of the Palazzo Mattei where Taddeo Zuccaro was painting the side façade.

Doc. 1

Letter from Nino Sernini to Cardinal Ercole Gonzaga, 19 November 1541:

... Io non trovo nissuno a cui basti l'animo di ritirare così in furia quello che nuovamente ha dipinto Michelagnolo per essere grande et difficile, essendovi più di cinque cento figure et di sorte che a ritrarne solamente una credo metta pensiero agli dipintori, anchor che l'opera sia di quella bellezza che po pensare V. Ill. S., non manca in ogni modo chi la danna; gli rmi Chietini sono gli primi che dicono non star bene gli inudi in simil luogo che mostrano le cose loro, benchè ancora a questo ha havuto grandma consideratione, che a pena a dieci di tanto numero si vede dishonestà. Altri dicono che ha fatto Christo senza barba et troppo giovane et che non ha in se quella maestè che gli si conviene, et così in somma non manca chi dica, ma il rmo Cornaro che è stato lungamente a vederla ha detto bene, dicendo che se Michelagnolo gli vuol dare in un quadro solamente dipinta una di quelle figure gli la vuol pagare quello ch'esso gli dimanderà, et ha ragione per essere al creder mio cose che non si possono vedere altrove. Il detto rmo del continuo vi tiene un suo dipintore a ricavare, et ancora che non vi perda punto di tempo non finirà il tutto in manco di quattro mesi, ma con tutto questo vedro d' havere almeno uno schizzo acciò che V. S. Ill. possa vedere il compartimento che ha fatto, che questo non credo la habbia in tutto a sodisfare, et che messer Julio si sarebbe fatto più honore, et sarà opera, quando la vedrà, assai diversa di quello che essa si pensa, perchè si conosce che tutto il suo sforzo ha messo in fare figure bizzare et in atti diversi, et se pure non potrò così tosto mandarle il disegno mi sforzaro di descriverle almeno il compartimento e ne pigliarà quello poco piacere che potrà.

L. von PASTOR, *History of the Popes*, XII, p. 659, no. 9.

In the abundant literature on this subject, the classic works are still: R. DE CAMPOS and B. BIAGETTI, *Il 'Giudizio Universale' di Michelangelo*, Rome, 1944 and C. de TOLNAY, *Michelangelo. V, The Final Period*, Princeton, 1960.

ROMEO DE MAIO, *Michelangelo e la Controriforma*, Bari, 1978, examines the Roman and European reactions to the *Last Judgement*, the ideas, friendships and enmities of Michalangelo in Rome and his relations, often difficult, with the Papacy after 1540. It contains a considerable amount of information, often little-known and sometimes unpublished, but with too many peremptory judgements, which one is not obliged to accept, and overweighted by an occasionally excessive erudition.

The identification of Biagio with the figure of Minos was recorded by Vasari. It is confirmed by a pasquinade contained in a Vatican MS, according to R. de Maio, op. cit., p. 47, n. 5.

Doc. 2

Letter from Don Miniato Pitti in Montoliveto to Giorgio Vasari, 1 May 1545:

Messer Giorgio Amantissimo, salute.

Sono stato piu giorni, che non u' ho scritto, perche non ho potuto, hauendomi bisognato attendere à burattare é (*i*) frati; et ui haueuo à dire un monte di roba, cio é: Com' io sto bene; é (*et*) come desidero intendere il simile di uoi; é (*et*) come io hebbi una uostra, che diceua, ch' ero ingoffito à Napoli; perche à Roma mi era piaciuto piu la uolta che la facciatá: Perche ui é mille heresie, massime della pelle di San Bartholomeo senza barba; é (*et*) lo scorticato ha il barbone: il che monstra, che quella pelle non sia la sua etc (*sic*).

K. FREY, *Der literarische Nachlass G. Vasaris*, Munich, 1923, vol. 1, p. 148, doc. no. LXIX.

Doc. 3

Letter from Aretino to Michelangelo, 6 November 1545:

Signor mio.

Nel vedere lo schizzo intiero di tutto il vostro dì del giudicio, ho fornito di conoscere la illustre gratia di Raffaello ne la grata bellezza de la inventione. Intanto io come battezzato mi vergogno de la licentia sì illecita a lo spirito, che havete preso ne lo esprimere i concetti, u' si risolve il fine, al quale aspira ogni senso de la veracissima credenza nostra. Adunque quel Michelagnolo stupendo in la fama, quel Michelagnolo notabile in la prudentia, quel Michelagnolo ammiranno (*sic*), ha voluto mostrare a le genti non meno impietà di irreligione, che perfettion di pittura? È possibile che voi, che per essere divino non degnate il consortio degli huomini, haviate ciò fatto nel maggior tempio di Dio? sopra il primo altare di Giesù? ne la più gran capella del mondo? dove i gran cardini dela chiesa, dove i sacerdoti riverendi, dove il vicario di Cristo con ceremonie cattoliche, con ordini sacri e con orationi divine confessano, contemplano et adorano il suo corpo, il suo sangue e la sua carne? Se non fusse cosa nefanda lo introdurre de la similitudine, mi vanterei di bontade nel trattato de la Nanna, preponendo il savio mio avedimento a la indiscreta vostra conscienza, avenga che io in materia lasciva et impudica non pure uso parole avertite e costumate, ma favello con detti irreprensibili e casti: et voi nel suggetto di sì alta historia mostrate gli angeli e i santi, questi senza veruna terrena honestà, e quegli privi d'ogni celeste ornamento. Ecco i gentili ne lo iscolpire non dico Diana vestita, ma nel formare Venere ignuda, le fanno ricoprire con la mano le parti, che non si scoprono: et chi pur è Christiano, per più stimare l'arte che la fede, tiene per reale ispettacolo tanto il decoro non osservato ne i martiri e ne le vergini, quanto il gesto del rapito per i membri genitali, che ancho serrarebbe gli occhi il postribolo per non mirarlo. In un bagno delitioso, non in un choro supremo si conveniva il far vostro. Onde saria men vitio che voi non credeste, che in tal modo credendo iscemare la credenza in altrui. Ma sino a qui la eccellenza di sì temerarie maraviglie non rimane impunita, poichè il miracolo di loro istesse è morte dela vostra laude. Si che risuscitatele il nome col far de fiamme di fuoco le vergogne de i dannati, et quelle de' beati di raggi di sole, o imitate la modestia Fiorentina, la quale sotto alcune foglie auree sotterra quelle del suo bel colosso; et pure è posto in piazza publica et non in luogo sacrato. Hor così ve lo perdoni Iddio, come non ragiono ciò per isdegno, ch'io hebbi circa le cose desiderate; perchè il sodisfare al quanto vi obligaste mandarmi, doveva essere procurato da voi con ogni sollecitudine, da che in cotale atto acquetavate la invidia, che vuole che non vi possin disporre se non Gherardi et Tomai. Ma se il thesoro lasciatovi da Giulio, acciò si collocassero le sue reliquie nel vaso de i vostri intagli, non è stato bastante a far che gli osserviate la promessa, che posso però sperare io? Benchè non la ingratitudine, non l'avaritia di voi pittor magno, ma la gratia et il merito del Pastor massimo è di ciò cagione. Avenga che Iddio vuole che la eterna fama di lui viva in semplice fattura di deposito in l'essere di se stesso, et non in altiera machina di sepoltura in vertù del vostro stile. In questo mezzo il mancar voi del debito, vi si attribuisce per furto. Ma conciosiachè le nostre anime han più bisogno de lo affetto de la devotione, che de la vivacità del disegno, inspiri Iddio la Santità di Paolo, come inspirò la beatitudine di Gregorio, il quale volse inprima disornar Roma de le superbe statue degli Idoli, che torre bontà loro la riverentia a l'humili imagini de i santi. In ultimo, se vi fuste consigliato nell comporre e l'universo e l'abisso, e 'l paradiso con la gloria, con l'honore et con lo spavento abbozzatovi de la istrutione, da lo esempio e da la scienza de la lettera, che di mio legge il secolo, ardisco dire che non pure la natura e ciascuna benigna influenza non si pentirieno del datovi intelletto sì chiaro, che hoggi in vertù suprema fanvi simolacro de la maraviglia, ma la Providentia, che vegge il tutto, terrebbe cura di opera cotale, sinchè si servasse il proprio ordine in governar gli emisperi. Di Novembre in Vinetia MDXLV.

Servitore l'Aretino.

Hor ch'io mi sono un poco isfogato la colera contra la crudeltà vostra usa a la mia divotione, et che mi pare havervi fatto vedere che se voi siate divino, io non so' d'acqua, stracciate questa, che anchio l'ho fatta in pezzi, e risolvetevi pur, chio son tale che anco e'Re e gli imperadori respondan a le mie lettere.

Al gran Michelangelo Buonarroti a Roma.

E. STEINMANN and H. POGATSCHER, 'Dokumente und Forschungen zu Michelangelo', *Repertorium für Kunstwissenschaft*, XXIX, 1906, pp. 491–2.
The 1547 version is in *Quarto libro delle lettere*, Venice, 1550, Cols. 83–4ᵛ, and E. CAMESASCA, *Lettere sull'arte di Pietro Aretino*, Milan, 1957, II, no. 364, pp. 175–7.

Doc. 4

Letter from Aretino to Enea Vico, January 1546:

Il *Dì del Giudicio* che la saputa diligenza del Bazzacco, uno dei buoni spiriti che abbia il disegno, ha ritratto dell' istoria del Buonaruoti, non è per mai sodisfare a la somma de la obligazione, che tiene a lo stilo, con la più salda, netta e morbida pratica di tratti leggiadri e dolci, lo intagliare in rame accurato e forbito. Imperò che lo starsi cotal istoria senza far di sé copia altrove, non serva il decoro appartenente a la religione che ella contiene; avenga che, dovendo essere per ordine d'Iddio il fine di tutto il mondo, è bene che il mondo tutto participi del suo tremendo e trionfante essempio. Per il che son certo che la virtù nostra in tal fatica ne ritrarrà premio da Cristo altissimo, e utile dal gran duca di Fiorenza. Sì che attendete pure a spedirvi da sì santa e laudabile impresa, che lo scandolo, che la licenzia de l'arte di Michelagnolo potria mettere fra i luterani per il poco rispetto de le naturali vergogne che in loro istesse discoprono le figure ne lo abisso e nel cielo; non è per tòrvi punto de l'onore che meritate per esser voi causa che ciascuno ne goda.

Di genaio, in Vinezia, 1546.

E. CAMESASCA, op. cit., no. 311, pp. 136–7.
On the copies after the *Last Judgement*:
L. STEINBERG, 'Michelangelo's Last Judgement as Merciful Heresy', *Art in America*, LXIII, 1975, pp. 48–63.

Doc. 5

G. VASARI, *Life of Michelangelo*, ed. Milanesi, VI, p. 455:

E nel vero la moltitudine delle figure, la terribilità e grandezza dell'opera è tale, che non si può descrivere, essendo piena di tutti i possibili umani affetti, ed avendogli tutti maravigliosamente espressi. Avvengachè i superbi, gl'invidiosi, gli avari, i lussuriosi, e gli altri così fatti si riconoscono agevolmente da ogni bello spirito, per avere osservato ogni decoro sì d'aria, sì d'attitudini, e sì d'ogni altra naturale circostanza nel figurarli; cosa che, sebbene è maravigliosa e grande, non è stata impossibile a questo uomo, per essere stato sempre accerto e savio, ed avere visto uomini assai, ed acquistato quella cognizione con la pratica del mondo che fanno i filosofi con la speculazione e per gli scritti.

See also: *La Vita di Michelangelo nelle redazioni del 1550 e del 1568*, ed. P. Barocchi, Milan–Naples, I, 1962, pp. 78–9.

Doc. 6

A. CATHERINI, *Commentaria in omnes divi Pauli et alias septem canonicas Epistolas*, Venice, 1551, p. 645, cited by R. de Maio, op. cit., p. 48, n. 15:

Est pictor et sculptor nostra aetate egregius, Michael-Angelus nomine qui admirabilis est in exprimendo nuda hominum corpora et pudenda. Commendo artem in facto: at factum ipsum vehementer vitupero ac detestor. Nam haec membrorum nuditas indecentissiem in aris et praecipuis Dei sacellis ubique conspicitur. Verum annumeretur et hic cum caeteris multis et magnis abusis, quibus foedatur ecclesia Dei sponsa Christi. Quod autem in meum praesentem usum sumere inde volui, istud est, non ea absoluta perfectione ab egregio isto pictore Michaele pingi nuda corpora turpia et obscoena (quae tunc vel natura ipsa in nobis tecta esse voluit) qua noster Apostolus haereticum nuda quaeque et pudenda vivo spiritus penicillo nobis expressit et in ostentum posuit.

On Michelangelo at S. Silvestro: R. de MAIO, 'Michelangelo e Paolo IV', *Riforme e miti nella Chiesa del Cinquecento*, Naples, 1963, p. 98.

Doc. 7

Luca Gauricus, *Michelangelo's Horoscope*, 1552:

Michael Angelus Florentinus.

Mercurius eous a Sole 27 gradibus elongatus, in Falciferi hospitio, ab ipsa Venere irroratus exagona radiatione platica, effecerunt ipsum Michaelem Angelum sculptorem & pictorem eminentissimum, Phidia, & Praxitele clariorem cum opibus affluentissimis, quam foelicitatem affirmare videtur Iuppiter secundae domus hospitator in horoscopo platice supputatus, & a Venere foeliciter irrigatus. Ex sui genij dotibus thesauros affluentissimos cumulauit, & a Principibus ecclesiasticis honores clarissimos.

L. GAURICUS, *Tractatus astrologicus*, Venice, 1552, p. 85.

Doc. 8

L. DOLCE, *Dialogo della pittura intitolato l'Aretino*, Venice, 1557:

Fab. – … odo dire che nell'ordine del suo stupendo Giudicio si contengono alcuni sensi allegorici profondissimi, i quali vengono intesi da pochi.
Aret. – [...] E questo vorrei io ancora credere che fosse stato l'intendimento di Michelagnolo, se non si vedessero nel medesimo Giudicio alcune cose ridicole.
Fab. – E quali cose ridicole sono queste?
Aret. – Non è cosa ridicola l'aversi imaginato in cielo, tra la moltitudine dell'anime beate, alcuni che teneramente si baciano? ove dovrebbono essere intenti e col pensiero levati alla divina contemplazione et alla futura sentenza, [...]. Poi, che senso mistico si può cavare dallo aver dipinto Cristo sbarbato? o dal vedere un diavolo che tira in giù, con la mano aggrappata ne' testicoli, una gran figura che per dolore si morde il dito? Ma di grazia, non mi fate andar più avanti, acciò che non paia ch'io dica male d'un uomo che per altro è divino.
Fab. – Vi ritorno a dire che la sua invenzione è ingegnosissima e da pochi intesa.
Aret. – [...] … poi che Michelagnolo non vuole che le sue invenzioni vengano intese se non da pochi e dotti; io, che di questi pochi e dotti non sono, ne lascio il pensiero a lui.

P. Barocchi (ed.), *Trattati…* I, pp. 190–1.

On the *paragone* Michelangelo–Raphael:
Letter from L. Dolce to G. Ballini, ibid., I, p. 785.

Doc. 9

Letter from Scipione Saurolo to Cardinal Borromeo:

[...] Imperò pregarò con ogni riuerentia Vostra Illustrissima et Reuerendissima Signoria che li piacia leggere questo mio discorso de la pittura de la Sacra Capella di Sua Santità et farui ufficio essendo cosa di quella importancia che è, et degna di consideratione. Dispiacque grandemente a Paulo Papa iij, santa memoria, et se più fosse campato l' haueria prouisto, come mi riferì il Cardinale Santa Croce, poi Marcello Papa, et il Cardinale di Carpo e Veralli, buona memoria; et so che il Cardinale Alessandrino mi disse che Pauolo iij ad ogni modo uoleua prouederlj hauendo in animo di agrandir la Capella tirandola in dentro nella Sacristia, hauendomi io fatto querella con tuttj; et so che l' ultim' anno di Paulo iiij Michel' agnolo hebbe a dir che la uoleua ad ogni modo conciare perchè si teneua di conscientia lassar da poi se una cosa tale...

B. NOGARA, 'Per la storia della cappella Sistina', *Monatshefte für Kunstwissenschaft*, III (1910), p. 161.

The short report in Latin appended to this letter deals exclusively with the point concerning the general nudity of Christ and the Saints, which is an offence against the Divine Majesty in such a sanctuary.

Doc. 10

P. LOMAZZO, *Il libro dei sogni* (*c.* 1563):

Dicesi che egli aveva pensato di fare in quella facciata una gabbia overo ciurma de fachini e de istrioni che andassero saltellando di là su, apponendo non star bene quei membri e coglioni si aparenti, non solamente ne' diavoli e fantasmi ma ne' Santi; e che poco ci manco che la no facesse mostrare a Cristo e la natura a Santa Catelina, che in certo atto sta che più lussuria genera nelle menti di riguardanti, insieme con molte altre femine, che di tremore [che in] un si terribile giorno, come serrà quello, aver si devrebbe. Dicessi ancora che quei biasci che di là su si fanno, che non se gli convengono, impero che elle sono cose da nozze e da bordelli; e molte altre cose dicono, non pensando né conoscendo come quella opera è il vero splendore de tutta Ittalia e de i pittori che sin, se ce ne fusse, dal estremo de Iperborei venir doverebbono per vederla e dessignarvi. Non sono molti mesi od anni che Papa Paolo quarto, detto il Tiatino, la volse far trare a terra, dicendo non convenirsi in Santo Pietro quelle apparenze forfantesche de membri con quelli atti istrionici.

R. P. Ciardi (ed.), *P. Lomazzo: Scritti sulle arti*, I, Florence, 1973, pp. 101–2.
See also R. de MAIO, op. cit., p. 39.

Doc. 11

G. A. GILIO DA FABRIANO, *Due Dialogi… Nel secondo si ragiona degli errori de' pittori circa l'Historie, con molte annotazioni fatte sopra il giuditio di Michelangelo et altre figure tanto de la vecchia quanto de la nuova Cappella et in che modo vogliono esser dipinte le Sacre Immagini…*, Camerino, 1564:

…Non penso che sia niuno, quanto si voglia goffo pittore, che non sappia o non pensi che Michelagnolo più tosto compiacer voluto si sia de l'arte, che de la verità istorica, e quello che egli non ha fatto non sia da ignoranza proceduto, ma dal voler mostrare ai posteri l'eccellenza del suo ingegno, e la eccellenza de l'arte che è in lui.

P. Barocchi (ed.), op. cit. vol. II, p. 55.

… Io fo molto più ingenioso quello artefice che accomoda l'arte a la verità del soggetto a la vaghezza de l'arte…

Ibid., p. 35.

Doc. 12

Payment to the heirs of Daniele da Volterra (Archivio di Stato, Rome):
R. DE CAMPOS and B. BIAGETTI, op. cit., p. 143.

…Constituunt summam scutorum sexaginta similium dicto quondam magistro Danieli pictori debitorum occasione mercedis laboreriorum per ipsum de anno 1565 factorum in tegendis partibus pudendis figurarum Cappellae pape Sixti…

Doc. 13

G. COMANINI, *Il Figino*, Mantua, 1591:

Fi. – ... Et a Michelangelo è stato parimente attribuito ad errore l'aver dipinto Cristo quasi senza barba nella rappresentazione dell'universal Giudicio, insegnandoci la teologia che gli uomini hanno a risorgere con la barba et a riformarsi secondo l'età della pienezza del Salvatore. Dal che si trae argomento che 'l Buonarotto scostossi in questa cosa dal verisimile. Perché, se la risurrezione di Cristo è, per parlar da teologo, cagione essemplare di quella degli uomini, i quali risorgeranno barbuti; assai manifesto è che egli non dovea dipingere il Redentor nostro col mento poco meno che ignudo. E quel baciarsi, che 'l medesimo pittore ha finto d'alcuni santi l'un l'altro in cielo, pur dà noia a' rigidi censori delle pitture, i quali dicono lui senza dubbio essere incorso nello sconvenevole in questa cosa, non essendo verisimile che i beati abbiano a baciarsi in quella maniera, quando saranno rivestiti de' loro corpi, quantunque s'ameranno insieme e gioiranno l'uno della gloria dell'altro.

Mar. – Sarebbevi modo alcuno da liberar Michelangelo da questa calunnia di sonvenevolezza? Percioché io lo stimo tanto grande uomo, che io vo imaginandomi lui non aver finto quell'atto del bacio tra le schiere de' beati se non con molto giudicio e con molto senno. [...]

«Bacimi (dice nella Cantica la Sposa al suo Sposo) col bacio della sua bocca». E come conviene che la Chiesa chiegga uno bacio al suo Sposo, il quale è Dio? che hanno a fare gli atti amorosi degli uomini nell'amor divino? Ma ecco che, col mezzo dell'allegoria, si fa dileguare ogni nebbia di sconvenevolezza, poscia che per questo bacio, desiderato con tanto ardor dalla Sposa, si dee intendere l'incarnazione del Verbo, nella quale si congiunsero le due nature, divina et umana, e si fece la communicazione degli idiomi dell'una e dell'altra, come nel bacio s'uniscono le due bocche, e si mischiano e confondono i fiati di quei che si baciano.

P. Barocchi (ed.), op. cit., vol. III, pp. 350–2.

F. Zuccaro: *Taddeo Zuccaro Copying the 'Last Judgement'*, drawing in the Uffizi, Florence (see Pl. 182). Taddeo Zuccaro's extensive activity as a copyist was recalled by his brother Federico in a series of panels destined for his house in Rome on the Pincio, built just before 1600. Only six out of the twenty-four panels remain (Palazzo Venezia), but the compositions are known from drawings, which give a real chronicle of studio life. See D. HEIKAMP, 'Vicende di Federico Zuccari', *Rivista d'Arte*, 1957, pp. 200 ff.; J. GERE, *Mostra di disegni degli Zuccari*, Florence, 1966, no. 75.

Doc. 1

C. RIDOLFI, *Le Maraviglie…,* Venice, 1648:

Ma quello, che maggiormente aggrandì il nome di Paolo furono quattro gran tele de' conuiti da lui in vari tempi dipinte in quella Città, nelle quali con inuentioni diuerse rappresentò sontuosi apparecchi ad vso di reali banchetti.

Il primo, ch'egli fece, fù quello del Refettorio di San Giorgio Maggiore [...] delle Nozze di Cana di Galilea [...].

Il secondo fù quello di San Sebastiano, ed è il conuito di Simone.[...]

Il terzo è in San Giouanni Paolo, da lui dipinto l'anno 1573 & è quello narrato da San Luca nella casa di Leui Vsuraio, che vi fù posto in luogo del Cenacolo di Christo fattoui da Titiano, che si abbrugiò; onde Frà Andrea de' Buoni, desideroso di veder rinouata la Pittura, offerì à Paolo per questo effetto certa quantità di danaro, che auuanzato di elemosine e di confessioni haueua, prezzo che per auuentura non si accettarebbe da vn galant'huomo ne' presenti tempi per lo imprimere vna così gran tela. Ma non potendo il pouero Frate spender di più, sforzato Paolo da preghi, lo volle in fine compiacere rassumendo così gran carica, spinto più dal desio della gloria, che dell'vtile.

210 Veronese. *Madonna of the Rosary.* 1573. Oil on canvas. Museo Vetrario, Murano.
A gathering of princes invoking the Madonna's protection.

L'apparecchio è finto sotto à spatiosa Loggia, in tre grand'archi compartita, fuor de' quali si mirano belle strutture de' Palagi, che rendono diletteuole veduta. Nel mezzo posa il Saluatore, al dirimpetto Leui vestito di purpurea veste, e seco siedono molti Publicani, & altri mescolati con gli Apostoli, ne' quali compose rarissime teste in singolari effetti, e vi ritrasse Frate Andrea sudetto in vn canto con la saluietta sopra la spalla, della cui effigie si trarebbe di vantaggio ciò, che fù speso nell'opera; e trà le cose d'ammiratione è la figura dell'Hoste appoggiato ad vn piedestallo, che oltre il diuisar singolarmente la qualità del personaggio, è di così fresche carni, che par viuo, e gli è vicino vn seruo Etiope con habito moresco e cesta in mano, che mostra di ridere, che muoue à riso, chi lo mira.

L'opera tutta in fine è maneggiata con grande maestria, quanto in questo genere si può fare, non volendo Paolo rimetterui di conscienza, ne dar materia à Frate Andrea di dolersi, di hauer mal impiegato il suo danaro.

Il quarto è posto nel Refettorio de' Padri Seruiti & iui espresse di nuouo il pranso di Simon leproso con Christo.

D. von Hadeln (ed.), Berlin, 1914, vol. I, pp. 313–4.

D. ROSAND, 'Theatre and Structure in the Art of Paolo Veronese', *Art Bulletin*, LV, 1973, pp. 217 ff.; reprinted in *Painting in Cinquecento Venice...*, New Haven, 1982, ch. 4. P. FEHL, 'Veronese's Decorum: Notes on the Marriage at Cana', in *The Ape of Nature. Studies in Honour of H. W. Janson*, New York, 1981, pp. 141 ff.
The list can be finally established as:
1563   *Marriage at Cana*, Refectory of the monastery of S. Giorgio (Louvre)
c. 1565   *Feast in the House of Simon*, SS. Nazzaro e Celso, Verona (Turin)
c. 1570   *Feast in the House of Simon*, Monastery of S. Sebastiano, Venice (Brera)
1572   *Feast in the House of Simon*, Servite monastery, Venice (Versailles)
1572   *Repast of St. Gregory the Great*, Monastery of Monte Berico, Vicenza (Vicenza)
1573   *Last Supper*, turned into *Feast in the House of Levi*, Monastery of SS. Giovanni e Paolo, Venice (Accademia)
The last picture of the series is thus the one for SS. Giovanni e Paolo.

On all these works:
T. PIGNATTI, *Veronese*, Venice, 1976.

According to Zanetti (1771) in the *Marriage at Cana* 'the double-bass player is Titian. Paolo painted himself as the cellist dressed in white. The other instrumentalist is probably Jacopo Tintoretto'. These identifications remain to be proved, for Zanetti's text has manifestly wrongly named figures in many places.

On the allegory of Lepanto:

S. SINDING-LARSEN, 'Christ in the Council-Hall. Studies in Religious Iconography of the Venetian Republic', in *Institutum Romanum Norvegiae Acta*, V, Rome, 1974.

Doc. 2

G. VASARI, *Life of Michele Sanmichele*, ed. Milanesi, VI, p. 370:

In Verona, nel refettorio di San Nazaro, monasterio de' monaci neri, ha fatto in un gran quadro di tela la cena che fece Simon lebroso al Signore, quando la peccatrice se gli gettò a'piedi; con molte figure, ritratti di naturale, e prospettive rarissime, e sotto la mensa sono due cani tanto belli che paiono vivi e naturali, e più lontano certi storpiati ottimamente lavorati.

Doc. 3

Interrogation by the Inquisition, 18 July 1573 (Archives of the Inquisition):

Die Sabbati 18m(ensi)s Julii 1573.
Constitutus in s(anc)to off(iti)o cora(m) sacro Tribunali D(ominus) Paulus
Caliarius Veronensis p(ictor) habitator in parochia S(anc)ti Samuelis
Et Int(errogatu)s de no(min)e et cogno(min)e: R(espon)dit ut s(upr)a. In(terrogatu)s De
professione sua. R(espon)dit Io depingo et fazzo delle figure
Ei dict(um) Sapete la causa p(er)che sete constituito: R(espon)dit S(ignor) no:

Sacri Trib(una)lis imponendis. Et ita deoreuerunt
o(mn)i mel(iori) m(od)o.

The text was discovered and translated (rather freely) by R. BASCHET, *Gazette des Beaux-Arts*, XXIII, 1867, pp. 378 f. Facsimile by G. DELOGU, *Veronese: the Supper in the House of Levi*, Milan, n.d. Critical edition in the excellent study by P. FEHL, 'Veronese and the Inquisition. A Study of the Subject Matter of the so-called *Feast in the House of Levi*', *Gazette des Beaux-Arts*, 1961, pp. 325 ff., app. pp. 349 ff., reprinted in T. PIGNATTI, op. cit., doc. 41, pp. 255–6.
G. FOGOLARI, 'Il Processo dell'Inquisizione a Paolo Veronese', in *Archivio Veneto*, 5th series, VII, 1935, pp. 352 ff.
E. SCHAFFRAN, 'Der Inquisitionsprozess gegen Paolo Veronese', in *Archiv für Kulturgeschichte*, 42, 2, pp. 178 ff.

One of the members of the tribunal, the Patriarch Giovanni Trevisan, had taken part in the Council of Trent. It will be seen that the Inquisition acted very differently in the affair of the miller Menocchio (1584), studied by C. GINZBURG, *Il formaggio e i vermi*, Turin, 1979.

On the iconography of the Last Supper: C. GILBERT, 'Last Suppers and their Refectories', in *The Pursuit of Holiness in Late Medieval and Renaissance Religion*, ed. C. Trinkaus and H. Oberman, Leyden, 1974.

On the function of the architecture in Veronese's grand scenographic compositions: D. ROSAND, art. cit. and op. cit., pp. 158 ff.

On the satirical engraving of the Pope at table: H. WÄSCHER, *Das deutsche illustrierte Flugblatt*, I, Dresden, 1955, p. 23.

Doc. 4

Johannes MOLANUS, *De Picturis et imaginibus sacris liber unus, tractans de vitandis circa eas abusibus et earundem significationibus*, Louvain, 1570, p. 64:

'Non sunt... prophanae historiae in ecclesiis pingendae, qui mos ethnicorum fuit, a christianis repudiandus, non imitandus.'

These precepts were taken up and endlessly amplified by the teachers of the Counter-Reformation. Thus, Comanini (*Il Figino*, 1591) says, still more simply: 'Non convenirsi dipingere in luoghi sacri cose naturali, che non servano alla pietà' (P. Barocchi (ed.), *Trattati*, III, p. 323). In this way principles were re-affirmed, although the applications were not always evident. The greatest treatise on the subject is incontestably the one by Cardinal PALEOTTI, *Discorso intorno alle imagini sacre e profane*, Bologna, 1582, studied by P. PRODI, 'Ricerche sulla Teorica delle Arti figurative nella Riforma cattolica', *Archivio italiano per la Storia della Pietà*, IV, 1962, pp. 121–212.

Doc. 5

Cristoforo SORTE, *Osservazioni nella Pittura* (Venice, 1580):

Dico bene che a questo bellissimo artificio, fra quante pitture mi ricordo d'aver vedute, s'è grandemente appressato M. Paolo Caliari nella Pala di S. Georgio qui in Verona, la qual opra Vostra Eccellenza et io abbiamo veduta insieme: perciò che alle figure fatte in quelle nubi ha maravigliosamente dato il suo decoro così in aver fatte esse figure de colori dolci, e divinamente illuminate dal sopraceleste splendore, come anco nell'aver intesa la prospettiva della distanzia, così nelle figure lontane come in quelle che sono nel piano che rappresenta com'è il naturale, le quali sono molto ben intese e con perfette ragioni condotte.

Cited from P. Barocchi, op. cit., I, p. 296.

Doc. 6

C. RIDOLFI, *Le Maraviglie...*, Venice, 1648:

Oltre le Pitture narrate, possiedono que' Signori ancora alcuni disegni sopra carte tinte illuminati di biacca, che lungo sarebbe il narrar le inuentioni tutte; ma solo faremo mentione di certi pellegrini pensieri, ch'egli di propria mano annotò nel rouerscio d'alcuni di quelli, inuiandogli per auuentura, à chi glie ne haueua fatta istanza, quali registreremo con l'ordine medesimo. [...]

Pittura quarta. Infinite sono le forme e le attitudini, con le quali è stata dipinta la Vergine, che fù da Alberto Durero ad vn medesimo modo quasi sempre rappresentata, facendola col figliuolino in braccio, e sempre nudo. Li Greci tutti lo faceuano inuolto nelle fascie, per non hauer eglino pratica di formare i corpi. Ogni figura puerile nondimeno si può dipingere nuda, come vestita. Il Buonarotti fece il bambino addormentato e la Madre, che leggeua vn libro; ne io la vidi giamai vicina al letticiuolo, vestendo il Saluatore. Io farei il bambino in culla con Angeli intorno, che tenessero panieri di frutti e di fiori in mano, e che suonassero vari stromenti, e chi di loro cantasse al dormiente bambino, e che la Vergine lo vezzeggiasse accompagnata da Sant'Anna. [...]

Pittura sesta. Se io hauerò tempo giamai, voglio rappresentare sontuosa mensa sotto à nobil loggia, oue entri la Vergine, il Saluatore e Gioseppe, facendogli seruire col più ricco corteggio d'Angeli, che si possa imaginare, che gli somministrino in piatti d'argento e d'oro regalate viuande e copia di pomposi frutti. Altri siano implicati in recar in tersi cristalli & in dorate coppe pretiose viuande, per dimostrare il ministero prestato da Beati spiriti al loro Dio, come meglio nel fine del libro sarà dichiarato, per intelligenza de' Pittori e per diletto degli amatori della Virtù; della qual inuentione io ne vidi un rarissimo disegno.

D. von Hadeln (ed.), Berlin, 1914, vol. I, pp. 320–1.

The interest of this text has been pointed out by J. von SCHLOSSER, *Materialen zur Quellenkunde der Kunstgeschichte*, vol. VI, *Die Kunstliteratur des Manierismus,* Vienna, 1919, p. 68.

On the drawing in the Louvre:
[Exhibition catalogue] J.-P. Mariette, *Le cabinet d'un grand amateur*, Louvre, Paris, 1967.

Index

Photo Credits

The author and the publishers wish to thank all those who have supplied photographs for this book. The numbers refer to the plates. The photo research was done by Ingrid de Kalbermatten.

Abano Terme, Foto Lufin   194
Ancona, Pinacoteca Civica   152
Antella (Florence), SCALA   1, 2, 20, 21, 24, 40, 41, 44, 48, 53, 54
Assisi, Basilica di San Francesco   50, 200
Berlin, Staatliche Museen Preussischer Kulturbesitz, Gemäldegalerie (Jörg P. Anders)   46, 57, 58
– Staatliche Museen Preussischer Kulturbesitz, Kupferstichkabinett (Jörg P. Anders)   102
Budapest, Museum of Fine Arts   142
Cambridge, Fitzwilliam Museum   158
Chicago, The Art Institute of Chicago   61
Florence, Alinari   4, 15, 22, 23, 25, 26, 30, 34–6, 49, 52, 56, 63, 111–13, 125, 145, 146, 198, 201, 203, 207
– Guido Sansoni   9, 47, 51, 66, 182
– Soprintendenza per i Beni Artistici e Storici, Gabinetto fotografico   3, 43, 60, 65
Gauting (Munich), Blauel-Bavaria   64
Holkham, Estate Office   140
Le Rove, Yann Thibault   121

Lille, Musée des Beaux-Arts   160, 161
London, British Museum   88, 89, 171
– A. C. Cooper   100
– Courtauld Institute of Art   162
– Lord Chamberlain's Office   5, 96 (1–6, 8, 9), 97, 99
– National Gallery   62, 67, 68, 103, 104, 128
– Victoria and Albert Museum   90, 154, 208
Madrid, Museo del Prado   87
Milan, Biblioteca Ambrosiana   39, 150
– Pinacoteca di Brera   95
– Mario Tornone   192
Naples, Soprintendenza ai Beni Artistici e Storici   177
New York, The Frick Collection   13, 14
– The Metropolitan Museum of Art   38, 144, 175
– Janos Scholz   101
Oxford, Ashmolean Museum   127, 137, 139
– Bodleian Library   33
Padua, Museo Civico   42
Paris, Anderson-Giraudon   11, 17, 18, 94
– Brogi, Giraudon   16, 19
– Gilles de Fayet   6, 7, 45, 92, 93, 96 (7), 109, 114, 115, 117, 120, 124, 135, 147, 148, 159, 163, 165, 172, 174, 181, 185, 191, 196, 197
– Photographie Giraudon   72, 153

– Réunion des musées nationaux   59, 105, 122, 123, 134, 141, 187, 195, 204
Rome, Anderson   119, 155, 167
Rotterdam, Museum Boymans-van Beuningen   10
Sansepolcro, Biblioteca Comunale   12
Siena, Fotografia Grassi   28, 29, 98
Urbino, Foto Moderna   110
Vatican, Biblioteca Apostolica   70, 71, 76, 77, 178, 180
– Monumenti Musei e Gallerie Pontificie   8, 69, 74, 75, 78–82, 84–6, 106, 168–70, 176, 183, 202
– Rev. Fabbrica di S. Pietro in Vaticano   37
Venice, Osvaldo Böhm   131, 132, 149, 156, 157, 166, 184, 189, 190
– Fotografia Giacomelli   210
– Soprintendenza ai Beni Artistici e Storici   188
Vienna, Österreichische Nationalbibliothek   73, 138, 209
Washington, D. C., National Gallery of Art   55, 91a, 91b, 107
Windsor, The Royal Library   133, 143, 173
Author's archives: Frontispiece, 27, 31, 32, 83, 108, 118, 126, 179, 193, 205

The following drawings were made by Atelier de création Ribes, Vevey: 116, 130, 186, 199

Color photolithographs: eurocrom 4, Treviso, and Schwitter A.G., Basle
Black/white photolithographs: Kreienbühl A.G., Lucerne
Design and production: Franz Stadelmann